Library Data

Empowering Practice and Persuasion

Darby Orcutt, Editor

LIBRARIES UNLIMITED
An Imprint of ABC-CLIO, LLC

A B C ⬥ C L I O

Santa Barbara, California • Denver, Colorado • Oxford, England

Library of Congress Cataloging-in-Publication Data

Library data : empowering practice and persuasion / Darby Orcutt, editor.
    p. cm.
  Includes bibliographical references and index.
  ISBN 978–1–59158–826–9 (acid-free paper) — ISBN 978–1–59158–827–6 (ebook)
1. Library statistics. 2. Library statistics—United States. 3. Academic libraries—Statistics. I. Orcutt, Darby.
Z669.8L54   2010
025.007′23—dc22   2009039781

14 13 12 11 10   1 2 3 4 5

This book is also available on the World Wide Web as an eBook.
Visit www.abc-clio.com for details.

ABC-CLIO, LLC
130 Cremona Drive, P.O. Box 1911
Santa Barbara, California 93116-1911

This book is printed on acid-free paper ∞

Manufactured in the United States of America

For my son, Cameron,
my love for whom cannot be quantified.

Contents

Introduction

DARBY ORCUTT

If you're actually reading this introduction, not only does it mean that you've opened this book on libraries and data, but it also means that you're interested in context. You may be curious what prompted the creation of this book, what drove the selection and organization of its contents, or how it all fits together. Strong data analysis begins with similar questions. In fact, data without context ceases to be data. Until units of information are brought together in such a way that they can be manipulated, interpreted, and used, they are not truly data.

The germ of this book—and the need for it—was made clear while I participated on the Association of College & Research Libraries's Educational & Behavioral Sciences Section's 2007 Program Planning Committee, chaired by Penny Beile, and I wish to thank her and the members of that committee for their encouragement and support. The resulting 2007 panel presentation stands as just one of a great many data-focused programs ubiquitously present at virtually all library conferences in recent years. In addition, I have met and corresponded with a growing number of professionals having new and major data responsibilities if not profiles, such as my own former position of Collection Manager for Data Analysis which I originated at The North Carolina State University Libraries (the second librarian in that position, my colleague Hilary Davis, is a contributor to this volume). Despite overwhelming interest and need, no publication thus far has sought to broadly and thoroughly address the obvious gap in the professional literature.

Especially in the digital age, libraries have grown more and more capable at generating data. Concurrently, the library profession has increasingly valued data as a—or even *the*—key component in decision-making. Whether we librarians will prove so adept at understanding and using data is still an open question, a positive future answer to which this collection will hopefully influence.

Given also the recent economic crisis of historic proportion, this book suddenly seems of even more immediate interest and value than its contributors may have realized at the time of writing. The strategies herein should prove useful in times when every decision within, and every persuasive argument about, the library could have especially lasting and defining consequences. The subtitle of this volume might appropriately be "Hard Data for Hard Times."

This book draws together research, theory, pragmatic reflections, honest assessments, and new ideas from a range of librarians: mostly academic and mostly American, but addressing issues as well as sharing ideas and practices that could be valuably applied within a wide variety of contexts. I have purposefully solicited contributions not only from seasoned researchers and senior administrators, but also from new and upcoming voices in the field—including many authors for whom this is their first publication.

"Data" is frequently equated in library circles with "quantitative information," and I have asked contributors to hold to this terminological convention wherever possible. Yet, in many instances it is necessary to challenge this potentially dangerous terministic screen, and I am pleased to open this volume with Jamene Brooks-Kieffer's excellent essay that does just that, problematizing this simplistic correlation. Comprising the remainder of Part I, "Approaching Data," Kate Zoellner's survey of sources for educational data will prove a handy reference and Anne C. Elguindi and Bill Mayer's tips for persuasive presentation offer practical guidance for all librarians.

Part II, "Evaluation of Monographic Collections," offers Lucy Eleonore Lyons's useful new matrix for planning evaluation in any context, as well as the results of a detailed use-study of approval versus librarian-selected titles at K-State, coauthored by Erin L. Ellis, Nikhat J. Ghouse, Monica Claassen-Wilson, John M. Stratton, and Susanne K. Clement. Turning to serials and e-resources, Part III opens with a thorough review of the literature on usage statistics in e-journal decision-making by Andrée J. Rathemacher, who next teams with colleague Michael C. Vocino to discuss the application of theory to a real-life serials cancellation project. Tracie J. Ballock, Carmel Yurochko, and David A. Nolfi articulate a theoretical yet practical guide to electronic resource decision-making, and Margaret Hogarth outlines sources, perspectives, and problems in collecting and understanding usage data.

Part IV casts a light on "Reference and Instruction." Danielle Theiss-White, Jason Coleman, and Kristin Whitehair detail an elegant system for capturing and interpreting transaction data from multiple reference points, while Erika Bennett, Sommer Berg, and Erin Brothen's similar approach within an online-only library complements and reinforces its usefulness. Wendy Holliday, Erin Davis, and Pamela Martin's system for outcomes-based assessment of instruction likewise offers a full and practicable way of measuring success in this aspect of library service.

Part V focuses on "New Methods" with Michael A. Crumpton's business-style perspective on data in libraries, David E. Woolwine's and Joseph A. Williams's fruitful application of sociology's "grounded theory" to interlibrary loan practices, and Tim M. McGeary's capital budgeting model for electronic resources. Lastly, Part VI, "Emerging Contexts" takes us into new library directions. Hilary Davis explores the use of data in developing and managing an institutional repository, Melissa Johnson outlines a project of using vendor-provided usage data to drive library home page design, and Samuel C. Utulu describes the increasingly important uses of data within the context of Nigerian university libraries.

My hope is that this volume will not be the last of its kind but rather will provoke further ideas and discussion of tools, methods, perspectives, and results of data analyses in library contexts. Data *is* the future of libraries; let's work together to shape that future.

PART I

Approaching Data

CHAPTER 1

Yielding to Persuasion: Library Data's Hazardous Surfaces

JAMENE BROOKS-KIEFFER

> If I was wrong in yielding to persuasion once, remember that it was to persuasion exerted on the side of safety, not of risk.
>
> — Jane Austen, *Persuasion*

INTRODUCTION

Anne Elliot, the sober and sedate heroine of Jane Austen's *Persuasion*, speaks at last to her longtime love Captain Wentworth as a woman whose reactions to acts of persuasion throughout her life have not left her entirely happy. Curiously, she defends the judgment of her persuasive friends rather than her own. She argues that Lady Russell's persuasive powers were intended to keep Anne safe at a time when Anne's own immature convictions led her into a risky engagement with the then younger and poorer Wentworth. Seven years later, Captain Wentworth's second offer of marriage, fortune, and consequence seems sensible rather than uncertain. Anne's years of loneliness have taught her that not all risk is dangerous, just as not all safety is comfortable. In the context of Austen's other novels this is a relatively radical conclusion. Dashing, risky suitors reward Austen's heroines with happiness and stability much less often than do ordinary, familiar, even offensive men. But in the unrelated context of libraries and their data, what can Anne Elliot teach us?

From *Persuasion*, we librarians may glean something from Anne's point of view. The blame or credit for an unhappy or a fortunate outcome does not lie with the persuader. The object of persuasion controls her own fate because she chooses to be convinced, or not, by the persuader's argument. Neither risk nor safety guarantees a happy ending. We librarians are often the objects of persuasion, exhorted by users, vendors, administrators, stakeholders, and others to do this, buy that, and produce thus-and-such. When we attempt to take on the role of persuader ourselves, we often restrict our persuasive powers by using inferior tools. The traditional ways in which librarians gather and process data often stop short of the analysis, processing, or mining techniques that would be considered a necessity in any other profession as data-rich as ours. Such techniques are not easy to employ but they produce remarkably informative, if at times uncomfortable, results. Instead, we prefer to deal with the surface, safe meaning of our data, relying on a predominance of quantitative variables and the simple, arithmetic conclusions we can draw from them. These conclusions are safe because they seldom yield unexpected results. For example, safe conclusions often occur during the serials renewal process. A subject librarian totals a long list of numeric usage data, assumes that a large total equals frequent use, and justifies a physics journal's renewal. Even if a thorough data analysis supports the opposite decision, cancelling the journal could jeopardize the librarian's relationship with the physics department.

ARGUMENT

This chapter is concerned with the data that libraries produce and analyze internally. A library's internal data does not reside in a vacuum; it is made relevant by the library's activities of evaluation and assessment. I do not intend to thoroughly investigate evaluation and assessment activities but to show that these pursuits succeed when they study carefully analyzed internal data. Many in-depth examinations of libraries' evaluation practices, assessment techniques, and cross-institutional data may be found in the current literature. While cross-institutional data is an important area of inquiry, I will only examine how it influences the internal collection of data.

Internal data gathered by libraries has long offered a wealth of information about interactions between a library and its users. Librarians who lay claim to this data attempt to inform their work of acquisition, deaccession, collection management, accessibility, and a host of other duties. Libraries' internal data often includes browse and checkout numbers (from the catalog); types and numbers of transactions at service desks; funds spent or available (from the integrated library system or ILS); requests and clickthroughs (from a link resolver or federated search tool); search and access logs and full-text downloads (from e-resource vendors); analysis of Web page activity; and logs of proxy server transactions. The acquisition and management of serial and electronic resource collections has contributed to the recent explosion in available data. Since many libraries spend a majority of their acquisitions budgets on these items, it comes as no surprise that data about serials and electronic resources is plentiful to the point of excess.

This plentiful data is often discussed at conferences and in the literature as a problem. Its very abundance creates compatibility and time management difficulties. Its quantity hinders a healthy question-and-answer relationship between libraries and their data. For example, librarians can often access usage data on a given journal title from at least three different sources: the ILS, the link resolver, and one or more e-resource vendors. When making journal renewal decisions, a librarian might choose to ask only one of these data sources, "Was this journal used?" rather than attempt to assemble one valid data pool from three distinct sets. Among librarians, the core problem seems to be extracting meaning from huge stores of internal records.

Many libraries' questions cannot be answered reliably by data from a single source:

- What are the consequences of changing library hours or other services?
- What resources and services do users value most highly?
- How do our users really use the library?

Only multiple sources of data can supply trustworthy answers to these and other questions. Transforming too-plentiful data from various sources into a truly valuable information source requires careful manipulation and analysis.

Unfortunately, data analysis is an area where librarians and libraries often perform poorly. Several pieces of current and historical literature support this assertion. Blake and Schleper claim that librarians "do not always use the information that we gather, preferring instead to point to the numbers themselves as evidence of our work" (2004, 460). Moroney (1956; cited in Allen 1985, 211) says, "there is something very sad in the disparity between our passion for figures and our ability to make use of them once they are in our hands." Allen's own lament (1985, 211), echoed by later authors (Ambrožič 2003; Hiller and Self 2004), is fairly damning: "Undoubtedly librarians are great compilers of statistical data, but exhibit poor abilities in its interpretation, manipulation or use." Each of these authors implies a slightly different meaning when invoking the word use in the dual contexts of librarians and data, but all are differentiating between a reliance on facts themselves and any scrutiny carried out on the collected information. These opinions span roughly 50 years of observing the profession and contain the same elemental criticism. Librarians' relationship with data is dysfunctional at best and pathologic at worst. We have far too much experience with and affinity for the safe activity of data gathering, and far too little experience with the risks of using it. In this chapter, using data means analyzing multiple inputs and feeding the results into the library's processes of decision-making, management, evaluation, and assessment.

Why do we have such difficulty with data analysis? A cynic might answer by pointing out other shaky foundations upon which libraries often base decisions. Some libraries stand firm in institutional tradition and when their methods are questioned, say, "We've always done it this way." Other libraries are quick to buy in to the newest heavily marketed trend and, when a topic of concern arises, say "Everyone else is doing it." Neither of these is a reason good enough for neglecting or foregoing data analysis. A different critic might fault organizations that supply their employees with ample tools for acquiring and amassing data but neglect to train them or allow them enough time to conduct data analysis. My own opinion is that librarians are confounded by data analysis because they assume that the common use of the word statistics is equivalent to the processes, skills, and outcomes associated with the discipline of statistics. This particular misunderstanding creates a path paved with inaccuracies and assumptions about data. Librarians happily trod this path, believing we are on the way to informed decision-making when we are really walking in circles.

In this chapter, I will examine libraries' bias in favor of quantitative data and clarify the relationships among quantitative and qualitative data, the popular definition of "statistics," and the discipline of statistics. I will also study the errors and assumptions made by librarians in their dealings with data. I will consider three models of data-supported persuasion and explore the misnomer that is data-driven decision-making. Finally, I will observe four risk-taking organizations that push various kinds of data through analysis, recommendation, and action.

DATA GOES BEYOND NUMBERS

Our discussion of data encompasses both quantitative and qualitative measures. Sullivan (2007) defines quantitative as giving "numerical measures" (6), explaining that arithmetic performed on these measures will produce meaningful results. Even though a phone number is numeric data, arithmetic performed on the numbers does not mean anything. On the other hand, qualitative "allows for classification . . . based on some attribute or characteristic" (6). The same phone number that is arithmetically nonsensical can be a meaningful trait in a qualitative context (7). Although both measures are useful, libraries seem to have a decided preference for quantitative data.

Libraries occasionally dip a toe in the waters of qualitative measurement by, for example, sending out surveys, organizing focus groups, participating in LibQUAL+, and so forth. However, the most commonly gathered data in a library is quantitative: gate counts; quantity of reference questions; number of circulated items; or amount of database usage. One reason for this biased practice is found by examining the measurements gathered by library-related agencies. The Association of Research Libraries (ARL) Statistics Interactive Edition lists 18 measures of expenditures, 15 of holdings, 6 of activities, and 5 of staffing, among others. The annually gathered Association of College & Research Libraries (ACRL) Statistics include 8 measures of print collections, 12 of expenditures, and 18 of electronic resource collections and usage. The National Center for Education Statistics (NCES) data on libraries gathered between 1976 and 2004 include 5 measures of collections, 7 of staffing, 1 of activities, and 26 of expenditures. Almost all of these measures are counts, totals, differences, or other arithmetic results. These agencies' emphasis on quantitative data sends an unsubtle message to libraries that it is the only significant kind.

The other glaring reason for quantitative data's takeover of the library is the sheer volume of numeric data our systems are capable of producing. In an age dominated by manual data collection methods, Allen wrote that decision-making was hampered by the slow pace of data extraction. He predicted that bringing computer systems into libraries would remove "physical obstacles to the assembly and digestion of data based on unit operations" (1985, 213). In one way, he was correct. Computerized, automated data collection has given nearly every library the ability to become a data warehouse. We now have the opposite problem, one of tonnage. White and Kamal point out that "managers are often overwhelmed with statistical numbers because digital technologies can be so efficient at capturing data" (2006, 14).

Gorman thinks about this onslaught of numeric data in the context of library stakeholders who have little time and short attention spans. He points out that these people are a primary audience for library data and a major source of library funding. Stakeholders, he says, prefer simple proof that X is bigger (and therefore better) than Y. When such stakeholders control a library's funding, the library may be forgiven for focusing on this data to the exclusion of all other types. Gorman also hypothesizes that the ease with which computing systems supply numeric data makes librarians more and more dependent on that data as the only means of evaluation. He points out that stakeholders' perception of computerized, numeric data as simple and quick to gather makes them more demanding of numbers as proof of value. Stakeholders assume that computerized methods of gathering and supplying quantitative data are accurate and easy for librarians to supply. Librarians assume that such data is efficient and effective at communicating progress to stakeholders. Such circumstances create a perfect storm of library preference for quantitative data, making it our default choice for empirical information (1999, under "The Problem with the Stakeholders . . . ").

DATA IS NOT STATISTICS

Having established the dominance of quantitative data in libraries, we must now consider librarians' equivalent treatment of data, "statistics," and statistics. This treatment first caught my attention during a forum sponsored by the National Information Standards Organization (NISO). During his talk, Bollen (2007) pointed out that usage data and usage statistics are not identical concepts. He characterized usage data as raw usage events and usage statistics as reports about those events. Even though Bollen defined these terms in the context of the MESUR project (Los Alamos National Laboratory), his very specific descriptions apply to many of the ways librarians speak about and work with data and statistics. Librarians' work with these topics is not limited to usage, but also incorporates collections, expenditures, and services—in short, any work of the library.

The discipline of statistics seems to take for granted the conceptual difference between the words statistics and data. Tietjen introduces statistics to the novice as "the accepted method of summarizing or describing data and then drawing inferences from the summary measures" (1986, 1). A recent introductory statistics textbook defines the topic as "the science of collecting, organizing, summarizing, and analyzing information to draw conclusions or answer questions" (Sullivan 2007, 3). This same author determines that facts describing characteristics of an individual are data (3). Both authors speak of statistics as a process that acts on all forms of data. This characterization supports Bollen's dividing line between data (raw events) and statistics (an analysis of those events). This professional treatment ignores the popular definition of "statistics" as a collection of numbers (e.g., the "stats" on a favorite ballplayer). This common usage echoes the definition of quantitative data, and it is how librarians use the word. But we are not only arguing semantics here. The usage of the word betrays the mind-set behind it—in this case, one that sees collections of quantitative data, or "statistics," as sufficient for evaluating our activities and setting our goals. This mind-set commits two major errors. It ignores the information available in collections of qualitative data. It also disregards the possibility that we can frame questions to be asked of data and have those questions answered by analysis. By engaging the process of statistics, we can analyze quantitative and qualitative date to find answers to our questions. Unfortunately, we are professionals at tending "statistics" while ignoring statistics.

The two most common recurring data collection projects in academic libraries are surveys taken for the ACRL Academic Library Statistics and ARL Statistics publications. Other data collection projects are carried out in academic, public, school, and state agency libraries by the Library Statistics Cooperative Program, which is jointly implemented by NCES, the National Commission on Libraries and Information Science (NCLIS), and the Institute of Museum and Library Services (IMLS). These surveys and publications use "statistics" in its popular sense: a collection of quantitative data on a particular topic. The "statistics" published by these agencies reinforce libraries' previously discussed bias toward quantitative data while offering few models of analysis.

Bentley (1979) writes a scathing critique of data gathered and supplied by NCES. She highlights faults with both the data and the agency's project goals. She censures NCES for undertaking a far reaching program to collect standardized survey information from a variety of libraries when their intention was to publish the results without first conducting any analysis of it. Her examination finds very little valuable information that libraries could use to compare their services with each other or to assess their own internal processes. She rebuffs the simple variables gathered by NCES, including volumes added, subscriptions held, and book expenditures; she determines that they are not "meaningful for evaluating or comparing libraries . . . beyond establishing that one library has more or less of something than another library" (143, 146–47). Such purportedly comparative data brings to mind the annual ARL rankings, which Bentley dismisses as equally useless as the NCES data: "An unstated assumption seems to be that if there are more volumes available, the library is better . . . . More useful could be information indicating the chances the user has of meeting his needs from a particular library" (148).

We might hope that Bentley's nearly 30-year-old findings are out of date, but an examination of current measures from the three agencies mentioned above proves otherwise. The national level sets of cross-institutional data offer libraries little in the way of actionable information. These agencies derive ratios and percentages from data and present them to librarians as analysis. Examples of these calculations include "Total Library Material Expenditures as Percent of Total Library Expenditures" and "Ratio of Items Loaned to Items Borrowed" (Association of College & Research Libraries 2006, categories 5, 7). This sad state of current affairs makes Bentley's calls for performance measures and cost-benefit analyses (1979, 150) all the more understandable. When national agencies send the message to U.S. libraries that meaningful statistics are collections of numeric data and simple calculations performed on that data, should we expect libraries themselves to think or act any differently?

Most libraries seem to have taken this message to heart, calling their own stores of collected numbers "statistics." Even works on library management urge readers to think about "administrative uses for library data" but focus on data collection (Faulkner 1988, 43). Currently available tools designed to assist librarians with data collection offer examples of this vernacular use of "statistics." An open-source program called Libstats provides a framework for service desk staff to gather data about service transactions. The increasingly popular ScholarlyStats product collects vendor-supplied usage data from electronic resources into a central warehouse for storage and analysis.

Understandably, one might look at these examples and claim that I am nit-picking over word usage. Perhaps I am, but my point is to demonstrate how pervasive is the idea within library culture that collections of quantitative data qualify as statistics. More importantly, I want to show how this treatment leads to a second, more dangerous idea. Since collections of quantitative data are considered "statistics," no work need be done, beyond the acts of collection and, possibly, simple calculation, to make meaning from the numbers. We might publicly deny the idea that data collection itself creates meaning, but our actions belie our words. Gumilar and Johnson found through interviewing managing librarians at eight large UK academic libraries that only one of the eight claimed to have "a formal and comprehensive system for library evaluation" (1995, 74). Just two of the remaining seven libraries had seriously investigated performance measurement for evaluating their services. Edem and Lawal performed a formal survey of academic librarians in Nigeria to determine their use of quantitative data in making decisions about acquisitions, storage, materials processing, staffing, and recruitment. Their conclusions resonate outside Nigeria as well as beyond the academy. The surveyed group faced many problems: not understanding the subject of statistics or its application and use; belief that librarianship does not require in-depth statistics or analysis; and no room in Nigerian library school curricula for teaching statistical methodology or practice (1997, 55). We may not wish to accept that these studies illustrate our own behaviors, but we cannot deny that the authors' conclusions, to a great extent, ring true in our own libraries.

TURNING DATA INTO PERSUASION

From this mistaken, though pervasive, idea that quantitative data alone is sufficient for evaluation and decision-making, librarians have evolved a number of misguided data-related practices. These practices promise dubious outcomes when they are used as the basis for any assessment project. Allen tells us how we err with data: not collecting appropriate data; not collecting accurate or cross-comparable data; not asking valid questions of the data; and not knowing how to manipulate the data into intelligible information (1985, 212). Shank more cynically tells us why we try to work with data in the first place: it might be worth something; to sustain tradition; just because it is there; to avoid embarrassment; to feed the public's demand for accountability; to overwhelm the administration with tables and reports; and to prove that the data-collectors are busy (1982, 3–4). Both summations are harsh, but at least one indictment from each list should ring true with every reader.

The results of extensive interviews with Digital Library Federation (DLF) members on assessment and use of electronic resources (Covey 2002) tend to reinforce the much older views of both Allen and Shank in identifying libraries' sometimes unfortunate relationships with data. Covey's respondents want to gather useful data that helps their libraries meet specified goals. However, they are worried that they gather some data because they have always done so or because it is easy to get. Some in the survey group are concerned that they spend large amounts of time gathering data but do not have the skills (or time to develop the skills) to manipulate it or make it useful. Covey writes that her respondents understand that data is only one piece of a complete assessment activity, and that the choice of what data to gather must evolve from the goals and objectives of a given project. She also reports that her subjects are aware of the need for prompt follow-through on a set of data. Once an analysis is complete, the organization should promptly follow up with action appropriate to the results. Covey warns that failure to follow through the actionable end of a project decreases staff morale and discourages cooperation with and participation in the next data collection project (2–4).

From Covey's report we could take away the discouraging message that Allen and Shank are correct, that this recently documented evidence proves librarians' ineptitude with data. We could also wonder what Jane Austen's Anne Elliot would tell us about Covey's report. She might recognize three methods of persuasion described by Covey's respondents. These three methods are my next area of examination. Two are havens of safety but are also, like Lady Russell's advice, pathways to stasis and stagnation. The third is fraught with risk but is, like Captain Wentworth's first proposal, decisive, active, and a bit of a gamble.

THREE METHODS OF PERSUASION

The first method of persuasion libraries are using is, I fear, the most common and least effective. Covey addresses it in her conclusion: "The results of the DLF study suggest that individually, libraries in many cases are collecting data without really having the will, organizational capacity, or interest to interpret and use the data effectively in library planning" (2002, 58). Flooded with data by our own computing systems, we may find it easier to collect the stuff than not. After all, someone might need it. But this collection phase is often where we stop, rather than start, dealing with data. Data collection itself is a difficult and tedious chore, so it is no surprise that shelving the data on the library's local area network, or worse, on an individual desktop computer, is seen as the end of the task. A library may believe that it is doing the right thing by gathering and storing its data, or it may be uncomfortably aware that its stashed data is not very persuasive to critical stakeholders. Librarians in this situation should ask themselves about the purpose data serves within the library. If the data is important enough to gather, why is it not important enough to use?

The second way librarians turn data into persuasion implies a more agonized, painstaking approach. Covey's survey respondents discuss the detrimental effects to a project caused by too many people working on it for too long (2002, 3–4). This hints at what I think of as analysis without end. Librarians can wreak havoc on an evaluation project even if their work includes analyzing the data at hand. Never wrapping up the analysis and proceeding to the results and recommendations for action can be just as destructive as not analyzing the data at all. Analysis without end can have several different causes, including ignorance of the best ways to query and manipulate data, no time to learn such techniques, and fear of declaring an analysis good enough to recommend action.

Before we move on to the third method of persuasion, I would like to take a broader look at the implications of these first two, stale and stagnant as they are. They are certainly not methods to be proud of, and they hold little hope of persuading internal or external stakeholders that some action must be taken. They do, however, shine a bright light on the place occupied by data in any organization where one or both of these methods are common practice. Think about it: would any piece of information that the organization considers vital for decision-making and strategic action be allowed to sit in storage or rot in committee? Is data such valuable information to your organization that it circulates endlessly among employees, is easily found when wanted, and is common knowledge even to new hires? Is any data that valuable? Perhaps the list of staff e-mail addresses? Here is a simple test to determine the value of data to your organization. Go to the person whose task it is to gather data about one of your library's services. If you have more than one such person, pick one at random. Ask that person why they collect data. Any response along the lines of "It's part of my job," or "It's just what I was trained to do," indicates the low regard in which your library holds data. In an organization that values and uses data, data gatherers will understand the rationale for their tasks and the purposes to which the data will be put.

The first two methods of persuasion are safe, in Austen's terms, because they hold very little possibility for change. It is difficult to feel threatened by impending change when the supposed evidence for that change is retired to a shelf or endlessly analyzed. In other words, data is not dangerous to the status quo until it is allowed to inform some action. Covey recognizes that developing skills and practices to act on data is very difficult given perpetual changes to the library's services and functions (2002, 58). Many changes made by libraries are imposed on us by external pressures, including administrative decrees, legislative gridlock, and budget freezes. We can allow our libraries' changes to be dictated to us, or we can take hold of our data and create our own change. This is the third, risky method of persuasion.

This method recognizes that data collection and analysis is part of a process that identifies specific problems, poses questions that data can answer, gathers data, analyzes it, proposes actions supported by the data, and carries out the actions. Many readers will recognize in this process the phases of an assessment cycle. Curiously, these steps look a lot like Sullivan's definition of the discipline of statistics: "The science of collecting, organizing, summarizing, and analyzing information to draw conclusions or answer questions" (2007, 3). In the previous paragraph I stated that data is not dangerous to the status quo until it is allowed to inform some action. I would now like to rework that statement: data is not meaningful to the organization until it is allowed to inform some action. This is the risky bit, since the data might not lead you in the direction you think you should go. I am not arguing for, as Allen puts it, "a tyranny [of statistical information] that would destroy the essence of professional judgment" (1985, 217). Rather, I am arguing for data to inform that professional judgment.

EVALUATE AND ANALYZE

Remember the person or people in your library whose task it is to gather data about the library's services? Suppose you have asked two people from different departments the question suggested above: "Why do you collect data?" To your surprise, you receive two different answers. From one person, you receive the telling answer, "It's a part of my job in this department." The implications of this response were discussed earlier. The other person stuns you with a neat summary of his department's reasons for collecting the data, the purpose to which it is put, and the actions that have been taken because of it. Both answers are possible within the same library because our organizations have a hard time enforcing consistent methods of evaluation throughout their component units.

Lancaster (1977) defines two levels of evaluation, which should be used together to best judge a system or service. Macroevaluation analyzes a system's level of performance, while microevaluation delves into how and why the system operates as it does (2). His examples of macroevaluation include determining how many books are checked out in a given time frame (13). This measurement tells something about the library's performance as a circulator of books if, say, 1/10 of the library's books are checked out at any given time. Lancaster's point is that this is all that macroevaluation can tell us. To draw any valid conclusions about the library's circulation services, we need to account for other factors that affect the number of checkouts, including users' abilities to find items on the shelf, user satisfaction with the quality of the library's books, the number of users studying a given topic at the same time, and so forth (13). Suddenly, knowing something about the library's circulation services seems more difficult than counting the number of books checked out.

Based on the above description, it might be easy to assume that macroevaluation is analogous to quantitative data because macroevaluation often performs arithmetic operations to investigate a data set. Similarly, one might imagine clear parallels between microevaluation and qualitative data because the questions microevaluation addresses are sometimes best considered in light of nonquantifiable information. In fact, neither assumption is true. Rather, Lancaster's terms characterize two different approaches to the process of statistics which, as we have discussed, is not the same as data. Both macro- and microevaluation require data analysis. Where macroevaluation is concerned with what a set of variables says about an organization, microevaluation addresses how that set of variables is impacted by other sets of variables and why the organization behaves as it does under the influence of these variables. Instead of providing endless (and endlessly confusing) definitions of these terms, I will offer a scenario that speaks to Lancaster's original idea of wanting to know something about a library's circulation services.

Let us suppose that we want to know how well our library's circulation services meet the needs of distance patrons. Because our ILS contains no single attribute that distinguishes "distance" from "local" patrons, we decide to use patrons' residential zip codes (qualitative data) to determine their distance from the library. We begin our study by asking whether a patron's distance from the library has any effect on the number of items they have checked out in the past year (quantitative data). To answer this question, we extract residential zip code and number of items checked out in the most recent 12 months for each active patron in our ILS. We arbitrarily determine that zip codes within a 40-mile radius of the library will be considered the "local" area, while zip codes outside that radius will be considered the "distance" area. After doing some research on our region's zip codes, we assign the zip code data to a "local" or a "distance" category. Within each category, we total the number of items checked out and count the number of patrons. We then obtain each category's ratio of total items checked out to number of patrons in the category and compare the ratios.

This simple (yet incomplete) data analysis follows the protocol of macroevaluation in that it examines one possible performance indicator: total items checked out by residential zip code. While this indicator might be a useful first step toward answering our original question, "How well are distance patrons' needs met by circulation services?" we cannot accept it as the answer. We cannot validly conclude anything beyond the analysis performed on the original data elements. To determine, for instance, why distance patrons check out items at a rate 75 percent less than that of local patrons, we need to conduct a microevaluation. We can gather other quantitative and qualitative data from the ILS and from distance patrons themselves to expand our original analysis. The practice of microevaluation requires that we also examine other issues that affect distance patrons' interactions with the library: library policies, scheduling constraints, course content, and so forth. While complicating the analysis a great deal, microevaluation provides a more complete answer to our question by attempting to consider factors outside the data's scope.

Even the straightforward analysis I described to demonstrate macroevaluation was not instant. It required thought and planning to construct, and space to explain. How much more effort, then, would be required to conduct our sketch of a microevaluation? Furthermore, I posit that to conduct the microevaluation, we must first conduct the macroevaluation. We could not otherwise intelligently frame the microevaluation because we would not know that distance patrons check out items at a rate 75 percent less than that of local patrons. In broad terms, we must know "What?" before we can ask "How?" or "Why?" During times of increased staff responsibilities and decreased budgets, who can devote the resources to such an undertaking? It is easier by far to focus on macroevaluation and pretend that it adequately provides the information demanded of us. Kyrillidou (2001) notes the pressures now put on higher learning institutions, including libraries, by politicians, agencies, and the general public to prove that the institutions consider public needs when meeting goals and objectives (7–10). Can we model our complex organizations using simple data analyses and thus prove to stakeholders that we recognize and meet their needs? Kyrillidou sums up our difficulty nicely, saying, "of course, what is easy to measure is not necessarily what is desirable to measure" (13).

Although the activities of macro- and microevaluation are difficult to coordinate, they must not only be conducted, but also conducted at multiple levels within the library. Organizations' assessment and evaluation activities often do not operate in this comprehensive way. Instead, each section within the library may endeavor to assess its performance very differently from endeavors of other sections. One department operates on clearly defined purposes and goals of data collection and analysis, whereas another collects data and forgoes analysis, and yet another department may ignore evaluation altogether. Departments have the option to base their actions on analyzed data (which is, after all, the point of evaluation), but they may do so inconsistently or not at all. When a library's units are not held accountable for their evaluations or encouraged to communicate with each other, the organization cannot claim to be carrying out a comprehensive assessment program. The groups' individual efforts in determining how well the system is operating at a given level are parallel to macroevaluation. Just like macroevaluation, these efforts are informative but insufficient for assessing the library as a whole. Organization-wide coordination of evaluation efforts, exploring how and why the system operates as it does, is parallel to microevaluation. When libraries desire to conduct assessment on this far-reaching level, their first concern should not be whether collected data is qualitative or quantitative, but whether all of the data is sufficiently and correctly analyzed to inform decision-making.

DRIVING DECISION-MAKING

I am pushing the limits of Lancaster's terminology to illustrate two things. First, the faddish phrase "data-driven decision-making" misleads many librarians into believing that they are acting correctly by basing their decisions on how many of something or what percentage it is of some other thing. Yes, these are decisions based on data analysis, but I hope I have shown that relying solely on such a minimal form of data analysis for organizational assessment is like trying to decode the human genome with a pocket calculator. Data-driven decision-making is a simplistic approach to a complex problem. It often bypasses all but the most basic forms of data analysis and ignores the possibility that decisions should consider factors other than quantitative data. In Lancaster's usage, this is decision-making based solely on macroevaluation.

Second, I want to probe the ideal nature of assessment. We commonly talk of the process as a cycle, where actions are singled out for evaluation, data is gathered and analyzed, the results acted upon, and the action submitted for more evaluation. This analogy is true as a simple model of assessment. But it is also true that the second round of evaluation is a bit different from the first, the third is different from either of these, and so forth. Each time an action is evaluated, the organization has learned more about the action itself and the organization's own process of evaluation. It would, therefore, be more accurate to describe assessment as a spiral, looping around while never quite retracing the same ground each time. Since we are trying to get at the ideal of assessment, this spiral process should occur for the library's services at all levels of the organization, and in a meta-spiral for the organization itself.

What should we do on the way to achieving ideal assessment? I have noted that data-driven decision-making is inaccurate. Let us instead consider the phrase analysis-driven decision-making as a respectable transition away from reliance on data alone as a source of persuasion. Bentley encourages us here, saying, "measuring is needed to determine the quantity of something. Evaluation is needed to determine its worth" (1979, 151). Libraries could take a huge leap forward by committing to analyze warehoused data and to make recommendations for actions based on those analyses. Such a move involves a mind-set that Austen's Anne Elliot would perhaps encourage—from one of safety and stasis, to one of risk and change.

THE ANALYZED LIFE

Some libraries already live and work in a daily environment of analysis-driven decision-making. I will leave to the reader to judge whether any of these libraries have achieved ideal assessment. The institutions mentioned below have been recognized by their peers, by national agencies, and in the library literature as leaders in the field of assessment. They are functioning proof that assessment is more than just a good topic for research papers.

Hiller and Self summarize assessment programs created and maintained at four specific institutional libraries (2004, 144–49):

- The University of Pennsylvania Libraries' Penn Library Data Farm (Zucca 2003)
- The University of Washington Libraries' work with user surveys, focus groups, and LibQUAL+ (Hiller and Self 2004)
- The University of Virginia Libraries' Balanced Scorecard (Self 2003)
- The University of Arizona Libraries' PEMS (Performance Effectiveness Management System) (Stoffle and Phipps 2003)

Each program has been documented in various publications (Stoffle and Phipps 2003; Self 2003; Zucca 2003; University of Pennsylvania Library (a); Hiller 2001; 2002a; 2002b; 2004). I will discuss how these libraries' approaches to assessment should encourage us that analysis-driven decision-making is an attainable goal.

The University of Pennsylvania Libraries

The University of Pennsylvania (Penn) Libraries Data Farm appears at first glance to be overwhelmed by quantitative data. The data farm began as a response to the frustrations many libraries continue to experience with their attempts to derive meaningful user behaviors from a flood of numeric usage data (Zucca 2003). These difficulties became a hole in Penn Libraries' accountability: "The lack of good management information . . . was viewed as a serious shortcoming . . . that could hamper the library's accountability to the university's schools and impede planning and budgeting" (175). The data farm started with attempts to capture and analyze Web usage logs and quickly expanded to incorporate data streams from other sources (176–77). Most critically for this discussion, the data farm rearranged its reporting mechanisms so that static summary reports were no longer the only option. Staff could request live, custom, detailed reports via a Web page without knowing SQL (177). A current examination of the Penn Library Data Farm Web page reveals that this capability is still in place (University of Pennsylvania Library (b)).

This capacity for custom reporting is important because it removes the data farm from the realm of the endless collection described earlier. The focus and intent of this library's data collection is making data available for analysis, according to Penn Libraries' Web page titled "About the Penn Library Data Farm." It is described as a utility, not treated as an end in itself, and the analyses derived from its data are targeted for use in "planning and the achievement of goals" (University of Pennsylvania Library (a)). The approach to data, analysis, and assessment prescribed by the Penn Library Data Farm shows us not only how we might begin to make some sense of our usage data, but also how we might begin to hold staff accountable for data analysis. This model is one way of making data available to staff in a way that eliminates excuses. When it is easier for staff to use the system and analyze the data than not, the data likely will be analyzed.

The University of Washington Libraries

The University of Washington Libraries shows particular strength and longevity in evaluating users' needs and the organization's responses to those needs. Triennial user surveys have been conducted since 1992; more recent inclusion of LibQUAL+ and targeted focus groups enhance this store of information (Hiller and Self 2004). Examination of the Libraries Assessment Group's Web site (University of Washington Libraries) reveals firm focus on assessment via qualitative data. Quantitative data is given second billing to results from user surveys, LibQUAL+, and usability testing. Given libraries' difficulties with qualitative data, the University of Washington Libraries' success is both impressive and inspiring. Their example demonstrates that working with qualitative data can be a feasible library undertaking.

The University of Virginia Libraries

Since 2001, the University of Virginia Libraries has conducted assessments using the Balanced Scorecard initiative (Self 2003). The Balanced Scorecard requires the Libraries to target their achievement goals into very narrowly defined objectives and allows the organization to work on only a few goals and objectives at a time. Self describes the technique and offers examples of actual assessment work within the Balanced Scorecard's four target areas: User; Finance; Internal Processes; and Learning and the Future (28). This laser-like approach to assessment offers the hope of alleviating libraries' helplessness in the face of a data onslaught. Self identifies this hope as one reason for Balanced

Scorecard's adoption by the University of Virginia Libraries: "It forces us to decide what is important, and to identify those numbers that . . . make a difference. It also introduces some balance into our statistical work . . . . We have collected many data regarding resources and user services, but other areas have not received the same attention" (28). As we have seen throughout our discussion, many libraries need some structure imposed on their data collection and analysis. Using a technique like Balanced Scorecard, they are not required to create that structure internally.

The University of Arizona Libraries

The University of Arizona Libraries created an assessment infrastructure known as PEMS in 1998 (Stoffle and Phipps 2003). The system is designed to bring accountability to every level of the organization. It aligns individual, group, and organizational goals and performance measures with objectives and outcomes outlined in the Libraries' strategic plan. Stoffle and Phipps speak of the critical element of cultural change that PEMS has brought to the Libraries. They point out that permeating the organization's culture with performance measures has broken down barriers to assessment that might otherwise have remained in place (26). The need for cultural change within libraries has been an undercurrent to the discussion of data and analysis in this chapter. The University of Arizona Libraries' example shows that a culture shift is achievable with consistent planning and reinforcement.

In creating and maintaining their different methods of assessment, these four libraries validate a statement made by Gumilar and Johnson: "Decision making is the conversion of information into action" (1995, 62). Both qualitative and quantitative data are gathered, housed, and analyzed in a variety of ways, including top-down alignment and individual, independent investigation. Each method's conversion of the information into action, however, is undeniable. These organizations' examples show that there is no one way of dealing with data or processing it into assessment.

CONCLUSION

In this chapter we have made a good case for Anne Elliot's idea of persuasion on the side of risk within libraries. Such persuasion begins in data, but it cannot end there. We investigated libraries' fixation with quantitative data over qualitative data and the problems caused by equating data with statistics. We picked apart three possible modes of persuasion through data and discovered that all but the riskiest are inherently flawed. With help from Lancaster's terminology, we inched closer to the notion that data collection and even analysis are of limited use unless feeding the broader activity of assessment. Finally, we landed firmly in the realm of assessment through the portals of four libraries that begin their assessments with data and maintain the spiral through analysis, recommendation, and action.

Looking again at the way things are rather than the way things could be, many of us are in the state described in Pink Floyd's rock album *The Wall* (1979) as "comfortably numb." Perhaps we do not wish to acknowledge that our customary practices are flawed, but we overlook the consequences to our organizations when we trot out surface data for external stakeholders. We present to people with powerful influence over the future of our libraries arguments and conclusions supported by data that looks the same as it always has. What persuasion is there in such data for stakeholders to award a library additional funding and support its new ventures? Is there enough power in this safe, predictable data to keep our libraries alive for the long term? I think not. Dependence on data's superficial meanings has made us complacent and wary of change, and our very complacency is hazardous to libraries' collective future. The deep meanings we will find in our data are risky because they will force us to change. But Anne's seven-year wait for Captain Wentworth proved to her that the risky outcome is not always the unhappy one. Perhaps it is time for librarians to embrace, through our data, risk and change in the hope of a happy ending.

REFERENCES

Allen, Geoffrey G. 1985. The management use of library statistics. *IFLA Journal* 11 (3): 211–22.

Ambrožič, Melita. 2003. A few countries measure impact and outcomes—most would like to measure at least something. *Performance Measurement and Metrics* 4 (2): 64–78. www.emeraldinsight.com/Insight/viewContentItem.do?contentType=Article&contentId=862316 (accessed January 2, 2008).

Association of College & Research Libraries. 2006. *ACRL library data tables 2006: Analysis of selected variables; institutions granting doctoral degrees (Carnegie code D).* http://www.ala.org/ala/mgrps/divs/acrl/publications/trends/2006/doc_analysis.pdf (accessed March 28, 2008).

———. *ACRL 2006 statistical summaries.* http://www.ala.org/ala/mgrps/divs/acrl/publications/trends/2006/index.cfm (accessed March 28, 2008).

Association of Research Libraries. *ARL statistics interactive edition.* http://fisher.lib.virginia.edu/arl/index.html (accessed March 28, 2008).

Austen, Jane. [1818] 1985. *Persuasion.* Ed. D. W. Harding. London: Penguin.

Bentley, Stella. 1979. Academic library statistics: A search for a meaningful evaluative tool. *Library Research* 1:143–52.

Blake, Julie C., and Susan P. Schleper. 2004. From data to decisions: Using surveys and statistics to make collection management decisions. *Library Collections, Acquisitions, and Technical Services* 28 (4): 460–64. http://dx.doi.org/10.1016/j.lcats.2004.09.002 (accessed January 2, 2008).

Bollen, Johan. 2007. Aggregation and analysis of usage data: A structural, quantitative perspective. Lecture, National Information Standards Organization (NISO) forum: Understanding the data around us; gathering and analyzing usage data, Dallas, TX. http://niso.kavi.com/news/events/niso/past/usage07/usage07bollen_plenary.pdf.

Covey, Denise Troll. 2002. Usage and usability assessment: Library practices and concerns. *Tools for practitioners.* Washington, DC: Digital Library Federation/Council on Library and Information Resources.

Edem, U. Selong, and Olu Olat Lawal. 1997. Utilization of quantitative methods in decision making among Nigerian university librarians. *Library Management* 18 (1): 53–58. www.emeraldinsight.com/Insight/viewContentItem.do;jsessionid=F9EEA6557F435497B6FB411569C4F0D3?contentType=Article&contentId=858832 (accessed February 10, 2008).

Faulkner, Ronnie W. 1988. Statistics and record keeping. In *The smaller academic library: A management handbook.* Ed. Gerald B. McCabe. New York: Greenwood Press.

Gorman, Gary E. 1999. Collecting data sensibly in information settings. Paper presented at the 65th International Federation of Library Associations and Institutions (IFLA) Council and General Conference, Bangkok, Thailand. www.ifla.org/IV/ifla65/papers/004-120e.htm (accessed February 10, 2008).

Gumilar, Dudung, and Ian M. Johnson. 1995. Management information systems in some academic libraries in Britain. *The New Review of Academic Librarianship* 1:57–84.

Hiller, Steve. 2001. Assessing user needs, satisfaction, and library performance at the University of Washington Libraries. *Library Trends* 49 (4): 605–25. http://proquest.umi.com/pqdweb?index=2&did=77808800&SrchMode=3&sid=1&Fmt=4&VInst=PROD&VType=PQD&RQT=309&VName=PQD&TS=1207527889&clientId=48067&aid=1 (accessed April 3, 2008).

———. 2002a. How different are they? A comparison by academic area of library use, priorities, and information needs at the University of Washington. *Issues in Science and Technology Librarianship*, no. 33 (Winter). www.istl.org/02-winter/article1.html (accessed April 6, 2008).

———. 2002b. The impact of information technology and online library resources on research, teaching, and library use at the University of Washington. *Performance Measurement and Metrics* 3 (3): 134–39. www.emeraldinsight.com/Insight/viewContentItem.do;jsessionid=F9EEA6557F435497B6FB411569C4F0D3?contentType=Article&contentId=862308 (accessed April 6, 2008).

———. 2004. Another tool in the assessment toolbox: Integrating LibQUAL+ into the University of Washington Libraries assessment program. *Journal of Library Administration* 40 (3–4): 121–37.

Hiller, Steve, and James Self. 2004. From measurement to management: Using data wisely for planning and decision-making. *Library Trends* 53 (1): 129–55. http://proquest.umi.com/pqdweb?index=0&did=771893151&SrchMode=1&sid=1&Fmt=3&VInst=PROD&VType=PQD&RQT=309&VName=PQD&TS=1207527781&clientId=48067 (accessed January 2, 2008).

Kyrillidou, Martha. 2001. An overview of performance measures in higher education and libraries. *Journal of Library Administration* 35 (4): 7–18.

Lancaster, F. W. 1977. *The measurement and evaluation of library services.* With the assistance of M. J. Joncich. Washington, DC: Information Resources Press.

Libstats: A simple Web-based app for tracking library reference statistics. http://code.google.com/p/libstats/ (accessed April 6, 2008).

Los Alamos National Laboratory. *MESUR: Metrics from scholarly usage of resources.* http://mesur.lanl.gov/ MESUR.html (accessed April 6, 2008).

Moroney, M. J. 1956. *Facts from figures.* 3rd ed. Harmondsworth, UK: Penguin.

National Center for Education Statistics. *Digest of education statistics: 2007.* http://nces.ed.gov/programs/digest/ d07/tables_7.asp (accessed March 28, 2008).

Pink Floyd. 1979. *The Wall.* Columbia Records. Pink Floyd Music Limited.

Self, Jim. 2003. Using data to make choices: The Balanced Scorecard at the University of Virginia Library, in New Measures. Special double issue, *ARL: A Bimonthly Report on Research Library Issues and Actions from ARL, CNI, and SPARC,* no. 230–31:28–29. www.arl.org/resources/pubs/br/br230/ (accessed January 2, 2008).

Shank, Russell. 1982. Management information and the organization: Homily from the experience of the data rich but information poor. In *Library automation as a source of management information: Papers presented at the 1982 Clinic on Library Applications of Data Processing.* Ed. F. W. Lancaster. Urbana, IL: Graduate School of Library and Information Science. http://hdl.handle.net/2142/1167 (accessed January 2, 2008).

Stoffle, Carla, and Shelley Phipps. 2003. Creating a culture of assessment: The University of Arizona experience, in New Measures. Special double issue, *ARL: A Bimonthly Report on Research Library Issues and Actions from ARL, CNI, and SPARC,* no. 230–31:26–27. www.arl.org/resources/pubs/br/br230/ (accessed January 2, 2008).

Sullivan, Michael, III. 2007. *Statistics: Informed decisions using data.* Upper Saddle River, NJ: Pearson Education.

Swets. ScholarlyStats. www.swets.com/web/show/id=80909/langid=42 (accessed April 6, 2008).

Tietjen, Gary L. 1986. *A topical dictionary of statistics.* New York: Chapman and Hall.

University of Pennsylvania Library. (a). About the Penn Library data farm. http://metrics.library.upenn.edu/ prototype/about/index.html (accessed April 2, 2008).

———. (b). Penn Library data farm. http://metrics.library.upenn.edu/prototype/datafarm (accessed April 2, 2008).

University of Washington Libraries. UW Libraries Assessment. www.lib.washington.edu/assessment (accessed April 2, 2008).

White, Andrew, and Eric Djiva Kamal. 2006. *E-metrics for library and information professionals: How to use data for managing and evaluating electronic resource collections.* New York: Neal-Schuman Publishers.

Zucca, Joe. 2003. Traces in the clickstream: Early work on a management information repository at the University of Pennsylvania. *Information Technology and Libraries* 22 (4): 175–79. http://proquest.umi.com/ pqdweb?index=1&did=535032681&SrchMode=1&sid=2&Fmt=4&VInst=PROD&VType=PQD&RQT =309&VName=PQD&TS=1207528569&clientId=48067 (accessed April 3, 2008).

CHAPTER 2

Using Educational Data to Inform and Persuade

KATE ZOELLNER

To make informed decisions and to advocate for libraries, information professionals should consider ways to enhance the information they use in decision-making and to present the value of libraries to external stakeholders. The use of educational data has gained prominence in the past 20 years for improving library evaluation, planning, and external communication. This chapter serves as a primer on the use of educational data to expand librarians' knowledge and skills on the use of data beyond library-generated statistics and service-area demographics. Educational data is first defined and a rationale for its use explained. Resources for locating the data, and the ways it is and can be used by library professionals, are then discussed.

EDUCATIONAL DATA

Definition

Educational data is used in this chapter to mean raw numerical data about schools, colleges, and universities in which libraries exist, or, in the case of public and special libraries, the educational institutions in their service communities, with a focus on American libraries and schools. Examples include budget allocations, enrollment figures, student test scores, and degree completion rates. Educational data also covers analyses of this raw data and data projections included in documents created by educational institutions, including government agencies. District curricula, plans for new degree-granting programs, accreditation reviews, and growth projections, for example, are encompassed by the term educational data.

The Need

Historically, libraries evaluated their work by collecting and reporting library input and output data, for example, budget line item figures or the number of monographs in a collection. During the past 20 years, the confluence of educational legislation; information seeking behavior and brain research; Internet information aggregators; and public funding pressures have led libraries of all types to evolve their roles and planning processes with a focus on education and accountability (Crowley 2005; Martin 2004). As a result, libraries have shifted their focus from the collection of library-generated statistics towards systematic evaluation practices that indicate planning and design, that contextualize the data collected, and that incorporate the perceptions of library users (Shi and Levy 2005). Educational data is constructive throughout this evaluation process, at the macro level in strategic planning and at the micro level in making decisions on specific library services. The new evaluation practices and measures used by libraries have led to the prominence of educational data as a means to contextualize library-generated data and to strengthen the role of libraries as informal educational institutions.

The movement within American libraries to align with larger educational institutions has been a determining factor in the growth of educational data as an evaluation measure and communication tool. This movement is evident in discussions of bibliographic instruction and learning outcomes, as well as the response of the profession to educational legislation and reports during the past 20 years. For example, the publication *Alliance for Excellence: Librarians Respond to "A Nation at Risk"* (Center for Libraries and Education Improvement 1984) presents libraries and librarians as essential to the educational reforms needed in the "Learning Society" deemed necessary in *A Nation at Risk: The Imperative for Educational Reform.*[1] The recommendations of the Center for Libraries and Education Improvement highlight the work of libraries with adult literacy, curriculum, information skills, media services, and professional training. Additionally, written in response to national education goals, *The Roles of Libraries in Education* identifies three roles that libraries play in education: providing access to education, ensuring equity in education, and impacting academic achievement (Boucher and Curry Lance 1992).

More recently, former American Library Association President Leslie Burger responded to "A First Look at the Literacy of American's Adults in the 21st Century" (National Center for Education Statistics 2006) with the following statement: "Libraries are the one institution that provides support for literacy before children enter kindergarten, throughout the school-age years and beyond retirement. Investing in literacy is an investment in our nation's future and investing in libraries supports lifelong learning for all" (2006, 7). Further, Bennett, in an article entitled "Charting the Same Future?" compares "A Test of Leadership: Charting the Future of U.S. Higher Education" (Commission on the Future of Higher Education 2006) with "Charting Our Future: ACRL's Strategic Plan 2020" (Association of College and Research Libraries 2006), concluding that librarians can use the recommendations in the commission's report in the areas of student learning, innovation, K-12 education, and lifelong learning "to accomplish the goals of the ACRL strategic plan" and "to take leading roles in the future of higher education" (Bennett 2007, 370, 372). In each of these instances the role of libraries and librarians are strategically aligned with those of formal educational institutions and placed within the larger context of social educational agencies.

Within this educational framework, the contributions libraries make to a community, school, college, university, or other organization are placed at the forefront of educators', public officials', and policymakers' agendas. In addition to informing and evaluating decisions and to communicating the library's story and vision, many librarians argue that the use of educational data is necessary for continued public funding and support of libraries.

RESOURCES

The majority of educational data can be accessed freely online, since the collection of this data is, in large part, legislatively mandated. Librarians must first determine what level of data they are seeking and then consider what educational institution might collect and document that data. For example, a public librarian seeking information on local elementary schools in the library's service area for outreach purposes should consult the state office of public instruction, which provides information on public schools by county and district. Also, the librarian could look to the National Center for Education Statistics (NCES), which tracks both public and private schools in the United States. Academic librarians needing information on new certificate and degree programs planned at their college or university would want to consult both their local institution's planning office as well as the state department of higher education that approves such degree proposals. The following section, organized by geographic coverage, outlines select key resources and approaches for locating educational data within them and the types of data each provides.

National

Sponsored by the U.S. Department of Education's Institute for Education Sciences (IES), two key resources for finding educational data at a national level are the NCES and the Education Resources Information Center (ERIC). Both function to increase and facilitate valid research and to disseminate it for the purpose of improving teaching practices, academic achievement, and closing achievement gaps (U.S. Congress 2002). Additionally, NCES is charged with collecting, reporting, analyzing, and disseminating statistical data on the condition and progress of education in the United States (ibid.).

The NCES Web site states that NCES is "the primary federal entity for collecting and analyzing data related to education" (U.S. Department of Education 2008b). The NCES site (http://nces .ed.gov) provides access to large data sets derived from NCES surveys that cover the broad areas of assessment; early childhood, elementary secondary, postsecondary, and international education; libraries; and educational resources. Their Common Core of Data (CCD) database includes elementary and secondary school data compiled by state education departments, including a general description of and contact information for schools and school districts, demographic data on students and staff, and fiscal data. NCES annually aggregates this data, along with data from other sources, for both *The Condition of Education* and *The Digest of Education Statistics*. The Integrated Postsecondary Education Data System (IPEDS) is the annual survey used by NCES to collect postsecondary education data. IPEDS includes enrollment figures, faculty and staff data, program completion and graduation rates, finances, institutional prices, and student financial aid information.

The NCES site provides quick access to educational data through faceted browsing and a variety of searching options. For example, one can search by name or city for public schools, private schools, or colleges; also, the ability to build data tables based on chosen parameters is possible through the "CCD Build a Table," "The Data Analysis System," and IPEDS' "Peer Analysis System." The NCES Web site is a valuable resource for locating aggregate data and analyses of national educational trends, as well as raw data on a particular state, school district, or school.

ERIC includes more than IES survey data and reports. The ERIC Web site (http://eric.ed.gov/) provides free searchable access to the bibliographic records of over one million journal articles (from over 600 journals), books, directories, research syntheses, conference papers, technical reports, policy papers, theses, and other education-related materials from 1966 to the present (U.S. Department of Education 2008a). Full-text literature is available for over 350,000 items, and a current effort to digitize ERIC microfiche documents is increasing full-text access. The site offers basic and advanced searching (subscriptions to ERIC via Ovid Technologies' OvidSP, ProQuest's CSA Illumina, or other vendors' discovery platforms provide additional search features and link to libraries' full-text materials indexed in ERIC). To locate numerical educational data, or analyses of such data, search by Descriptor (ERIC's controlled vocabulary subject term) for one or more of the following publication types:

- 102 machine-readable data files,
- 110 numerical/quantitative data,

- 140 reports: general,
- 141 reports: descriptive,
- 142 reports: evaluative, or
- 143 reports: research.

ERIC is a valuable database for locating analyzed educational data on American education, as well as on specific states, individual schools, and school districts. ERIC provides wider access than NCES to educational research, as its scope not only includes documents published by the U.S. Department of Education but also journal literature and myriad education-related materials from scholarly organizations, professional associations, research centers, policy organizations, and university presses (U.S. Department of Education 2008a). While the depth of analysis is greater in most ERIC items, access to raw data is easier to find through the NCES Web site.

State

State-level educational data can be found through the educational governing bodies of each state. These entities coordinate the educational system of a state and provide a statewide perspective for planning, policy development, and program review. In most states, these administrative functions are separated, thus one department exists for K–12 schools and another for postsecondary educational institutions. While the names of these offices vary by individual state, the functions and types of data they provide are consistent.

A state's department of education or office of public instruction provides aggregate state data as well as data on specific K–12 school districts and schools. For example, the Montana Office of Public Instruction Web site provides annual accreditation data used in school accreditation and state and federal reporting, fiscal data, state and individual school report cards, a statewide education profile, and more.

Similarly, a state's board of higher education, board of regents, higher education commissioner, or university system provides education data on colleges and universities in the state. For example, the Illinois Board of Higher Education collects educational data in three areas: demographic information about enrolled students and degree recipients, faculty and staff information, and characteristics of individual colleges and universities. Additionally, the Board conducts studies for policy decision-making and for examining issues of importance to the state.

Local

The Web sites of school districts, colleges, and universities include educational data and reports at a local level. While this data may be available through a state or national office, if one is only seeking local data it may be easier to access from local sites. For example, Seattle Public Schools, the North Kansas City Schools, The School District of Philadelphia, and other school districts provide data at both the district and school levels. Most elementary and high schools have Web pages within district Web sites, as opposed to a freestanding Web presence. College and university Web sites provide educational data at both the institutional level and frequently the individual school or college level, too. For example, the University of California, Berkeley, provides a statistics page that links to the "Common Data Set" for the university, campus statistics, student and personnel data, comparisons of the university with peer institutions, and more. Often this data is accessible through a campus office of planning and analysis.

Most educational data is easily and freely accessible via the Internet at the sites listed above. Two subscription databases that are education-specific, the Inter-university Consortium for Political and

Social Research (ICPSR) and LexisNexis Statistical, are additional resources for locating educational data. Education librarians, government documents specialists, and researchers at NCES and in university offices of institutional research can provide additional assistance and expertise on the use of this data.

USING THE DATA

Educational data can be effectively used with internal library data to guide decision-making regarding library services, to forecast library needs, and to communicate to stakeholders. Educational data is not meant to stand alone or to eliminate the need for other evaluative measures; it is meant to complement quantitative and qualitative data on library use, users, and service communities.

Examples

Looking to research studies and the work of other libraries as models can be a great starting place in determining how educational data can best support the work of a library. The following three examples show how libraries may use educational data to evaluate services, inform library decision-making, plan for the future, or communicate the value of the library to external stakeholders.

Academic.   Mezick (2007) correlates NCES student retention data with library input data to determine the relationship of library expenditures and of professional library staff to student retention and graduation rates. According to Mezick, "Library administrators can demonstrate the academic library's positive impact upon institutional outcomes. Such evaluative techniques may also be used to identify areas where use of limited economic resources may have the greatest impact" (2007, 565). Through the use of national-level educational data on colleges and universities, this study was able to reveal a positive correlation between library expenditures, library professionals, and student achievement: "The study demonstrates that library expenditures and professional staff have a significant positive effect on student retention" (ibid.). Additionally, the study serves as a model for analyzing the relationship of other library services with student achievement, for the purpose of budgetary allocations and communicating the value of the library to administrators.

Public.   The King County Library System (KCLS) conducts community studies of their libraries roughly every 10 years for service planning and, currently, for construction purposes. The KCLS Web site (www.kcls.org/about/communitystudies) provides the following description: "The community study process involves identifying each library's service area, collecting school and demographic statistics, analyzing the community and developing recommendations for improved library services and collections" (2008a). The *Auburn Library 2008 Community Study* includes school enrollment and ethnicity statistics; reading, math, writing, and science test scores by school; and a narrative section ("Education, Schools & Children") detailing changes in school administration, academic achievement of students, and successful educational partnerships (KCLS 2008b).

The study's sections on current and future library services for children, teens, and adults, as well as the recommendations section, clearly indicate that the library's service projections were in part based on the community's educational institutions. For example, the study states, "Maintaining good communication with the staff of the Auburn School District . . . about available library services continues to be a high priority. Staff will continue to write and send out eNews and hope to augment these with demonstrations of KCLS databases, Assignment Alert options and the Accelerated Reader section of our library catalog" (2008, 13). Additionally, the study recommends that the library "Welcome new teachers with informational packets and library tours" and "Expand the standardized test preparation program for SAT," among other educational initiatives (16). In the *Auburn Library 2008 Community Study*, KCLS used educational data available from the local school district, alongside internal library data and information on other community services, to develop a holistic scan of the Auburn Library service area. Educational data in this example played a key role in informing the library of present and growing educational needs in the community, towards the goal of service planning.

School.   According to McGriff, Harvey, and Preddy, "The library media specialist can analyze reading strengths and weaknesses in order to design a recreational reading program that will help improve student academic achievement," and can further use achievement data to evaluate the program's success (2004, 27). The authors advocate the use of educational data, specifically data on the reading achievement of students, to both inform a library reading program and to assess the impact of that service. Similar to this recommendation and the Mezick study, the funding, staff, and collections of school library media centers have been shown to positively impact the academic achievement of students through the use of educational data. In *How School Librarians Help Kids Achieve Standards*, statewide reading scores from the Colorado Student Assessment are correlated with library media center data (Lance, Rodney, and Hamilton-Pennell 2000). The results of the analysis show that all of the following positively increase reading scores: student visits to the library media center, professional media specialist collaboration with classroom teachers, and information technology (ibid.). In this study, statewide testing achievement scores are utilized as a measure to show the effect of library media centers on student academic achievement.

Moving Forward

The above examples provide models for the ways in which educational data can assist librarians in making informed decisions and communicating their library's vision and successes. The examples cover the use of educational data to support and evaluate library expenditures and professional staffing, to inform an environmental scan for forecasting service needs, and to describe the connection between elementary student academic achievement and school library media center funding, staffing, and collections. Educational data has the potential to enhance decision making for, and communication of, all library services. What follows are a few ideas of other ways in which educational data could be incorporated into library evaluation and communication practices:

- *Collections and access*: Identify new programs at colleges and universities, or changes in curricula in schools. Analyze collection to ensure it will meet the new learning and research needs of the students and teachers. Based on the collection analysis, develop a collection development plan for the relevant subject area. Communicate plans to instructors.

- *Library instruction and reference services*: Review school achievement or university retention data. Identify subject areas, specific academic departments, or key grade levels where students are underperforming. Find out, based on internal data, what services the library has provided to those areas where students are struggling. Based on results and communications with school or university instructors, focus library services and outreach efforts to meet struggling students' needs.

- *Physical facility*: Evaluate student assignments to determine the prevalence of group assignments and if there is a need for the library to adjust group study rooms or to provide presentation technology in the rooms. Based on findings and resulting changes made in the library, market library study rooms.

In each of the scenarios above educational data is used alongside other quantitative and qualitative information to evaluate and, in turn, inform library services.

CONCLUSION

The use of educational data with internal library data can enhance the evaluation, planning, and communication of library goals and services. Since the documentation and collection of educational data is in large part legislatively mandated, it is easily accessible to librarians online. Educational data is valuable because it can provide a measure for evaluating the effects of library services and can be used to contextualize libraries as educational institutions. Within this educational framework, the contributions libraries make to the education of their communities, larger educational institutions, or other organizations are placed at the forefront of educators', public officials', and policymakers' agendas. For this reason, librarians should consider how they could use educational data to focus and improve their libraries' services, to strengthen their communication to external constituencies, and to advocate for continued public funding and support of libraries.

ENDNOTE

1. *A Nation at Risk*, published in 1983 by the National Commission on Excellence in Education, reported on the quality of education in the United States and recommended educational reforms based on the findings.

REFERENCES

2006. News fronts. *American Libraries* 37 (2): 5–8.

Bennett, Miranda. 2007. Charting the same future? The ACRL strategic plan and the report of the commission on the future of higher education. *C&RL News* 68 (6): 370–72, 377.

Boucher, Julie J., and Keith Curry Lance. 1992. *The roles of libraries in education*. Denver, CO: Library Research Service, State Library and Adult Education Office, Colorado State Dept. of Education.

Center for Libraries and Education Improvement. Office of Educational Research and Improvement. 1984. *Alliance for excellence: Librarians respond to "A nation at risk."* www.eric.ed.gov/ERICWebPortal/contentdelivery/servlet/ERICServlet?accno=ED243885.

Crowley, Bill. 2005. Save professionalism. *Library Journal* 130 (14): 46–48.

King County Library System. 2008a. *Community studies*. www.kcls.org/about/communitystudies (accessed April 3, 2008).

———. 2008b. *Auburn library 2008 community study*. Issaquah, WA: Author. www.kcls.org/about/community studies/Auburn%20Library%20Community%20Study.pdf (accessed April 3, 2008).

Lance, Keith Curry, Marcia J. Rodney, and Christine Hamilton-Pennell. 2000. *How school librarians help kids achieve standards: The second Colorado study*. Denver, CO: Colorado State Library, Colorado Dept. of Education.

Martin, Robert S. 2004. Libraries and learning. *Advances in Librarianship* 28:83–93.

McGriff, Nancy, Carl A. Harvey II, and Leslie B. Preddy. 2004. Collecting the data: Monitoring the mission statement. *School Library Media Activities Monthly* XX (7): 24–29.

Mezick, Elizabeth M. 2007. Return on investment: Libraries and student retention. *Journal of Academic Librarianship* 33 (5): 561–66.

Shi, Xi, and Sarah Levy. 2005. A theory-guided approach to library services assessment. *College & Research Libraries* 66:266–77.

U.S. Congress. 2002. *Education Science Reform Act of 2002*, Public Law 107-279, U.S. Statutes at Large 116:1940–87.

U.S. Department of Education. 2008a. About the ERIC collection. Education Resources Information Center. www.eric.ed.gov/ERICWebPortal/resources/html/collection/about_collection.html (accessed April 3, 2008).

———. 2008b. Welcome to NCES. National Center for Education Statistics. http://nces.ed.gov/ (accessed April 3, 2008).

BIBLIOGRAPHY

Eaton, Gale. 1985. "A nation at risk" & the library community's response. *School Library Journal* 32 (4): 28–31.

England, S. Randle. 2007. The consequences of promoting an educational role for today's public libraries. *Public Libraries* 46 (2): 55–63.

Farrell, Maggie. 2005. Trends in higher education: How will they impact academic libraries? Paper presented at the 12th National Conference of the Association of College & Research Libraries, Minneapolis, Minnesota. www.ala.org/ala/mgrps/divs/acrl/events/pdf/farrell05.pdf (accessed April 3, 2008).

Lance, Keith Curry, and Becky Russell. 2004. Scientifically based research on school libraries and academic achievement. *Knowledge Quest* 32 (5): 13–17.

Neuman, Susan. 2002. The role of school libraries in elementary and secondary education. *Teacher Librarian* 30 (1): 74–5.

Sager, Donald. 1992. The best of intentions: The role of the public library in the improvement of public education. *Public Libraries* 31 (1): 11–17.

Todd, Ross. 2008. The evidence-based manifesto for school librarians: If school librarians can't prove they make a difference, they may cease to exist. *School Library Journal* 54 (4): 38–43.

CHAPTER 3

Telling Your Library's Story: How to Make the Most of Your Data in a Presentation

ANNE C. ELGUINDI AND BILL MAYER

Numbers—administrators want them so they can make good funding decisions, and you want them so you can express your library's needs and goals clearly and convincingly. But many things need to fall into place before these objectives can be achieved, including meaningful data collection, relevant analysis, and thoughtful, easily comprehensible display. There is also one key technique that can translate data into a convincing argument: providing context. Whether it is provided by showing trends over time, appropriate comparisons, or reference to established standards, context is what translates a simple number into a persuasive story. It is also what helps others understand what you are trying to achieve. You may be close to your data, and therefore assume that other people can easily see the conclusions you've reached by looking at your graphs, spreadsheets, and/or cocktail napkins. Be careful! The people you are trying to convince are often the people who have the least time to dive deep into complex data and interpretation. They are also often from outside the library world; your colleagues in the library already know what you've been working on for so long, but they aren't the ones who will approve your budget requests.

What follows are three case studies from American University Library, each highlighting a different aspect of the process of transforming simple numbers into an argument for change. Each of these case studies also highlights a different challenge common to many libraries:

1. print-to-digital migrations are happening all around us, and good data is what enables you to manage the politics of change effectively while still accomplishing your goals;

2. the move to a 24-hour library, an expensive change in services and therefore a hard sell to some administrators, is one example of the need for writing clear funding justifications that is endemic to library operations;

3. the effective management of library instruction statistics is critical to a deeper understanding of library services and can help incorporate that understanding into the decision-making process.

These three cases studies are different in that the first is a political problem, the second an operational problem, and the third a programming development problem. All three, however, are linked by data and its innovative presentation, capture, and analysis. We hope that these case studies will help you see new potential in data you already have or give you added insight into how you could present your data as influential evidence to your library community and administrators.

CASE STUDY ONE

The library that does not have space problems is rare these days. Demands on space are numerous and range from traditional needs, including physical storage and study space, to more recent needs, including multipurpose and community-based technology services. Our library is no different; our shelves are full, our chairs and tables are full, and our computers are full. The space crisis came to a head when our off-site storage was unable to accept new shipments for over a year; the crunch was felt throughout the library and the use and potential of space was a constant topic of discussion.

Recently, when off-site storage became an option again, the opportunity for real change presented itself. With the increasing use of and preference for electronic periodicals, and with the need for truly dramatic action that would open up a great deal of space, it was decided to move all bound journals to off-site storage. However, because all academic libraries exist in the context of the larger institution, the problem changed from "What decision should we make?" into "How do we sell this decision to the university community?" As the decision to move out the bound journals had come from the analysis of some highly divergent sources of data (shelving statistics; usage statistics of print and online journals and monographs; computer use statistics; physical plant statistics; and an examination of what makes a library), it seemed best to use data to paint a full picture to the university community.

There are a number of ways to represent the space crunch of a given collection to the university community. At the most basic level, you can show actual pictures of the packed shelving or you can simply present the numbers in a table. Even if only the numbers are presented, details like changing a number's size (as seen in Figure 3.1) or color, or highlighting certain portions that you want your audience to focus on, can be used to make your point more clear. Numbers can also be made more effective through visual representation. The chart in Figure 3.2 is one way to show that if the current trend continued, the books owned would rapidly exceed the amount of space the library has available for them.

Another way to express the situation is to focus on the small number of shelves available for growth and express them visually in the context of the total shelving, as shown in Figure 3.3. This is also a good example of what can be done if you are presenting your data in electronic rather than paper format. If it is in a PowerPoint presentation, for example, you could animate the bars with the "available shelves" bar climbing up to the top, followed by the "full shelves" bar. To see the full shelves come nearly to the mark of complete capacity in a dynamic display would make a more lasting impression. It is important to recognize that chart animation in a live presentation can be effective in the moment, but the chart might need to be adjusted if it used in a printed report; a static image has to stand on its own.

Sometimes the numerical balance of needs can be expressed effectively by highlighting the general idea rather than trying to offer precise quantities. In terms of space, there is simply only so much room

Figure 3.1
Available Shelving

Shelves required for current collection:	21,253
Total shelves available:	21,871
Shelves available for growth:	21,871 - 21,253= **618**

Figure 3.2
Monographs: Space Projections

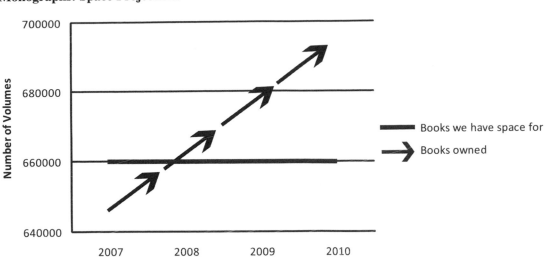

in a given library, and filling one demand will by necessity compromise another. A visual expression of this, as in Figure 3.4, can convey this point in a more engaging way than could a simple statement.

In the case of the bound periodicals, although the space crunch created the need behind their removal, they were selected for removal because of the shift from paper to electronic. The argument for why they should go instead of another collection of materials within the library can be effectively shown with a chart that demonstrates the downward trend of use statistics (Figure 3.5). Our library is lucky that these statistics had been kept for enough years to show a consistent trend. The numbers you need are not always available, but in the case of a fairly universal trend like the drop in paper periodical use, you can always look for a source in the library literature.

Figure 3.3
Shelf Capacity and Shelf Usage

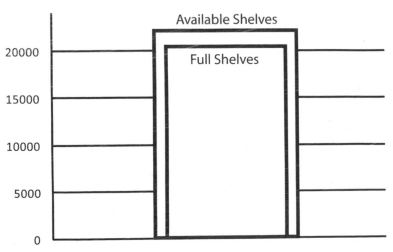

Figure 3.4
Allocation of Space

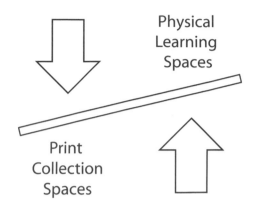

CASE STUDY TWO

Twenty-four-hour access is becoming the norm for library services. Librarians at the frontline of information delivery have long suspected that their main customers are not the ones they might encounter over the reference desk between 9 and 5. Certainly in undergraduate education late-night study groups are essential to the landscape, and libraries which offer online chat services see traffic at all hours of the day and night. Although American University Library's separately housed computer center was open 24 hours during the semester, the call for the library to be open 24 hours had been heard for years. In fall 2007, the library shortened its hours in the computer lab to fund the library's desire to stay open 24 hours from Sunday through Thursday evenings for the entire semester.

Figure 3.5
Print Journals Use Statistics

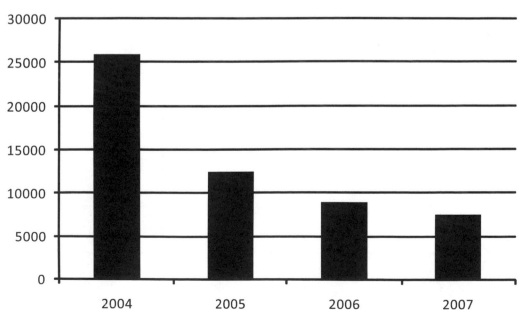

As is often true, with increased funding came the need to justify it. The libraries' access services group was already taking some entrance count statistics, but those were merely gate counts and did not tell much beyond the number of gate-clicks as someone entered or exited the library. The statistics did not tell a story that was compelling or exciting to the university librarian, which meant the university librarian would not be able to easily make a case to the provost for the success of the new 24-hour program.

In collaboration with the evening supervisor, the university librarian developed a system for counting users manually. This provided a number of benefits: evening and late night staff had an important hourly activity to perform that was measurable and noticeable if it was not completed; the task of walking through the library on regular rounds furthered the staff's sense of "what was going on" inside the library, particularly in the wee hours; and an entirely unexpected opportunity for data collection and interpretation was presented that eventually provided the university librarian with a new way of seeing laptop use and computer support in the library.

A display of the number of users in the building, shown in Figure 3.6, is made more effective by clearly showing maximum, minimum, and average numbers. When looking at the steady decrease in users as the night progresses, however, administrators would consistently ask the same question: "Is it worth staying open through 4 A.M.?" Therefore, new tracking was implemented to capture data regarding *what users were actually doing at nighttime*.

Figure 3.7 compares the number of people present and the number of laptops being used. We can infer from the data provided that one out of every two students brings his or her own laptop into the library at the beginning of overnight hours, but by the time 3 A.M. rolls around, most users are working on their own equipment. This gives insight into computer usage in the library. For example, based on the data collected, the library may be well advised to lend laptops overnight—instead of having them due at midnight—and invest in more laptops rather than fixed workstations. This data spurred the

Figure 3.6
24/5 Services Launch—Fall 2007

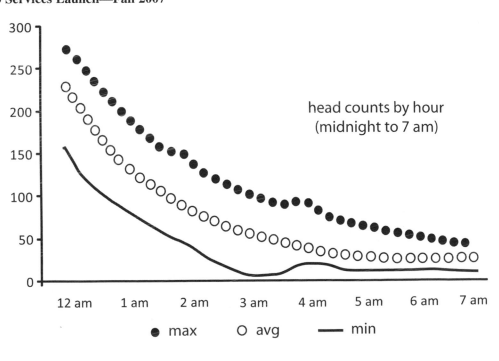

Figure 3.7
Users and Laptops Overnight

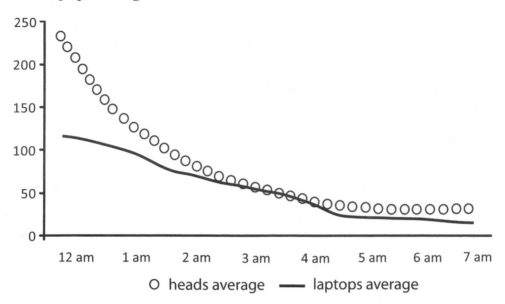

university librarian to ask students how they used their laptops; most reported that they did not carry their laptops around during the day, as they were too heavy, but when they knew they had a long night ahead in the library they would make the effort to take their laptops with them.

Plans are now underway to provide more 24-hour services. The student body has applauded the library's increased hours of operation, but it has also lamented the closing of the computer lab overnight. "Why does the campus always take away with one hand what they are giving with the other?" one student asked the university librarian during an open forum with student government leaders. Critical to the planning for changes to library services will be the capture and meaningful interpretation of data. With measurable data, you can gain insight into how well the service is succeeding, and without it, you might miss the unexpected discoveries that can emerge.

CASE STUDY THREE

The process of compiling and analyzing library instruction statistics had been problematic for years. An old paper-based system had been replaced by a Microsoft Excel file, but with no true data controls, the file had become a jumble of information. In the column labeled "group/time," for example, some library instructors would put the number of minutes the class was taught, some would put the minutes and the relevant program, and some would put the time range of the class. Sorting through the data and compiling it was a tedious chore, and only the most basic statistics could be gleaned from the data (e.g., the number of classes and students taught).

In order to overcome the limitations of this system and get a better picture of who in the university community was being reached through library instruction, the library instruction team decided to move to a Microsoft Access database. One of the members designed the database and its entry forms, with all members participating in exactly what should be recorded and how. In the end, there were fields for library instructor(s), date and time of the session, location, type of attendee, and type of instruction session (in-class session, walk-in workshop, personal appointment, tour for a particular

Figure 3.8
Library Instruction Classes by School

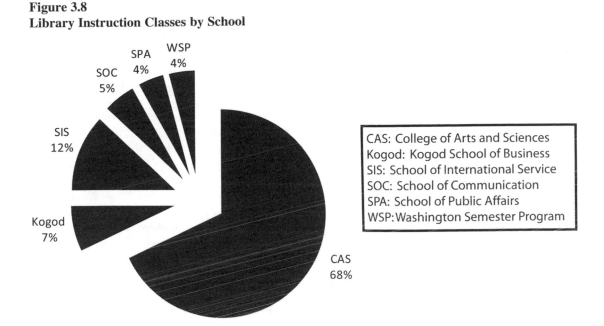

CAS: College of Arts and Sciences
Kogod: Kogod School of Business
SIS: School of International Service
SOC: School of Communication
SPA: School of Public Affairs
WSP: Washington Semester Program

program, or personal research appointment). For each type of instruction session, further clarifications were allowed; for an in-class session, for example, the curriculum course code, professor's name, class title, and school (e.g., College of Arts and Sciences) were listed, all with controlled vocabularies (except for the course title, which was included for the needs of individual instructors and not intended to be part of any analysis). In effect, any item that was intended to be used for analysis, even how many minutes a class was taught, was kept clean using a controlled vocabulary. Subforms that were accessed directly from the main form allowed individuals to add to controlled vocabularies as needed, including adding a new professor or a newly developed walk-in workshop they had developed.

Figure 3.9
Library Instruction Classes by CAS Department

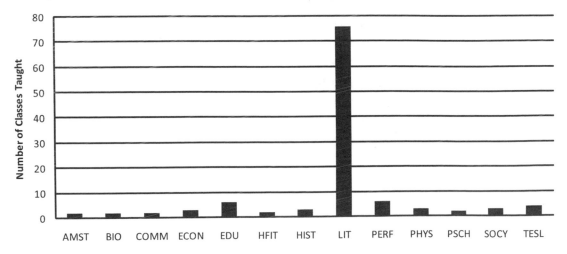

This new repository of library instruction data allowed for greater ease of access—once a report had been written, it could quickly produce up-to-date statistics with a few clicks—and greater detail of results. Because each in-class session was associated with a school and a course code, library administration and the library instruction team were now able to track which schools and disciplines had received library instruction. They could also track the relative prominence of undergraduate versus graduate classes, outside groups, and which walk-in classes were well attended. For example, Figure 3.8 shows the predominance of students from the College of Arts and Sciences (CAS) who attended library instruction sessions, and Figure 3.9 shows that the majority of library instruction classes taught within the CAS were for literature and writing courses. Not a surprise, but this clear difference between library instruction for CAS and for the rest of the schools and colleges provides evidence that the library could consider promoting library instruction more to other departments.

An example of a change that came about due to greater ease of access to statistics was the adjustment of the walk-in class schedule. The database made it possible to quickly see which classes were well attended (Figure 3.10) as well as which days of the week had been more popular (Figure 3.11). The schedule for the following year was adjusted accordingly: some classes were cut and others were

Figure 3.10
Average Attendance for Individual Walk-in Classes

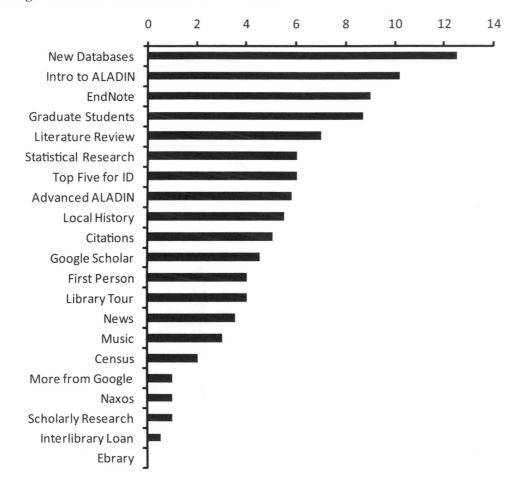

Figure 3.11
Average Walk-in Attendance by Day of the Week, Fall 2007–Spring 2008

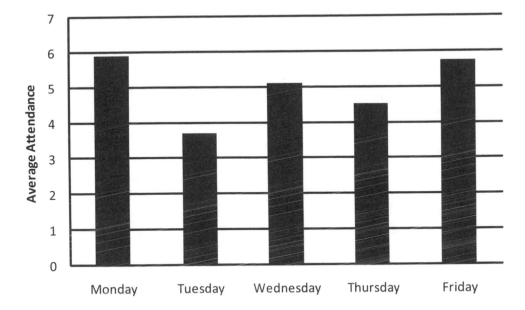

moved to days that had received higher attendance. Overall, because it was much easier to generate summary statistics and reports that showed the patterns among the instruction sessions, the database led to a better understanding of the library's relationship with the university community with regard to instruction.

CONCLUSION

Drawing meaningful outcomes from data about library services is now a requirement for any academic library. University accreditation organizations demand it, campus administrators demand it, and most importantly, students benefit from seeing how services are operating so they can understand where campus dollars go; we see immediate responses from students in the library's online suggestion box when they like (or dislike) changes that the library has made. Yet merely counting widgets or tallying tick marks are not enough in today's competitive environment. Contextualizing your data and showing its relevance to the university's mission is essential to libraries in order to get funding for new student-centric operations. Simple steps to transform your data from mere numbers into easily read and understood charts and graphs can go a long way towards ensuring your next budget request is endorsed by the campus administrator who needs to balance a world of competing priorities.

Data can tell stories for you, and it can lead your audience to new interpretations that may surprise you and, in turn, further spur your thinking. Contextualizing data is much like beginning a conversation; once you present your data, it is open for all manner of interpretation, and how you manage that conversation will make the difference. Busy campus executives will not have the time or patience to scroll through a lengthy spreadsheet, but if you give them the bottom line, in easily digested and comprehensible ways, their appreciation of your work will come through in support for your proposals.

PART II

Evaluation of Monographic Collections

CHAPTER 4

Collection Evaluation: Selecting the Right Tools and Methods for Your Library

LUCY ELEONORE LYONS

INTRODUCTION

This chapter, a guide to conducting collection evaluations, demonstrates that *all* libraries are capable of conducting assessments. This can be accomplished by adhering to three essential steps: (1) the level of analysis must be established; (2) the working environment must be weighed; and (3) the above must be matched to appropriate collection analysis tools and methodologies. In short, the steps to successful collection assessment answer these three questions: What *must* be done? What *can* be done? And *how* can it be done?

Efficiency and economy are always valued when applied to collection evaluation. These are particularly important when collection assessment is not a routine task, but a special project. In such circumstances, time and resources must be shifted to accommodate the work. Hence, it is important that the tasks are kept to a minimum. Section I (step 1), "Level of Analysis," explains how to align the level of analysis with the purpose of the analysis itself, and why it is important to do so.

The most viable collection analysis for any given library can be discovered by recognizing the true state of the library's circumstances. It is not enough to simply choose an assessment tool or methodology. To be successful, there are also genuine and sobering utilitarian calculations that must first be considered. Section II (step 2), "Working Environment," provides schemata for identifying your library among situational types.

After following the first two steps, establishing the level of analysis for the evaluation and gaining an understanding of the potential for assessment in your library, it is time for step three: a consideration of tools and methodologies. While there is no shortage of creative analytical approaches to collection evaluation, many are too costly, too time consuming, or too difficult to replicate. Section III (step 3), "Matching Tools to Environment," is the largest of the sections and provides concrete suggestions for carrying out collection evaluations under all types of situations, from relatively more expensive commercial software products to simple, low-cost research programs which are capable of fulfilling workaday assessment needs. I do not attempt to provide a comprehensive list of evaluation tools, but rather seek to encourage librarians to approach assessment with imagination, creativity, and originality while simultaneously maintaining the integrity of quantitative research.

LEVEL OF ANALYSIS: WHAT *MUST* BE DONE?

Initial planning for collection evaluation should consider the purpose of the assessment. That may sound obvious, but it is often overlooked because librarians do not always recognize that there are different levels of analysis and choosing the appropriate level depends upon the purpose of the evaluation.

There are innumerable reasons to conduct evaluations of collections. New hires of faculty often precipitate new directions within an academic department, thereby leading to a subject-specific collection assessment and changes in collection development policies. When staff changes (e.g., turnover, retirement, or promotion) cause responsibility shifts, an assessment of the subject specific collection may serve as an introduction for the new bibliographer or selector as well as an opportunity to reevaluate an area that, having been under the long-term care of the previous selector, perhaps has not been closely examined in years. Internal and external academic program reviews, accreditation reports, grant applications, discussions with faculty, advanced research assistance to graduate-level students, selective subject development, and gift solicitations are but a few more examples of situations that may require the library to describe, display, and analyze current holdings of specific subject areas. These types of assessment may arise at any time, as in: "Hi. We in the Department of Sociology are working on a grant and it requires data from the library. We need your data by Friday."

The purpose of the assessment, then, will determine the level of analysis. It is helpful to ask: Is it truly necessary to evaluate the library's total holdings? If, for example, the library wishes to solicit donations, it may be possible that concentration on a particular subject area (e.g., theatre) will be more profitable than a vaguely defined campaign for support for all types of library materials. A very close analysis of the theatre collection, including both what it contains and titles it does not, may be more useful to and have more effect upon donors than an overwhelming overview of all holdings.

On the other hand, if the library wishes to argue with the institution's administration for a higher base allocation, aggregate statistics demonstrating the ranking of the collection compared to that of peer libraries may be most persuasive. Assessments of total holdings are invoked whenever it is necessary to capture the "big picture." Although one may wish to cite subject specific needs (e.g., demands brought about by a new nanotechnology program), it is imperative to demonstrate that a mere reallocation of existing resources will not suffice for the needs of the library. Likewise, review of internal budget appropriations for collections requires total collections data in hand. Major projects (e.g., stacks shifts) call for an analysis of the entire physical collection so that decisions can be made in regard to weeding or the removal of materials to storage facilities. Furthermore, evaluations of total holdings can be used to test and discuss the fulfillment of the library's mission or strategic or annual plans. Such assessments may also be used to create or reassess collecting responsibilities among consortium members, to define local or regional needs, and to identify collection cooperation or partnership opportunities between libraries.

It is imperative to think hard about the purpose of the assessment and to choose the proper level of analysis, because it will require a great deal more of the library's resources to assess all collections rather than a specific one or a set. As will be seen in Section II, taking an account of your library's resources, or its current working environment, is an equally important step in preparing to conduct a collection assessment.

WORKING ENVIRONMENT: WHAT *CAN* BE DONE?

It may be that the newest collection analysis tool on the market seems tailored to answer your library's collections questions, but the most technologically advanced product will fail to provide the needed assessment if the library, while just able to afford the product, cannot spare the staff time to learn to use it. Hence, the next step toward successful collection assessment is to understand the assets and liabilities of your library's working environment. This understanding should, in turn, help to guide your decision about which assessment tool to choose. In short, it is necessary to assess what is *possible*, given the resources available, *before* attempting to assess the collection.

All research methodologies contain assumptions—not only suppositions having to do with the objectivity of the process, but also assumptions having to do with its execution. Makers of electronic collection assessment tools, for example, implicitly assume that there are libraries that can afford to pay for these products. Sometimes the costs are less obvious. If the library does not create a new position for a collection analyst, it may appear as though the project can be carried out without affecting the overall budget. That is, of course, an illusion. The reference librarian who is asked to execute a collection evaluation sets aside other tasks to take on the special assignment. In addition to expenses in terms of staff time, many projects carry other costs (e.g., for new software or color printers). Hence, essential areas of your library that need to be analyzed include (1) staff, in terms of analytic and technical skills, as well as time, and (2) the budget, in terms of overall available funds and special costs for assessment tools, hiring, and/or new equipment.

The mere mention of expenditures may scare some librarians away from considering a collection assessment. However, the following will demonstrate that all libraries can afford assessment projects. The first key element to doing so is to systematically identify the library's assets and develop an awareness of the potential costs of any given method. With this knowledge, it is possible to identify compatible collection evaluation projects for all types of libraries. This section provides a schematic approach to recognizing structural constraints and to matching methodologies to environments.

The ideal collection evaluation situation is one in which the library has adopted a "culture of assessment" (Nardini 2001). If the resources are available, collection evaluation will become an embedded value and assessment will be viewed as routine rather than exceptional. This is cost effective, because when staff time is dedicated to assessment, the learning curve becomes increasingly low; in addition, the cost is routinely absorbed, and the funding becomes established and recurring. Hence, in the ideal environment, both time and money are in place. Unfortunately, there are other types of library environments.

Figure 4.1 is a simple diagram of library types. Even libraries with the best intentions sometimes cannot afford a culture of assessment and instead simply cope with assessment when the demand arises. In addition to libraries with plenty of staff resources and funds (Type A libraries), some have available funds but not the staff time to devote to skills enhancement and research tasks (Type B). In other cases, staffing and skills are plentiful, but there is a scarcity of funds (Type C). Finally, in many libraries there is a shortage of both time and money (Type D). After reading this section, you should be able to identify your library's type in Figure 4.1.

Figure 4.1
Library Types Defined by the Demands of Assessment Tools

		Intensity of Time and Skills	
		High	Low
	High	Type A	Type B
Cost			
	Low	Type C	Type D

Type A Libraries

Figures 4.2 through 4.5 expand on what one needs to evaluate in terms of your library's circumstances. Figure 4.2, for example, under "Current Working Environment," describes Type A libraries as well endowed with both staff and funds. Therefore, as noted under "Acceptable Demands of Evaluation Tool," Type A libraries can consider employing tools that require a high degree of analytic and technical skills, or staff who can develop these skills, as well as tools that carry added costs.

The more sophisticated and complicated the assessment project, the greater will be the need for strong analytical skills. While many librarians are capable of data manipulation and able to deftly use software applications (e.g., Access or Excel), fewer have the knowledge and experience necessary to interpret, to judge, to articulate relationships, to provide context, or otherwise analyze the impressive tables, graphs, and charts that are easily produced. The electronic WorldCat Collection Analysis (WCA) product, for example, includes over 5,000 subject descriptors. With these and other variables, it is possible to create elaborate tables that rank subjects by rate of growth within a 10-year period. Northwestern University Library thereby discovered a phenomenal 631 percent rate of growth in the acquisition of monographs on "plant physiology" between 1990 and 2000. However, in 1990, the collection contained only 16 books; 10 years later, there were 117. Is this significant growth for a collection in a research level library? Staff who possess experience or education in statistics might suggest that criteria be applied to provide meaning to the results, e.g., that only those subject collections with at least 500 books in 1990 be considered for rate-of-growth analysis.

Type A libraries, then, can and should consider purchasing or subscribing to an online collection assessment tool, employing a full-time analyst who possesses strong analytical skills, and fully incorporating assessment into the organization so that collection assessment becomes a routine part of the library's operations.

Type B Libraries

If, on the other hand, your library is a Type B with money but little staff time, slightly different outcomes must be considered (see Figure 4.3). When staff time is restricted, assessment cannot be incorporated as a routine task. Even if the library has operational or collections funds to pay for statistical software for collection analysis, it must also possess significant staff time to achieve mastery of the

Figure 4.2
Library Type A: High Intensity and High Cost

The Current Working Environment
- Staff time availability: high
- General funds availability: high

Acceptable Demands of Evaluation Tool
- Analytic/technical skills: high

- Learning curve tolerance: high
- Financial outlay: high

Suggested Methodology
- Purchase commercial assessment software
- Create full-time collection assessment position to establish a "culture of assessment"

interface and methodology. And while some work can be safely handled by student assistants (who are nonetheless also "staff time"), organizing massive amounts of data into coherent sense and interpreting and reporting it is extremely labor intensive and calls for robust analytic skills. Thus, while professional staff time may not be required for all portions of an evaluation project, much will be needed for its completion.

In this case, with the funds available, the library can still obtain the expensive electronic tools that Type A libraries can purchase, but new personnel (e.g., a part-time consultant) will need to be hired to do the work. And because staff time is always a problem in Type B libraries, the idea of continuous assessment will have to be abandoned. It is possible, however, to establish a modified culture of assessment. An evaluation of the total collection could be scheduled, for example, to be performed every three years.

Type C Libraries

Library Type C is descriptive of the current reality within many libraries (see Figure 4.4). In Type C libraries, there are sufficient personnel with sufficient time wishing the library had more money. It could be argued that Type C's staff time is of equal value to Type B's resource budget. Expensive as well as "free" assessment tools can carry considerable costs in terms of staff skills and hours. Many libraries make use of their own internal operating management system for collection evaluation. While this resource requires no new financial outlay, it can be expensive in terms of time intensity. The "Create list" function, for instance, within the Innovative Interfaces Inc. (III) system provides a relatively easy way, for those with medium skills and understanding, to extract reports on collection size and other data; on the other hand, Endeavor's Voyager offers no such ease of extraction. To gather the same data from Voyager requires an able computer programmer or someone with advanced Access application skills. Unlike Type B libraries, Type C libraries have sufficient staff time to learn to use complex tools. With enough foresight and planning, Type B libraries can, of course, use their funds to temporarily hire experts. Nonetheless, Type C libraries might be considered only slightly less fortunate than well-managed Type Bs.

In the case of Type C libraries, then, it is possible to consider methodologies that require specific skills and a high learning curve, and little or no extra expenses. With access to the public catalogs of other libraries and ample staff time available, even peer comparison analyses can be performed. Many libraries also have access via FirstSearch to Worldcat, which (it will be shown) can be used as

Figure 4.3
Library Type B: Low Intensity and High Cost

The Current Working Environment
  • Staff time availability: low
  • General funds availability: high

Acceptable Demands of Evaluation Tool
  • Analytic/technical skills: low

  • Learning curve tolerance: low
  • Financial outlay: high

Suggested Methodology
  • Purchase commercial assessment software
  • Hire an analyst on a per-project basis to interpret results and generate reports every two or more years

Figure 4.4
Library Type C: High Intensity and Low Cost

The Current Working Environment
- Staff time availability: high
- General funds availability: low

Acceptable Demands of Evaluation Tool
- Analytic/technical skills: high

- Learning curve tolerance: high
- Financial outlay: low

Suggested Methodology
- Rely on resources currently available
- Rely on current staff to learn new analytic skills and enhance or learn technical skills

---

an instrument of assessment. These are examples of collection evaluation tools which do not carry costs above what the library currently pays.

Type D Libraries

Finally, Type D libraries consist of overworked staff and few funds. Although poor in staff time and poor in funds, Type D libraries can carry out assessments with tools including the local catalog and the Internet, both available to all college and research libraries. These tools do not require new training or skills, and they are easy to use.

MATCHING TOOLS TO ENVIRONMENT: *HOW* CAN IT BE DONE?

Once the level of analysis has been identified (total holdings versus subject-specific) and your library's work environment has been recognized (Types A–D), you can begin to look for assessment

Figure 4.5
Library Type D: Low Intensity and Low Cost

The Current Working Environment
- Staff time availability: low
- General funds availability: low

Acceptable Demands of Evaluation Tool
- Analytic/technical skills: low

- Learning curve tolerance: low
- Financial outlay: low

Suggested Methodology
- Rely on resources currently available for subject-specific only projects
- Rely on current staff skills, not on the development of new skills

---

Figure 4.6
Selecting the Right Tools and Methods for Your Library Type

Assessment Tool Type	Maximum Analysis Level	Type A Toleration: high cost and high intensity	Type B Toleration: high cost and low intensity	Type C Toleration: low cost and high intensity	Type D Toleration: low cost and low intensity
commercial products	total holdings	preferred	preferred	too costly	too costly
library vendor's database	subject holdings	universe too limited	limited universe and high learning curve; request standard reports	no new costs; customize own reports	high learning curve; request standard reports
vendor Web site title lists	subject holdings	limited universe	limited universe and time-consuming process	no new costs	no new costs or skills; time consuming, use for small subject areas
FirstSearch	subject holdings	worthwhile for peer comparisons	worthwhile for peer comparisons	preferred, if access is already available	preferred, if access is already available
booksellers' databases	subject holdings	limited and somewhat unknown universe	limited and somewhat unknown universe and time-consuming process	no new costs	no new costs or skills; time consuming, use for small subject areas
booksellers' lists	subject holdings	not necessary	not necessary	no new costs and useful as qualitative measure	no new costs and useful as qualitative measure
rankings and peer comparisons	total holdings	worthwhile for aggregate statistics	quick, easy access to aggregate statistics	no new costs and worthwhile for aggregate statistics	no new costs or skills and quick, easy access to aggregate statistics
vendor reports	total holdings	worthwhile for special purposes	readily available and worthwhile for special purposes	worthwhile as supplement to local data	readily available and can use as substitute to local data
local collections data	total holdings	worthwhile to collect on regular basis	worthwhile to collect on staggered schedule	worthwhile to collect on regular basis	worthwhile and possible to collect occasionally on specific subjects
local budgetary data	total holdings	worthwhile to collect on regular basis	worthwhile to collect by hired analyst on staggered schedule	worthwhile to collect on regular basis	possible to cautiously report core spending
core and other collections	subject holdings	only for particular purposes	only for particular purposes	worthwhile, no new costs	worthwhile, no new costs or skills

tools to match. Figure 4.6 is a guide to, as well as a rough outline of, all of the components of this chapter. It matches library work environments and the level of analysis to a variety of suggested tools and methods.

Figure 4.6 assumes two high priorities in collection assessment: (1) the ability to analyze the largest possible universe, i.e., the most comprehensive collection of titles; and (2) the ability to make comparisons with peers or other libraries. Thus, Type A libraries would choose access to the WorldCat database via WCA software rather than a bookseller's prize-winner list. So, too, would Type D libraries, but not all things are equal. Due to a lack of funds, staff time, and staff skills, and with the WCA out of reach, Type D libraries may find bookseller lists quite satisfactory, affordable, and easy to use as assessment tools.

The tools and methods listed in Figure 4.6, both quantitative and qualitative, are described in detail in the following sections. They are roughly listed in order of cost and complexity, e.g., high intensity/high cost to low intensity/low cost. Though it may be obvious, it should be noted that every methodology available in the Type D environment is possible in Types A, B, and C; all options for Type C are plausible choices for Type A and B; and so on. Since the reverse is not true, this work focuses mainly on lesser-known options for Types C and D. Note, too, that depending on the tool used, results will differ accordingly, so it is important to thoroughly understand the content of the data as well as to thoroughly describe it in the assessment report.

Commercial Collection Assessment Products

As indicated earlier, an option for Type A and Type B libraries is to subscribe to an electronic or online collection assessment tool. There are several from which to choose, including Bowker's Book Analysis System, Spectra CRC, and WCA (Collection Tools 2008). All three are subscription-based products and thus recurring commitments on the library's budget.

In general, these products purport to provide gap analyses, overlap analyses, and comparisons with other libraries or with title lists. The WCA advertises these features. It is an OCLC (Online Computer Library Center) produced software program that manipulates data from the WorldCat database. Analyses can be performed on three levels: broad "Divisions" (e.g., anthropology); subfields of divisions called "Categories" (e.g., ethnology and ethnography); and thousands of "Subjects" within the categories (e.g., culture and cultural processes). Like all electronic collection assessment software, it has advantages and disadvantages. It is a powerful tool but requires training to use and to maximize its potential. The learning curve is quite high; one must understand exactly what the database contains, ensure consistency of the data, and have good Excel skills to clean the data, compute statistics, and develop decent tables, graphs, and charts. It also requires keeping informed, as the software is still evolving and the results change after each update to the database. The tools in the next list require fewer demands on library personnel, though one is also less comprehensive and the other less flexible than the commercial products.

Prevalent In-House Tools

Approval Plan Vendor Databases.   Major approval plan vendors, including Blackwell Book Services, Yankee Book Peddlar (YBP), and Harrassowitz, have searchable databases that can be considered "universes" of publication. Although many librarians now order books using online slips via vendor databases, their potential use as assessment tools has been much less explored. For example, in YBP's database, GOBI, it is possible to run various reports showing the percentage of books the library has obtained in specific call number ranges, out of the entire YBP universe and within a given time period. It is also possible to search for titles by subject heading, retrieve the overall number of titles, then limit the same search to books the library has received, and thereby obtain a percentage of coverage of a particular subject. If GOBI contains 200 books related to the U.S. presidency, published in the past 10 years, and the library received 90 percent of these, it could be stated that this is an indication of a collection that is robust (in terms of the GOBI universe). As follow-up, the 10 percent not received can be studied as a gap analysis. For at least the past eight years, GOBI records have also included a field called "Interdisciplinary Topics." It is very useful for an analysis of, say, Hispanic American collections, which are scattered and untraceable through call number ranges and almost impossible to capture using subject headings. It is also important to note the limitations of the universe (e.g., what books might be absent from the YBP database?), and to know the library's profile well (e.g., is that really a gap in the collection or were those titles, present in GOBI, received through vendors other than YBP?).

Because approval plan databases were not designed as assessment tools, to use them as such takes time to explore, innovate, and customize the reports. Hence, while library Types A and C might make use of such tools, it will be more difficult for Types B and D. In the case of the latter two, it will be worthwhile to request standard reports from the vendor. And although major vendor databases are impressively large, they have a smaller universe than WorldCat. Thus, when possible and given the choice, the latter is preferable as an evaluation tool.

Libraries that are not customers of approval plan vendors can still make use of some analytic features on vendors' Web sites, as opposed to their databases. YBP offers free access to "University Press Bestseller Lists" as well as the "YBP Core 1000" and "Lindsay and Croft Core 300" (for UK imprints), and to "aid academic libraries in assessing current collections and to allow smaller academic libraries the opportunity to benefit from participation with a seasoned vendor in collection development" (YBP 2008b). The latter two lists are helpfully divided into subject areas. Thus Type B and D libraries, with little staff time, can search a manageable subset of the "Core 1000" instead of cutting and pasting 1,000 titles into their local catalogs.

One general lesson that can be extrapolated from thinking of approval plan databases as assessment tools is that there are many universes of publications which can be compared to a library's holdings. More of these are listed below.

FirstSearch.   Libraries with access to WorldCat via FirstSearch have one of the most powerful collection assessment tools. It is not only useful for Types C and D but also may on certain occasions be of more use to Types A and B than the commercial analysis products. For Type D libraries, the advantages of FirstSearch include the fact that new staff skills will not be required (staff will presumably already be familiar with the interface) and the learning curve associated with using it as an assessment tool will be low.

Due to both the numerous search limits allowed by FirstSearch as well as the categorization of the results, the simplest search will provide a wealth of rich information. If the English literature department wishes to know the library's strength in terms of books as well as sound recordings related to William Shakespeare, a "Basic Search" instantly provides the figures for all libraries in WorldCat. Record these statistics, then limit the results to your library, and the requested proportion can be reported.

More sophisticated analyses are possible from the "Expert Search" page. If an institution's economics department has expertise in women and employment, and inquires (for the sake of a program review) about the library's collection in this broad subject, a search can be run using expert search to retrieve an indication of collection strength. With a little extra effort, much more can be reported and interpreted, including information regarding existing resources held and not held by the library, trends in the publication of this subject, and collecting patterns of the library over the years. To create the table in Figure 4.7, "women" and "employment" were listed as descriptors, date and language limits were set, and juvenile readership and fiction were excluded. This search will retrieve numbers on the universe of bibliographic records within these parameters.

Figure 4.7
FirstSearch Results

Women and Employment	Total WorldCat Holdings	# of Holdings in Library X	% of Holdings in Library X
1980–1989	6,933	962	7.28%
1990–1999	5,693	420	13.88%

Though the table in Figure 4.7 appears simple, it provides more information than a first glance may recognize. It indicates, for example, that fewer records in the 1990s were classified or described with the terms "women" and "employment" than in the 1980s. This could be an indication that fewer such books were published. The table also suggests that Library X has a relatively weak collection of such works, but that, over the last decade, the pattern has been to collect a higher proportion of the published titles on this topic.

FirstSearch also provides easy analyses of interdisciplinary subjects. On the top of the "Basic Search" page is a predefined list of "Hot Topics." Like YBP's GOBI search, these are generally interdisciplinary or other topics which cannot be easily retrieved via call numbers, subject headings, or the OCLC conspectus of the WCA. After running the basic search on a topic, it is possible to limit the results to holdings in any library, and thus obtain the relative strength of a particular collection. This handy feature is more comprehensive in terms of the searched universe than that which is accessible through GOBI. On the other hand, it is less comprehensive in terms of the number of interdisciplinary subjects available to search. Hence, GOBI's interdisciplinary search feature may prove to be useful on more occasions.

Why would library Types A and B make use of FirstSearch capacities? Although FirstSearch and WCA manipulate largely the same data, it is possible with the former to make peer comparisons that are sometimes time consuming, cumbersome, or impossible with the latter, especially when permission from comparison libraries must be solicited in advance or is denied.

Free Data from the Internet

Comparisons with Booksellers.   Although there is no one database that represents every publication in the world, there are nonetheless many that contain large quantities of titles. Amazon, Alibris, and the Web sites of other booksellers are such databases and access to them is free. Library holdings can be compared against these lists. It is, however, more efficient for library Types A and B to use the WorldCat database and bypass the trouble of searching individual titles. If those databases are not available for Type C libraries, bookseller databases are a good substitute. They may also be useful to Type D libraries, depending upon the number of titles that must be compared in the local catalog.

It is important to know the specialization or general characteristics of the booksellers' lists and find one that coincides with characteristics of your research. Amazon is useful for exploring the strength of the library's collection in recent publications or in popular works. To narrow the results, it provides useful breakdowns of subjects, e.g., biographies of women, in the United States, and in the nineteenth century. In addition, there is a good, though limited, "Advanced Search" feature. This advanced search allows one to set limits, but Amazon's options are not as useful as those of FirstSearch. For example, the choices under "Reader Age" are either "juvenile" or "all"; thus, it is not possible to limit by adult only. Likewise, the choices under "Language" are limited to English, French, German, and Spanish. It is worthwhile, however, to check back from time to time (two years ago, the language choices were "All" and "Spanish").

It should be no surprise that the total results from Amazon are much smaller than that of WorldCat, as the latter contains larger quantities of older titles and all formats. Depending on the purpose of the analysis, this might be an advantage for Type D libraries that have very limited staff time in which to be comparing the retrieved titles to the library's catalog.

Amazon also offers a large array of prize-winner lists, many of which go back to the first award issued. Against these lists the holdings of the library can be compared and the richness of the collection analyzed. Prize winners can be said to represent quality within the collection. When analyzing a literature collection, it would be of interest to see what percent of Mann Booker Prize finalists and winners are in the collection, whether there is a high percentage of all back to the first in 1969 or from just the past two years. Or, check out how many of the mystery books nominated for the Edgar Award (including one entitled *The Librarian*) are on the library's shelves. These percentages are quick and simple to calculate and provide a good indication of the quality of the collection.

Rankings and Peer Comparisons.   Free sources of peer comparisons can be found online via associations. Those institutions which are members of the Association of Research Libraries can use ARL statistics to describe not only their own holdings but also their ranking among peers, aspirational peers, or against all other ARL libraries (ARL 2008). Comparisons may be made on overall library collection sizes, expenditures, staffing, and other variables. In a report on these statistics, a description of ARL and qualifications for membership should be included. Few faculty, administrators, proposal evaluators, program reviewers, or others who read the report may be aware of the criteria for qualification of ARL designation.

A lesser-known alternative for both ARL and non-ARL libraries is the peer comparative data found online for free from the Academic Libraries Survey of the National Center for Education Statistics (NCES 2008). This organization collects much of the same data as the ARL including collection size, library staff size, expenditures, online services, interlibrary loans, and more. The interface is simple to use.

Vendor Reports

Regardless of whether or not the library has a working relationship with a major monograph vendor, statistics from YBP and BBS can be used to supplement an analysis of local data. YBP's "New Book Price and Output Report" and BBS's "Coverage and Cost" are freely available online annual reports based on the large universes of books these vendors handle on approval (YBP 2008a; BBS 2008). The data are variously broken down by subjects, disciplines, and publisher types (e.g., university versus trade presses). Note that the data represent primarily English language books distributed in the United States and United Kingdom. Within those parameters, the data indicate how much publishing is occurring in particular subject areas and provide average book prices. This information can be useful, even to Types A and B libraries, to calculate and discuss the probable costs of a new graduate program in anthropology or of building up a weak collection in American literature. Furthermore, they provide a helpful narrative regarding pricing indicators and forecasts on prices.

Local Catalogs

If the library can afford absolutely nothing else, local data can be used very effectively as an assessment tool. The following demonstrates that sophisticated analyses can be derived from simple data. It describes ways to enrich results by organizing your local data around particular analytical concepts. In short, if you know how many the library has of what, as well as publication dates, you can describe the collections in terms of strength, growth, currency, and age.

Collection Strength.   All libraries should be able, at the very least, to generate a measurement of the size of their collections broken down by classification ranges and/or some other variable. Some may have the capacity to do this on a regular basis (every year), while others only on occasion (once every five years). While some can look at total holdings, others might need to rotate analyses to particular collections each time. The numbers representing collection size can be useful as indicators of collection strength—the relative strength of subfields within subject ranges, the strength of subject areas relative to the library's entire collection, or the library's collection strength in comparison with peer libraries.

Although it is possible to have a very large, poor quality collection, librarians tend to give size the benefit of doubt; in which case, the bigger, the better. However, in the absence of comparative data with other libraries, size can be difficult to interpret. Furthermore, size is increasingly tricky to establish. Print monographs, microforms, videos, and a few other format types are easily counted. E-books and e-journals in large serials packages, databases with partial full-text, and large e-collections not cataloged at the title level make counting collection size much more troublesome. Additionally, it is not uncommon for vendors to add and drop titles from large databases without notification to customers. The risks of underrepresenting the resources available to scholars are great. Hence, in circumstances of restricted time and money for assessment, when it comes to measuring strength, it may be best to limit the analysis to print monographs and/or to qualitative measurements against core lists or core collections (as described below).

All caveats aside, local data can provide illuminating information. If the generation of comparative peer data is prohibitively time consuming, as it is sometimes for Type B libraries and always for Type Ds, relative strengths within a single collection may be addressed. Is a higher percentage of the collection found in just one call number subrange or subject heading, e.g., 50 percent of the economics books are related to economic theory? Or, are the percentages almost the same across subranges? In the case of the former, the collection could be described as specialized, with its strength in theory; in the latter case, one might describe the collection as generalized, with a somewhat even distribution of titles across subject headings. In either case, the results can be both interesting and useful.

A simple method for obtaining comparisons of peer collection strength is to search by LC (Library of Congress) subject headings in your local catalog and repeat the same search in the online public catalogs of peer institutions. Although this is less rigorous than some other methods (e.g., those which map titles to call numbers), it can be said to result in at least an indication of collection strengths and requires only the resource of time, which is available to Type C libraries.

Collection Growth.   With the addition of one more variable, publication date, it is possible to analyze collection growth. All librarians think of collection size as a variable in assessment, but not all realize that growth can be articulated as a by-product of size. The degree of difficulty in providing this statistic will depend on the library's management system and history. At most libraries, order records in the acquisitions module are erased at some point in time. Thus, the received date in the order record cannot be used as a count of yearly acquisitions. Likewise, virtually all libraries have not only changed from card to computerized systems, but many have switched from one computerized system to another over time. Quite frequently it is the case that information on original received dates did not migrate from one system to another. Although "growth" subsequently becomes a slight misnomer, the solution is to treat publication dates as acquisition dates.

When publication dates are used to represent acquisition dates, it is possible to track growth by gathering statistics within a certain call number range with publication dates prior to, for example, 1995; repeat this same process with publication dates up to 2005; and report the percentage of change or growth over that decade. Various combinations of years can be utilized for comparisons, e.g., to demonstrate the percentage of change within the last two years as compared with the two prior, or to track growth over time from the 1950s to the present.

Though relative strength and growth are simple statistics, these are powerful statistics, especially when the two are combined. The measurement of relative subject collection strengths helps to clarify whether or not the emphasis within the collection matches research and teaching in corresponding academic departments. That is important information; however, it is possible that the results demonstrate the effects of past collecting practices and more important information is hidden. By tracking relative strength over time (collection sizes within subranges sorted by publication dates) it is possible to analyze whether or not collecting in the last 10 years has been going in the same direction as research interests.

The weakness of a methodology that relies on publication date as an acquisition date is that it will not record retrospective buying. It is therefore important to know the history of the library and its collections. It is nonsensical to treat books with 1880 publication dates as acquisitions in the nineteenth century if the library itself is only 50 years old. It is also imperative to have knowledge of the library's collecting practices. It is not uncommon to institute a retrospective buying project for the purpose of building up a weak, new, or small collection. If, between 2000 and 2001, the selector for the new Southeast Asian collection was given extra funds to concentrate more on purchasing older titles (published in the 1970s) than contemporary titles (2000s), the data could easily be misinterpreted. It would appear as though the collection has been in existence for the last 30 or more years and, depending on the proportions, it may also appear as though the collection had steady growth in the 1970s and a drop in growth in the early 2000s. If retrospective buying has been minimal, however, then there is no reason to fear grave misinterpretation of the data.

Currency and Age.   Publication dates may also be used to measure collection age. How this data is interpreted will depend on the mission of the library as a whole or on the purpose of a particular subject area. While demand and space may call for the weeding of older collections in some libraries or within particular collections (e.g., undergraduate collections), it would be contrary to their mission for research libraries to weed old works. So, while the books in one library's collection may be described as outdated, the same books in another library would be considered core.

On the other hand, all libraries need to keep their collections current. This data can help determine the currency of collections. Perhaps the overall number of books in engineering is large, but that number really reflects a high amount of purchasing prior to 1998. Unlike publication dates, the overall collection size reveals nothing about current acquisitions or whether or not the collection is dated. Publication dates can also help uncover small and interesting subcollections, such as a small subcollection of German language literature of the eighteenth century within a very large general literature collection.

By using local collections data within a preexisting analytical framework, it can be seen that all library types (A through D) can produce important and useful collection assessments. However, if local data remains a challenge to work with, even in a preexisting framework, there are still other options (below) for all types of libraries.

Budgetary Data

Analyses of collections have as much to do with examining titles as with examining expenditures. The funds allocated to and expended on a particular subject area can be just as important to a description of the collection as numbers of titles. This is especially true if the purpose of the analysis is to show support for research and teaching in a particular field or to justify a request for budget increases. However, in many libraries, the total amount of funds expended per subject may be more difficult to uncover than anticipated. Many bibliographers and selectors underestimate the library's support for specific subjects. Oftentimes, those who select materials treat the funds spent at their discretion as the total budget. However, all large libraries pay for and receive materials through multiple routes.

And in some budgets, the most expensive resources are often the most interdisciplinary and least likely to be charged to a particular subject (especially in the social sciences and humanities). Hence, true collections budget analysis—which accounts for resources per subject area received through approval plans, firm orders, standing orders, subscriptions, or in large aggregated databases, and paid for via allocated funds, endowments, gifts, and grants—may realistically be available only to library Type A and periodically to Type B (when an analyst is hired). A modified version, which accounts for "core" spending (e.g., discretionary spending by subject selectors) might be cautiously reported on a regular basis by Type C and D libraries.

Core and Other Collections

Along with data on "core" expenditures, libraries Type C and D who cannot afford full-scale analyses may be able to report on and measure the "core" literature of any field. The measurement of core collections is also a useful analysis technique for all library types when it is necessary to assess certain interdisciplinary subjects. If relevant literature on the subject is scattered throughout LC or Dewey classifications, it may be necessary to refer to that which is countable as "core."

There are several methods for measuring core collections (including the vendor lists already discussed). One is to simply describe the strength of the reference collection by checking the library's holdings against the list of reference works in the definitive, well-established ALA's (American Library Association) *Guide to Reference Books*. Although this may not sound exciting, the Department of Spanish and Portuguese was very interested to learn from one Type D that of the 285 definitive reference works listed by the *Guide*, the library held 94 percent, yet only 70 percent of the bibliographies. Note, too, that the *Guide* includes lists relevant to interdisciplinary studies, which is beneficial because such lists can be difficult to find. While the *Guide*, 11th edition, is now dated, according to the publisher, the 12th edition should be ready shortly—and online, which will greatly improve the efficiency of this work as an assessment tool (English 2008).

The Web pages of some Association of College and Research Libraries sections and other library organizations keep up-to-date core lists. There is a set of core lists of monographs provided by the Collection Development Committee of the Women's Studies Section of ACRL (Women's Studies Section 2008), for example. One library let it be known that it had a solid collection of 395 of the 412 core monographs in women's studies. Not only did the quality of the collection sound impressive, this finding created an opportunity to encourage funding for the missing 4 percent.

Collection assessment is not only numbers and statistics, but also the narrative story of collections (although relevant to all library types, this is an especially cost- and time-efficient approach for Type D libraries). For a highly interdisciplinary subject or one which has no historical classification range per se, an analysis of collection size alone could be misleading—an analysis of the women's studies collection that only provides counts within the Dewey classification of 305 would greatly underestimate and underrepresent works related to this subject. It would be important to note, in the narrative story of the collection, that works related to women's studies are also found within the broader classifications of history, political science, literature, and almost all other humanities and social sciences.

Even the most sophisticated collection assessment tools will leave out information about collections. In the case of large academic libraries, in particular, there are often many older, unique works whose records have not migrated to WorldCat, or that will be relegated to the "unknown classification" within WCA because their call numbers are not recognized. Most libraries also have backlogs and "hidden collections" of uncataloged materials. In addition, there are major microform sets which often contain large collections of monographs whose individual titles may not appear in the local catalog. The same holds for some e-book collections. Although it may be difficult to quantify the number of full-text monographs in these collections, it is important to acknowledge their relevance to the subject under analysis.

To reiterate, assessment should not be just numbers. Descriptions of manuscripts and archives, e-books, and microform sets will help provide a broader, richer, and truer picture of the collection, all without a great expenditure of time or funds.

CONCLUSION

This guide to conducting collection evaluations for libraries demonstrates that collection assessments can be carried out under all types of circumstances. This can be achieved by first taking a few essential steps to clarify what must and can be done, and how. In providing examples of assessment tools, this guide also illustrates that, just as there is a wide range of available resources within different libraries, from the richly endowed to severely restricted, so too is there a wide range of evaluation methods and tools, from expensive to free, and a comprehensive list has not been compiled here. On the contrary, this guide aims to inspire all librarians, regardless of library type, to invent new and imaginative evaluation procedures and to approach collection assessment as an opportunity to be creative.

REFERENCES

American Research Libraries. 2008. "ARL statistics & measurement." www.arl.org/stats/annualsurveys/arlstats/index.shtml.

BBS. 2008. "Coverage and cost." www.blackwell.com/librarian_resources/coverage_and_cost.

Collection Tools. 2008. "Bowker's book analysis system." www.bbanalysis.com/bbas/; "Spectra CRC." www.librarydynamics.com/default.aspx?page=services&service=Spectra_CRC; "WorldCat collection analysis." www.oclc.org/collectionanalysis/default.htm.

English, Catherine, Marketing Manager, ALA Editions. 2008. E-mail response in inquiry regarding the 12th edition (April). "The new online version of Guide to Reference will be available shortly."

Nardini, H. K. G. 2001. Building a culture of assessment [workshop at the 2001 ACRL conference]. *ARL*, no. 218 (October): 11.

National Center for Education Statistics, Library Statistics Program, Academic Libraries. http://nces.ed.gov/surveys/libraries/academic.asp.

Women's Studies Section, ACRL, ALA. 2008. "Core lists in women's studies." http://digicoll.library.wisc.edu/ACRLWSS/.

YBP Library Services. 2008a. "Annual book price update." www.ybp.com/book_price_update.html.

YBP Library Services. 2008b. "YBP core 1000." www.ybp.com.

CHAPTER 5

Comparing Approval and Librarian-Selected Monographs: An Analysis of Use

ERIN L. ELLIS, NIKHAT J. GHOUSE,
MONICA CLAASSEN-WILSON,
JOHN M. STRATTON, AND SUSANNE K. CLEMENT

ABSTRACT

This chapter will demonstrate that monographic materials acquired at the University of Kansas (KU) through the approval plan and firm orders are, in some cases, being used for research more extensively than originally believed. A circulation analysis of approval plan and librarian-selected monographs and a review of use by different user groups reveal a surprising mixture of monographic usage patterns among the disciplines under consideration. Additionally, departmental dissertation output provides further indication that some of these disciplines still make substantive use of monographs. In this chapter, business, psychology, religious studies, and sociology collections are compared and discussed. Further, this chapter describes our analysis methodology, presents potential implications for approval and firm ordering, and makes suggestions for using and collecting similar data in the future.

INTRODUCTION

Subject librarians at the University of Kansas, a comprehensive research institution, expend considerable time engaging in collection development activities with the usual aim of supporting the research and teaching mission of the colleges, schools, and departments they serve. The physical book has, for generations, formed the body of the collections within KU libraries. At KU, monographs are acquired in two general ways: on approval via YBP Library Services,[1] a subsidiary of the Baker & Taylor Company; and through the firm order acquisition activities of individual subject librarians, who represent a significant number of academic disciplines in the humanities, social sciences, sciences, and technological fields.

In the library science literature, a number of articles about collection development activities pursued by academic librarians are available.[2] Many of these articles focus on collection use by various patron groups or provide recommendations for focusing or improving collection development plans and policies. This is not surprising given that expenditures devoted to acquiring, cataloging, marking, storing, and circulating monographs represent a large portion of any library budget. Collection analysis and assessment are ongoing, since this activity comprises one of the central responsibilities of library administrations in academe, regardless of institution size.

At KU, several methods have been employed to determine the use of monographs acquired for our constituent groups (university faculty, students, and staff). Some of these methods have included review and analysis of circulation data, individual subject collection analysis, and review of approval plans. While the current study is informed by some of these previous analyses, the authors of this chapter reviewed the circulation data for a smaller cross-section of the collection for a relatively narrow time frame; our analyses concentrate exclusively on those items with imprint dates of 2004–2007, in the areas of business, psychology, religious studies, and sociology, acquired through the approval plan and through the acquisition activities of individual subject librarians.

METHODOLOGY

As noted above, monographs are acquired at the KU Libraries in two primary ways: via the YBP approval plan and through the activity of subject librarians responsible for collecting in their respective disciplines. The number of titles added to the collection in a particular year can vary depending on several factors, including the parameters of the approval plan, number of monographs published in the discipline, price/inflationary factors, availability of funds to purchase materials, and total number of orders placed by subject librarians through their collecting activities.

Scholarly monographs are added to the collection based on their potential use and long-term scholarly value. Thus, there is a balance to be struck in trying to meet both immediate scholarly needs as well as institutional and societal informational needs. While these are not necessarily mutually exclusive collection development goals, one enduring goal is to ensure that the allocation of institutional resources is done in a way to maximize the impact of limited financial resources. In some instances, analysis of collections to determine use is one method of discovering whether current levels of financial allocations for certain disciplines are adequate to meet immediate and long-term scholarly needs. Analyses can also reveal other trends, including whether or not use justifies an adjustment in funding levels.

In order to understand how recently acquired items have been used by patrons (including KU faculty, staff, and students; resident and guest borrowers; and interlibrary loan requestors), titles were examined in terms of both individual title use and total circulation transactions for items with an imprint date of 2004–2007. Imprint date was used rather than acquisitions date for consistency of data. In addition, both titles and circulation transactions were reviewed for items added to the collection on the approval plan or through direct order by the subject librarian. In the sections below, information is presented about both title use and circulation transactions of monographs. In addition, both titles and circulation transactions were reviewed for items added to the collection on the approval plan or through direct order by the subject librarian. In the sections below, information is presented about both title use and circulation transactions of monographs.

The following parameters apply to all analyses:

- Data for the years 2004–2007 only is included.
- Only titles with imprint dates of these years are included.
- Analysis has been informed by applying the 80/20 rule to the circulation transaction data collected: that is, for any given year, data was sifted to discover how many circulation transactions comprised either 20 percent or 80 percent of the transactions for that year (Britten 1990).

DATA COLLECTION

The list of titles acquired on the approval plan was provided by YBP in three separate databases, covering receipts for fiscal years 2005, 2006, and 2007.[3] Because fiscal year overlaps calendar year, these three databases were then combined into a new database that was then compared against holdings in KU's Voyager circulation system using the International Standard Book Number (ISBN).

A master table was created from Voyager with all titles having a publication date of 2004–2007. This date range assured that no title had been transferred to the library annex and that all titles would be on the shelves in the main circulating collections. A second assumption in using this date range was that it would not include any titles that had been transferred to the library annex, and that all titles would be on the shelves in the main circulating collections. A query was run against Voyager to search for the ISBN in the 020N, or Normal Heading, in the Index Code field. This table with the titles and ISBNs was compared to the YBP table, and BIB_IDs (bibliographic record identification numbers) were added to all of the YBP titles to allow them to be used to gather circulation data. Another query was run to eliminate the duplicates between the YBP and Voyager master tables, and each table was then used to pull circulation data from the Voyager system.

The next challenge was determining how to categorize titles into the respective subject areas being examined. Because of variations between how YBP and the Library of Congress define subject head ings, YBP's "Aspect" field and Voyager's subject headings (Library of Congress subject headings) were quickly dismissed due to the labor involved in normalizing these to match each other. Figure 5.1 shows Library of Congress call number classifications used.

Figure 5.1
LC Classifications Used

Subject Subheading	Call Number
Philosophy	B
Psychology	BF
Religions, Mythology, Rationalism	BL
Religious Studies	BL-BX
Judaism	BM
Islam, Baha'ism, Theosophy, etc.	BP
Buddhism	BQ
Christianity	BR
The Bible	BS
Doctrinal Theology	BT
Practical Theology	BV
Christian Denominations	BX
Business	HD-HJ
Sociology, General	HM

The limitations of this approach are that the YBP approval plan allows for the selection of items based on YBP categories, which do not always match the LC classification for a given subject, and subject selectors do not purchase titles within strict call number ranges, but often choose materials that fall into other categories.

Circulation data was generated using queries that provided patron group/affiliation and charge dates. The final data was broken down in several ways to present a broad picture of use. Overall use was displayed by showing the total number and percentage of titles that had circulated or not circulated. Use of titles by patron groups was generated based on a count of titles with one or more charges. Finally, an analysis was conducted based on Richard Trueswell's 80/20 rule which predicts that 20 percent of a library's holdings will account for 80 percent of the total use or transactions (Burrell 1985).

A Voyager-based "title charged table" was created to reveal whether a particular title had circulated at least once since the item was acquired. Titles counted in the Voyager-based "total charged" column may have multiple transactions associated with them, but all titles included had at least one transaction. For the 80/20 analysis, where transactions per title are counted, a transaction is defined as a single charge on a given title. For example, a given title is considered to have circulated if it was charged at least one time. That same title may have been charged multiple times, resulting in multiple transactions associated with that title. In some cases, a title may also have multiple items (CD, other media) or copies associated with it, which could also result in a greater number of transactions for that single title.

A preliminary examination of the circulation data reveals a pattern of use that is unusually high for some business titles housed in Anschutz Library (one of two main libraries on the KU Campus). Further analysis revealed this had to do with internal procedures related to charging items on interlibrary loan. Following this discovery, and in an effort to ensure greater consistency across the data, all charges to the Interlibrary Loan/Binding patron group were excluded from the circulation data. Whenever conducting circulation analysis, it is important to investigate whether any internal procedures may skew the data.

USE BY TITLE AMONG DISCIPLINES

Average circulation of monographs acquired on the approval plan tends to be markedly different for some disciplines compared to others in this study. Figure 5.2 shows these average percentages of circulated versus noncirculated titles acquired under the approval plan during this period.

It should be noted that in some of the disciplines in this study, librarians often transmit orders received from the faculty and do not have to make a significant number of decisions regarding which

Figure 5.2
Approval Plan Acquired Titles

Subject	# Titles received 2004–2007	% YBP titles circulated	% YBP titles not circulated
Business	2,633	37%	63%
Psychology	660	63%	37%
Religious Studies	2,981	48%	52%
Sociology	593	63%	37%

particular items to add to the collection. In other instances, librarians often generate orders without significant input from the faculty. These realities also affect the average use of monographs in any one discipline.

Comparatively speaking, business titles acquired on the approval plan are used less by all patron groups than titles in other disciplines in this study, and in some cases, significantly less. Sociology and psychology monographs are, comparatively, in much greater demand from patrons during this period, followed by religious studies.

Average circulation percentages for nonapproval plan acquired monographs reveal somewhat dissimilar patterns of use. Comparing the disciplines used in this study, Figure 5.3 shows the average percentages of circulated versus noncirculated items acquired through subject librarian acquisition activities during this period.

Only about one-third of all business monographs acquired during this period were used at least once. Psychology and sociology titles, on the other hand, enjoyed much higher use, followed by monographs in religious studies, which displayed only slightly higher use than business. This pattern of less frequent usage is important because it shows that scholarly information presented in the monographic format may be less germane than other kinds of information important to current Business researchers. For example, most undergraduates seem to prefer information available in electronic format when conducting research for class assignments or research projects. Such information is usually in the form of articles or other statistical or financial data available from business databases or specific statistical Web sites.

For business monographs, circulation by title is remarkably similar whether the title was ordered by the subject specialist or arrived via the approval plan. However, circulation data for monographs in the other disciplines generally reflect greater use of items acquired via the approval plan than via the acquisition activities of individual subject librarians. These data may hold some implications for librarians to consider. For example, it may be that in this particular discipline, titles added via the approval plan are generally sufficient to support the needs of the faculty and students in the program. That is, there may be limited value in having the librarian devote substantial amounts of time toward actively searching for and acquiring individual titles. The approval plan could instead be monitored and adjusted on a regular basis to meet departmental needs, based on circulation analysis and patterns of usage among various patron groups.

If this were the approach, the subject specialist would be more free to concentrate on other aspects of her position, including offering more instruction and providing enhanced reference and research support. Further, the collection-related work of the specialist could be focused not as much on acquiring monographs as other areas and formats vital to the program, including the acquisition of databases, electronic journal titles, and harvesting of relevant Web-based resources already being

Figure 5.3
Nonapproval Plan Acquired Titles

Subject	# Titles received 2004–2007	% Non-YBP titles circulated	% Non-YBP titles not circulated
Business	4,279	34%	66%
Psychology	749	57%	43%
Religious Studies	2,838	35%	65%
Sociology	548	48%	52%

prominently used by a number of students in the program. Given the reliance of users on the discovery and delivery of current business information in electronic form, the activities of the Business Librarian may reasonably require a fresh look.

For psychology monographs, too, use by title is remarkably similar regardless of how individual items were added to the collection. For example, about two-thirds of the monographs in psychology were circulated over a four-year period, whether selected by the subject specialist or added to the collection via the approval plan. On the other hand, sociology monographs acquired via the approval plan circulate far better than those acquired through librarian selection.

For religious studies, the similarity continues. Over half of the monographs in this subject were used over a four-year period. As with business and psychology, religious studies monographs acquired via the approval plan demonstrate greater use of items than those acquired via librarian selection. This is particularly noteworthy, for the majority of the nonapproval plan monographs in religious studies are recommended by the teaching faculty of that department and purchased with the final approval of the subject librarian. Traditionally, the religious studies faculty at KU has been intimately involved in selecting monographs for the discipline. The fact that the teaching faculty of this department plays such an integral role in selection is not unusual. After all, most faculty want collections in support of their specific subfield. What may be unexpected is that the materials they have requested are not circulating as much as the materials received from the approval plan.

USE BY PATRON GROUP

Use by Title and Number of Transactions

Five patron groups were identified by the authors of this study as being the most active users of monographs across the disciplines of business, religious studies, psychology, and sociology: graduate students, undergraduates, faculty, interlibrary loan patrons, and "other" (which includes resident borrowers, KU affiliates, classified staff, library processing staff, and reciprocal borrowers). These groups were consistently the five groups most responsible for the greatest circulation of monographs in this study.

Business. In the case of both approval plan acquired items and nonapproval plan acquired items for business, patron group analysis demonstrates that use among the top five user groups is remarkably similar regardless of the source of acquisition (see Figure 5.4). That is, while the level of use varies among each group, the top five patron groups using either approval plan or librarian-acquired materials are, as noted above, the same groups during the years 2004–2007. Please note that the interlibrary loan "group" reflects the third-highest number of transactions for nonapproval plan acquired materials. The authors believe this is due to the renewal of interlibrary loan monographs, which added additional transaction counts to individual items. It is the authors' contention that since interlibrary loans are given for shorter periods (six weeks) the renewal rate may be higher, especially for graduate and faculty borrowers. Typically these users enjoy considerably lengthier loan periods at KU when borrowing monographs from the libraries (e.g., semester-long loans, which can be renewed online up to five times).

Psychology. Of the top user groups of approval monographs in psychology, graduate students are clearly the heaviest users, with faculty and then undergraduates rounding out the top three (see Figure 5.4). Nearly 37 percent of the approval plan monograph circulation (monographs that circulated one or more times) is attributable to graduate student use. The remaining 63 percent is made up of faculty (21 percent of total circulation), undergraduate (16 percent of total circulation), ILL (interlibrary

Figure 5.4
Monographs/Use by Title and Number of Transactions

YBP	Total # transactions	80% of total # of transactions	Titles	# of titles = 80% of transactions	% of total titles	# of titles = 20% of transactions	% of total titles
Business	1,651	1,321	2,633	639	24.3%	1,994	75.7%
Religious Studies	2,657	2,126	2,992	912	30.5%	2,080	69.5%
Psychology	864	691	660	251	38.0%	409	62.0%
Sociology	811	649	593	231	39.0%	362	61.0%

Non-YBP	Total # transactions	80% of total # of transactions	Titles	# of titles = 80% of transactions	% of total titles	# of titles = 20% of transactions	% of total titles
Business	2,657	2,126	4,521	778	17.2%	3743	82.8%
Religious Studies	2,662	2,130	4,029	868	21.5%	3161	78.5%
Psychology	1,082	866	818	258	31.5%	560	68.5%
Sociology	919	735	826	230	27.8%	596	72.2%

loan) use (11 percent of total circulation), and other smaller patron groups, including resident borrowers and other KU affiliates.

Use of nonapproval plan monographs is much the same. Graduate students, again, are clearly the heaviest users of material, representing 32 percent of total circulation. And, again, faculty and undergraduates round out the top three, with 19 percent each of total circulation. Together, these three groups represent 71 percent of total circulation. The remaining 29 percent is made up of ILL use (11 percent of total circulation), resident borrowers (10 percent of total circulation), and other smaller patron groups.

Religious Studies.   Faculty represent the heaviest users of approval plan acquired monographs in religious studies, followed by graduate and undergraduate students (see Figure 5.4). Over 29 percent of the approval plan monograph circulation (monographs that circulated one or more times) is through faculty use, but the highest use, in terms of the number of transactions, is actually from graduate and undergraduate students (28 percent for each group). This is a reversal from business and psychology.

With regard to nonapproval plan religious studies monographs, the heaviest users are faculty (29 percent), graduates (27 percent), and undergraduates (23 percent). Though faculty represent the heaviest circulation, undergraduates have the highest nonapproval plan transaction count of 28 percent to the faculty transaction count of 26 percent. This transaction count may be related to faculty involvement in collection development. Because of this involvement faculty have an excellent knowledge of the collections that are available for teaching and research and include titles they have recommended for purchase in their students' reading lists.

Sociology.   Of the top user groups of approval plan monographs in sociology, graduate students are, again, clearly the heaviest users (see Figure 5.4). However, in this case, undergraduates make up a substantial amount of use, too. Faculty use rounds out the top three. Graduate student use is 37 percent of the circulation of approval plan monographs (monographs that circulated one or more times). The remaining use is made up of undergraduates (26 percent of total circulation), faculty (25 percent of total circulation), interlibrary loan (7 percent of total circulation), and other patron sets (4 percent of total circulation). Together, graduates, undergraduates, and faculty groups are responsible for 89 percent of total circulation.

With relatively the same number of titles circulating, the nonapproval plan monographs enjoy slightly more transactions than the approval plan monographs. Again, graduate students are the heaviest users, making up 35 percent of total circulation. Faculty and undergraduates follow, with 26 percent and 25 percent of total circulation, respectively. Interlibrary loan comprises 9 percent of total circulation, and other patron groups comprise the remaining 5 percent.

Circulation of Titles by Subject

As expected, the longer a title is available, the more likely it is to be used by patrons. Thus, titles with an imprint date of 2004 should have higher circulation statistics than titles with imprint dates of 2005, 2006, or 2007 (i.e., those titles available for a shorter amount of time). Some of the disciplinary differences seen in the previous section are also apparent here. Business titles have the fewest titles circulating, whether acquired through the approval plan or not; sociology and psychology titles circulate the most; and religious studies titles circulate neither the most nor the least. Where the approval plan brings in traditional and basic academic material, the librarian-selected material tends to be more specialized. This may explain why this category of material, overall, circulates less than approval material.

Business.   For the years 2004–2007, KU libraries received 2,633 individual business titles on the approval plan. Figure 5.5 illustrates circulation by individual title per year in business and provides a percentage of the total titles received that either circulated or did not circulate. Please note that for purposes of this study, "circulated" means a title has circulated at least once since the date of acquisition. Conversely, for this study, "not circulated" denotes titles that have not circulated ever.

Business titles with imprint dates of 2004, which represent that part of the collection that has been available to users on the shelves for three years, have circulated the most; 47 percent circulated at least once from 2004 to 2007. As noted in Figure 5.5, after 2004, items acquired in each subsequent year from 2005 to 2007 have circulated less each year (6.6 percent less each year). On average, for the period of time under consideration for this study, 37 percent of all business titles acquired via the approval plan circulated at least one time. Therefore, on average, 63 percent of titles did not, resulting in a low level of use.

For the years 2004–2007, KU libraries received 4,279 individual titles through nonapproval channels, chiefly through acquisition activities of the subject librarian assigned as liaison to the Business School. Figure 5.5 illustrates circulation patterns for titles per year for business. Like approval plan acquired titles, those acquired from nonapproval avenues with imprint dates of 2004, which represent that part of the collection that has been available to users on the shelves for three years, have circulated the most; 48 percent have circulated at least once from 2004 to 2007. As with the approval-acquired titles, monographs acquired after 2004 have circulated 9.6 percent less each year through the year 2007. On average, 34 percent of all business titles acquired via the nonapproval plan circulated at least one time. Therefore, 66 percent of titles did not—again, a low level of use.

Figure 5.5
Circulation of Approval and Nonapproval Titles by Subject

| Patron group | Business | | | | | | Psychology | | | | | | Religious Studies | | | | | | Sociology | | | | | |
| | YBP | | Non-YBP | | | | YBP | | Non-YBP | | | | YBP | | Non-YBP | | | | YBP | | Non-YBP | | | |
	# titles circulated	# transactions	# titles circulated	# transactions			# titles circulated	# transactions	# titles circulated	# transactions			# titles circulated	# transactions	# titles circulated	# transactions			# titles circulated	# transactions	# titles circulated	# transactions		
Graduates	409	531	607	856			238	407	243	486			733	982	633	868			564	870	573	904		
Undergraduates	327	432	452	645			165	207	166	246			615	965	551	954			379	486	423	538		
Faculty	307	358	456	561			105	141	141	260			763	907	688	858			398	637	402	800		
Interlibrary loan*	170	220	270	566			69	81	80	147			313	411	343	475			105	123	154	197		
Other†	73	78	109	120			65	68	134	150			163	188	156	201			68	124	79	142		

*Interlibrary loan transactions in this row reflect greater activity for non-YBP acquired material possibly due to renewal of interlibrary loan monographs—adding additional transaction counts to individual items.

†Other groups include resident borrowers, KU affiliates, classified staff, library processing staff, and reciprocal borrowers.

Psychology.   A total of 660 monographs were acquired through the approval plan in psychology with imprints of 2004–2007. Of these titles, 416 circulated at least once (63 percent). Only sociology titles circulate similarly. Figure 5.5 illustrates circulation by individual title per year in the psychology call number range and provides a percentage of the total received that either circulated or did not circulate.

For this discipline, titles with imprint dates of 2004, which represent that part of the collection that has been available to users on the shelves for three years, have circulated the most; 73 percent have circulated at least once. Monographs acquired after 2004 have circulated 5 percent less each year through 2007. Thus, a total of 63 percent of this material has circulated, leaving 37 percent of titles that did not circulate. This indicates substantial use of monographic material. Psychology titles in the nonapproval purchases circulate, on average, only slightly less than those coming in through the approval plan. Monograph acquisitions with imprint dates of 2004–2007 totaled 769. Of these titles, 437 (57 percent) have circulated. No other social science discipline analyzed came close to this level of circulation in the nonapproval selections. Figure 5.5 illustrates circulation patterns for titles per year in the psychology call number range.

Like approval plan acquired titles, those acquired from nonapproval avenues with imprint dates of 2004 have circulated the most; 76 percent circulated at least once. Use dropped considerably during 2005, but then in the year 2006, circulation increased again to a level similar to approval plan materials. For the year 2007, circulation again dropped, but this could be due to the fact that the items were simply newly acquired and had not had time to be discovered by users. On average, 42 percent of all titles did not circulate, indicating a fairly substantial amount of use.

Religious Studies.   For the years 2004–2007, KU libraries received 3,072 religious studies titles via the approval plan. Figure 5.5 illustrates circulations by individual title per year in the subject range, and provides a percentage of the total received that either circulated or did not circulate. For the discipline of religious studies, 54 percent of the collection with an imprint date of 2004 circulated extensively during 2004–2007, while monographs acquired after 2004 circulated on average 3.74 percent less each year. When analyzing the circulation of religious studies titles acquired via the approval plan during this period of study, 48 percent circulated at least once. Thus, 52 percent did not circulate even one time, meaning that just over half of the approval plan collection is not being utilized.

For the years 2004–2007, KU libraries received 4,272 religious studies titles through nonapproval plan channels, chiefly through faculty selections and requests for monographs that specifically address faculty research and curriculum needs. Figure 5.5 shows circulation patterns for titles in this range by imprint year.

For nonapproval plan monographs in religious studies, 45 percent of the collection with an imprint date of 2004 circulated extensively during 2004–2007, while items acquired after 2004 circulated 10–20 percent less each year. On average, of all religious studies titles acquired through the acquisition activities of the subject librarian during this period, nearly 35 percent circulated at least once.

Sociology.   In the sociology call number range, a total of 593 monographs were acquired through the approval plan. Of these titles, 375 circulated at least once (63 percent). Again, in more recent years, we see a circulation decline of 8–9 percent, possibly due to the items being available for less time. Only an average of 37 percent of materials from this call number range did not circulate, indicating a fairly substantial amount of use overall.

Sociology titles that were selected by the subject specialist circulated less than those added via the approval plan. Nonapproval monograph acquisitions with imprint dates of 2004–2007 totaled 762 in number. Of these titles, 388 (51 percent) have circulated. This is significantly less than approval plan acquired titles, which displayed a circulation rate of 63 percent. Figure 5.5 illustrates circulation patterns for titles per year in the sociology call number range.

Unlike those items acquired through the approval plan, circulation rates of nonapproval plan sociology monographs show a steady and significant decline from 2004 to 2007. From highest use in 2004 (66 percent), there is an average of a 13 percent decline in use per year for the years 2005–2007. As expected, only a little more than one-third of the monographs with imprint dates of 2004–2007 circulated in 2007.

Use by Transactions

Figures 5.6 and 5.7 illustrate the total number of transactions per year for the period 2004–2007 for those items acquired by the approval plan (Figure 5.6) and by the subject librarians (Figure 5.7). Note that the authors here define "transaction" as the total number of circulations per year for all monographs in the range. Individual titles may have circulated multiple times and these transactions are reflected in the two figures. For purposes of analysis, the authors also presented data to show the number of titles that accounted for both 80 percent of all transactions and 20 percent of all transactions. No attempt has been made in this study to map this information to existing patron groups.

Transactions for Approval Plan Acquired Monographs

Of the four disciplines, business shows the closest adherence to the Trueswell 80/20 rule. As noted in Figure 5.6, of the 2,633 titles received for business, 639 (or slightly over 24 percent) account for 80 percent of all transactions for this time period. The rest of the monographs added during this time for business, or nearly 2,000 titles, account for the remaining 20 percent of all transactions. Psychology and sociology statistically have the same use pattern and neither adheres to the Trueswell rule, as 40 percent of titles account for 80 percent of use. In psychology, of the 660 titles received, 251 titles (or nearly 40 percent) account for 80 percent of all transactions for this time period, and the remaining 409 titles account for the remaining 20 percent of all transactions. In sociology, of the 593 titles received, 231 (nearly 40 percent) account for 80 percent of transactions and the remaining titles, 362 (or 60 percent), account for the remaining 20 percent of transactions. This indicates that a very high proportion of approval plan books are being used in psychology and sociology research. Use of religious studies approval plan monographs is between that of business and that of psychology and sociology. Of the 2,992 books received on approval in religious studies, 912 (or 30.5 percent) account for over 80 percent of all transactions for the period reviewed. The remaining 2,080 books (nearly 70 percent of the collection) account for 20 percent of use.

Transactions for Nonapproval Plan Acquired Monographs

Though the transaction pattern noted in Figure 5.7 is similar between the disciplines, those monographs acquired by the subject librarian were used much less over the period under review.

Again, business has the lowest level of use. Of the 4,279 total monographs selected by librarians, 746 individual titles (or 17 percent) comprise 80 percent of the total transactions from 2004 to 2007. Conversely, just over 3,500 monographs of the total acquired were circulated for the remaining 20 percent of all transactions recorded. Religious studies is again in the middle. Of the 4,029 titles received, 868 (or nearly 22 percent) account for 80 percent of all transactions in 2004–2007. The remaining 3,161 titles account for 20 percent of all transactions. Although the religious studies faculty is actively

Figure 5.6
80/20 Rule for Approval Plan Titles

YBP				NON-YBP		
Year	# Titles received	Circulated/ % total	Noncirc/ % total	# Titles received	Circulated/ % total	Noncirc/ % total
Business						
2004	467	220/47%	247/53%	1,358	660/48%	698/52%
2005	734	315/43%	419/57%	1,195	452/37%	743/63%
2006	923	309/33%	614/67%	939	283/30%	656/70%
2007	509	140/27%	369/73%	787	155/19%	632/81%
Psychology						
2004	95	69/73%	26/27%	207	158/76%	49/24%
2005	224	150/67%	74/33%	169	84/49.7%	85/50.3%
2006	213	128/60%	85/40%	211	131/62%	80/38%
2007	128	69/54%	59/46%	162	64/40%	98/60%
Religious studies						
2004	671	362/54%	309/46%	1,103	497/45%	606/55%
2005	1084	563/52%	521/48%	1,244	437/35%	807/65%
2006	944	405/43%	539/57%	937	338/36%	599/64%
2007	361	155/43%	206/57%	822	187/23%	635/77%
Sociology						
2004	115	78/68%	37/32%	214	142/66%	72/34%
2005	197	135/68%	62/32%	185	98/53%	87/47%
2006	201	121/60%	80/40%	188	89/47%	99/53%
2007	80	41/51%	39/49%	175	59/34%	116/66%

involved in the selection of monographs outside the approval plan, overall transactions do not differ significantly from the Trueswell rule.

Following the pattern of approval monographs, albeit it with lower percentages, nonapproval monographs in psychology and sociology are still used more than their counterparts in business or religious studies. Of the 749 total monographs selected for psychology, 239 (32 percent) of titles account for 80 percent of the total transactions from 2004 to 2007. Conversely, 510 monographs circulated, for the remaining 20 percent of transactions. For sociology, a total of 762 titles were acquired by librarian selection, and 218 (30 percent) represent 80 percent of use. The remaining 544 account for the remaining 20 percent of use.

Figure 5.7
80/20 Rule for Nonapproval Plan Titles

	Total # transactions 2004–2007	80% of total # of transactions	Title count	# of titles to account for 80% of transactions	% of total titles	# of items representing remaining 20% of transactions	% of total titles
Business	1,651	1321	2,633	639	24.30%	1,994	75.70%
Psychology	864	691	660	251	38.00%	409	62.00%
Religious Studies	2,657	2,126	2,992	912	30.50%	2,080	69.50%
Sociology	811	649	593	231	39.00%	362	61.00%

DISSERTATION ANALYSIS

Though social science research is predominantly journal driven, monographs still represent an important research source for these disciplines. This is evident in dissertation bibliographies. In order to measure effectiveness of monographic selection, a review of recent dissertations accepted by the disciplines was undertaken. The goal was to gauge the level of monographic material included in dissertation research and, more importantly, to discover to what extent dissertations included citations to material acquired through the approval plan and through subject librarian selection.

Dissertations submitted and accepted for degree requirements in business, psychology, and sociology at KU from 2005 to 2007 and available in the ProQuest Dissertations and Theses database were considered (religious studies is not a doctoral program at KU, only a baccalaureate and master's degree program and thus not pertinent for this aspect of the discussion). For each dissertation, the bibliography was reviewed and all monographic material with an imprint date of 2005, 2006, or 2007 recorded.

Of the 15 dissertations in psychology, three (20 percent) had no references to monographic material published between 2005 and 2007. Thirteen dissertations (80 percent) had recent monographic content, with nine using material published in 2005; three dissertations used material from 2006; and six dissertations used material published in 2007.[4] Over 50 percent of these titles were from publishers on the approval list. Thus, the conclusion for psychology is that monographic material is still very important and that the approval plan is meeting students' needs. A review of bibliographies also revealed that many students in psychology used a significant number of monographs with much earlier imprint dates, indicating that it is important to continue to acquire monographic material in psychology for future researchers.

Of the dissertations produced between 2005 and 2007 in business, only three included monographic material published between 2005 and 2007. Excluding two dissertations that were not available through the ProQuest database (at their authors' requests), 80 percent of the dissertations had no current monographic content. Though one contained no monographic material at all, most included earlier monographs published in the last 20 years. One of the dissertations had a very short bibliography and included only four citations to monographs, of which the newest was dated 1995, and the remaining from 1954, 1977, and 1984, and all from publishers included in the approval plan profile. Another dissertation relied heavily on large quantities of unpublished working papers from professors around the world, as well as government documents, thus using neither approval plan nor librarian selected monographs. Overall, it would appear that, for business, traditional monographic material has become less important for doctoral research, and that we may be able to be more selective in acquiring monographs in support of business.

Only two dissertations from 2005 to 2007 in sociology were available in ProQuest, and neither used monographic material that had been published during these same three years. However, both heavily cited monographic material published in the last 20 years, each with a 2004 imprint as the most recent. Due to the small number of available dissertations in sociology, the dissertation analysis is inconclusive for this discipline.

As Pancheshnikov (2007) shows, students tend to rely more heavily on monographic content in their research than do faculty members. It is not surprising that most dissertations in all the disciplines made use of monographic content. The literature review is generally completed early in the research process and thus, the majority of dissertations do not include a significant amount of current monographic material—that is, material published within the two to three years prior to the dissertation being submitted for the degree requirement. Variations occur when the topic is very contemporary or more data-driven or statistical in nature, as illustrated in the analysis of psychology dissertations.

It has always been difficult to measure the impact of current monographic acquisition activities, and bibliometric analysis of dissertations is only one way of measuring how well collections are meeting user needs. For most disciplines, a certain amount of time needs to pass before monographs are cited in any meaningful numbers in dissertations and other research products. If that is the case, how do librarians determine whether monographic use is actually declining or whether individual monographs are simply not yet being utilized for scholarly work? If libraries reduce monographic acquisitions too much it will require future researchers to use interlibrary loan instead of local collections. But if monographic use is declining, then libraries may be acquiring monographs that will never be cited in future research. Bibliometric analysis should therefore not be conducted annually for each discipline, since results can vary significantly. However, if librarians review their respective disciplines, say, every five years, patterns and trends may be seen, thus enabling all concerned to make better collection development decisions in the future.

CONCLUSIONS

This chapter presents findings about the use of monographic materials by academic users in four disciplines within a comprehensive research institution over a four-year period. Data about the number of titles circulated over time, in addition to the number of transactions recorded, for monographs acquired via the approval plan and those acquired by subject specialists, were analyzed and compared. Conclusions drawn from these analyses both confirm and belie expectations.

For example, in the areas of psychology and sociology, use of monographs exceeded the expectations of the authors, both in terms of individual title use and number of transactions recorded over time. The use of monographs in religious studies seems to have been lower than expected, while the use of monographs selected for business, which generally saw the lowest use among all for disciplines, was not entirely unexpected. This pattern in business, in particular, may be attributed to the greater reliance on journal articles and other forms of research information more readily available in electronic formats (for example, financial or economic data).

It is generally shown that items acquired via the approval plan were used more than those acquired through nonapproval plan methods; that is, largely through the selection activities of individual subject specialists, at least in the disciplines under consideration in this study. This may be due to the fact that approval plans tend to acquire a broad spectrum of general academic monographs, whereas those acquired by the subject specialist are either specifically requested by faculty or students in the discipline or are identified by the librarian to fill more specialized gaps in the collection. Either way, across all four disciplines included in this chapter, items acquired on approval tend toward higher use than those acquired by librarians.

When resources are limited, both in fiscal and human terms, it is important to be able to ascertain whether the approval plan is meeting current needs. If it does, then the library is able to justify the allocations made to the approval plan. If it does not, then adjustments should be made. It is also important to ascertain if the time spent by librarians in selecting monographs outside the approval plan is reflected in the circulation data and also in research production (e.g., dissertations). If the data indicates that material selected by librarians is being used, then the library will probably want the librarian to continue to spend time selecting monographic material. On the other hand, if the data indicates that librarian-selected material is not being used, then presumably the organization will want to use the librarian's time for other critical work or services. As previously discussed, the librarian may be able to offer more instruction, provide additional reference services, or focus on other areas of collection development. This could include focusing on acquiring other formats or resources, depending upon the specific needs of the discipline being supported.

It is interesting to note that the use of monographs in dissertation research tends to correlate with overall collection use in a particular discipline. For example, while psychology and sociology dissertations revealed higher numbers of monographic citations in bibliographies that were examined, business dissertations revealed low levels of monographic use. The final conclusion reached by the authors is that monographs are still robust for some disciplines but seem to be in a state of transition, if not decline, for others. Future implications for library collections are difficult to predict with certainty, given the nature of this analysis, but it seems likely that a study such as this could be replicated among other disciplines to further understand actual monographic collection use. Analysis of circulation patterns of monographs may help budget planners more efficiently allocate scarce institutional resources and ultimately may allow for greater and more efficient allocation of valuable library faculty time.

ENDNOTES

1. YBP Library Services was formerly known as Yankee Book Peddlar.
2. See this volume's bibliography for readings on this topic.
3. We thank YBP Library Services for providing the datasets used in analysis for this chapter.
4. Imprint dates were not compared against year received. For example, we did not check if all the monographs with an imprint of 2007 had been received only in 2007 and not in 2006 or 2008.

REFERENCES

Britten, William A. 1990. A use statistic for collection management: The 80/20 rule revisited. *Library Acquisitions: Practice and Theory* 14 (2).

Burrell, Quentin L. 1985. The 80/20 rule: Library lore or statistical law? *Journal of Documentation* 41 (1): 24.

Pancheshnikov, Yelena. 2007. A comparison of literature citations in faculty publications and student theses as indicators of collection use and a background for collection management at a university library. *Journal of Academic Librarianship* 33:6, 674–83.

BIBLIOGRAPHY

Baker, Sharon L., and F. Wilford Lancaster. 1991. *The measurement and evaluation of library services*. Arlington, VA: Information Resources Press.

Bartolo, Laura M., Don A. Wicks, and Valerie A. Ott. 2002. Border crossing in a research university: An exploratory analysis of a library approval plan profile of geography. *Collection Management* 27 (3/4): 29–44.

Beile, Penny M., David N. Boote, and Elizabeth K. Killingsworth. 2004. A microscope or a mirror? A question of study validity regarding the use of dissertation citation analysis for evaluating research collections. *Journal of Academic Librarianship* 30 (5): 347–53.

Black, Steve, and Amy Sisson. 2003. Bradford's distribution, the 80/20 rule, and patterns of full-text database use. *Against the Grain* 15 (6): 20–23.

Britten, William A. 1990. A use statistic for collection management: The 80/20 rule revisited. *Library Acquisitions: Practice and Theory* 14 (2): 183–89.

Burrell, Quentin L. 1985. The 80/20 rule: Library lore or statistical law? *Journal of Documentation* 41 (1): 24–39.

Emanuel, Michelle. 2002. A collection evaluation in 150 hours. *Collection Management* 27 (3/4): 79–91.

Gabriel, Michael R. 1995. *Collection development and collection evaluation: A sourcebook.* Metuchen, NJ: Scarecrow Press.

Gorman, Michael. 2003. Collection development in interesting times: A summary. *Library Collections, Acquisitions, & Technical Services* 27 (4): 459–62.

Grover, Mark L. 1999. Large scale collection assessment. *Collection Building* (2): 58–66.

Intner, Sheila. 2003. Making your collections work for you: Collection evaluation myths and realities. *Library Collections, Acquisitions, & Technical Services* 27 (3): 339–50.

Kingsley, Marcia S. 1996. Circulation statistics for measuring approval plan effectiveness. *Against the Grain* 8 (4): 1–17.

———. 2000. Evaluating approval plans and other methods of book selection through system management reports. In *Acquiring Online Management Reports*, edited by William E. Jarvis, 57–64. Binghamton, NY: Haworth.

Knievel, Jennifer E., Heather Wicht, and Lynn Silipigni Connaway. 2006. Use of circulation statistics and interlibrary loan data in collection management. *College and Research Libraries* 67 (1): 35–49.

Littman, Justin, and Lynn Silipigni Connaway. 2004. A circulation analysis of print books and e-books in an academic research library. *Library Resources & Technical Services* 48 (4): 256–62.

Lorenzen, Elizabeth, and Suzanne Kapusta. 2007. Long live the approval plan, even in a time of financial constraints. *Against the Grain* 19 (3): 40–43.

Mortimore, Jeffrey M. 2005. Access-informed collection development and the academic library: Using holdings, circulation, and ill data to develop prescient collections. *Collection Management* 30 (3): 21–37.

Mueller, Susan. 2005. Approval plans and faculty selection: Are they compatible? *Library Collections, Acquisitions, & Technical Services* 29 (5): 61–70.

Pancheshnikov, Yelena. 2007. A comparison of literature citations in faculty publications and student theses as indicators of collection use and a background for collection management at a university library. *Journal of Academic Librarianship* 33 (6): 674–83.

Pasterczyk, Catherine E. 1988. A quantitative methodology for evaluating approval plan performance. *Collection Management* 10 (1/2): 25–38.

Stoller, Michael. 2006. A decade of ARL collection development: A look at the data. *Collection Building* 25 (2): 45–51.

Wagner, Celia Scher. 1988. Academic book trends—approval plans and library collections—do they all look alike? *Against the Grain* 10 (5): 73.

PART III

Serials and E-Resources Management

CHAPTER 6

E-Journal Usage Statistics in Collection Management Decisions: A Literature Review

ANDRÉE J. RATHEMACHER

Over the past several years, the online availability of scholarly journals has grown. Many research libraries now subscribe to journals in online format, either instead of or in addition to print subscriptions. In the electronic environment, it is possible to measure how many times online journals are used. Statistics on usage can be requested from publishers or generated by local systems. These statistics can be used for collection management decisions, including whether to cancel or retain subscriptions. This chapter reviews the literature on employing usage as a factor in journal cancellation projects. It examines sources of e-journal usage data, issues in working with the data, the relevance of usage data of large e-journal packages, and the objectivity of the statistics themselves.

USAGE-BASED JOURNAL CANCELLATION AND RETENTION DECISIONS

Journal use statistics have long been used by libraries in deciding which journals to cancel and which to retain. Medeiros reports that "Goehlert, Maxin, and Broadus have described the value of usage statistics when making collection development decisions about print journals. Impetus for these studies of the late 1970s and early 1980s was the rising cost of serials, especially scientific/technological/medical (STM) journals" (2007, 234). Jaguszewski and Probst note that "Usage and especially cost per use are central in determining whether a print title is a likely candidate for cancellation or withdrawal" (2000, 801). Kraemer adds, "For libraries with expensive journal subscriptions, use data has been a mainstay for justifying the purchase of new journals and the cancellation of no longer cost-effective subscriptions" (2006, 164).

Usage as a Proxy for More Meaningful Data

Despite the widespread analysis of use data in making collection management decisions, many authors have noted that usage is a proxy for more meaningful but elusive data. According to Oliver Pesch, Chief Architect at EBSCO Publishing, "Statistics are a measurement of users' actions that we try to correlate to their intentions" (2004, 153). Peters adds, "What is usage, and what do we really know with confidence about how persons use information? . . . We need to be careful about any inferences we make from an analysis of usage data about the needs, interests, and preferences of users. How do users actually apply library resources and services to the information and learning projects of their lives?" (2002, 44).

Some authors have commented that the retrieval of an article (removing a journal issue from the shelf or successfully accessing a full-text article online) may not correspond to the article actually being read or cited at a later point in time. Best explains, "The library assumes that the article met the need, but for a heavy undergraduate population that may rely on the title only to judge an article's relevancy (often without looking at the abstract), students may not discover the inadequacy of the article until later in their research process" (2007, 205). Medeiros notes that "clearly there is some number of e-journal uses that merely meet a professorial requirement (e.g., a certain number of journal articles necessary in a bibliography) versus satisfying an information need" (2007, 240). According to Conger, usage measures an interaction with the material, but beyond this, "the librarian has no way to interpret the reality of the user's expectation before the interaction, the degree to which that expectation was met after the interaction, or the outcome, or impact, of that interaction on the user's life as a researcher" (2007, 265).

There is also a question about whether all use is "created equal." Is the value of an article dependent on who is using it, or for what purpose? Boots and her coauthors state, "We do not know who within the organization is using any given journal, and whether it is used a little by many staff members or a lot by only a few staff. We do not know what value is attached to an article by the person who has downloaded it, and who is using it for their work" (2007, 197). Duy and Vaughan conducted a study at Concordia University Libraries in Montreal and found that "although reading an article and citing an article are different activities, and perhaps indicate different usefulness of an article, there is an overall correlation between journals that are looked at online, and those that are cited by local researchers." Nonetheless, they note that this might not be the case "at an academic institution where non-publishing students are presumably a large population of online journal readers" (2006, 516–17). Luther, in her heavily cited 2001 white paper on electronic journal usage statistics, concludes, "Both publishers and librarians emphasize that measures of the level of activity do not indicate the value of an article. It is dangerous to assume that a popular title that is used by many students is worth more than a research title that is used by only a few faculty members working in a specific discipline. Other factors need to be considered" (2001, 123).

All in all, as Conger states, "Decisions that rely only upon usage data or inferential data suffer from a vacuum of experiential data about customer experience or customer outcomes" (2007, 265). Noonan and McBurney add, "Gathering usage data . . . will provide the staff only with quantitative data, which lends nothing to the assessment of a publication's quality or its intended use by the patron" (2007, 158).

Other Criteria

Perhaps because of the shortcomings of usage data, total use and cost per use are seldom the only factors considered in the cancellation or retention of periodical subscriptions. Enssle and Wilde examined the literature regarding what other information is used in decisions to cancel journals. While they found that "use is an integral part of the majority of serials cancellation projects," libraries also employ such measures as questionnaires and surveys, faculty journal preferences, interlibrary loan data, and citation and impact data (2002, 260). Other sources of information include subjective evaluation by subject specialists and checks against external benchmarks. Colorado State University Libraries also used Local Journal Use Reports (LJUR) from the Institute for Scientific Information (ISI), in which "ISI analyzes the information from its citation database and provides the institution with information about the journals in which their faculty have published or which their faculty have cited" (Enssle and Wilde 2002, 264).

At the Owen Science and Engineering Library (OSEL) at Washington State University, use and cost per use are the "primary evaluation factors for making retention decisions" (Galbraith 2002, 80). Yet "retention decisions are based on the following factors: use patterns over the last five years, population served, availability of other titles covering the same topic, impact factor, coverage in indexes owned by OSEL, availability in other local libraries, available document delivery options, and faculty input" (Galbraith 2002, 85). Kraemer, at the Medical College of Wisconsin, "compiles an annual journal evaluation package that includes complete usage reports, low-use reports, high cost-per-use lists, a list of high-demand interlibrary loan (ILL) journals, and a list of requested journals." A Web-based survey of titles that were requested through interlibrary loan is then made available to all patrons (Bordeaux, Kraemer, and Sullenger 2005, 297). A survey was also used by the Lee Graff Medical & Scientific Library in Duarte, California; they designed a survey to combine with their usage statistics to determine what their users really wanted and needed (Wood 2006).

Enssle and Wilde conclude that, "On the surface, usage seems to be a good justification for canceling periodicals, however, upon closer examination, one soon discovers that this is not always the case . . . . The primary problem with usage statistics is that they fail to take into consideration the impact of a journal in an individual subject area" (2002, 267). Best adds, "Usage data . . . is not and should not be the main driver for decisions on selection and retention. Selection and retention decisions . . . must be made with a proper understanding of the users being served, the users' needs, and the overall strength of the resources of the entire collection" (2007, 200). According to Jaguszewski and Probst, "The librarian's knowledge of the collection, faculty research and teaching interests, user expectations, and current and future trends in research in related fields are equally important in ensuring that appropriate choices are made" (2000, 800).

While it is necessary to look at other factors and not make decisions based on usage statistics alone, usage has been and will remain an important criterion in cancellation and retention decisions. As Gatten and Sanville acknowledge, "We now have a much more concrete measure of relative value, which is the number of uses (downloads). While sheer volume of use (i.e., cost-use analysis) is not the only measure of value, to fail to recognize use as the dominant starting point is to deny reality" (2004).

SOURCES OF USAGE DATA FOR ONLINE JOURNALS

Vendor-Supplied Usage Data

Once a library decides to employ usage data as a factor on which to base e-journal cancellation and retention decisions, the library must decide whether or not to use vendor-provided or locally produced data. The majority of libraries rely on vendor-supplied usage data, which are readily available from a large number of publishers. In their 2004 survey of academic libraries in New Zealand, McDowell and Gorman found that 65 percent of libraries surveyed used vendor-supplied usage statistics to aid in collection management decisions. That number is sure to have increased significantly by 2008.

Previously, the literature was rife with complaints about the inconsistency of vendor-supplied usage data. McDowell and Gorman found in 2004 that the standardization of usage statistics across vendors through COUNTER or International Coalition of Library Consortia (ICOLC) guidelines had not yet been adopted by vendors. They found, for example, that there was no common definition of "use" among vendors: "Some vendors defined it as accessing the home page of the e-resource, some as downloading the full text article, and others itemized use counts of a number of different activities including searching or accessing table of contents, abstracts, or full text" (2004, 338).

Fortunately, since then the widespread adoption of COUNTER compliant statistics has largely solved these problems of inconsistency. COUNTER does a great deal to standardize these statistics and help make statistics between different publishers and platforms comparable. According to the

COUNTER Web site, COUNTER was launched in 2002 in order to set "standards that facilitate the recording and reporting of online usage statistics in a consistent, credible, and compatible way."

A 2006 study by Duy and Vaughan concludes that COUNTER-compliant statistics are a valid method to determine electronic journal use. Morrison adds that, thanks to the efforts of initiatives including COUNTER and the ICOLC Guidelines for Statistical Measures of Usage of Web-based Information Resources, "librarians are now beginning to see usage statistics based on these standards that are comparable across resources and platforms." Morrison acknowledges that a great amount of work still needs to be done, yet she concludes that "there are currently enough quality usage statistics available that this is now a factor in making financial decisions, such as the cancellation and retention of journals" (2007, 174).

Most libraries measuring the use of online journals will use the COUNTER Journal Report 1, "Number of Successful Full-Text Article Requests by Month and Journal." Boots and her colleagues at Cancer Research UK (CRUK) have "been persuaded that the number of full-text downloads is the most important statistic to measure" (2007, 189). They write, "CRUK has developed a very simple model of cost-per-download by dividing usage statistics into journal costs. We have proposed to use this technique as part of the annual review of journal titles for cancellation or renewal" (2007, 187). Galbraith, at the OSEL at Washington State University, has concluded that "one use equals one access of a full text article" (2002, 81). In some cases, it is possible to examine other COUNTER reports, for example Database Report 3, which provides total searches and sessions on the vendor's platform, or the optional Journal Report 3, which offers additional measures including views of tables of contents, abstracts, and references (and which, in COUNTER Release 3, will also measure requests of supplementary data sets, images, and videos). However, without a sophisticated statistics management system, so much data can lead to information overload and the inability to interpret any of it in a meaningful way.

If Publisher Does Not Provide Statistics

When relying on vendor-provided usage statistics for collection management decisions, one problem libraries encounter is the fact that some publishers do not provide usage statistics at all. Noonan and McBurney note that "there are a handful of small publications purchased individually that provide no statistics whatsoever" (2007, 156). Galbraith found that "most publishers who are not providing statistics are publishing just one or two e-journals" (2002, 85). Noonan and McBurney point out that the unavailability of usage statistics "makes it very difficult for the library to make informed collection development decisions" (2007, 156).

It may be to a publisher's advantage to not offer usage statistics when it comes to retaining subscribers; if a journal has low usage, it might get cancelled, but if a journal does not report usage at all, it is likely safe, at least from cancellations based on usage statistics. Peters speculates, "Some vendors may be reluctant to supply usage statistics, because they are fearful that low or uneven usage may cause libraries or consortia to demand changes in pricing, terms, and scope of content when license agreements come up for renewal" (2002, 43). Of course, it is conceivable that some libraries would consider the availability of COUNTER-compliant usage statistics to be an important factor in deciding whether or not to subscribe to an online journal in the first place, or whether to retain a subscription.

Locally Generated Usage Statistics

Instead of vendor-provided usage statistics, some libraries have chosen to rely on local statistics that measure links to publisher sites through a journal A–Z list, an OpenURL link resolver, a proxy server, or in some cases, accesses to content hosted locally. Such practices have the advantage of providing statistics in cases where vendor-supplied statistics are not available, as discussed above. Kraemer explains, "For a shrinking number of electronic journals, locally gathered click-through counts from an A to Z list are the only statistics available" (2006, 166). For example, libraries that subscribe to Serials Solutions can access "click-through" statistics, which represent "any instance where a user clicks on a journal link within Serials Solutions. Thus, an institution can get a decent idea of how many times each database, each journal title within that database, or each journal title individually has been accessed using the Serials Solutions interface" (Fowler 2007, 137). At the Medical College of Wisconsin, Kraemer has created a program that uses OpenURL linking data to track journal usage by year of publication, a measure that is not available in COUNTER-compliant reports (Bordeaux, Kraemer, and Sullenger 2005, 296–97).

It is important to keep in mind, however, that not all researchers at an institution access subscribed resources through the library's interface, preferring to navigate directly to the journal or linking from e-mailed tables of contents or other sites (for example, Google Scholar). Therefore, these click-through statistics are not accurate. Ralston found a correlation between click-through statistics from a list of online journals and vendor-supplied statistics, yet he found that the "usage counts from the online journal list were not accurate enough to use with cancellation decisions" (2007, 51). He determined that "the correlation breaks down at the low use end of the online journal list statistics, precisely where it is needed to make accurate cancellation decisions" (2007, 60). Ralston further discovered that accesses from an A to Z title list could not be equated with articles downloaded, as his study "found an average ratio of 5.73 articles downloaded for each title access recorded on the list" (2007, 63). Kraemer offers a possible solution: "Since click-throughs represent only a fraction of the total use, that count is multiplied by a factor that has been derived from journals for which both click-through counts and publisher-provided COUNTER compliant data was available" (2006, 166).

There appears to be a consensus that vendor-provided usage statistics, for all their weaknesses, are the most complete and accurate data available. Fowler, in his study of Serials Solutions click-through data, found that

while the breadth and depth of the statistics it provides are impressive, they do not, as yet, serve as an alternative or replacement for the site statistics provided directly by journal providers, or journal platforms, such as Ingenta or MetaPress. They can, however, provide valuable adjunct statistics to complement and fill out these other statistics. In the cases where a particular journal title has no statistics provided by its platform or producer, Serials Solutions may, in fact, be the only resource available for providing any usage statistics at all (2007, 149).

LABOR OF GATHERING

Regardless of their source, usage statistics for electronic resources take a great deal of time and effort to acquire and compile into a useful format. Despite their increased availability, vendor-supplied statistics have to be gathered, platform by platform. As Anderson explains, "The majority of vendors provide Web sites dedicated to usage statistics and, often, other administrative functions. This practice simplifies access to various data repositories, although the library must maintain a list of the access points for vendor statistics" (2007, 248). Weintraub rightfully complains, "Yale must maintain dozens of passwords to various databases in order to get usage statistics" (2003, 32). Fortunately, Release 3 of the COUNTER Code of Practice for Journals and Databases, effective January 2009, incorporates the SUSHI protocol. According to the COUNTER Web site, "Implementation of the SUSHI protocol by vendors will allow the automated retrieval of the COUNTER usage reports into local systems, making this process much less time consuming for the librarian or library consortium administrator." However, libraries will need an electronic resource management (ERM) system capable of fetching the statistics in order to take advantage of SUSHI.

Even after statistics have been gathered, they must be organized in such a way as to make them easily usable for decision-making purposes. Medeiros puts it well:

> Despite the adoption of COUNTER compliant usage statistics by a growing bloc of e-journal providers, the maintenance of usage statistics is a labor-intensive activity .... Merely accumulating spreadsheets of e-journal usage, however, does not provide the kind of immediate and longitudinal analysis libraries need, in order to make both informed and on-demand collection management decisions. Still the practice of storing countless spreadsheets of usage data predominates among statistics maintainers, since no agreeable alternative presently exists (2007, 236).

Anderson adds, "Excel spreadsheets work well for cost-per-use analyses and for more sophisticated reports linking budget data and usage. Access and Oracle offer additional reporting capabilities, but ... with a higher cost in time and personnel to develop that functionality" (2007, 251). Fortunately, a number of ERM systems now available offer an alternative to multiple spreadsheets for the storage and analysis of usage data.

WORKING WITH THE NUMBERS

Once usage statistics have been compiled, how should they be used and interpreted? How should the data be used to help make collection management decisions?

How Many Years of Data to Examine?

One question to consider when making decisions based on usage data is how many years of data to examine when making cancellation or retention decisions. Some libraries, like the Owen Science and Engineering Library at Washington State University, calculate both an average and a sum of all years of use available for each title (Galbraith 2002, 83). Other libraries compare data from the current year against past years. According to Peters, this answers the question, "How is usage of the e-resource evolving over time? After a year's worth of usage data have been compiled, the usage statistics for a month or quarter can be compared to those for the same month/quarter of the proceeding year" (2002, 44). Advanced comparisons or calculations will be easier with the use of an ERM or similar system.

In most cases, better decisions will be made by consulting multiple years of data. Comparing use over a few years will help avoid any aberrations in the data that occur during a limited time period. For example, a decrease in the use of a particular journal during a period of a few months to a year might be because a faculty member who made particularly heavy use of the title was on sabbatical, or has retired and not yet been replaced. On the other hand, a decline in use that is sustained over more than a year might reflect changing research interests in a department, in which case the journal should not be retained but perhaps traded for another title. Open lines of communication between librarians and researchers can help in the interpretation of these variations in usage.

Another factor to take into consideration is how long the library has subscribed to a particular online journal. In 1999, Townley and Murray wrote, "Usage rates are positively related to length of use. The longer a database has been available, the more likely it is to be used. A minimum of twelve to eighteen months seems to be necessary before heavy use will be observed. Libraries should commit to support any database for at least one year before assessing use" (1999, 38). Whether this is still the case is uncertain. As of 2008, it seems that journals and other electronic resources with print counterparts are more likely to be used online than in print. For instance, Kraemer found in 2005 that "electronic usage has quadrupled in four years, while reshelving of print journals has dropped by more than half" (Bordeaux, Kraemer, and Sullenger 2005, 297). If there is no print alternative to an online journal, as is the case when libraries support only one format, online use might not take very long at all to reach a peak. Nonetheless, it is probably wise to take the amount of time a journal has been online into consideration when examining usage for cancellation purposes, giving more weight to usage from later years in cases where usage has grown over time.

Creating a Benchmark

Many libraries that rely on usage data for cancellation and retention decisions will rank their subscriptions by total use and/or cost per use and begin with a cutoff point, or benchmark, above or below which decisions will be made. In preparing to cancel journals, Enssle and Wilde at the Morgan Library at Colorado State University picked a "benchmark statistic to use for the initial cut. This benchmark statistic served to shorten the list of titles and eliminated the need to compile a complete set of statistics for each subscription in the collection." From there they compiled additional information for each title on the list of potential cancellations (2002, 266). Likewise, the Owen Science and Engineering Library at Washington State University maintains a database of inhouse use statistics. Galbraith explains, "On a regular basis OSEL's selection librarians run a list of titles from the database that have received less than a designated number of uses during the year. The librarians then evaluate these titles in order to decide which to cancel and which to retain" (2002, 85).

Benchmarks used for cancellation decisions can be based on total use, cost per use, or both. In fact, these strategies were used long before usage statistics for online journals became readily available. In 1996, the Management and Economics Library at Purdue University developed a decision support system for a journals cancellation project based on duplication, price inflation, and use. Use was measured by scanning the bar codes of reshelved journals for one semester, and titles were identified as candidates for cancellation if they were circulated or used inhouse fewer than five times during the study (Nixon 2000). Likewise, The Washington University School of Medicine in St. Louis looked at use of print, incorporating online use when available, and drew "a line . . . at a certain use level based upon the available funding" (Mercer 2000).

Benchmarks for cost per use are based on dollar amounts rather than times used. According to Hiott, "In 2003, the Houston Public Library used full-text units examined to measure the cost per use of its databases and to renegotiate prices for databases with high costs. With no information on what a unit should cost, the library set five dollars as an upper acceptable limit for a full-text article because the article cost for all but a few of its databases fell under this figure" (2004, 445). Galbraith at the OSEL uses a cost per use benchmark of $100 in addition to a benchmark for total use: "Use of a journal may be in the acceptable range, but the cost of the journal may make the cost-per-use unacceptable" (2002, 85). Sometimes the benchmark for cost per use can be based on an external factor. For example, CRUK compares cost per download "with the average cost of obtaining a copy of a journal article from document supply sources" (Boots et al. 2007, 183).

In the electronic environment, before cancelling any title based on low use, the library should verify whether or not access to that title is working and that the content is accessible. If not, low use could be due to lack of access rather than lack of interest. Similarly, if a particular title or platform has had problems with connectivity during the year, this should be taken into account when interpreting the total usage for the time period.

Context Needed

One recurring theme in the discussion of benchmarks, however, is that they are inherently arbitrary unless placed into some kind of context. In 2001, before usage statistics were as prevalent, Luther commented, "Publishers are concerned that the data they share with librarians lack context. If, in the absence of such a context, usage data seem low, the publishers fear that librarians may use such information as a basis for canceling subscriptions" (2001, 121). Kraemer adds, "Complete as well as estimated or projected data requires a context before decisions can be derived from the data. Given the occasional contentiousness of journal budgeting negotiations, misrepresenting data unintentionally can have a lasting, damaging impact. The strength or weakness of data must be clearly identified" (2006, 164).

The need to place usage statistics into context by discipline is one of the key issues that has been raised. Luther writes, "Known differences in information-seeking behavior among users in various scientific disciplines warrant additional study to identify usage patterns. As more data are examined on use and behavior, it may be possible to establish average levels of use for different subject areas or user groups" (2001, 123). Enssle and Wilde agree that

when examining the statistics, it quickly becomes evident that there is no uniform standard for "low-use"; it is best to compare journals within individual disciplines rather than across the board. In some cases "low-use" journals had been used fewer than twice a year, while for other disciplines "low-use" journals had been used fewer than 15 times a year. Intra-disciplinary comparisons help ensure that the cancellations are more evenly spread among the departments, and that the collection will not lose its diversity (2002, 267).

Another context suggested to help make sense of usage statistics is that of peer institutions. Peters writes, "Just as there are basic ways to analyze e-resource usage statistics, so too are there basic contexts into which these usage reports can be placed. . . . Usages statistics for the same e-resource from peer institutions can be compared" (2002, 44). Best concurs: "There is no universal consensus as to what constitutes acceptable or adequate amounts of usage. Without access to data for peer institutions with similar collections, it is doubtful that we will ever be able to provide proper benchmarks for usage rates" (2007, 200). At least one vendor, Serials Solutions, already provides benchmarks of click-through usage data by peer institutions. Fowler explains that subscribers can use benchmarking data available from Serials Solutions to compare and contrast the median statistics at their institutions with those at peer institutions that are also Serials Solutions subscribers. Peers are divided into categories by library type (academic, public, and special). Public libraries are then broken down by number of residents served, and academic libraries are grouped by Carnegie class (2007, 143–46).

Other options for creating context have been proposed as well. Luther suggests the possibility of benchmarking by journal price or number of articles available. She writes, "To base comparisons on the use of large or very popular journals (e.g., *Nature*, *Science*, or *Cell*) sets an artificially high benchmark for other titles with fewer articles available for use. This raises the question of whether the measure of activity should be relative to another factor, such as the price of the journal or the number of available articles, which puts the measure in a context" (2001, 123). Finally, some have suggested that e-resource usage statistics would be more meaningful if placed in the context of institutional population. Relating use levels to the number of potential users would allow for an examination of the growth in use over time of a library's e-resources by its users (Blecic, Fiscella, and Wiberley 2001; Peters 2002).

Titles with Very Low or No Use Are Not Unusual

In relation to benchmarks, it should not come as a surprise when a library finds that a substantial number of their subscriptions receive very low or even no use. In 1969, Trueswell posited that a well-known rule of inventories, the "80:20 Rule," applied to libraries, in that 80 percent of circulation requirements are satisfied by 20 percent of a library's holdings. Trueswell's findings have been reproduced in subsequent studies. In their 2000 study of the usage of 194 titles available both in print and online at the Norris Medical Library at the University of Southern California, Morse and Clintworth note that "the concentration of usage on the most popular titles was almost identical for the print and electronic lists. In both cases just 20 percent of the titles accounted for nearly 60 percent of the usage, and, conversely, the bottom 40 percent of both ranked lists accounted for only 9 percent of total usage." Kraemer, at the Medical College of Wisconsin, finds that "the highest use journals make up eighty percent of the total journal use" (Bordeaux, Kraemer, and Sullenger 2005, 297). Galbraith at the Owen Science and Engineering Library writes: "OSEL data collection has shown that it cannot be assumed that all electronic journals are heavily used. The database has revealed some titles that have received no uses in the time that they have been available" (2002, 88). Morse and Clintworth (2000) sum up the issue when they conclude that studies like theirs indicate "that the large spread in usage levels between titles, which librarians have long observed in the print domain, is being duplicated in the electronic one."

REFLECTIONS ON PUBLISHERS AND PACKAGES

One situation that results in a lack of meaningful usage data, at least for cancellation purposes, is the bundling by publishers of a large number of their journal titles into packages, often referred to in the literature as "portfolio packages" or the "big deal." While the price of the journals included, especially of those journals a library already subscribes to, is often used to calculate the initial cost of a portfolio package, most packages do not subsequently break down the package cost by title. Even if they do, the ability of a library to cancel individual titles in a package is usually contractually curtailed.

Because these packages are priced at a discount, costing much less than the combined list price of all included titles, it is usually the case that the aggregate cost per use for the entire package is low compared to nonpackaged e-journals. The lower cost per use suggests that these packages are a good value overall. However, critics of these packages, most notably Frazier (2001, 2005), have written in depth on the hazards of the "big deal," which can be summarized as follows:

- Libraries lose much of their ability to shape their collections according to local needs. "Big deal" packages monopolize library budgets, preventing money from being used for other resources, for example journals from smaller publishers and the "big deal" publisher's competitors.
- Libraries have less flexibility in response to budget cuts. In order to avoid the disruption that would be caused by cancelling the portfolio package, they will instead cancel journals from smaller, not-for-profit publishers. This punishes the small publishers, which are for the most part not responsible for the crisis in serials costs, while favoring the large, for-profit publishing corporations that raise prices indiscriminately. As stated by Jaguszewski and Probst: "The prospect of canceling journals published by learned societies and professional associations in order to support lesser-used titles from commercial publishers is one most librarians will want to avoid" (2000, 804).
- Diversity among library collections decreases, as many libraries subscribe to the same packages.
- These trends in turn enhance the market power and market share of the large "big deal" publishers.

Regardless of one's stance toward these packages, it is hard to argue with Best's contention that "aggregators do bundle their weaker titles with their strongest titles. As a result, libraries end up paying for titles they neither want nor need" (2007, 206). It is likely for these reasons that the Committee on Institutional Cooperation (CIC), a consortium of 12 research universities (the 11 members of the Big Ten Conference and the University of Chicago), recommended in 1998 that, "Bundling of titles as a provider's 'all-or-nothing' electronic journal product is not the best solution for all libraries and should not be the sole model for licensing these titles. Title-by-title purchase may be preferred and this option should be available," and "Cancellation of electronic journals should be possible on a title-by-title basis."

While many "big deal" packages offer COUNTER-compliant usage data, these data are of limited use to subscribers. Although usage statistics are provided on a title-by-title basis, restrictions on cancelling individual titles mean that such data serve only to alert the library to journals that are either more or less used. If a large number of journals in the package do not receive much use, the library may consider cancelling the package or attempting to renegotiate the price at the end of the contract period.

Cost per use data for these packages is also less useful than similar data for individually subscribed e-journals. Meaningful cost per use data can only be calculated for the package as a whole, since the relative cost of the journals in the package is not known, although some libraries (and ERM statistical software) divide the total package cost by the number of titles to determine an average cost per title. As Boots and her coauthors explain, "the cost of individual journals cannot easily be separated from the overall total. In these cases, the total cost is divided equally across the number of titles in the deal" (2007, 191). In any case, as Noonan and McBurney state, "Usage statistics availability does not mean the library can always utilize them if it has purchased bundled packages, or if the library is locked into a multiyear deal" (2007, 156).

NOT AS OBJECTIVE AS THEY APPEAR

Although usage statistics are not the only criterion on which to base cancellation decisions, at first glance they appear to have the advantage of being straightforward, objective measures that reflect the value that a given institution's users place on a journal. However, a closer look reveals that usage statistics are not as simple as they seem; in fact they could easily be characterized as "dirty data." There are many factors that can distort usage statistics or make comparisons between them invalid. While most of the problems identified below relate specifically to vendor-supplied usage statistics of online journals, some are equally relevant when using locally generated online journal statistics or in the print environment.

Title Changes

One problem in working with usage statistics is that publishers are inconsistent about how they handle title changes, split titles, and merged titles. Are the usage statistics for a particular journal consolidated under the new title of a journal, divided between new and old titles based on the date of the article downloaded, or duplicated for each title? To accurately compare journals by use, usage data for current and former titles of a journal must be merged to reflect total use, otherwise there is a risk that use for the new title will be artificially low. With a large subset of journals, this is a daunting task. It may not be necessary to consolidate the usage data for all changed titles on a regular basis, although some libraries do (see Galbraith 2002; Wulff and Nixon 2004), and ERM systems can help in this task. Certainly, however, before a journal is cancelled based on low use, it should be checked for a recent title change on the chance that use has accrued on the basis of the previous title. Henle and Cochenour sum up the problem with statistics when journals change titles, split into multiple parts, merge, or change publishers: "Any of these issues produces fractures in a journal's usage statistics that may go unnoticed and, thus, produce a false picture of the actual importance of a title for the local collection. While such detailed statistics are valuable, compiling them to ascertain the use of a given subscription and/or subject becomes a complicated affair. The task of integration across titles . . . is too manually cumbersome to justify routine processing and is better saved for specific requests" (2007, 18–19).

Bundled Titles

Some e-journal subscriptions are bundled such that a subscription to one title includes a small number of additional titles. This is on a much smaller scale and not at all comparable to the portfolio or "big deal" packages discussed above. For example, a 2008 subscription to Wiley-Blackwell's *International Studies Quarterly* includes four other titles from the International Studies Association: *International Studies Perspectives, International Studies Review, International Political Sociology,* and *Foreign Policy Analysis.* These additional titles are not priced individually or even available as separate subscriptions; they are simply included with a subscription to the "mother" title.

As is the case with "big deal" packages, the total number of successful full-text article requests will be available on a title-by-title basis, but calculating cost per use for each title is complicated. Libraries have to decide whether to divide the cost of the bundle equally between all the titles and then calculate cost per use for each title based on this average cost, or whether to perform a separate calculation for the package as a whole, with an aggregated number of article requests divided into the total price. Librarians should also think about whether or not it is important to apply the same methodology to all such bundles. Is it important to be consistent? Or should this decision be made on a case-by-case basis? For example, if all of the journals in a bundle are desired subscriptions, the value of the bundle could be calculated as one unit. In another case, perhaps the library has determined that only one title in a package is important to the collection. In that instance, cost per use could be calculated for the important title only, while the data for the other titles is ignored.

Either way, these small bundles can easily be overlooked, resulting in inaccurate cost per use calculations. Since the price for the bundle is actually the price of the mother title, it is easy to accidentally ignore the child titles and calculate cost per use of the mother title based on the use of the mother title alone. This makes each use of the subscription appear more expensive than if use for all titles were included in the calculation. If cancellations are being made based on cost per use, the mother title (along with the children) might be slated for cancellation based on this inflated cost per use number.

Multiple Platforms

Electronic access to a given journal is often available to an institution's users through multiple platforms, and this content may or may not reflect more than one subscription. For example, a subscription to the current volume of a journal might be available on the publisher's own platform as well as on IngentaConnect and EBSCOhost EJS. To further complicate matters, the same title may have back volumes available through JSTOR and/or a full-text indexing and abstracting database, for example EBSCOhost's Academic Search Premier. Multiply this situation by the number of titles a library accesses online and the scope of the problem becomes clear.

Many librarians have struggled with these problems. Luther writes, "Constructing a complete picture of use is further complicated by the existence of journals in multiple formats that are available through multiple sources or distribution channels" (2001, 123). Boots and her colleagues faced this problem when Cell Press switched from their own platform to Science Direct and the usage for the same time period was reported differently for each platform. It was not clear whether to combine the statistics, or if that would be double counting. They note, "Problems occur when a publisher launches a new Web site, or moves to a new aggregator platform. This frequently requires a complete change in the method whereby usage statistics are counted, and the format in which they are displayed. If this occurs midyear, it becomes very difficult to merge the new usage data with the old" (2007, 190).

Amount of Content Available Online

While missing or double counted usage statistics resulting from title changes, bundling, or platform variations can impact the validity of usage statistics, with enough effort the data can be adjusted to account for these anomalies. A more serious shortcoming of vendor-supplied online usage statistics as they currently stand is the varying number of years of content available online for different titles, which makes accurate comparisons between titles based on use impossible.

To illustrate: if articles from Journal A are available online back to 1950, while articles from Journal B are available online only for the last 10 years, it is not surprising that total usage for Journal A will be higher than for Journal B, with related effects on cost per use, even though researchers may be using articles from current issues of both journals at the same rate. It is interesting to speculate whether the increased use that results from access to more online content motivates in part the common practice of publishers providing online access to the latest 10 years or so of a journal, even if a library has subscribed in online format for a much shorter time. This might also be one motivating factor behind the move by many publishers to digitize their backfiles.

Luther writes, "A collection becomes more useful when the amount of archival content available online increases, especially if it is well indexed. When backfiles are included with the current subscription or basic service, the user has more articles to view, and this will affect usage" (2001, 124–25). Medeiros points out that, since cost per use is calculated with the cost of one subscription year only, the "calculation is inherently flawed . . . , since publisher-provided statistics do not reveal the percentage of . . . uses that were of [the subscription year] journal issue content only" (2007, 237). Holmström (2004) makes a similar point: "Currently ROI [return on investment] of 2003 expenditures is calculated relating the money invested to gain access to the journals published in 2003 to the total number of downloads in 2003 from the publisher's collection for all years. This way ROI appears to be larger than it actually is by including downloads that should not be included. However, the current method also neglects future downloads to older articles and therefore makes ROI appear smaller than it actually is." Usage studies of print journal collections often suffer from the same flaw (Galbraith 2002, 81), yet in many cases it is possible to track use by publication date for print journals by scanning barcodes of bound volumes or counting use of unbound issues only.

A number of solutions to this problem have been suggested. Many have called for publishers to provide usage statistics not only by date of use, but also by date of publication. In their survey of New Zealand academic libraries, McDowell and Gorman found that the least commonly provided vendor usage statistic in responders' libraries was "publication date of material accessed," yet librarians identified this as important (2004, 336). Pesch adds, "When a library can determine how frequently various subsets of their user community are accessing full text based on age of articles, they can make more informed decisions on the relevance of subscribing to backfile collections versus paying for on-demand access" (2004, 150).

Providing monthly and annual usage data for each journal by year of publication would add a great deal of complexity to the data, yet it would allow for the number of uses of the current volume to be separated out. This would enable a more accurate calculation of cost per use and basis for comparing total use between journals, especially in relation to decisions about cancelling or retaining current subscriptions.

A step in this direction will come with COUNTER Release 3, to be implemented in 2009. COUNTER Release 3 is slated to require a new report, "Journal Report 1a: Number of Successful

Full-Text Article Requests from an Archive by Month and Journal" (currently an optional report in Release 2). Journal Report 1, "Number of Successful Full-Text Article Requests by Month and Journal," will still include all use of a journal. By subtracting use of an archive from all use, an estimate of current, or "nonarchive" use could be made. While not precise, this would at least remove the effects of backfiles from the usage data of some journals. One problem is that the new report is required only of vendors "who provide separately purchasable journal archives" (COUNTER). There is also no uniform definition of exactly what an archive is. More helpful would be a report that separated out the use of material published a given number of years ago (for example, five years).

Indeed, although a breakdown of usage statistics by a fixed time period is not currently available, it would go a long way toward making usage statistics more comparable. It would then be possible to calculate and compare the use of the latest five years of content evenly across all journals. Five years is a good cutoff point, since a study of monthly publications by Maxfield and her colleagues found that "use peaks at three months after publication. By eighteen months after publication, fifty percent of use has occurred, and by five years after publication, ninety percent of use has occurred" (1995, 76). Holmström (2004) cites similar data from Tenopir and King that breaks down percentage of articles read by how recently they were published and suggests that this can be used to estimate the number of uses by year of publication. For example, according to Holmström's adaptation of data from Tenopir and King, 58.5 percent of all readings of scholarly articles by university scientists occur for articles that are one year old or newer. By multiplying total use by 58.5 percent, one could estimate the amount of that use which occurred in the current year, and thus match current use with current subscription price to better calculate cost per use. Medeiros makes a similar claim: "Given the limitation of current statistics-reporting capabilities, cost-per-use should be derived from a Tenopir-King-like formula, which factors in all uses of an e-journal over the lifetime of that e-journal" (2007, 238). Yet such an approach assumes the presence of available backfiles for all online journals, which is not the case. Holmström (2004) acknowledges this when he states, "the reliability of these estimates is affected by the lack of backfiles . . . . In order to accurately measure ROI, we need download statistics by time period published."

Others have suggested a slightly different approach: to create a ratio comparing usage of a journal in a given time period to the total number of articles available online from that journal. Luther wonders "whether the measure of activity should be relative to another factor, such as the price of the journal or the number of available articles, which puts the measure in a context" (2001, 123). Hahn and Faulkner elaborate on this idea by introducing a metric called "content adjusted usage," which is calculated by dividing the number of full-text accesses by the total number of articles online for that journal. This is a way to "compare the usage of journals that offer widely differing numbers of articles online" (2002, 218–19). To calculate "content adjusted usage" would require publishers to provide data on total number of articles available or lengthy studies to count or estimate total articles, and such data would need to be updated on a regular basis. Whether to make the calculation using total articles available online or only the number of articles available to an institution is another issue to consider. All in all, without more data from vendors as well as the assistance of staff with programming skills to create a database to store and manipulate this kind of data, a "content adjusted usage" calculation, while useful, would be extremely difficult and time consuming to produce on a large scale.

In the face of this problem, some libraries have given up on vendor statistics altogether and use data from their local systems. For example, Kraemer, at the Medical College of Wisconsin, has resorted to using OpenURL data to track journal usage by year of publication (Bordeaux, Kraemer, and Sullenger 2005, 296–97). The problem with this approach, besides requiring technical expertise in tracking and converting OpenURL data into a tally of uses by journal and year, is that not all researchers access the library's resources using the library's link resolver; many researchers navigate directly to the journal or use services like Google to identify articles. Kraemer, too, believes that requiring COUNTER reports to group usage by year of publication would be the best solution (Bordeaux, Kraemer, and Sullenger 2005, 297).

Technical Issues

Even if usage statistics as provided by vendors were normalized for title and platform changes and were broken down by year of publication, there are other behind-the-scenes ways in which usage statistics may fail to record the true use of a journal.

Full-Text Delivered During Article-Level Linking. The measure of successful full-text downloads may be inflated if HTML full text is displayed with the initial citation display or when a user is directed to an article through a linking mechanism (e.g., CrossRef). Oliver Pesch, Chief Architect at EBSCO Publishing, explains, "If a user is merely browsing the 'detailed' display of a list of articles, they may well be accumulating the full text retrieval count by virtue of this being shown automatically. The user may not even have cared about the article, but the count is still accumulated" (2006, 153). After viewing the HTML, the user may then view, print, and/or e-mail the PDF version, and these actions may be counted as additional uses (Pesch 2004, 148). A study by Davis and Price in 2006 found the ratio of PDF to HTML views, even after controlling for differences in publisher content, to be inconsistent across publisher interfaces, which may have been the result of this phenomenon.

COUNTER Journal Report 1, "Number of Successful Full Text Article Requests by Month and Journal," provides separate year-to-date totals for HTML and PDF articles requested. This allows for any large discrepancies between HTML and PDF to be noted. As Pesch explains, "By separating out HTML and PDF, the institution can make better informed decisions related to a given journal" (2006, 153). However, there is still some confusion on how best to handle the data. JSTOR, for example, only has articles in PDF format, and counting only HTML would exclude them. As Hiott asks, "Does a library add together PDF and HTML articles examined, and how much double counting does that represent?" (2004, 450). It is probably best to use total articles downloaded without making a distinction between PDF and HTML, with the understanding that the usage of some journals may be inflated if the full text of any format is set to display automatically when linking to the article. Perhaps as a result of the awareness of this problem, many of the major publishers and platforms have recently set their article-level links to display only a citation, or a citation with abstract and/or list of works cited, with links to full text in HTML or PDF format. While not providing one-click access to full text might inconvenience the user, it certainly results in more realistic usage statistics.

Federated Search Engines, Robots, and Crawlers. Metasearch or federated search products can dramatically affect usage statistics, primarily for searches and sessions as opposed to article requests. However, full-text articles requested can also be inflated if the full text is retrieved automatically with the search results. Hits by Internet robots and crawlers, as well as LOCKSS systems, can also be registered as full-text article requests. Fortunately, the forthcoming COUNTER Release 3 includes "new protocols that require activity generated by internet robots and crawlers, as well as by LOCKSS and similar caches, to be excluded from the COUNTER reports" (COUNTER). Vendors must comply from the beginning of 2009.

Prefetching and Double-Clicking. Other technical issues that have been addressed by COUNTER are prefetching and double-clicking. Prefetching occurs when Google or other services improve performance by automatically fetching the full pages for the first few results of a search. As Pesch explains, "When the user does click the link, another header request is made, that could be considered yet another full-text request. Without some kind of control, this activity could result in significant over-counting" (2006, 159). COUNTER Release 3 should fix this issue, as it contains "a new protocol that requires prefetched full-text articles to be excluded from the figures reported in all reports containing full-text requests" (COUNTER).

Double-clicking by impatient users with slow connections can also increase the tally of full-text requests. Different publishers may filter multiple clicks according to different rules, which can affect usage. According to the Joint Information Systems Committee (JISC), the COUNTER Code of Practice has specified a filter to eliminate this problem. In sum, COUNTER compliant statistics should no longer be affected by prefetching or double-clicking; however, librarians should be aware of these issues when working with non-COUNTER-compliant usage statistics.

Effects of Site Interface.   Many authors have commented on the potential of the design and functionality of the vendor's Web site to influence usage. Davis and Price studied general levels of usage across journal publisher platforms and compared the use levels of identical content on different platforms, finding that "the design of a publisher's electronic interface can have a measurable effect on electronic journal usage statistics" (2006, 1243). Kraemer maintains that "electronic journal use is more dependent on the range of access mechanisms available, than was the typical use scenario for print journals. If, for example, the access infrastructure for electronic journals is poorly developed, the data will show use levels well below their potential" (2006, 171).

Most of the effect of interface on usage levels appears to center around convenience. Usage will be higher as ease of access increases, while additional steps in retrieving content will cause use to be lower. In explaining the popularity of electronic access over print in the late 1990s, Morse and Clintworth (2000) concluded that "there is no question that a substantial percentage of the electronic journal usage reported here is attributable to the convenient full-text links provided in the heavily used Ovid databases. User preference for electronic versions of articles that are not similarly linked to popular databases would be much less pronounced than that observed in this study." Luther comments, "the user's experience of the interface also will significantly affect the results. Both Academic Press and the American Institute of Physics (AIP) noted that they experienced surges in usage after they introduced new platforms that simplified navigation and access" (2001, 125). Wulff and Nixon find that researchers show "the same relative behavior in the electronic environment as in the print environment, especially when multiple steps [are] not required to locate the electronic journal. One-click electronic access from citation to article is important to users and an important factor in electronic journal usage. At times, users find that the best article is the most convenient article, and they choose to end their search at that point" (2004, 321).

Publisher Manipulation.   Value-added features on a site can also contribute to higher use than might otherwise be the case. In a review of journal use data at the Medical College of Wisconsin Libraries, Kraemer found that "the rate of increase in use for individual electronic journals appears to show higher rates for those journals with advanced linking features, e.g. linked references, OpenURL support, and other features that 'enhance the presence' of a journal in an electronic environment" (2006, 169–70). It is interesting to note that this phenomenon, if true, could privilege the content from large, commercial publishers with substantial resources to devote to interface design over smaller publishers with less sophisticated platforms. Davis and Price acknowledge that "it is entirely possible for a publisher to optimize its interface to maximize the total number of article downloads. In an environment that requires justifying price per download, this may be an understandable goal" (2006, 1247).

Numerous authors have raised the related concern of whether publisher-provided usage statistics are inflated. Luther writes, "Publishers who make usage data available are aware that this information will be used to assess the value of their journals. Consequently, they want to ensure that usage is high so that the cost per use is low compared with that of other publications. Publishers and librarians with experience in electronic databases agree that marketing to users—whether librarians or library patrons—and making them aware of the availability of the resource and its features have a noticeable impact on usage" (2001, 124). A common way in which publishers are able to market to researchers is through encouraging them to create accounts on the publisher's site by registering their e-mails.

This allows users to opt in to added features (for example, the ability to save searches or sign up for e-mail tables of contents for their favorite journals), which are likely to increase use.

In a study at North Carolina State University, Duy and Vaughan (2003) found evidence that publisher-provided usage statistics overstated use in comparison to inhouse data. The researchers compared journal use as measured by library Web server logs to vendor-supplied data for a 12-month period. Fewer than half of the library's vendors were reasonably close to the inhouse use data. However, it is not safe to assume that all users are connecting through the library's site. Many users may navigate directly to the vendor site to retrieve content; thus, it makes sense that vendor-supplied data would show higher use. Nonetheless, as Medeiros states, "It is not hard to imagine some publishers padding actual use as a way of enticing renewal of certain middle-tier journals. Perhaps in response to this concern, COUNTER employed a rigorous auditing requirement to ensure the authenticity of statistics" (2007, 239).

When cancelling journals based on usage data, therefore, using COUNTER compliant data is essential to ensure a level playing ground across publishers. While value-added Web site features may encourage researchers to make greater use of a publisher's content, with COUNTER compliance we may assume that use is *bona fide*. Since cancellation decisions are made based on *low* usage (either as a direct measure or by calculating cost per use), publisher attempts to inflate usage would be more likely to result in an underutilized journal being retained than in a heavily used title being cancelled based on low use.

CONCLUSION

This chapter has reviewed the literature related to the use of electronic journal usage statistics in cancellation and retention decisions. It found that usage is largely a proxy for more meaningful information that is difficult to measure, and that most libraries base collection management decisions on other factors in addition to usage. It explored the sources of usage data for electronic journals (retrieving statistics from a vendor and generating them inhouse) and showed that each method is labor intensive and notes that ERM systems under development will assist with these tasks. Questions related to working with the data were addressed: how many years of usage data to examine, the need to create benchmarks for decision-making, and the desirability of placing the data in a larger context (for example, by discipline or peer institution). Also examined was the effect of the bundling of e-journals into large packages on the ability to make decisions based on usage levels. Selected characteristics of usage statistics were revealed that might require adjustment of the data or at least care in its interpretation. These include the effects of title changes, the bundling of titles, the availability of journal content on multiple platforms, the number of years of content online, and technical issues that might result in inflation in usage. Throughout, the importance of the COUNTER standard in ensuring reliable and comparable data was emphasized. Many of the difficulties of working with usage data, as well as shortcomings in the data itself, will likely be resolved by evolving standards, including COUNTER, and by the evolution of ERM systems for tracking and manipulating data.

REFERENCES

Anderson, Elise. 2007. The next steps in developing usage statistics for e-serials. In *Usage statistics of e-serials*, edited by David C. Fowler, 245–60. Binghamton, NY: Haworth Information Press.

Best, Rickey. 2007. Lies, damn lies, and usage statistics: What's a librarian to do? In *Usage statistics of e-serials*, edited by David C. Fowler, 199–214. Binghamton, NY: Haworth Information Press.

Blecic, D. D., J. B. Fiscella, and S. E. Wiberley, Jr. 2001. The measurement of use of Web-based information resources: An early look at vendor-supplied data. *College & Research Libraries* 62 (5): 434–53.

Boots, Angela, Julia Chester, Emma Shaw, and Chris Wilson. 2007. E-journal usage statistics in action: A case study from Cancer Research UK. In *Usage statistics of e-serials*, edited by David C. Fowler, 183–98. Binghamton, NY: Haworth Information Press.

Bordeaux, Abigail, Alfred B. Kraemer, and Paula Sullenger. 2005. Making the most of your usage statistics. *Serials Librarian* 48 (3/4): 295–99.

CIC Collection Development Officers and CIC Electronic Resources Officers. 1998. Preferred practices for CIC licensing of electronic journals. Committee on Institutional Cooperation (CIC) Center for Library Initiatives. www.cic.uiuc.edu/programs/CLIConsortialAgreementProgram/archive/BestPractice/Prefered Practices.pdf (accessed July 2008).

Conger, Joan E. 2007. Usage statistics in context: Develop effective assessment practices through collaboration. In *Usage statistics of e-serials*, edited by David C. Fowler, 261–73. Binghamton, NY: Haworth Information Press, 2007.

COUNTER: Counting Online Usage of Networked Electronic Resources. www.projectcounter.org.

Davis, Philip M., and Jason S. Price. 2006. eJournal interface can influence usage statistics: Implications for libraries, publishers, and Project COUNTER. *Journal of the American Society for Information Science & Technology* 57 (9): 1243–248.

Duy, Joanna, and Liwen Vaughan. 2003. Usage data for electronic resources: A comparison between locally collected and vendor-provided statistics. *Journal of Academic Librarianship* 29 (1): 16–22.

———. 2006. Can electronic journal usage data replace citation data as a measure of journal use? An empirical examination. *Journal of Academic Librarianship* 32 (5): 512–17.

Enssle, Halcyon R., and Michelle L. Wilde. 2002. So you have to cancel journals? Statistics that help. *Library Collections, Acquisitions, & Technical Services* 26 (3): 259–81.

Fowler, David C. 2007. Serials Solutions and the art of statistics gathering. In *Usage statistics of e-serials*, edited by David C. Fowler, 129–49. Binghamton, NY: Haworth Information Press.

Frazier, Kenneth. 2001. The librarians' dilemma: Contemplating the costs of the "big deal." *D-Lib Magazine* 7 (3) (March). www.dlib.org/dlib/march01/frazier/03frazier.html.

———. 2005. What's the big deal? *Serials Librarian* 48 (1/2): 49–59.

Galbraith, Betty. 2002. Journal retention decisions incorporating use-statistics as a measure of value. *Collection Management* 27 (1): 79–90.

Gatten, Jeffrey N., and Tom Sanville. 2004. An orderly retreat from the big deal: Is it possible for consortia? *D-Lib Magazine* 10, (10). www.dlib.org/dlib/october04/gatten/10gatten.html (accessed April 20, 2008).

Hahn, Karla L., and Lila A. Faulkner. 2002. Evaluative usage-based metrics for the selection of e-journals. *College & Research Libraries* 63 (3): 215–27.

Henle, Alea, and Donnice Cochenour. 2007. Practical considerations in the standardization and dissemination of usage statistics. In *Usage statistics of e-serials*, edited by David C. Fowler, 5–23. Binghamton, NY: Haworth Information Press.

Hiott, Judith. 2004. Collecting and using networked statistics: Current status, future goals. *Library Quarterly* 74 (4): 441–54.

Holmström, Jonas. 2004. The return on investment of electronic journals: It is a matter of time. *D-Lib Magazine* 10 (4). www.dlib.org/dlib/april04/holmstrom/04holmstrom.html (accessed April 20, 2008).

Jaguszewski, Janice M., and Laura K. Probst. 2000. The impact of electronic resources on serial cancellations and remote storage decisions in academic research libraries. *Library Trends* 48 (4): 799–820.

Joint Information Systems Committee (JISC). COUNTER Filter: Improving the Comparability of Usage Statistics. Joint Information Systems Committee. www.jisc.ac.uk/whatwedo/programmes/programme_pals2/project_counter.aspx (accessed May 14, 2008).

Kraemer, Alfred. 2006. Ensuring consistent usage statistics, part 2: Working with use data for electronic journals. *Serials Librarian* 50 (1/2): 163–72.

Luther, Judy. 2001. White paper on electronic journal usage statistics. *Serials Librarian* 41 (2): 119–48.

Maxfield, Margaret W., Rebecca DiCarlo, and Michael A. DiCarlo. 1995. Decreasing use of monthly serials after publication date. *Serials Librarian* 27 (4): 71–77.

McDowell, Nicola, and G. E. Gorman. 2004. The relevance of vendors' usage statistics in academic library e-resource management: A New Zealand study. *Australian Academic & Research Libraries* 35 (4): 322–43.

Medeiros, Norm. 2007. Uses of necessity or uses of convenience? What usage statistics reveal and conceal about electronic serials. In *Usage statistics of e-serials*, edited by David C. Fowler, 233–43. Binghamton, NY: Haworth Information Press.

Mercer, Linda S. 2000. Measuring the use and value of electronic journals and books. *Issues in Science and Technology Librarianship* 25. www.istl.org/00-winter/article1.html (accessed March 27, 2008).

Morrison, Heather, 2007. The implications of usage statistics as an economic factor in scholarly communications. In *Usage statistics of e-serials*, edited by David C. Fowler, 173–82. Binghamton, NY: Haworth Information Press.

Morse, David H., and William A. Clintworth. 2000. Comparing patterns of print and electronic journal use in an academic health science library. *Issues in Science and Technology Librarianship* 28. www.istl.org/00-fall/refereed.html (accessed March 27, 2008).

Nixon, Judith M. 2000. Using a database management program as a decision support system for the cancellation of business periodicals and serials. *Journal of Business & Finance Librarianship* 5 (4): 3–21.

Noonan, Christine F., and Melissa K. McBurney. 2007. Application of electronic serial usage statistics in a national laboratory. In *Usage statistics of e-serials*, edited by David C. Fowler, 151–60. Binghamton, NY: Haworth Information Press.

Pesch, Oliver. 2004. Usage statistics: Taking e-metrics to the next level. *Serials Librarian* 46 (1/2): 143–54.

———. 2006. Ensuring consistent usage statistics, part 1: Project COUNTER. *Serials Librarian* 50 (1/2): 147–61.

Peters, Thomas A. 2002. What's the use? The value of e-resource usage statistics. *New Library World* 103 (1172/1173): 39–47.

Ralston, Rick. 2007. Assessing online use: Are statistics from Web-based online journal lists representative? *Journal of Electronic Resources in Medical Libraries* 4 (1/2): 51–64.

Townley, Charles T., and Leigh Murray. 1999. Use-based criteria for selecting and retaining electronic information: A case study. *Information Technology and Libraries* 18 (1): 32–99.

Trueswell, R. L. 1969. Some behavioral patterns of library users: The 80/20 rule. *Wilson Library Bulletin* 43:458–61.

Weintraub, Jennifer. 2003. Usage statistics at Yale University Library. *Against the Grain* 15 (6): 32–34.

Wood, Elizabeth H. 2006. Measuring journal usage: Add a survey to the statistics? *Journal of Electronic Resources in Medical Libraries* 3 (1): 57–61.

Wulff, Judith L., and Neal D. Nixon. 2004. Quality markers and use of electronic journals in an academic health sciences library. *Journal of the Medical Library Association* 92 (3): 315–22.

BIBLIOGRAPHY

Bevan, Simon, Pete Dalton, and Angela Conyers. 2005. How usage statistics can inform national negotiations and strategies. *Serials* 18 (2): 116–23.

Botero, Cecilia, Steven Carrico, and Michele R. Tennant. 2008. Using comparative online journal usage studies to assess the big deal. *Library Resources & Technical Services* 52 (2): 61–68.

Chisman, Janet K. 2007. Electronic resource usage data: Standards and possibilities. In *Usage statistics of e-serials*, edited by David C. Fowler, 275–85. Binghamton, NY: Haworth Information Press.

Davis, Philip. 2003. Why usage statistics cannot tell us everything, and why we shouldn't dare to ask. *Against the Grain* 15 (6): 24–26.

Fischer, Karen. 2006. eJournal interface can influence usage statistics: Implications for publishers, libraries, and Project COUNTER. *Against the Grain* 18 (1): 64.

Fowler, David C. 2007. *Usage statistics of e-serials*. Binghamton, NY: Haworth Information Press, 2007. Co-published simultaneously as *Serials Librarian* 53, suppl. 9.

Haddow, Gaby. 2007. Level 1 COUNTER compliant vendor statistics are a reliable measure of journal usage. *Evidence Based Library & Information Practice* 2 (2): 84–86.

Howard, Mark. 2002. Ejournals not cancelled. *Information World Review* 176 (January): 10.

International Coalition of Library Consortia. Guidelines for statistical measures of usage of web-based information resources (update: December 2001). International Coalition of Library Consortia. www.library.yale.edu/consortia/2001webstats.htm.

Jasper, Richard P. 2006. 21st century shell game: Cutting serials in the electronic age. *Acquisitions Librarian* 18 (35/36): 161–66.

Johnson, Peggy. 1997. Collection development policies and electronic information resources. In *Collection management for the 21st century: A handbook for librarians*, edited by G. E. Gorman and Ruth H. Miller, 83–104. Westport, CT: Greenwood Press.

Kent, Allen, et al. 1979. *Use of library materials: The University of Pittsburgh study.* New York: Marcel Dekker.

Metz, Paul, and John Cosgriff. 2000. Building a comprehensive serials decision database at Virginia Tech. *College and Research Libraries* 61 (4): 324–34.

National Information Standards Organization. ANSI/NISO Z39.7-2004: Information services and use: Metrics & statistics for libraries and information providers—data dictionary. Appendix B: measuring the use of electronic library services. www.niso.org/dictionary/toc/appendices/appendixb/.

Pesch, Oliver. 2007. Usage statistics: About COUNTER and SUSHI. *Information Services & Use* 27 (4): 207–13.

Peters, Thomas A. 2001. What's the big deal? *Journal of Academic Librarianship* 27 (4): 302–4.

Rhine, Leonard. 1996. The development of a journal evaluation database using Microsoft Access. *Serials Review* 22 (4): 27–34.

Rous, Bernard, ed. 2004. *Online usage statistics: A publisher's guide.* New York: Association of American Publishers.

Shim, W., and C. R. McClure. 2002. Improving database vendors' usage statistics reporting through collaboration between libraries and vendors. *College and Research Libraries* 63 (6): 499–514.

Ward, Randall K., John O. Christensen, and Elizabeth Spackman. 2006. A systematic approach for evaluating and upgrading academic science journal collections. *Serials Review* 32 (1): 4–16.

CHAPTER 7

Perspectives on Using E-Journal Usage Statistics in a Serials Cancellation Project

ANDRÉE J. RATHEMACHER
AND MICHAEL C. VOCINO

INTRODUCTION

In fall 2007, the University Library at the University of Rhode Island (URI) found it necessary to cancel over $200,000 in serial subscriptions. We had been aware since late summer that our fiscal year 2008 budget was inadequate to cover the cost of our subscriptions, but we were told by the University to refrain from cancelling any journals in the hope that supplementary funds for the library could be identified. In early October, when no additional funding had been made available, we proceeded with the cancellation of journals. Given that our list of titles to renew was already overdue to our subscription agent, we had only two weeks to identify titles to cancel. Lacking the time to involve librarian subject specialists and university faculty in the decision, we decided to base the cancellation on what we thought was the most objective measure available to us at that time: usage statistics of electronic journals. This chapter reviews our process and examines a number of problems and issues that we encountered in using usage statistics as a basis for cancelling electronic journals.

BACKGROUND

The University of Rhode Island holds the Carnegie Classification of RU/H (research university with high research activity). The University Libraries serve the full time equivalent (FTE) of 13,790 students and 713 faculty and consist of the University Library, serving the main campus in Kingston, and two branches: The College of Continuing Education Library in Providence, and the Pell Marine Science Library in Narragansett, which serves the Graduate School of Oceanography.

In fiscal year 2007, the materials budget for the University Libraries was approximately $2.9 million. Of this, over $2.6 million, or about 89 percent, was spent on serials and other continuing resources, including online databases. A large portion of the Libraries' continuing resources were in electronic format. If online databases are included, we devoted 75 percent of our serials budget and

67 percent of our total materials budget to online resources. Excluding online databases (but including all electronic journals purchased either individually or in packages), 56 percent of our serials budget and 50 percent of our total materials expenditures were for online journals.

These numbers are quite high compared to other research libraries, large or small. In terms of serials expenditures as a percentage of total library materials expenditures, the median value for libraries surveyed by the Association of College and Research Libraries in 2006 was 65.74 percent, compared to our 89 percent. Summary data gathered from ACRL's 2006 survey reveal that ACRL libraries spent approximately 14 percent of their total materials expenditures on electronic serials (including online databases), compared to URI's 67 percent. Even when the URI Libraries are compared to much larger Association of Research Libraries, we see that a relatively large portion of our budget is devoted to online journals. In 2006, according to statistics gathered by ARL, approximately 37 percent of the material expenditures of ARL libraries were for electronic serials, not including electronic databases, while the URI Libraries spent 50 percent.

The fact that such a large portion of our materials budget is spent on online resources is largely due to the fact that in early 2002, the Libraries' management team adopted a policy of converting print subscriptions to online-only, provided online was available and did not cost substantially more than the print. Beginning in subscription year 2003, we incrementally converted a large number of our subscriptions to online-only format. While some of our print titles were converted to online through the purchase of packages including Elsevier's Science Direct, the *Institute of Electrical and Electronics Engineers (IEEE)* All Society Periodicals Package, American Chemical Society Web Editions, and Project Muse, a large number were converted as individual, online-only subscriptions from Blackwell, Wiley, Taylor & Francis, Cambridge University Press, Springer, Sage, and other publishers. When a title was changed to online-only format, the corresponding print was cancelled; staffing and budget levels did not allow us to maintain multiple formats. By fall 2007, excluding titles accessed through full-text indexing and abstracting databases, about 60 percent of our electronic serials dollars (representing 70 percent of our e-journal titles) were spent on packages, while 40 percent of our electronic serials dollars (representing 30 percent of our e-journal titles) went toward individually subscribed e-journals.

METHOD

In previous years when the University Library undertook large serials cancellation projects, library subject selectors typically consulted with academic departments over a period of months to identify titles to cut. In 2007, due to delays by the University administration in finalizing the Libraries' budget, we did not have the luxury of time. Faced with the need to identify over $200,000 worth of serials to cut in a two-week period, we decided to cut individually subscribed, online-only journals based on usage statistics. We did not consider cancelling online reference databases, since we subscribe to them on a July–June cycle and they had already been renewed. We also did not look at cancelling any of our large packages of online journals like Science Direct or Cambridge Journals Online, because we had signed multiple-year contracts for many of these packages, and because cancelling packages requires an "all or nothing" approach; cancellation of part of a package is not possible. Fortunately in this case, due to chronic budget shortages, we had not been able to participate in many of the "big deal" packages. Thus many of our online journals were individually subscribed, giving us a fairly large pool of titles that we were free to cancel.

We briefly considered cancelling print periodicals, but realized that identifying which titles to cancel was not possible in such a short time because we had no readily available data on which to base a cut. As mentioned above, we had no time to seek input from faculty. Other libraries use interlibrary loan statistics and citation and impact data in their cancellation processes (Enssle and Wilde 2002;

Galbraith 2002; Bordeaux, Kraemer, and Sullenger 2005), but we did not have such information at hand. In addition, the University Library at URI has not circulated print journals since a brief period in the mid-1980s, and we have never kept statistics on the reshelving of print periodicals, so usage data for print was nonexistent. We were also aware of the fact that cancelling those titles that remained in print-only format would disproportionately punish small, independent, and/or nonprofit publishers who are not responsible for the crisis in serials costs.[1]

Since 2006, we have been tracking usage statistics for our online journals when such statistics are available. For each database and platform, we download the Counting Online Usage of Networked Electronic Resources (COUNTER) Journal Report 1: Number of Successful Full Text Article Requests by Month and Journal. We merge all of the reports into one large spreadsheet and add columns for journal price and cost per use. This lets us calculate cost per use by title for individually subscribed titles. For e-journal packages and full-text databases, we calculate a total cost per use for the package but not for the titles within the package.

We decided to cancel titles based on number of uses rather than cost per use, primarily because looking at number of uses was simpler and faster given our time constraint (see further discussion below). We sorted the titles in our 2006 usage spreadsheet by total number of articles downloaded and began identifying titles to cancel starting with those with zero uses for 2006, and continuing until we reached our goal of cancelling over $200,000 in subscriptions. In practice, this resulted in cancelling titles with 10 or fewer uses. Any titles in packages or databases that could not be individually cancelled were skipped.

The list was then double-checked to make sure all usage for each title had been counted. For example, if usage for a particular title was recorded on both the MetaPress and informaworld platforms, or on both Blackwell Synergy and EBSCOhost Electronic Journals Service (EJS), the usage from each platform was combined. Usage from JSTOR and full-text databases (for example, ABI/Inform and Academic Search Premier) was not included, although it is likely that the availability of a journal through JSTOR or a full-text database cannibalized usage on the platforms we tracked, making it more likely that the journal would be cancelled.[2]

Finally, 2007 usage (through October 2007) was gathered for those titles on the cancel list. The number of months for which 2007 usage data was available varied by platform, so it was "prorated" to convert available 2007 usage to the equivalent of 10 uses or fewer. For example, if data were available through May 2007, a journal would be cut if used four or fewer times (5/12 of a year × 10 uses = 4 uses per year). If a title had been used five or more times through May 2007, it would be removed from the cancellation list, "saved" by its 2007 usage data. This was a crude process, but one which served to compensate for growth in use of a journal over time or for discrepancies in the 2006 statistics. In cases where anomalies cropped up (for example, if we found that a journal had changed platforms midyear and access had not been activated on the new platform), we gave the journal the benefit of the doubt and removed it from the cancellation list, choosing to take a conservative approach and decrease the possibility of cancelling a title in error. When this process was complete, we had identified 304 titles to cancel, totaling $219,000.

PROBLEMS AND ISSUES WE FACED

Throughout the process of identifying titles to cancel based on low levels of use, we struggled to compile complete usage information on our electronic journal subscriptions and to normalize irregularities in the data. In the process, we were confronted with a number of problems to solve and choices to make before we could proceed. We also found that our decision to cancel based on usage unequally impacted different subject areas and academic departments.

Labor of Gathering

When we started the cancellation project, we had already gathered 2006 e-journal usage data from most of our vendors. Combining 2006 usage from all of our e-journal platforms from which we were able to retrieve statistics resulted in a spreadsheet of over 4,500 lines. Adding usage from full-text indexing and abstracting databases in order to see the full usage for every title brought the total number of lines to over 10,000. Since vendor-supplied usage statistics don't include local cost data, the price paid and subject-based fund code for each title needed to be looked up in our library system and added to the sheet, and a cost per use calculated. Fortunately, this step was easier for titles in packages and databases, since these titles aren't priced individually. Nonetheless, this process was time consuming.

We found that the data needed further modification if we were to use it as the basis for sound decisions on titles to cancel. We needed to be able to sort the spreadsheet by title, ISSN, total uses, journal price, cost per use, and subject-based fund code. This was difficult because some vendors use leading articles such as "The" in the title, and Excel does not ignore leading articles when sorting. Using find and replace to eliminate these articles was cumbersome, as each instance needed to be corrected individually so that the article was not deleted if it appeared elsewhere in the title. Some platforms also provided alternate versions of a title; for example, a title from the IEE might be listed as "IEE electronics systems and software" on one platform and "Electronics systems and software" on another. ISSNs appeared with and without dashes, and in some cases leading zeroes needed to be added in order to allow the spreadsheet to be sorted by ISSN. As Kraemer notes, "The formats and contents of publisher-provided use data reports vary widely, even if many of them comply now with the COUNTER requirements. Seemingly small variations, e.g., an unusual ISSN format [no dash just numbers] require special attention before that data can be merged with other data, for example, prices from invoices" (2006, 165–66).

Creating a usable spreadsheet was also complicated by the fact that many platforms provide usage statistics for unsubscribed titles. It was difficult to tell if a title had zero uses because the library was not subscribed, or if the journal was simply not used. Verifying the status of all these titles was a huge task. An alternative would have been to disregard usage data for any title with zero uses, but this could have resulted in ignoring an unused but subscribed title. Another issue, as noted by Noonan and McBurney (2007, 155), is that many vendors do not include titles with zero hits in their statistics. During our cancellation project, for example, we found that Taylor and Francis's new platform, informaworld, instead of reporting zero uses for subscribed titles that were not used at all during the year simply excluded zero-use titles from our institutional report.

To further complicate matters, most journals offer free access to selected articles, especially highly cited articles, and some publishers, notably Sage, offer free trial periods for all their journals during the course of a year. It is inevitable that a library's users will access free articles at some point, and these uses will be tallied in the statistics. We found it confusing when payment data for these "free" journals could not be found. We needed to decide whether to remove the usage data for "free" titles from the spreadsheet or to retain it with a notation that access was not paid for. Boots and her colleagues report similar experiences: "The sheer variety of different formats in which journals usage statistics are available makes it very difficult to select, collate, and use them effectively . . . . Just to give a flavor of the practical issues that are faced, in many cases it is necessary to wade through the statistics for unsubscribed titles in order to navigate to the ones we want" (2007, 189–90).

Fortunately, there are a growing number of products and services available to help libraries with the task of gathering, normalizing, and analyzing usage data; this will undoubtedly be a growing market in the future, especially as vendors become SUSHI (Standardized Usage Statistics Harvesting Initiative) compliant. These products are not inexpensive; however, their cost may be justified by staff time saved and sophistication of analysis offered. At the University of Rhode Island, we look forward to using our newly acquired Innovative Interfaces electronic resource management (ERM) module during future analyses of serials usage to accomplish many of the tasks detailed above.

If Publisher Does Not Provide Statistics

Like Noonan and McBurney (2007, 156) and Galbraith (2002, 85), we encountered the problem of publishers that do not provide usage statistics for their online journals. At the URI, only a small number of the publishers whose journals we subscribe to do not offer usage statistics, and they tend to be smaller publishers. As of this writing, for example, the following are some of the publishers from whom we are unable to get usage journal statistics: the American Mathematical Society, the American Society of Limnology and Oceanography, the Canadian Mathematical Society, the History Cooperative, Human Kinetics, Inter-Research, Liverpool University Press, the National Council of Teachers of English Journals, New Left Review, the Rocky Mountain Mathematics Consortium, the Royal Society of New Zealand, Slack, and the Society for the Experimental Analysis of Behavior. When asked, some of these publishers indicated that they are in the process of developing usage statistics reporting capabilities, while others were unaware of the existence of usage statistics or simply had no plans to provide them.

It is interesting to note that in at least some cases, publishers appear to be unwilling to provide usage statistics. For example, the URI Libraries subscribe to titles from a number of societies, published by Allen Press. Some Allen Press societies (such as the American Association on Intellectual and Developmental Disabilities, the American Meteorological Society, the Ecological Society of America, and the Geological Society of America) offer access to usage statistics on the Allen Press platform. Other Allen Press affiliated societies do not offer statistics (for example, the American Fisheries Society, the American Society of Mammalogists, and the Wildlife Society). Since usage statistics are generated by the Allen Press platform, on which the journals are hosted, providing usage data requires no additional technological capabilities on the parts of these societies; it would seem, therefore, that Allen Press societies not providing usage statistics simply do not want to.

As Noonan and McBurney state, "This lack of information makes it very difficult for the library to make informed collection development decisions" (2007, 156). In our cancellation project at the URI Libraries, online journals without usage data were not considered for cancellation. A lack of statistics shielded these titles from being cut. It may be to a publisher's advantage to not offer usage statistics when it comes to retaining subscribers; if a journal has low usage, it might get cancelled, but if a journal does not report usage at all, it is likely safe, at least from cancellations based on usage statistics. Peters speculates, "Some vendors may be reluctant to supply usage statistics, because they are fearful that low or uneven usage may cause libraries or consortia to demand changes in pricing, terms, and scope of content when license agreements come up for renewal" (2002, 43). Of course, it is conceivable that some libraries would consider the availability of COUNTER-compliant usage statistics to be an important factor in deciding whether or not to subscribe to an online journal in the first place, or in whether to retain a subscription.

Publisher Packages

A similar problem occurs with large packages of e-journals from a single publisher, known as "portfolio" or "big deal" packages. Although usage statistics are available for individual journal titles in the package, licensing agreements prevent the selection or deselection of journals on a title-by-title basis.

As could be expected, at the University of Rhode Island, our ability to cancel e-journals based on use was constrained by the portfolio packages to which we subscribed. At the time of our cancellation project, we subscribed to Elsevier's Science Direct Freedom Collection, Sage Premier, Cambridge Journals Online, the IEEE All-Society Periodicals Package, and the American Chemical Society's Web Editions. Since we were not prepared to cancel any of these all-or-nothing packages, we could only select titles for cancellation from among our individually subscribed e-journals. Interestingly, those publishers hit the hardest in our cancellation (Blackwell, Springer, and Taylor and Francis; see Figure 7.1) also offer large packages of titles; however, we had not subscribed to any. Our experience offers a clear illustration of how titles in the big deal packages were "protected," while unpackaged titles were cut. While the big deal packages offer convenience of administration and low cost per use, the fact that we subscribed to them made it impossible for us to cancel the lowest use titles across the board. To a large extent, we have lost our ability to shape our collection to the demonstrated needs of our users as indicated by usage statistics.

Could the trend among publishers toward creating these large packages of preselected titles be connected to the demand for and increased availability of COUNTER-compliant usage statistics? No doubt, to a large extent publishers have been motivated to create packages as a way to stem losses incurred by libraries cancelling subscriptions due to budget constraints and journal price increases. However, given the shift toward online journals and the availability of usage statistics, libraries are now better able to see evidence of the truism that a relatively small number of journal titles account for the majority of use, while a large number of titles receive very little use.[3] Might another incentive for publishers to create these packages have been to avoid the possibility that librarians would cancel individual titles revealed to have low use?

Total Use or Cost Per Use?

One of the most difficult decisions we needed to make was whether to rank journals for cancellation by total use (defined as number of full-text articles retrieved) or by cost per use (defined as the price of the journal divided by the number of full-text articles retrieved during the subscription period), or both. Total use is a measure of the importance placed on the journal by the library's users, while cost per use is essentially a measure of the journal's "bang for the buck." Each has its advantages and disadvantages, both practical and philosophical.

Total Use.   At the University of Rhode Island, we made cancellation decisions based on total use because of our sense that it was more clear-cut than cost per use, and less subject to error. Ideally, total use for a journal should be calculated by combining the use of that title on all platforms on which it appears, including any full-text databases or archival products like JSTOR. Even though the use of a title in JSTOR or a full-text database is distinct from the use of the title on the publisher's platform (and may not cover the same dates of publication), it is likely that use on the publisher's platform is diminished by the availability of the title through other providers. The most sound decisions will therefore be made on complete usage data. Of course, use of the journal on different platforms should be examined individually as well. Any title changes that might cause split usage should be accounted for. The consolidation of usage data for each title is time consuming unless performed by an automated system, but it is procedurally uncomplicated and presents a fairly accurate measure of how much a journal has been used by a library's clientele. We also found total use to be simpler to work with than cost per use when totaling or averaging data across multiple usage periods (for example, over 18 months or two years).

Cost Per Use.   We discovered that correctly calculating cost per use, on the other hand, is far more difficult, if not impossible. There are many factors which can cause errors when calculating cost per use. Title changes and platform changes can result in split use numbers which must be consolidated for an accurate cost per use figure to be calculated. The failure to consolidate split usage might

Figure 7.1
Cancelled Titles by Publisher from Among Individually Subscribed E-Journals

Publisher	No. of titles cut	Approximate dollar value cut	% of total value cut
American Counseling Association	1	$94	0.04%
American Physical Society	1	$612	0.29%
American Society of Plant Taxonomists	1	$177	0.08%
Annual Reviews	3	$635	0.30%
American Statistical Association	1	$482	0.23%
Baywood	4	$1,340	0.63%
Blackwell	94	$40,749	19.11%
Brill	1	$1,058	0.50%
Cornell University Press	1	$232	0.11%
Haworth	9	$4,120	1.93%
IEST (Institute of Environmental Sciences & Technology)	1	$135	0.06%
IET (Institution of Engineering and Technology)	22	$8,529	4.00%
INFORMS	3	$1,429	0.67%
IOS Press	1	$600	0.28%
M.E. Sharpe	2	$2,344	1.10%
Maney	2	$584	0.27%
MIT Press	2	$526	0.25%
Modern Humanities Research Association	1	$376	0.18%
National Association for Music Education	1	$42	0.02%
Nature Publishing Group	1	$1,086	0.51%
Oxford University Press	4	$1,225	0.57%
Palgrave	1	$529	0.25%
PNG Publications	1	$198	0.09%
ProEd	2	$256	0.12%
Professional Engineering Publishing	16	$25,620	12.01%
Psychonomic Society	3	$850	0.40%

SIAM (Society for Industrial and Applied Mathematics)	12	$3,904	1.83%
Springer (and imprints)	40	$61,889	29.02%
Taylor & Francis	41	$43,404	20.35%
Thomas Telford	13	$6,230	2.92%
Transaction	1	$202	0.09%
University of California	7	$1,004	0.47%
University of Chicago	10	$2,597	1.22%
University of Wisconsin	1	$231	0.11%
TOTAL	**304**	**$213,289**	**100.01%**

result in a title being cancelled due to high cost per use; for example, if the title changed midyear and the cost per use were calculated on the use of the current title only, the cost per use number might be twice as high as it should be. If some of a journal's use comes from a full-text database (such as Academic Search Premier or ABI/Inform) or from an archival product (for example, JSTOR), the uses from these products should *not* be used to calculate cost per use of the journal as subscribed directly from the publisher, as these products have their own costs and costs per use. Yet it is inevitable that the use of the journal on the publisher platform will be lower due to the full text also being available through these aggregator products. Simply put, most cost per use numbers are likely to be inaccurate, as it is usually impossible to accurately match the total use of a journal with the journal's price. Basing decisions on total use instead of cost per use allows the use on all platforms to be combined into a total measure of how heavily the journal is used, independent of how the content has been paid for, or even if the content has been paid for (in the case of free back files).

Furthermore, in most cases cost per use is calculated on the price of the current year's subscription. In almost all cases, however, total uses as reported in vendor-provided usage data are for multiple years of content. The amount of content available online varies for each title, and usage data are not broken down by year of publication. Technically, to arrive at a correct cost per use number, the subscription prices for every year for which content is available should be added together and only then divided by total use. For this reason alone, cost per use numbers are inherently flawed.

Cost Concerns.   Ranking journals for cancellation or retention based on cost per use means that if two journals are used the same number of times, the less expensive title might be retained while the more expensive title might be cut. In this way, higher priced journals with less use will be penalized. It is important to note in such a case, though, that while one journal is less of a value dollar-wise, the actual use-value of the two titles is the same; articles from both were used the same number of times.

We librarians have always known that one use of a chemistry journal costs more than one use of a literary magazine, or that one use of a business journal costs more than one use of a history journal. We've accepted this disparity in price between journals in different disciplines as part of the environment in which we work. A strict examination of usage data by cost per use would tend to favor journals in disciplines with lower journal costs and threaten with cancellation journals in disciplines with more expensive journal titles. For this reason, if cost per use is to be used as the basis of a cancellation decision, it should be done discipline by discipline, not across the board. Ideally, cancellation decisions based on total use should also be made by discipline, since different disciplines use journals with different levels of intensity.

However, if one of the goals of a cancellation project is to eliminate overpriced journals, an alternative method to ranking subscriptions by cost per use would be to start by ranking all of the library's subscriptions by price. Then, total usage for the most expensive titles could be examined more closely to see if these titles were used heavily enough to make subscriptions worthwhile.

What Difference Does It Make?.   It is certainly true that cancelling based on cost per use rather than total use results in higher-priced journals being cut. Since the goal of most serials cancellation projects is to reduce the library's budget by a set dollar amount, cancelling based on cost per use will result in cancelling fewer titles, while cancelling based on use will result in a greater number of titles being cut.

At the URI Libraries, we cancelled based on total use. As a result, to save approximately $219,000 dollars, we cut 242 subscriptions, or 304 titles, since some titles were bundled. As a comparison, a rough examination of our usage data sorted by cost per use indicates that if we had cancelled on cost per use instead, to save the same amount of money we would have cancelled only 160 titles. These 160 titles were more heavily used by our researchers and students than the 242 we actually cut, but they provided less use per dollar spent. Only 34 percent of the 242 subscriptions cancelled based on total use would have been cut if the criterion had been cost per use, while 53 percent of the titles that would be cut based on cost per use would also have been cut based on use. Together, there was only 26 percent overlap among the 402 titles identified for cancellation by each method.

Effect Across Disciplines of Cutting Based on Usage

The mechanics of working with usage statistics aside, cancelling journals based on usage is likely to mirror and exacerbate resource inequalities between disciplines. At the University of Rhode Island, as at many universities, faculty have been under pressure to secure grant support, which usually funds release time for their research. In terms of resource allocation, the University has placed a particularly strong emphasis on biotechnology and related fields in the applied sciences. Meanwhile, student enrollment has grown, and many faculty in the humanities and social sciences face increasing class sizes and therefore presumably less time to conduct research. These disparities are doubtless reflected in the usage statistics for online journals. If journals in the humanities and social sciences with low usage are cut because faculty in these areas haven't had the time or resources to engage in research, losing access to these journals will only perpetuate and intensify the problem, leading to future discrepancies if resources are allocated based on research productivity.

In fact, the most heavily hit departments in our usage-based cut were those that have been struggling. The Department of Economics lost 21 titles, the largest number of any department. This is not surprising, given that during the period of usage examined, of nine total faculty positions, the department had one vacancy, one faculty on sick leave, two approaching retirement, and two working on a temporary basis for other departments or programs. Other hard-hit departments were History (16 titles), Political Science (14 titles), Education (12 titles), Biological Sciences (12 titles), and Mathematics (11 titles).

It is clear that basing usage statistics on only one or two years of data, as we did at the URI Libraries, disadvantages a department that has had a retirement or sabbatical, especially of a researcher who worked in a specialized subject area. In this case, the specialized field may still be important to the department and the curriculum, but due to the vacancy, not be reflected in current usage statistics. Other authors have noted similar fluctuations in usage patterns based on research activity and differences between disciplines. Noonan and McBurney, of the Pacific Northwest National Laboratory (PNNL), state that, "Research trends change periodically at PNNL because of new scientific fields emerging, funding from the Department of Energy fluctuating, the ebb and flow of grant proposal cycles, etc. Usage statistics often mirror the research landscape—its natural ups and downs and the changing of directions into new emergent areas" (2007, 155).

The effects of these anomalies in usage statistics could be lessened by basing cancellations on an average of total use or cost per use over a period of several years, or by following trends in the usage of each title over time. As systems are developed to better help libraries track and manipulate usage data, and as more years of data become available, this will become feasible. One alternative is to compare usage of a particular e-journal or set of e-journals to usage at a peer institution (Peters 2002, 44). Another possibility is to compare the usage of journals within disciplines (Enssle and Wilde 2002, 267), subject areas, or user groups (Luther 2001, 123). In any case, "in a large and multidisciplinary institution, it may be important to protect the needs of small user groups" (Boots et al. 2007, 185).

Beyond the realm of an individual library, it is possible that widespread cancellation of journals based on usage could have far-reaching effects. Morrison addresses the potential problems caused by the cumulative effects of many libraries cancelling journals based on popularity: "At any given time, some areas of scholarly endeavor are likely to be more popular and/or better funded that other endeavors, regardless of their underlying merit" (2007, 176). Morrison states further,

There are some real potential pitfalls if usage becomes prevalent as the basis for selection and cancellation decisions. There is reason to suspect that the cumulative effect of such decisions, made separately by many libraries, could create a tendency toward an overall increase in scholarly conservatism; the loss of important, but less popular or less well-funded areas of research; detrimental effects on smaller research communities; and less linguistic and cultural diversity. Journals allowing open access options such as self-archiving could also be adversely affected. Happily, open access not only can, but almost certainly will, counter many of the unfortunate effects of such decisions (2007, 181).

Of course, the commercialization of scholarly communication and the consolidation of scholarly journals into the hands of an ever-smaller number of for-profit, multinational publishing conglomerates is probably an even greater threat to the diversity of scholarly research (as well as the primary cause of the price inflation that makes journal cancellation projects necessary). Nonetheless, Morrison's points are thought provoking and worthy of consideration.

CONCLUSIONS

We have outlined in this chapter the consequences of cancelling electronic journals based on usage statistics. We have demonstrated that it can be done, but that such a project has flaws and drawbacks. Cancelling based on usage statistics alone disregards other factors, perhaps most importantly, the input of faculty and the professional judgment of librarians. Decision-making based on usage data in isolation also lacks the context that might be provided by examining the statistics by discipline or in relation to peer institutions. Usage-based journals cancellations might perpetuate inequalities among disciplines within an institution and academia at large.

Furthermore, an in-depth look at usage measures shows that they are not as objective as they seem. To make meaningful decisions, it is essential to normalize the data to take into account many factors, including title changes, multiple platforms, and varying amounts of online content. Fortunately, working with usage data will become easier in the future with the further development and increasing sophistication of systems to gather, store, and manipulate the data, as well as with the continued refinement of standards for its collection.

ENDNOTES

1. According to Crow (2006), "Commercial publishers now play a role in publishing over 60 percent of all peer-reviewed journals . . . . While the for-profit segment comprises a relatively small number of large commercial publishers, the non-profit segment represents a large number of mostly small publishers . . . . The prices for commercially-owned journals average four to five times higher than for journals published by societies." See also ARL (2004); Bergstrom and Bergstrom (2001, 2006); McCabe (2002; 2004); Susman et al. (2003); and White and Creaser (2004).

2. This leads to a dilemma: If a journal's total use is high in part because of its availability through a full-text database, should the individual subscription be retained because of high total use or cancelled because much of that use comes from another subscribed service that will continue to provide (at least partial) access to the journal after it is cancelled?

3. See Trueswell (1969); Morse and Clintworth (2000); Bordeaux, Kraemer, and Sullenger (2005); and Galbraith (2002).

REFERENCES

Association of College and Research Libraries. 2006 statistical summaries. Association of College and Research Libraries. www.ala.org/ala/mgrps/divs/acrl/publications/trends/2006/ALA_print_layout_1_449220_449220.cfm.

Association of Research Libraries, Office of Scholarly Communication. 2004. Framing the issue: Open access. Association of Research Libraries. /www.arl.org/bm~doc/framing_issue_may04.pdf.

———. ARL statistics: Interactive edition. University of Virginia Library. http://fisher.lib.virginia.edu/arl/.

Bergstrom, Carl T., and Theodore C. Bergstrom. 2001. The economics of scholarly journal publishing. http://octavia.zoology.washington.edu/publishing/intro.html.

———. 2006. The economics of ecology journals. *Frontiers in Ecology and the Environment* 4 (9): 488–95.

Boots, Angela, Julia Chester, Emma Shaw, and Chris Wilson. 2007. E-journal usage statistics in action: A case study from Cancer Research UK. In *Usage statistics of e-serials*, edited by David C. Fowler, 183–98. Binghamton, NY: Haworth Information Press.

Bordeaux, Abigail, Alfred B. Kraemer, and Paula Sullenger. 2005. Making the most of your usage statistics. *Serials Librarian* 48 (3/4): 295–99.

Crow, Raym. 2006. Publishing cooperatives: An alternative for non-profit publishers. *First Monday* 11 (9). www.firstmonday.org/issues/issue11_9/crow/index.html.

Enssle, Halcyon R., and Michelle L. Wilde. 2002. So you have to cancel journals? Statistics that help. *Library Collections, Acquisitions, & Technical Services* 26 (3): 259–81.

Galbraith, Betty. 2002. Journal retention decisions incorporating use-statistics as a measure of value. *Collection Management* 27 (1): 79–90.

Kraemer, Alfred. 2006. Ensuring consistent usage statistics, part 2: Working with use data for electronic journals. *Serials Librarian* 50 (1/2): 163–72.

Luther, Judy. 2001. White paper on electronic journal usage statistics. *Serials Librarian* 41 (2): 119–48.

McCabe, Mark J. 2002. Journal pricing and mergers: A portfolio approach. *American Economic Review* 92 (1): 259–69.

———. 2004. Law serials pricing and mergers: A portfolio approach. *Contributions to Economic Analysis and Policy* 3 (1): 1–29.

Morrison, Heather. 2007. The implications of usage statistics as an economic factor in scholarly communications. In *Usage statistics of e-serials*, edited by David C. Fowler, 173–82. Binghamton, NY: Haworth Information Press.

Morse, David H., and William A. Clintworth. 2000. Comparing patterns of print and electronic journal use in an academic health science library. *Issues in Science and Technology Librarianship* 28. www.istl.org/00-fall/refereed.html (accessed March 27, 2008).

Noonan, Christine F., and Melissa K. McBurney. 2007. Application of electronic serial usage statistics in a national laboratory. In *Usage statistics of e-serials*, edited by David C. Fowler, 151–60. Binghamton, NY: Haworth Information Press.

Peters, Thomas A. 2002. What's the use? The value of e-resource usage statistics. *New Library World*103 (1172/1173): 39–47.

Susman, Thomas M., David J. Carter, and Ropes & Gray LLP. 2003. *Publisher mergers: A consumer-based approach to antitrust analysis*. Washington, D.C.: Information Access Alliance. www.arl.org/bm~doc/whitepaperv2final.pdf.

Trueswell, R. L. 1969. Some behavioral patterns of library users: The 80/20 rule. *Wilson Library Bulletin* 43:458–61.

White, Sonya, and Claire Creaser. 2004. Scholarly journal prices: selected trends and comparisons. *LISU Occasional Paper, number 34*. Leicestershire, England: LISU, Loughborough University. www.lboro.ac.uk/departments/ls/lisu/downloads/op34.pdf.

BIBLIOGRAPHY

Carnegie Foundation for the Advancement of Teaching. The Carnegie classifications of institutions of higher education. Carnegie Foundation for the Advancement of Teaching. www.carnegiefoundation.org/classifications/.

COUNTER: Counting Online Usage of Networked Electronic Resources. www.projectcounter.org.

O'Malley, William T. 2001. 2000–2001 annual report of the Department of Technical Services. University Library, University of Rhode Island.

———. 2002. 2001–2002 annual report of the Department of Technical Services. University Library, University of Rhode Island.

———. 2002. Report of the Department of Technical Services to the library faculty, November 2002.

University of Rhode Island, Office of Information Services, Institutional Research. Just the facts sheet: Fall 2007 campus highlights. University of Rhode Island. www.uri.edu/ir/pdf/factsheet07.pdf.

University of Rhode Island, University Libraries. Historical serials cancellations at the University Library. University of Rhode Island. www.uri.edu/library/serials/serials_cuts/serialscuts.html.

———. Library statistics. University of Rhode Island. www.uri.edu/library/statistics/stats.html.

CHAPTER 8

Using "Meta-Analysis" in Electronic Resource Decision-Making

TRACIE J. BALLOCK,
CARMEL YUROCHKO, AND DAVID A. NOLFI

INTRODUCTION

In response to increasing user expectations and changing program needs, libraries are spending a rapidly growing portion of their limited budgets on electronic resources (Zhang and Haslam 2004). Collection expenditures must support diverse needs, including undergraduate learning as well as highly specialized graduate student and faculty research. It can be difficult to balance these needs while maintaining the core collection necessary for a viable academic library. These competing demands make it imperative for libraries to effectively analyze relevant data in an effort to allocate funds wisely.

Effective evaluation of electronic resources calls for intellectual flexibility, requiring quantitative analysis coupled with careful assessment of qualitative factors. Since it is impossible for any single library collection to meet all user and program needs, libraries must weigh available data in light of institutional mission, goals, and values. Libraries need to adopt a kind of meta-analysis, pooling disparate data in order to make sound decisions representing their constituents' needs.

Meta-analysis is a method of analyzing "the results of several studies for the purposes of drawing general conclusions" (Konstantopoulos and Hedges 2004, 281). In this chapter, we propose using a modified type of meta-analysis that includes both quantitative data and qualitative factors. Utilizing this modified meta-analysis, libraries can identify the most reliable quantitative measures of electronic resource use, choosing among data sources including link resolvers, Web page clickthroughs, and vendor reports. While analysis of quantitative data is essential, it presents an incomplete picture. Libraries must also utilize qualitative factors to make decisions about electronic resources, including institutional mission and identity, political considerations, administrative priorities, and teaching and research needs. Librarians need to implement a decision-making process that includes a continuing two-way conversation between the library and its constituents.

This chapter includes detailed descriptive examples of a modified meta-analysis process that can be applied to individual subscriptions. Additionally, two aggregator databases are analyzed and compared using further adapted meta-analysis. This chapter represents an academic library perspective.

Many of the methods we describe are likely to be useful for public, school, and special libraries. Other libraries will need to take into account somewhat different factors; however, the basic approach remains the same.

PRINT VERSUS ELECTRONIC

In many academic institutions, journal collections are evolving from print to electronic (Easton 2001; Zhang and Haslam 2004; Franklin 2005). There are a number of driving forces behind this movement including low print journal use, space issues, and associated costs (e.g., claiming and binding). Many libraries are reexamining space requirements of print journal collections due to increased demand for collaborative work spaces, computers, and seating. As institutions offer more online courses, it is imperative that resources be provided to remote users. Few libraries can afford to subscribe to both print and electronic versions of journals (Vaughan 2003). Electronic journals seem to provide a solution for all of these challenges while meeting user needs. Librarians need to use data to help faculty, administrators, and other stakeholders understand why it is necessary to shift collections from print to electronic.

As a general rule, libraries abound with statistics from exit numbers, to printer use, and virtually everything else imaginable (Hiller and Self 2004). As good stewards of their institutions' finances, librarians must ask why they continue to spend thousands of dollars on underused print journals. In order to make informed decisions, libraries rely on one or more of the well-established use-study methods, including the "sweep method," removable labels, and paging journals.

Print Journal Use Statistics and the Foundations of Modified Meta-analysis

When libraries had mostly print journals, they had a paucity of use statistics; now in the electronic journal era they have an overabundance of use statistics. In either case, libraries need to determine which use statistics are most meaningful and avoid overreliance on any single measure.

The first step in any use statistics project is to identify the scope of the study. Will the use of only current subscription titles be addressed, or will specific disciplines be addressed overall? There are a number of methods that can be used for gathering print journal use statistics. Libraries have long utilized the "sweep" method, in which print journals removed from the shelves are gathered from throughout the library and then staff members count the numbers of issues and volumes for each specific title to provide an approximation of use. Removable labels provide another option for estimating use. In this method staff attach a label to an unbound issue and then count as a "use" each time the label is broken (after counting the use, the staff attaches a new label and reshelves the issue). Some libraries choose to close their periodical stacks and then require users to request journals from library staff who "page" the needed volumes. The staff count each volume paged in order to approximate use for each title.

The statistics produced by each method lead to additional questions. They require large amounts of staff time and can potentially inconvenience users. Potential human error and staff motivation must be taken into consideration. Does the staff understand how important it is for them to complete these tasks accurately and routinely? Do they fully understand the purpose of the use study? If the answer to either question is "No," the resulting use statistics could be skewed. For example, unsupervised student employees might decide that it is more important to quickly reshelve journals than to count use and enter statistics, thereby undercounting use. User behavior can further skew the statistics. Sometimes users try to be helpful by reshelving journals, but in actuality "interfere" with the library's attempt to count use. Removable labels might solve this problem, but other issues can arise (for example, labels that do not adhere properly can lead to overcounting).

Most of the methods mentioned above are time consuming and produce statistics that inform the library that the item was "used" in some manner. The sweep or paging methods would count a journal volume removed from the shelf as "one use." Yet, a student could have photocopied five articles or might have never opened the volume. In order to discover "real use," staff need to employ multiple methods, which can be quite costly and time consuming. One additional approach is interviewing the user. This approach completely depends on the user's willingness to cooperate and be truthful. Some users will recognize that inflating use statistics can help to protect subscriptions from being cut. Another important consideration is whether users would view being interviewed as a violation of their privacy.

While the above mentioned methods of gathering usage statistics for print journals provide some degree of data, they are not foolproof. When using any of these methods, the library still would not know how the journal was used or how many articles were used. Generally speaking, print use statistics offer an incomplete picture, lack depth, and are often unreliable. In order to ensure user needs are being met cost effectively, the library must embrace print journal use statistics as part of the collection decision-making process (Jewell 2001). Yet, the library cannot make sound decisions on print subscriptions based solely on use statistics. Evaluating which quantitative data is meaningful and tempering it with qualitative factors is the foundation of modified meta-analysis as defined in this chapter.

Changing from Print to Electronic

As serial collections evolve from print format to electronic format, libraries generally see an increase in overall serials use (Zhang and Haslam 2004). Access to electronic journals is generally more convenient and reliable than print. Print issues or volumes are sometimes unavailable because they are missing, checked out, or at the bindery. This is usually not the case with electronic journals, unless a source is experiencing temporary technical difficulties. Simultaneous users can access electronic journals from the library or remote sites 24 hours a day, seven days a week. Many electronic journals are included in more than one database. Users can gain access to these journals even when one of the databases is unavailable. All of these factors combine to make the electronic journal experience a marked improvement over print.

From a workflows point of view, skills and duties change with the onset or addition of electronic journals to the collection (Zhang and Haslam 2004). Purchasing electronic journals is intrinsically more complex than purchasing print journals. When starting new electronic subscriptions, libraries must negotiate licenses (with the possible exception of consortial deals), investigate technological compatibility, and provide support for numerous end-user platforms. Publishers and other library vendors undergo corporate mergers and takeovers, resulting in changed relationships between libraries and vendors. These changes have an impact on library workflow. In the print world, that might have meant a simple change in invoice management. In the electronic world, mergers or takeovers can be more complex, changing crucial elements including end-user platforms, authorized users, license terms, interlibrary loan rights, packages offered, archival rights, systems interoperability, invoicing, and payment options. A good working relationship with a vendor can lessen the effects of these changes, simplify communication, and help the library staff to work more efficiently. A poor relationship can have the opposite effect.

All of these changes lead to a continuous learning curve for library staff managing electronic journals as well as for patrons. While print was more consistent, electronic resources are constantly changing, and so are the methods used to collect, manage, and analyze statistics. Regardless of the format, libraries still have the same obligation to see that institutional funds are well spent.

QUANTITATIVE DATA

When considering the merits of electronic resources, it is never a problem to find quantitative data. If anything, there are too many statistics available, from vendors' use data, to link resolvers, click-throughs, costs, calculated statistics, and more. Perhaps the toughest question is how to make sense of all these data sources and use them in a way that supports effective decision-making. In order to make informed decisions libraries must embrace electronic use statistics in some form, regardless of their flaws and shortcomings (Medeiros 2007).

For the purposes of this chapter, we are using the following terminology:

- *Session*: "an interaction between a user and database at a given time to fulfill information need" (Coombs 2005, 599). A session ends when the user logs out or closes the resource.
- *Search*: a distinct query entered to obtain needed information (Coombs 2005).
- *Clickthrough*: an instance when a user clicks a link to open an electronic article, journal, or database.

Multiple Access Points to Electronic Journals

While print journals have one point of access, the physical library, often electronic journals can be accessed from a vendor's site, an electronic resource page, an A–Z journal title list, or from an integrated library system (ILS). Furthermore, a library might have multiple instances of access for a single journal; for example, a library may have electronic access to *Newsweek* (counted as one unique title), with instances available from more than one source (EBSCOhost, ProQuest, and Gale). The wide variety of access points and access instances complicates the process of tracking use statistics.

Vendor Use Data

Electronic use statistics provided by vendors are gathered or harvested in an automated fashion. Vendors employ numerous and sophisticated ways of counting use, producing an abundance of data, varying from highly useful to problematic. One of the most difficult issues for librarians is trying to interpret the meaning of vendor-reported usage data. Vendors often fail to report use data uniformly. The vendor might not be able to explain whether reported "use" indicates sessions, searches, or full-text article accesses, leaving the library to speculate on the meaning of the data reported.

Data Reporting Standards. Both librarians and vendors have recognized the importance of having a consistent manner of counting and reporting electronic resource usage. With the emergence of the Counting Online Usage of NeTworked Electronic Resources standard in 2002, consistency of data began to improve. COUNTER describes itself as "an international initiative to improve the reliability of online usage statistics. It is supported by the vendor, intermediary and librarian communities. COUNTER's objective is to ensure that vendor online usage reports are credible, compatible and consistent" (COUNTER 2007). COUNTER-compliant reports enable libraries to compare usage reports across vendors. Comparability is a key to being able to make decisions because libraries need to know that they are comparing apples to apples.

The National Information Standards Organization has developed the Standardized Usage Statistics Harvesting Initiative (National Information Standards Organization 2007). SUSHI's function is to help automate the collection of COUNTER-compliant statistics. It can be integrated into electronic resource management systems (ERMs) or homegrown systems. Some libraries choose to contract with a third party vendor, e.g., ScholarlyStats, which uses SUSHI to compile a single report with data from numerous vendor sources.

Protocols, systems, and services that automate the data compilation process can help libraries manage the very large number of statistics available. The numbers of databases and electronic journals that must be tracked can be daunting for librarians and staff if they need to manually gather and input the data.

Link Resolver Statistics

Link resolvers make electronic resources more widely available. According to the Online Dictionary of Library and Information Science, a link resolver is "application software that uses the OpenURL standard to provide context-sensitive linking between a citation in a bibliographic database and the electronic full text of the resource cited" (Reitz 2007). Commonly used commercial link resolvers include Ex Libris' SFX and ProQuest's Serials Solutions.

Link resolver statistics provide a great deal of information about the pathways users are taking to access electronic resources. Link resolvers can track how often users attempt to find full text for a given journal and how often they click through to resources. This information tells the library which resources patrons are trying to use and how often they are successfully accessing those resources. For example, if the library sees that patrons are unsuccessfully trying to access *The European Journal of Medicinal Chemistry*, it can make subscribing to the journal a priority.

A key limitation of link resolvers is that they cannot count use when the link resolver is not engaged to access full text. Some circumstances include

- when patrons go directly to full-text journal collections,
- when a researcher connects via a publisher link in PubMed, and
- when a Google Scholar user clicks an article title and goes directly to the publisher site.

Reviewing link resolver statistics shows that patrons make a "request" via the link resolver, which means that they started the process of trying to view full text but then stopped the process before connecting to the online journal, ILS, or ILL system. In link resolver terminology this next step would be a clickthrough. For example, at Duquesne University we have observed that link resolver requests are almost always significantly higher than clickthroughs. This pattern is predictable when journal titles are available through multiple databases, since multiple requests are generated. However, a user is unlikely to click through to find full text in more than one resource.

Link resolvers offer unique data that demonstrate which resources are most frequently directing users to the library's electronic full text. Using link resolver statistics, one library was able to determine that Google Scholar had surpassed all other databases in directing users to electronic full text (Nolfi and Yurochko 2007). By integrating interlibrary loan systems with link resolvers, it is also possible to track ILL requests generated from specific research databases. Link resolvers offer additional options for generating statistics beyond those mentioned here. Libraries can find creative ways to use these statistics to learn more about electronic resource use.

Web Site and Online Catalog Clickthroughs

In addition to using a link resolver, many libraries choose to catalog electronic resources, and virtually all libraries provide links to research databases via library Web sites. Additionally, many libraries provide links to databases that include collections of electronic journals, e.g., ProQuest Research Library Complete or EBSCOhost Academic Search Premier.

Each point of access the library provides is capable of generating a use statistic. These statistics help the library to get a somewhat different picture of use. A library might look at the collection of titles available in ProQuest Research Library Complete and determine that several are not used. Yet, click-throughs from the library Web site might show that ProQuest Research Library Complete (as a whole) is being heavily used. Since Web site clickthrough data is collected by the library's own systems, many libraries trust it more than similar data provided by the vendor. Catalog clickthroughs illustrate how frequently patrons use the online catalog to connect to electronic full-text. Together with the other usage statistics, catalog clickthroughs help to present a fuller picture of use.

USING DATA IN DECISION-MAKING

A key challenge is to create a decision-making process for electronic resources that works for the library and institution (Booth 2006). This decision-making process will depend on the institution's curriculum and research needs, political factors, institutional values, and many other factors beyond statistics. In this section, we examine a few pertinent factors and primarily focus on the issues of comparing electronic resources.

Cost Data

Journal and electronic resource prices have risen steadily for more than 20 years (Dougherty 1999; Association of Research Libraries 2004). As a result, many libraries are finding that the cost of subscriptions is crowding out other collection needs, including books and audiovisuals. When charting subscriptions as a portion of their total budgets, many libraries experience the "Pac-Man effect" (Yurochko, Nolfi, and Ballock 2006), with Pac-Man's mouth closing over the book budget.

Figure 8.1
Pac-Man

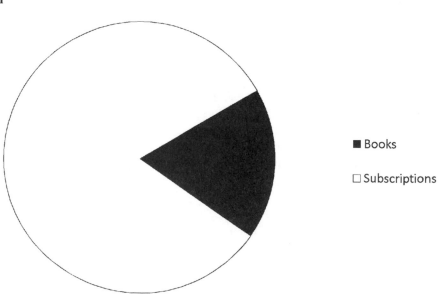

■ Books

☐ Subscriptions

Many libraries have allowed this situation to occur due to the strong need for electronic resources and other subscriptions. But they need to ask whether they are getting value for their money. One possible measure of value is cost per use.

Cost Per Use.   The potential value of cost per use calculations is that they enable comparisons using a common scale. The library can divide the subscription cost by the total number of uses over a given time period. For example, a library might subscribe to *Tetrahedron Letters* for $13,500 per year and *Organic Letters* for $4,300 per year. If the library finds that *Tetrahedron Letters* was used 300 times in a year, it can calculate a cost per use of $45. If *Organic Letters* is used 86 times in a year, its cost per use would be $50. Thus, the more costly subscription is the better value according to this measure.

Although this calculation seems relatively straightforward, there are several practical issues to consider:

- Is the subscription cost the true cost of the resource or should the library take into account other costs, including licensing, serials maintenance, and instruction support?
- Is a resource too new to have generated adequate use data? Have patrons had adequate time to learn that it is available?
- Are subscriptions with backfiles being compared to subscriptions without backfiles?

The library also needs to consider whether other factors skew usage data. Does the resource have a prime location on the library's Web site or public workstation desktops? Is the resource required for a class that has a very large number of students? Does the resource have a name that might inflate its usage statistics? For example, several years ago Duquesne University students consistently chose OCLC FirstSearch before other database packages; when questioned, they said that they selected it over other databases because they believed that its name implied "search here first."

Verifying Congruence in Use Statistics.   Before beginning cost per use calculations, libraries need to feel confident about the use data. The question is how to assess its reliability. Although it might be impossible to fully answer this question, it is possible to compare statistics and determine whether they are congruent. A common problem is that vendor statistics are usually significantly higher than link resolver statistics. One solution to correcting these differences is to create a logarithmic chart using a spreadsheet program like Microsoft Excel. Creating a logarithmic chart can show whether the peaks and valleys align for each source (see Figure 8.2) (Yurochko, Nolfi, and Ballock 2006). When they align, the data sources are congruent.

When there are not significant differences between link resolver and vendor statistics, it is possible to create charts using the actual use numbers. Libraries can also confirm congruence using correlation tests if they have access to SPSS or SAS, which are systems capable of data storage and mining as well as statistical and predictive analysis. North Carolina State University Libraries compared locally collected electronic resource use data to vendor electronic resource data and found significant correlations (Duy and Vaughan 2003).

Confirming that the statistics are congruent makes it possible to choose combinations of statistics in order to develop a more complete calculation of cost per use. For example, EBSCOhost Business Source Premier is an abstracting and indexing source that contains a large number of full-text journals. Patrons searching the database can access these journals without using a link resolver. However, journals purchased directly from the publisher depend on link resolvers to connect from the abstracting and indexing database to the full text. Using combined statistics can be a way to correct these differences in usage patterns.

Figure 8.2
Logarithmic Chart

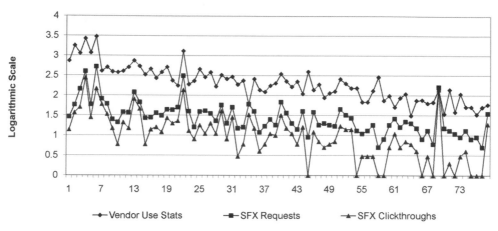

Once satisfied with the reliability of usage data, it is possible to calculate cost per use. Some libraries take further steps by factoring in operational costs including maintaining servers, managing holdings, retraining staff, and hiring staff with new skills sets (Franklin 2005).

Limitations of Cost Per Use Data. Despite the importance of cost per use, it has limitations. Journals are not merely commodities, and some journals have no peers. Some electronic resources support an institution's mission or values so strongly that it would not be possible to replace them regardless of what the cost per use data suggests. In these cases, it might not be worth the time and effort to do the cost per use analysis, but from an assessment standpoint it is still important to track use. When mission critical resources show zero use, it is time to investigate why! Conversely, journals sometimes have temporarily high usage statistics in a given year and then drop substantially in following years. A few reasons that these spikes in usage statistics occur in either journals or research databases include the following:

- A faculty member writing a textbook or review article.
- Preparation for a grant.
- Requirement to use a database or journal within a course.
- Placement on a link resolver menu or the library Web site.
- Promotion of a resource through publicity efforts or library instruction.

The use analysis in one year may lead to a purchase decision that may change the following year (Medeiros 2007). It is important to look at the trend of use over several years.

USING "META-ANALYSIS" TO ANALYZE DISPARATE DATA SOURCES

Meta-analysis is a useful construct when studying electronic resource data. It has become commonly used in health and social sciences research. As already cited above, "Meta-analysis refers to an analysis of the results of several studies for the purposes of drawing general conclusions" (Konstantopoulos and Hedges 2004, 281). A broader definition is "the entire process of quantitative research synthesis" (281). For our purposes, we are going one step further by including qualitative factors in "meta-analysis." We suggest that libraries bring together varied sources of quantitative data while taking qualitative factors into account in the final decision-making process.

Meta-analysis Introduced

Libraries must consider both quantitative and qualitative issues when interpreting cost per use data. It would be a mistake to blindly use cost per use to make all decisions. Perhaps the most fundamental issue is which use data to count. There is much concern about the merits of various vendor usage reports (Jewell 2001). While COUNTER-compliant reports represent the ideal, some have asserted that even COUNTER data can lack reliability (Chawner 2006; Davis 2003). Given these doubts, and since not all electronic resources are COUNTER compliant, libraries need to choose the usage data that makes the most sense in their environments.

One possible solution is to use only vendor data or only link resolver data. Another possibility is to combine these data sources with library Web site or online catalog clickthroughs. This approach has the benefit of including several data sources but duplicates some data (presumably, the vendor report counts all uses). Comparing the various statistics to each other might also bring potential discrepancies to light. It is essential to understand what constitutes use for each data source. It might be necessary to question vendors or library information technology staff to discover whether a particular data source is meaningful. Most importantly, the library must carefully examine how its patrons are using resources in order to determine which data sources provide the most useful data for a specific resource. However, when dealing with large numbers of subscriptions, it may be necessary to choose a consistent approach that works well for most resources.

Applying Basic Meta-analysis to Individual Subscriptions

Basic meta-analysis of two or more sets of use statistics can be applied to the decision-making process for "pick and choose" (or individual subscription) electronic journals. It is possible to combine varied statistics into a single list using a calculation of cost per title or cost per use to provide a common scale (Anderson 2005; Franklin 2005). The examples below show how cost per use data may be employed in the decision-making process.

One method is comparing cost per use data to estimated document delivery or ILL costs. These estimates can be based upon figures provided by document delivery providers or by calculating the library's average ILL cost. It might be necessary to vary the estimate depending on the types of journals under consideration (e.g., document delivery is more expensive for science journal articles). For purposes of these examples, we arbitrarily use a document delivery cost of $50 per article.

Figure 8.3 shows titles that were considered for renewal. Three of the four fell well below the break-even point (document delivery cost of $50). If basing the decision only on analysis of vendor cost per use data, *Polyhedron* would not have been renewed. It is also reasonable to add the link resolver statistics since, as Figure 8.4 shows, the use data is congruent yet the resulting cost per use is still much higher than the break-even point. Regardless, it is possible to imagine a scenario in which a library keeps the subscription due to a strong need that cannot be easily quantified (see further discussion of qualitative factors below). Please note that the journal *Tetrahedron*, referred to in Figures 8.3 and 8.4, is a different title than *Tetrahedron Letters*, referred to in an earlier example in this chapter.

Figure 8.5 shows a list of titles that a library did not renew. All of the titles fell above the break-even point, even after adding the link resolver statistics; Figure 8.6 shows congruence.

Figure 8.3
Table of Titles Renewed

Title	Approximate Cost	Vendor Use Statistics	Cost Per Use (Vendor)	Link Resolver Use Statistics	Vendor + Link Resolver Use Statistics	Cost Per Use (Both)
American Journal of Emergency Medicine	$377.10	46	$8.19	55	101	$3.73
Lancet	$872.10	428	$2.03	511	939	$0.92
Polyhedron	$7,378.20	55	$134.14	13	68	$108.50
Tetrahedron	$16,641.90	725	$22.95	211	936	$17.77

Applying Meta-analysis to Aggregator Databases

Meta-analysis can also be applied to the decision-making process for aggregator databases (for example, when comparing ProQuest Education Complete to ProQuest Psychology). The process is a bit more work, and a bit more complicated, because there are often large numbers of overlapping titles between aggregator databases. It is possible to compare the overall use and cost of one database versus another. However, this comparison would not take into account what makes each database unique.

Figure 8.4
Graph of Titles Renewed

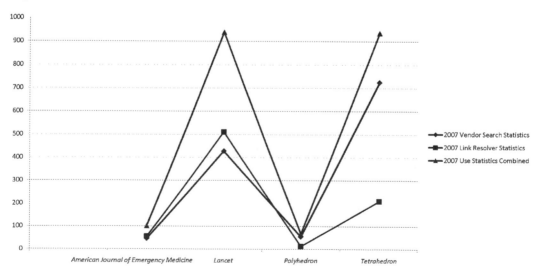

Figure 8.5
Table of Titles Not Renewed

Title	Approximate Cost	Vendor Use Statistics	Cost Per Use (Vendor)	Link Resolver Use Statistics	Vendor + Link Resolver Use Statistics	Cost Per Use (Both)
Chemico-Biological Interactions	$3,353.00	17	$197.23	13	30	$111.77
Computer Physics Communications	$6,154.00	20	$307.70	20	40	$153.85
Journal of Experimental Social Psychology	$803.00	13	$61.77	0	13	$61.77

Comparing Two Aggregated Collections.   As seen in Figure 8.7, the cost of a database can be divided by the number of titles to determine each aggregator database's cost per title. The number of titles is based on an Ulrich's Serials Analysis System count of ISSNs on March 6, 2008. Ulrich's counts only those ISSNs that are in its database. ProQuest Psychology's cost per title is $4.36 higher than that of ProQuest Education Complete. Further analysis can illustrate other differences between the two databases.

Figure 8.6
Graph of Titles Not Renewed

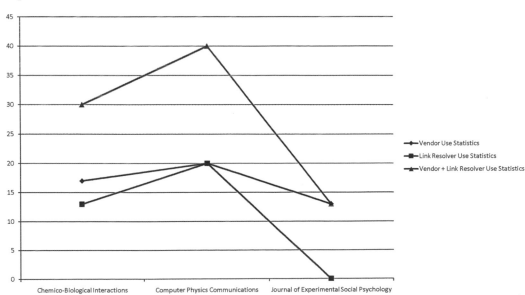

Figure 8.7
Database Cost Per Title

Database	Approximate Cost	Number of Titles	Cost Per Title
ProQuest Education	$12,520	518	$24.16
ProQuest Psychology	$12,520	439	$28.52

In Figure 8.8, the analysis is based on overall cost per use, incorporating use statistics from both the vendor and the link resolver. The cost of the database is divided by the total number of searches performed in 2007. Once again, the differences in cost per use are minimal.

Comparing Unique Titles Using Meta-analysis.   While the two methods above provide useful statistics, neither represents the full picture. To reveal additional details, create a list of each database's ISSNs and journal titles. Comparing the lists using a spreadsheet or a serials analysis system (e.g., Ulrich's) shows the number of titles common to both databases and the number of unique titles found in each. Dividing the cost of the entire database by the number of unique titles provides a basic cost for each unique title (see Figure 8.9). Once again, the costs are relatively close.

In Figure 8.10, dividing the database cost by the vendor use statistics for unique titles produces a cost per use for unique titles in each database. ProQuest Psychology unique titles cost $0.42 more per use than ProQuest Education Complete titles. Put another way, ProQuest Psychology's cost per use is approximately 42 percent greater than that of ProQuest Education Complete.

ProQuest Education Complete has a large number of titles, making it a popular tool for undergraduate research. In this case, the use statistics might reflect uses of convenience rather than the need for unique journals. However, the link resolver use statistics show that a researcher took the step of connecting from an abstracting and indexing database in order to obtain the full text. One could argue that the link resolver use demonstrates a unique need for the journal title. Even if there is a unique need for the journal, there is not necessarily a unique need for the database. In this scenario, the link resolver lists more than one Pro-Quest full-text database for journals that are in more than one collection. When this occurs, the link resolver statistics can be skewed by the order of the databases on the link resolver menu (Figure 8.11).

Figure 8.12 lists the five most used titles in ProQuest Education Complete based on vendor statistics. Somewhat surprisingly, *Journal of Nursing Education* is the most highly used title in ProQuest Education Complete. Subtracting link resolver statistics from vendor statistics shows that *Journal of Nursing Education*'s unique use within the database is significantly lower. This example shows that four of the five highest used titles were more closely related to education. It further suggests that the high use for *Journal of Nursing Education* in ProQuest Education Complete is probably a result of the link resolver database order.

Figure 8.8
Cost Per Use by Vendor

Database	Approximate Cost	Number of Titles	Vendor Use Statistics	Cost Per Use (Vendor)	Link Resolver Use Statistics	Cost Per Use (Both)
ProQuest Education	$12,520	518	155,991	$0.080	2,880	$0.079
ProQuest Psychology	$12,520	439	143,155	$0.087	1,162	$0.086

Figure 8.9
Comparison of Database Costs

Database	Approximate Cost	Number of Unique Titles	Cost Per Unique Title
ProQuest Education	$12,520	313	$40.00
ProQuest Psychology	$12,520	302	$41.46

Figure 8.10
Unique Titles within Databases

Database	Approximate Cost	Vendor Use Stats for Unique Titles
ProQuest Education	$12,520	12,379
ProQuest Psychology	$12,520	8,755

Figure 8.13 lists the most used ProQuest Psychology titles. Unique use is calculated by subtracting the higher reported use from the lower reported use.

Interpreting these statistics will help the decision-making process. The statistics shown in Figures 8.12 and 8.13 help to shed light on the uniqueness of each collection but do not necessarily address needs in a particular library. Examining qualitative factors (see Figure 8.14) for each collection can help to determine which database best suits a particular library.

In order to make the best decision for a specific library at a specific institution, it is necessary to examine electronic resource subscriptions in light of institutional needs and qualitative factors.

QUALITATIVE FACTORS

The modified meta-analysis process for electronic resource collection development involves more than just quantitative data. Even though cost and use are extremely important, qualitative factors must also be taken into consideration. These factors can be both internal and external to the library and the institution. Examples of external factors include

• journal impact factor and times cited,
• lack of publisher competition in certain subject areas,
• key literature for given disciplines, and
• availability of open access alternatives for scholarship.

Libraries must also take into account several internal factors when judging the importance of electronic resources to their institutions. For example, does an electronic resource support an institution's

• regional, disciplinary, or internal accreditations?
• mission and identity?
• administrative priorities and goals?
• research and teaching needs?
• current research grants?

Figure 8.11
SFX Menu, Courtesy of Ex Libris Group

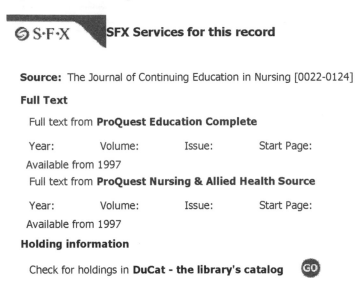

Impact Factors

Against the backdrop of proliferating journal titles and constantly changing technologies, the ability to find external measures of quality is paramount (Bauer and Bakkalbasi 2005). One such measure is the journal impact factor maintained by Thomson Scientific's Institute for Scientific Information. A journal's impact factor is a measure of the frequency with which the "average article" in a journal has been cited in a particular year or period (Garfield n.d.). The assumption is that the higher the impact factor, the better the quality of the journal. However, it is important to note that there is much debate on the worth of impact factors (Garfield 1999).

Journal impact factors can help librarians see which journals in specific fields are being most heavily used by researchers. Across academia, faculty are being pressured to publish in scholarly, peer-reviewed journals and to secure grant money for their research in order to receive tenure. For this reason, faculty aspire to publish in journals with higher impact factors. ISI's Journal Citation Report

Figure 8.12
ProQuest Education Complete Table

Title	Vendor Use Statistics	Link Resolver Use Statistics	Unique Use
Journal of Nursing Education	542	384	158
The Chronicle of Higher Education	403	114	289
Phi Delta Kappan	387	91	296
Library Journal	386	53	333
Booklist	365	0	365

Figure 8.13
ProQuest Psychology Table

Title	Vendor Use Statistics	Link Resolver Use Statistics	Unique Use
The Lancet	707	373	334
New England Journal of Medicine	657	507	150
American Journal of Psychiatry	441	350	91
American Journal of Public Health	327	205	122
Nature	276	171	105

(JCR) lists journal impact factors for thousands of titles in the sciences and social sciences. However, it is limited to only those journals indexed in ISI's Web of Science, and some disciplines are badly underrepresented. Worse still, almost no humanities journals are covered in JCR.

The impact factor should not be used as the sole measure of a journal; it should be used in combination with other measures discussed in this chapter. Perhaps the impact factor's greatest value is providing another point of comparison when examining two journals that are relatively equal in other measures.

Even assuming that the impact factor is a completely reliable measure of a journal's quality, basing collection decisions solely on this measure would be ill advised. The open access title *PLoS Biology* has a 2007 journal impact factor of 13.501, while *FASEB Journal* comes in at 6.791. Yet, we suspect few libraries would cancel the well-respected *FASEB Journal* simply because they have free access to *PLoS Biology*. Highly recognized and prestigious journals are often deemed sacrosanct by faculty, requiring the library to maintain subscriptions.

Internal Indicators of Quality

There are many internal factors that each individual library must take into consideration when reviewing any part of its collection. Internal factors are characteristics unique to each institution and in some cases are important enough to be incorporated into most library collection development policies.

Figure 8.14
ProQuest Comparison Table

Analysis of ProQuest Education Unique
- 117 unique titles in the subject area of education—13 with ISI Impact Factors
- 66 titles with ISI Impact Factor ratings (13 are unique education titles)
- 173 titles that are refereed (peer reviewed)
- 21 unique library and information sciences titles
- 6 unique medical sciences titles
- 5 business/economics titles
- Others in subjects including biology, computers, and geography
- 17 titles were unused

Analysis of ProQuest Psychology Unique
- 127 unique titles in the subject area of psychology—48 with ISI Impact Factors
- 193 titles with ISI Impact Factor ratings (48 are unique psychology titles)
- 269 titles that are refereed (peer reviewed)
- 64 unique medical sciences titles
- 21 business and economics titles
- 10 social services and welfare titles
- Other subjects including public health and safety, gerontology, and drug abuse and alcoholism
- 14 titles were unused

Mission and Identity.   One of the most important factors that librarians must keep in mind is the mission and identity of their institution. The mission is the cornerstone of any organization because it gives the institution meaning and purpose, while providing guidance in the decision-making process. A good example of this would be a Catholic university whose mission and identity is rooted in Catholic beliefs and teachings. In support of its Catholic mission, the library may retain all materials that support Catholic teaching, regardless of format, use, and even cost. Administrative priorities and strategic plans develop out of an institution's mission, and the library may purchase resources in support of such initiatives. At times, the library might purchase low-use resources that support a unique discipline that is closely related to the mission.

Since academic libraries exist to support the teaching and research needs of a university community, it is essential to maintain resources that support the institutional curriculum. This may include maintaining underused resources required for disciplinary, professional, or regional accreditations and program reviews.

It is equally important to sustain student and faculty research needs. Faculty research can be more complicated and costly to support. In an effort to support faculty, research librarians need to be aware of many such things, including the following:

• What are the key areas of research across campus?
• Which faculty members are involved in the research?
• How much grant money is coming into the institution because of the research?

The answers to these questions can have an impact on a library's decision to retain a title or not. At one institution, Elsevier's title *Brain Research* was maintained at the cost of approximately $19,913 a year to support one faculty member's research. In another case expensive subscriptions were continued in print instead of moving to electronic, due to a few researchers' dissatisfaction with the image quality in the electronic equivalents. All of these factors were taken into consideration due to the fact that these faculty members' research brought in millions of dollars in grants.

Essential Titles

Although it is often possible to draw a line from faculty needs to library subscriptions, certain journals are not as directly connected to an institution's research or teaching efforts. Libraries need to provide access to many journals regardless of whether they are clearly tied to the curriculum. At Duquesne University, we call these "stupid library" titles, as in, "What kind of a stupid library would not have this journal?" When a library does not provide access to these titles, it can foster the perception that the library collection is inadequate. An academic library supporting any kind of science program should almost certainly have a current subscription to the journal *Science*, since it is considered to be one of the most prestigious peer-reviewed journals in the sciences.

But what are the "stupid library" titles for a particular institution? When trying to determine which journal titles are most important to acquire or maintain, librarians often look for core title lists for specific subjects or disciplines. These core lists can be extremely varied. Some accrediting bodies, professional organizations, and researchers have created lists that many consider to be useful guidelines for libraries in supporting their disciplines. Some examples of these lists include NAHRS Mapping the Literature of Nursing and Allied Health projects (Allen, Jacobs, and Levy 2006; Schloman 1997), American Chemical Society Guidelines for Bachelor's Degrees (American Chemical Society 2003), and the American Association of Colleges of Pharmacy Basic Resources for Pharmaceutical Education (Bowman and Nanstiel 2009).

When a core list is compiled by an accrediting body or professional organization it takes on a higher level of importance because it can be recognized as a measure of the library's collection. However, most disciplines have not developed "official" core lists. For this reason, faculty and librarians attempt to develop core lists using a variety of methods. As Corby notes, many problems develop when libraries try to follow this path, because the definition of a core list can vary based on who is compiling it. She notes that a core list for undergraduate needs would differ from a core list for faculty interested in publishing (Corby 2003).

The bottom line is that a library needs to weigh the factors within its institution to determine which titles are the most essential to the students and faculty it serves. Once a library determines its essential titles, it should create a "protected from cancellation" list (Corby 2003). The list should include all subscriptions regardless of format and should be tailored to a particular institution and its needs (Zhang and Haslam 2004).

In the end, dealing with internal qualitative factors can be quite complex. It is not simply a matter of meeting needs or cutting resources that are underused. Administrative priorities and organizational politics can quickly complicate the issues. Since libraries typically do not generate revenue, they must strive to keep the administration and other stakeholders happy. Many libraries purchase aggregated databases in an effort to maximize the number of electronic journals available while minimizing costs.

Aggregated Databases

Libraries must consider the pros and cons of aggregated databases. In most cases these databases are collections of hundreds, sometimes thousands of journal titles that vendors bundle and sell using cost-effective pricing models. These packages normally consist of a smaller number of significant titles bundled with a larger number of less important titles. Aggregated databases allow libraries to obtain access to larger numbers of titles for a relatively low cost. They are often heavily used by undergraduates doing general research because they offer a wide range of full texts. Aggregated databases are typically sold as "all or nothing" agreements, so libraries lose the ability to drop or add titles. As shown above, it is possible to do meta-analyses on aggregated databases like ProQuest Education Complete, but the final decision is on the database as a whole, and not on individual titles.

A disadvantage of aggregated databases is that the journal content is often not owned by the vendor, thus the vendor is bound by the journal publishers' stipulations. Many publishers license their journals to aggregated databases, but sometimes abruptly pull their content in order to start their own online packages, leaving libraries with access gaps. Therefore, libraries cannot rely on aggregated content for critical titles. In some cases, aggregated databases include only selected full-text articles or lack the most current issues, due to embargoes. Some embargoes include up to a year's worth of current issues, forcing libraries to continue individual subscriptions. Some publishers delay providing content to aggregators even when there is no embargo, and at other times, provide lesser quality formats. For example, *The New England Journal of Medicine* provides ASCII text to many aggregators but provides searchable PDFs to direct subscribers. In some aggregated databases, format changes have occurred over the years, leading to a single journal's articles being available in varying formats, including ASCII, HTML, and PDF.

Interface Considerations

With so many resources and formats to choose from, it is very important that librarians learn as much as possible about their patrons. This issue becomes complicated when comparing the very different research needs of undergraduates, graduate students, and faculty. When factoring in the preferences of the specific disciplines, the issue becomes further convoluted. All of this information assists librarians in making well-informed decisions when purchasing or renewing subscriptions.

Undergraduates typically use what is most convenient to them (Wulff and Nixon 2004). They normally begin by choosing familiar resources that are easy to use, e.g., Google Scholar, EBSCOhost, or ProQuest, confident that they will find relevant full texts. Graduate students are heavy users of electronic journals in general. Faculty have core lists of discipline specific electronic journals that they consult routinely. In some instances faculty feel that it is important to maintain the core titles in their field both in print and electronically (Tenopir, Hitchcock, and Pillow 2003).

The number of research database interfaces offered by a library can be daunting to students and faculty. Libraries must try to limit the number of interfaces they offer in order to help their patrons to search more effectively. The problem with limiting interfaces is that interfaces are not always completely comparable. MLA International Bibliography is available through both Gale and EBSCOhost, but each has unique full text in its interface. For the sake of convenience, undergraduates (and probably others) are more likely to use journals whose full text is readily available in the databases they are searching.

One-click access from citation to article is important to users, and an important factor in electronic journal use. At times, users find that the best article is the most convenient article, and they choose to end their research at that point (Wulff and Nixon 2004). These situations skew use numbers for those journals. One solution is to use a federated searching system, e.g., Ex Libris' MetaLib, Serials Solutions' CentralSearch, or WebFeat Express. Cervone writes, "When patrons have multiple databases available to them, they typically prefer to use a single interface rather than having to learn different interfaces for each database" (Cervone 2007, 67). He further notes, "The end result is that students and faculty often will find many significant citations of which they were not previously aware" (68). For libraries that cannot afford federated searching, Google Scholar, coupled with a link resolver, offers an alternative solution. However, Google Scholar does not always offer the same level of completeness or currency found in specific databases (Neuhaus et al. 2006).

Contract/License Issues

A notable new task for librarians working with electronic resources is dealing with contracts and license agreements. Librarians must become familiar with legal concepts while making sure that their libraries' needs are met and their institutions protected. Although reviewing license agreements can seem burdensome, it is essential because it addresses points that the library must negotiate, including

- authorized users,
- terms of use,
- interlibrary loan permissions,
- technological requirements, and
- perpetual access and/or archival rights.

Since these negotiations can be time consuming, adding new resources onto existing license agreements is cost effective, time saving, and convenient. One way that a library can provide access to large numbers of journals using a single license agreement is by pursuing a "big deal," which is "an online aggregation of journals that publishers offer as a one-price, one size fits all package" (Frazier 2001). The price tags on these deals are generally deeply discounted and may seem too good for a library to turn down. The "big deals" generally offer an abundance of titles in a variety of disciplines; however, they have many of the same pros and cons as aggregated databases.

Frazier (2001) notes that the "big deal" not only causes libraries to subscribe to unneeded journals but also makes them increasingly dependent on specific publishers. "Big deals" require libraries to maintain a set spending level with the publisher. In some circumstances, if the library decides to cancel the "big deal," the prices of the publisher's other resources are subject to substantial increases. Libraries agree to "big deals" for a number of reasons, such as affordability, value for the money spent, consortial arrangements, and the quality of titles offered. Quite often one vendor or publisher may have a monopoly on the scholarly research being published in a specific subject area. This is extremely common in the areas of science, technology, and medicine. Many of the publishers in these areas have inflated the prices for these journals at such an alarming rate that some libraries are forced to make hard collection decisions. Usually the choices include either paying exorbitant subscription costs for needed resources or dropping these subscriptions and depending on interlibrary loan or document delivery.

COMMUNICATION AND ENVIRONMENTAL SCANNING

When analyzing usage statistics and costs, it is important to remember that these are not the only relevant data. It is critical to continually and actively seek user feedback.

Two-Way Communication with Faculty

Faculty members are the library's key stakeholders for virtually all journal subscriptions. They frequently use journals for their own research, steer graduate research, and guide undergraduates. Faculty members directly influence how heavily a journal is used. They are in the best position to evaluate a journal's importance within a discipline as well as its impact on departmental accreditation and program review. Academic libraries must engage faculty in two-way conversation about subscription decisions. One of the greatest challenges is finding a good way to communicate with faculty. Some options are

- faculty e-mail lists,
- library Web site,
- university committees,
- contacts between librarian liaisons and their faculty counterparts,
- comment forms or user surveys, and
- faculty focus groups or informational meetings.

Regardless of the method, libraries need to find ways to inform faculty of the challenges they face. A key consideration is that the library needs to maintain a positive approach, particularly when discussing potential journal cuts or replacements. While more closely aligning subscriptions to teaching and research needs, the library should emphasize its goal to act as a responsible steward of valuable university resources.

Open communication carries an element of risk. Some libraries might be reluctant to share subscription costs and budgets with a wider audience, but being up-front about this information enables the faculty to be informed and act in partnership with the library. The library might also choose to share its cost per use data with faculty. Once they understand this data, faculty are more capable of looking at the big picture (i.e., an institution-wide view) and are more likely to support the hard decisions that libraries must make. There will always be a few faculty members who insist on getting what they want regardless of the cost to the library or their colleagues. In these cases, the library needs to carefully weigh other qualitative factors.

Staying in Touch with Students and Other Users

The library needs to provide opportunities and pathways to facilitate input from the campus community beyond the faculty. Some examples include

- campus committees,
- comment cards (print and Web),
- student government,
- open forums, and
- focus groups.

It is critical to keep open these avenues of communication. Otherwise the library could miss the opportunity to learn about new needs, new trends, changing expectations, and other developments that might not be obvious from within the library's four walls.

Keeping Track of Changes on the Campus

An unfortunate reality on many campuses is that important information is not always communicated to the library. When a faculty member doing a unique type of research leaves the institution, she is unlikely to notify the library. University curricula are constantly evolving, and often schools do not consider the impact on the library. Students' interests, capabilities, and needs change over time. Some ways that libraries can stay on top of this information follow:

- Maintain a strong liaison program.
- Lead campus initiatives.
- Participate on campus committees.
- Partner with faculty on teaching or research projects.
- Get to know faculty in informal settings, e.g., the cafeteria or coffee shop.
- Become involved with student organizations.
- Create formal channels to communicate program changes to the library.
- Provide opportunities for student dialogue with the library (e.g., town halls, focus groups, or meet and greets).

As the library gathers information from all these sources, it develops a more complete understanding of changing needs. Armed with this information, the library can then identify new resources needed. It can also identify resources that are no longer needed and then proactively develop "hit lists" of subscriptions earmarked for cancellation to share with faculty and other stakeholders. If the library does its homework well and identifies resources that are truly no longer needed, it is more likely to get faculty agreement. Librarians need to be sensitive to demands on faculty time and avoid overwhelming them with too many numbers and options.

Opportunity Cost

Even after receiving all faculty input, the library still needs to make hard choices since no library can afford to buy everything. The library must take into account opportunity cost. For example, choosing to buy *Brain Research* for $19,913 per year to support one faculty member's research could cause the library to forego the purchase of additional resources that could satisfy the needs of many others. The library could have purchased several different resources instead of

Brain Research. In making these decisions, libraries need to balance many of the factors discussed above and to consider alternatives, including ILL. It might be more cost effective to get articles via ILL for a single high-priced journal than it would be to get them for numerous lower priced journals. Given delays associated with ILL, somebody will be unhappy if their journal is not available. Part of the "political calculus" may be the difference between making one superstar unhappy at the expense of several students and faculty. That kind of calculation is hard to make, and will differ from library to library.

Applying "Meta-analysis"

Before gathering data, it is important to determine if the library is ready and willing to make tough decisions. If not, this process will be an exercise in futility. When ready, develop a plan and a time frame that outlines how to use the data in decision-making. Begin by asking pertinent questions:

- Will the data help to achieve specific goals?
- How might the data be used as part of the decision-making process?
- Which data sources will contribute to the decision-making process?
- Are there resources protected from cancellation that do not require review?
- Is it feasible to gather the data needed? If not, are there alternative data sources?

Answering these questions will help to determine the most relevant data sources. It might also be beneficial to purchase services that gather data more efficiently (for example, ScholarlyStats). It is important to keep an open mind and be willing to question assumptions when analyzing the data. Try to avoid bringing personal biases to the process, and be willing to move out of comfort zones. Look at what the numbers suggest when forming conclusions.

After analyzing quantitative data, weigh the conclusions against the most important qualitative factors. Regardless of what the numbers say, institutional priorities and political realities should be taken into consideration. As Figure 8.3 showed, sometimes it is necessary to make decisions that conflict with the quantitative data. At other times, budgetary realities might force different decisions. When a very limited pool of funds is available, it might be necessary to drop even very heavily used resources.

Statistics gathering, analysis, and decision-making comprise a cyclical process. The first time through the cycle will be a learning process. Be prepared to rock a few boats because some will argue for the status quo. Issues can arise within the library, including turf battles, questions about work processes, differing points of view, and difficulty finding ways to share information. Outside the library, faculty can be protective of resources that support their work. Recognize these challenges up front and acknowledge that first attempts will not be perfect. This process is cyclical, so learn from mistakes. It will become easier with practice!

Using "Multivariate Analysis"

Multivariate analysis suggests a solution for making sense of all the use statistics, cost data, and other factors when trying to get a grasp on a large amount of data—let alone trying to use it for calculations. It is possible to begin examining a question using limited data sources. For example, in trying to decide whether to retain one journal subscription or another, the following sources are available:

- vendor use statistics,
- catalog clickthroughs,
- Web site clickthroughs,
- link resolver use requests and clickthroughs,
- interlibrary loan requests,
- subscription costs,
- estimated staff costs to provide access (e.g., via catalog, link resolver), and
- training costs.

It would be a challenge to use all of the above data sources to make decisions for even a small number of journals. When multiplied by hundreds of journals, the task becomes daunting. Using data selectively makes the analysis and decision-making processes more manageable. The key is to examine the resources in question and logically determine which variables can be eliminated, such as the following:

- For some resources the vendor data could be the most reliable, making it possible to eliminate all clickthroughs from consideration.
- Some costs might be relatively equal for all resources considered (for example, staff, training, and platform fees).
- Interlibrary loan might not be relevant for a given journal if access is available through other local libraries.

STRATEGIES FOR USING STATISTICS TO MAKE DECISIONS

In order to make sound collection decisions, libraries must develop a plan of attack (Booth 2006). Specify goals and how to accomplish them before jumping in. The meta-analysis process can be overwhelming, so do not try to do it all at once. When involving multiple players, increase efficiency and expedite the process by assigning specific tasks, including harvesting statistics, organizing data, communicating with stakeholders, and decision-making.

A less overwhelming approach is to review only one portion of the collection at a time. Perhaps tackle all individual electronic journal subscriptions first, move on to the electronic journal packages, and then review the aggregated databases and full-text databases. Libraries must be proactive in keeping, reviewing, and analyzing statistics. In order to avoid getting caught flat-footed, do not wait until it is absolutely necessary to make subscription cuts. Libraries should develop "wish lists" in addition to "hit lists," and review them regularly.

While subscription changes have the potential to upset users, well-intentioned librarians should not shy away from making necessary changes. Given pressing student and faculty needs and limited budgets, librarians must sometimes make hard decisions.

Paradigm Shift: Marriage versus Speed Dating

In this new reality, low-use electronic journal subscriptions can quickly be identified and then very easily dropped, and new subscriptions added in their place. Unlike in the print world, libraries no longer need to be "married" to journals that are not being used. Electronic titles purchased directly from the publisher or through a subscription agent can be swapped out at the yearly renewal (in some multi-year contracts, titles can be switched more frequently, as long as the overall spending level is maintained). Libraries might need to change their philosophy of journal collection development from "marriage" to "speed dating." Although archival access is the ideal, not every library can collect as comprehensively as an Association of Research Libraries member. Other libraries must make difficult choices to meet the needs of their students and faculty in the present day.

Taking the "speed dating" approach requires a library to be agile and prepared with a safety net in place in case it make a less than perfect decision. Some possible safety nets are

- reciprocal agreements with local libraries,
- free interlibrary loan (for the library's patrons),
- subsidized document delivery, and
- reserve funds for new/replacement subscriptions.

Recognizing the Limits of Statistics

Recognize at the beginning of the process that all statistics are flawed in some way. It is impossible to maintain perfect statistics. The key is to determine whether it is feasible to make a decision using the flawed or imperfect data that is available (Medeiros 2007). Libraries can keep additional statistics to improve data collection, but at what cost? No matter how automated the statistics tracking, keep the human element in mind. Each library needs to take into accounts its own unique institutional factors and determine how they impact decision-making. Ideally the numbers will suggest obvious decisions, but sometimes libraries face a choice between the "lesser of two evils."

CONCLUSION

Current usage statistics need to do a better job of answering the questions of who is using electronic resources, as well as what, when, and why they are using them. No matter how detailed or precise usage statistics are, they cannot provide information on who is using the resources (Medeiros 2007; Davis 2003). Vendor data usually indicates that resources were used, but not which publication years used. Being able to answer these questions will help libraries to make better decisions about electronic resources. More importantly, we need to learn more about user behavior (without jeopardizing privacy).

Usage statistics are not an end in and of themselves. The process of analyzing usage statistics should lead librarians to ask new questions and to begin thinking about why those questions matter to their libraries. What are the implications for how collections are developed and made available, services offered, and user education provided? Librarians must be willing not only to ask these new questions but also to do the research necessary to gather evidence needed to answer them.

One of the biggest remaining questions is how usage of subscription-based resources compares to use of free internet resources. We can answer some of these questions with link resolvers. For example, it is possible to see how many link resolver requests or clickthroughs were generated by Google Scholar. The more interesting question is, when do students use free Internet resources that do not connect to the library? We need to know our competition. If we can get a sense of how, when, and why students turn to Internet resources instead of the library, we can do a better job of building and making accessible high-quality collections that meet students' needs and expectations. This information might lead to further integration of high-quality free Internet resources and to the selection of different subscription-based resources.

A key consideration is always how long it takes to compile the data. Some libraries might not have the staff or the time to examine more than vendor supplied data. However, systems like ScholarlyStats, ERMs, and federated searching can make this process more efficient, while providing additional benefits. Although it is tempting to conclude that a particular library does not have the money to hire staff or purchase additional systems, given the size of the investment in electronic resources, the need for reliable measures seems self-evident.

Librarians should decide what data to harvest and assume the responsibility for analyzing the mountains of data gathered. Librarians *must* use this data in decision-making, particularly given the significant commitment of resources necessary to maintain electronic subscriptions. Since analyzing these data sets requires skills that might be new, librarians should consider taking classes to learn more about statistics. However, decision-making is not simply a matter of mathematics. It should speak to other factors that are unique to a particular library and institution.

Marcum and George (2003) ask, "Is our campus adapting in ways and at a rate that is appropriate to meet needs and expectations of our particular students and faculty?" The more pertinent question for us is, "Is the library changing in ways that meet the needs and expectations of our unique students and faculty?" If done properly, statistical analysis should be able to help us answer this critical question. If the meta-analysis of all the quantitative and qualitative data is done well, we should better be able to answer this question with "Yes!"

REFERENCES

Allen, Margaret (Peg), Susan Kaplan Jacobs, and June R. Levy. 2006. Mapping the literature of nursing: 1996–2000. *Journal of the Medical Library Association: JMLA* 94 (2): 206–20. www.pubmedcentral.nih.gov/picrender.fcgi?artid=1435835&blobtype=pdf.

American Chemical Society. 2003. ACS guidelines for bachelor's degrees: Library requirements. http://portal.acs.org/portal/PublicWebSite/about/governance/committees/training/acsapproved/degreeprogram/WPCP_010224.

Anderson, Elise. 2005. Maximizing the value of usage data. *Against the Grain* 17 (5): 20–21.

Association of Research Libraries. 2004. Monograph and serial expenditures in ARL libraries. www.arl.org/bm~doc/monser04.pdf.

Bauer, Kathleen, and Nisa Bakkalbasi. 2005. An examination of citation counts in a new scholarly communication environment. *D-Lib Magazine* 11 (5). www.dlib.org/dlib/september05/bauer/09bauer.html.

Booth, Andrew. 2006. Using research in practice. *Health Information and Libraries Journal* 23:298–303.

Bowman, Leslie Ann, and Barbara Nanstiel, eds. 2009. *Basic resources for pharmaceutical education.* Alexandria, VA: American Association of Colleges of Pharmacy. www.aacp.org/governance/SECTIONS/libraryeducationalresources/Documents/2009%20Basic%20Resources.pdf.

Cervone, Frank. 2007. Federated searching: Today, tomorrow and the future. *Serials: The Journal for the Serials Community* 20 (1): 67–70.

Chawner, Brenda. 2006. LITA blog: SUSHI: The NISO standard usage statistics harvesting initiative. http://litablog.org/2006/10/28/sushi-the-niso-standardized-usage-statistics-harvesting-initiative/ (accessed February 14, 2008).

Coombs, Karen A. 2005. Lessons learned from analyzing library database usage data. *Library Hi Tech* 23 (4): 598–609. www.emeraldinsight.com/Insight/ViewContentServlet?Filename=Published/EmeraldFullTextArticle/Articles/2380230412.html.

Corby, Katherine. 2003. Constructing core journal lists: Mixing science and alchemy. *Libraries and the Academy* 3 (2): 207–17.

COUNTER: Counting Online NeTworked Electronic Resources. 2007. COUNTER FAQs. www.projectcounter.org/faqs.html (accessed February 13, 2008).

Davis, Phil. 2003. Why usage statistics cannot tell us everything, and why we shouldn't dare to ask! *Against the Grain* 15 (6): 24–26.

Dougherty, Richard M. 1999. Reflections on 25 years of JAL and academic libraries. *Journal of Academic Librarianship* 25 (1): 3–8. www.sciencedirect.com/science/article/B6W50-3YCDKSR-2/2/e674bff519338a0f0e4247628e699745.

Duy, Joanna, and Liwen Vaughan. 2003. Usage data for electronic resources: A comparison between locally collected and vendor-provided statistics. *Journal of Academic Librarianship* 29 (1): 16–22. http://dx.doi.org/doi:10.1016/S0099-1333(02)00400-7.

Easton, Christa. 2001. Doubly bold—replacing print journals with electronic versions. *Serials Review* 24 (3/4): 97–101. http://dx.doi.org/10.1016/S0098-7913(99)80106-3.

Franklin, Brinley. 2005. Managing the electronic collection with cost per use data. *IFLA Journal* 31 (3): 241–48.

Frazier, Kenneth. 2001. The librarians' dilemma: Contemplating the costs of the "big deal." *D-Lib Magazine* 7 (3). www.dlib.org/dlib/march01/frazier/03frazier.html.

Garfield, Eugene. n.d. The Thomson Scientific impact factor. http://scientific.thomson.com/free/essays/journalcitationreports/impactfactor/ (accessed February 20, 2008).

———. 1999. Journal impact factor: A brief review. *Canadian Medical Association Journal* 161 (8): 979–80. http://proquest.umi.com/pqdweb?did=46270199&Fmt=7&clientId=65345&RQT=309&VName=PQD.

Hiller, Steve, and James Self. 2004. From measurement to management: Using data wisely for planning and decision-making. *Library Trends* 53 (1): 129–53. http://search.ebscohost.com/login.aspx?direct=true&db=tfh&AN=15289212&site=ehost-live.

Jewell, Timothy D. 2001. *Selection and presentation of commercially available electronic resources: Issues and practices*. Washington, DC: Council on Library and Information Resources. www.clir.org/pubs/reports/pub99/contents.html.

Konstantopoulos, Spyros, and Larry V. Hedges. 2004. Meta-analysis. In *The SAGE handbook of quantitative methodology for the social sciences*, edited by David Kaplan, 281. Thousand Oaks, CA: Sage.

Marcum, Deanna B., and Gerald George. 2003. Who uses what? *D-Lib Magazine* 9 (10). www.dlib.org/dlib/october03/george/10george.html.

Medeiros, Norm. 2007. Uses of necessity or uses of convenience? What usage statistics reveal and conceal about electronic serials. In *Usage statistics of E-serials*, edited by David C. Fowler, 233–43. Binghamton, NY: Haworth Press. http://eprints.rclis.org/archive/00012558/.

National Information Standards Organization. 2007. ANSI/NISO Z39.93—The Standardized Usage Statistics Harvesting Initiative (SUSHI) Protocol. www.niso.org/kst/reports/standards?step=2&gid=None&project_key=2de0e3e04f3a7e32d45db8ee87574c3c8206ddcb (accessed October 7, 2009).

Neuhaus, Chris, Ellen Neuhaus, Alan Asher, and Clint Wrede. 2006. The depth and breadth of Google Scholar: An empirical study. *Portal: Libraries and the Academy* 6 (2): 127–41. http://muse.jhu.edu/journals/portal_libraries_and_the_academy/v006/6.2neuhaus.pdf.

Nolfi, David A., and Carmel Yurochko. 2007. Using Google to provide access to scholarly resources: Meeting students where they live online. Poster presented at the 4th Annual Teaching and Learning Conference, Pittsburgh, PA.

Reitz, Joan M. 2007. *ODLIS: Online dictionary for library and information science*. Westport, CT: Libraries Unlimited. http://lu.com/odlis/index.cfm (accessed February 13, 2008).

Schloman, Barbara F. 1997. Mapping the literature of allied health: Project overview. *Bulletin of the Medical Library Association* 85 (3): 271–77. www.pubmedcentral.nih.gov/picrender.fcgi?artid=226270&blobtype=pdf.

Tenopir, Carol, Brenda Hitchcock, and Ashley Pillow. 2003. Use and users of electronic library resources: An overview and analysis of recent research studies. Washington, DC: Council on Library and Information Resources. www.clir.org/pubs/reports/pub120/pub120.pdf.

Vaughan, K. T. L. 2003. Changing use patterns of print journals in the digital age: Impacts of electronic equivalents on print chemistry journal use. *Journal of the American Society for Information Science and Technology* 54 (12): 1149–52. http://proquest.umi.com/pqdweb?did=417061351&Fmt=7&clientId=65345&RQT=309&VName=PQD.

Wulff, Judith, and Neal D. Nixon. 2004. Quality markers and use of electronic journals in an academic health sciences library. *Journal of the Medical Library Association: JMLA* 92 (3): 315–22. www.pubmedcentral.nih.gov/picrender.fcgi?artid=442173&blobtype=pdf.

Yurochko, Carmel, David A. Nolfi, and Tracie J. Ballock. 2006. Using evidence to build faculty participation in serials collection development. *LibraryConnect* 4 (1): 6.

Zhang, Xiaoyin, and Michaelyn Haslam. 2004. Movement toward a predominantly electronic journal collection. *Library Hi Tech* 23 (1): 82–89.

BIBLIOGRAPHY

Cowgill, Allison, Joan Beam, and Lindsey Wess. 2001. Implementing an information commons in a university library. *Journal of Academic Librarianship* 27 (6): 432–39. www.sciencedirect.com/science/article/B6W50-44G8NW7-2/2/4b952adca1ea6cf4d624ea4a38440b60.

Davis, Philip M., and Jason S. Price. 2006. E-journal interface can influence usage statistics: Implications for libraries, publishers, and Project COUNTER. *Journal of the American Society for Information Science and Technology* 57 (9): 1243–48.

Luther, Judy. 2000. White paper on electronic journal usage statistics. Washington, DC: Council on Library and Information Resources. www.clir.org/pubs/reports/pub94/contents.html.

MacDonald, Brad, and Robert Dunkelberger. 1998. Full-text database dependency: An emerging trend among undergraduate library users? *Research Strategies* 16 (4): 301–7. www.sciencedirect.com/science/article/B6W60-40H08VB-6/2/742ed3d55f14fd713ab5bc869408449d.

McMullen, Susan, Patricia B. M. Brennan, Joanna M. Burkhardt, and Marla Wallace. 2006. Collection development strategies for online aggregated databases. In *Handbook of electronic and digital acquisitions*, edited by Thomas W. Leonhardt, 61–90. Binghamton, NY: Haworth Press. http://digitalcommons.rwu.edu/librarypub/6/ (accessed February 20, 2008).

Plum, Terry. 2005. Evaluating the usage of library networked electronic resources. Paper presented at the International Developments in Library Assessment and Opportunities for Greek Libraries conference, Thessaloniki, Greece. www.libqual.org/documents/admin/PlumEvaluating%20Networked%20Electronic%20ResourcesGreece050527.doc.

Shepherd, Peter. 2003. Keeping count. *Library Journal* 128 (2): 46. http://web.ebscohost.com/ehost/detail?vid=5&hid=116&sid=66dac666-2344-44d7-96e4-fc1c21c3a419%40sessionmgr106.

Strong, Carolyn. 1997. The question we continue to ask: How do organisations define their mission? *Journal of Marketing Practice* 3 (4): 268–83.

Svenningsen, Karen. 1998. An evaluation model for electronic resources utilizing cost analysis. *The Bottom Line: Managing Library Finances* 11 (1): 18–23. www.emeraldinsight.com/Insight/viewPDF.jsp?Filename=html/Output/Published/EmeraldFullTextArticle/Pdf/1700110104.pdf.

CHAPTER 9

Usage Statistics: Resources and Tools

MARGARET HOGARTH

INTRODUCTION

Libraries have long had a tradition of tracking use of resources and services. Usage statistics are used to guide collections decisions, spending, infrastructure, service decisions, strategic plans, and many more areas of interest. Empirical evidence can trump other information but must be interpreted in context. Publisher usage statistics, OpenURL Linker statistics, Journal Use and Journal Citation Reports, and Web site clickthroughs are captured by many libraries. COUNTER, SUSHI, and other standards continue to enrich harvesting opportunities. These reports can tell us about the use of library resources and unmet user needs. Can libraries draw conclusions from what the data portrays? How can this information be leveraged into decisions about collections and services? Which data and accompanying calculations are recommended? How can this data be best interpreted and used?

WHY ARE USAGE STATISTICS IMPORTANT?

Libraries, publishers, vendors, and system providers each have a stake in usage statistics because funding for resources is never guaranteed. Usage statistics can be used to guide decisions. A library can confirm high use of resources or identify print and electronic cancellation targets, point out new areas for collection development and research, justify expenses and programs, and prioritize acquisitions and support functions. Usage statistics inform resource budget and subject fund allocation decisions, the number of seats in a subscription, cost-benefit analyses, "big deal" decisions, strategic plans, selection guidelines and policies, usability issues and training, and resource contract negotiation, along with providing empirical data describing trends on local and consortial levels. In a survey on "Electronic Resource Usage Data from Vendors" sent to 284 directors of research libraries, Baker and Read document that 94 percent of the 92 respondents depend on review and analysis of usage statistics for subscription decisions, 86 percent for justifying expenditures, and 61 percent for meeting reporting requirements. Usage data can provide insight into access and interface issues, monitor the availability of and demand for purchased items, and identify areas for instruction and training. It also can illustrate content or interface improvement. When we capture and analyze usage, we can gain critical insight into our user communities and enable all of the stakeholders to provide better systems, services, and resources (Anderson 2004, Anderson 2007; Moen, Oguz, and McClure 2004; Sullenger 2005; Stemper and Jaguszewski 2003; McDonald 2006; Baker and Read 2008).

JSTOR USERS GROUP AND ICOLC

The JSTOR Users Group created a Web Statistics Task Force in 1997 in response to the variability in vendor-provided usage statistics. After studying the varying resources licensed by task force members' institutions, guidelines were recommended for vendors providing usage statistics. These suggestions heavily influenced the International Coalition of Library Consortia "Guidelines for Statistical Measures of Usage of Web-based Indexed, Abstracted, and Full Text Resources" (ICOLC Guidelines), released in November 1998 (Medeiros 2007).

Vendor reports require counts of the number of queries (searches), where each search is considered an intellectual inquiry. Subsequent browsing and reviewing records retrieved are not considered additional searches, although a resubmission of the search form is. If the interface has menu selections (e.g., alphabetic or subject menus), these choices should be counted. Sessions or log-ins should be counted. Turnaways (those requests that exceed the simultaneous user limit) should be counted. The number of items examined (including viewed, marked, downloaded, e-mailed, and printed) should be counted. For abstracting and indexing databases, the number of citations displayed should be counted. Full-text displayed should fully break down tables of contents, abstracts, and articles (HTML or PDF) that are downloaded, viewed, and e-mailed. Other materials (e.g., audiovisual files) should also be counted. The guidelines suggest that data be collected for each specific database from the provider, by institutionally defined IP sets and by consortium. If an account number (I.D.) or other specific data element is sent from subscriber to resource provider, it should be counted, as should the time period (ICOLC 1998).

USAGE STATISTICS IN A NUTSHELL

Usage can be tracked in several ways. By intercepting clickthroughs in the library catalog and Web site, a library can see which resources patrons are choosing to use. Data is collected in a database. Some ILSs require table setup with a specific list of resource URLs to be counted instead of capturing use through scripting. Library Web site log files can also be stored, processed, and analyzed. These approaches require programming support, as the data captured is loaded into a database. Another approach is to use vendor- or publisher-provided usage statistics. Some publishers provide usage data; others don't. File formats are varied and include Microsoft Excel, text files, XML (extensible markup language), or HTML (hypertext markup language). Data can be in standards-based forms or not. Often data is accessed separately for each platform, publisher, or vendor through a secure site, registered e-mail delivery, or other method. Administrative site management requires tracking of access URLs, user names, passwords, and other administrative information (Anderson 2006).

There are advantages and disadvantages to each approach. Intercepting clickthroughs in the library catalog and the library Web site requires programming and analysis resources not all libraries have. While this captures the initial choice of the patron, the subsequent navigation once the patron gets out into the publisher or vendor's site is not captured. This approach also misses what the patron is looking at: articles, tables of contents, or other parts. Log files on the use of the library's Web site can provide a lot of information on the use of the site, navigation tendencies, most-used resources, and similar information, but misses where the patron goes once she leaves the library domain. Specialized log analysis tools are needed to manage the data, and staff time and expertise are needed to analyze it. Vendor-provided usage statistics, while frequently informative about what our patrons are looking at and downloading, as Shim points out, can be inconsistent, inaccurate, unreliable, incomparable between vendors, time consuming, and staff intensive to download, process, and analyze (Stemper and Jaguszewski 2003; Shim 2004).

Here is a typical search sequence, which ICOLC defines as a unique intellectual inquiry:

1. Execute a simple search across multiple databases using a simple search screen from a library portal (Searchlight, MetaLib, WebFeat).
2. View the hit count.
3. View the summary results in the native database environment.
4. Find the record of interest.
5. View the full bibliographic record.
6. Print the record from the native environment.
7. Refine the search using the search capabilities of the native environment.
8. View the summary results.
9. Refine the search further.
10. View the summary results.
11. View three full records.
12. Export two results (Pringle 2004, 77).

The above could be counted as nine searches.

Here is another scenario:

1. Perform the search.
2. Select a record.
3. View the HTML.
4. View the PDF.
5. Download the PDF.
6. E-mail the file to two colleagues.

How many searches were executed? In the second example, five searches are counted. In simple, typical search interactions such as these, it is possible to see the critical need to define database, searches, sessions, downloads, articles, tables of contents, and other parts of the record, as well as the originating location of the user. Also, multiple clicks must be filtered out (Anderson 2004).

PROJECT COUNTER

Project COUNTER (www.projectcounter.org/about.html) was launched in March 2002 in an attempt to further standardize usage statistics. Developed through a collaborative effort of librarians, vendors, and publishers, Project COUNTER is a not-for-profit, member-owned company based in the United Kingdom. COUNTER is a National Information Standards Organization (NISO) standard for counting, recording, and reporting use of online journals, databases, books, and reference works. COUNTER allows comparison of usage statistics from different vendors and publishers and gives different perspectives of the use. In order to be COUNTER compliant, publishers must complete an audit in which usage is counted according to the definitions set by the standard. One can easily see the influence of the ICOLC Guidelines. Reports from Release 2 of the COUNTER Code of Practice for Journals and Databases (published April 2005) include the following:

- Journal Report 1: Number of Successful Full-Text Article Requests by Month and Journal (full journal name, print ISSN and online ISSN are listed).
- Journal Report 2: Turnaways by Month and Journal (full journal name, print ISSN, and online ISSN are listed).
- Database Report 1: Total Searches and Sessions by Month and Database.
- Database Report 2: Turnaways by Month and Database.
- Database Report 3: Total Searches and Sessions by Month and Service.

Release 2 included standards for consortia:

- Consortium Report 1: Number of Successful Full-Text Requests by Month (XML only).
- Consortium Report 2: Total Searches by Month and Database (XML only).
- Journal Report 3: Number of Successful Item Requests and Turnaways by Month, Journal, and Page Type (full journal name, print ISSN, and online ISSN are listed).
- Journal Report 4: Total Searches Run by Month and Service (includes saved searches, modified searches, and searches with zero results).

Books and Reference Works Release 1 (March 2006) specifies the following reports:

- Book Report 1: Number of Successful Title Requests by Month and Title (full title and ISBN are listed).
- Book Report 2: Number of Successful Section Requests by Month and Title (full title and ISBN are listed).
- Book Report 3: Turnaways by Month and Title (full titles and ISBN are listed).
- Book Report 4: Turnaways by Month and Service.
- Book Report 5: Total Searches and Sessions by Month and Title (full title and ISBN are listed).
- Book Report 6: Total Searches and Sessions by Month and Service (ProjectCOUNTER 2008a).

COUNTER reports have done much to drive the development of e-metric systems. Standardized data means machine actionable data and opportunities for automation. A list of COUNTER-compliant publishers can be found at www.projectcounter.org/articles.html.

COUNTER

COUNTER Release 3 was made available in draft form in March 2008 and was finalized and released in August 2008. The following specific improvements were added:

- Definitions now include "federated search," "Internet robot," and "sectioned HTML."
- SUSHI (discussed below) is incorporated.
- Usage reports must be provided in XML, in addition to the existing prescribed formats (Excel and CSV).
- Journal Report 1a: Number of Successful Full-text Article Requests from an Archive, by Month and Journal, will be required.
- In Database Report 1 and Database Report 3, search and session activity generated by federated search engines and other automated search agents must be reported separately.
- There will be two new library consortium usage reports.
- Federated searches are to be isolated from bona fide searches by genuine users.
- New protocols will require activity generated by internet robots and crawlers be excluded.

- A new protocol will require prefetched full-text articles to be excluded from the figures reported in all reports containing full-text requests (Project COUNTER 2008b).

There are still issues with COUNTER data. For example, vendors may or may not include searches that result in zero results or when the number of search results displayed exceeds a predefined (e.g., 1,000 results) threshold. COUNTER permits some vendor variation in counting searches and sessions. COUNTER recommends a 30-minute session time-out, but time-out length varies by platform. A shorter time-out could mean inflated session counts. This may result in statistics that show more session counts than searches. Usually the number of searches is greater than the number of sessions. Some federated search tools generate one session and one search per resource searched. Search and citation alerts, table of contents searches, RSS (really simple syndication) feeds, and other features may not be counted, or may be folded into other search reports (Project COUNTER 2008b; Pesch 2008; Blecic, Fiscella, and Wiberly 2007; Anderson 2006).

Baker and Read recommend the addition of a "product name" field to Journal Report 1 so that different databases from the same vendor and platform can be distinguished. Nonsubscribed titles and data from trials should be excluded. All subscribed titles, even those without use, should be included in the report. Nonjournal titles should be reported elsewhere and not in the Journal 1 report. In this way, use studies will be more accurate. ISSNs should be in the hyphenated format to ensure intrasystem analysis. It would be most helpful if data by date range (across years) could be easily extracted for reporting needs (Baker and Read 2008).

COUNTER-compliant (and other) usage statistics cannot tell us the motive for use. Impatient students will often choose a lesser but full-text article instead of a more appropriate article available in print or by ILL (Medeiros 2007). Phillip M. Davis and Jason S. Price found that interface design affects counts of items in COUNTER-compliant reports. OpenURL linking is also a significant factor resulting in higher full-text downloads (Blecic, Fiscella, and Wiberly 2007; Davis and Solla 2003). There has also been discussion about article-level statistics and if they should be included in COUNTER (Anderson 2004). Peter Shepherd would like to see the year of publication included with the journal reports (2006). This would do much to inform actual use.

SUSHI

SUSHI, another NISO standard (see www.niso.org/committees/SUSHI/SUSHI_comm.html), was developed in 2005 by a group of librarians and vendors and was accepted by NISO in November of that year. SUSHI is based on the SOAP (Simple Object Access Protocol) request response Web service that serves as a wrapper and fetch mechanism for COUNTER reports. Reports are transmitted in XML format. SUSHI works like this:

- A transaction is initiated between a client service (e.g., an ILS with SUSHI capability or a usage data consolidation service) and a data provider, usually a publisher's administrative Web site where the usage statistics are stored.
- Using preinput administrative data, the client service identifies the customer's statistics and specifies the type of report.
- In response, the data provider returns a report in XML, along with requester and customer information, or if applicable, an error message (Chandler and Jewell 2006).

When all connections are working optimally and the system is programmed with the necessary connection information, reports can be automatically fetched on a monthly basis. This data may be regularly incorporated into an electronic resource management system. COUNTER Release 3's insistence on including the SUSHI standard in the vendor audit will do much to encourage vendors to become SUSHI compliant (Pesch 2008).

ERMI

The requirements for ERMs were set forth in the Digital Library Federation's (DLF) Electronic Resource Management Initiative (ERMI) (www.diglib.org/standards/dlf-erm02.htm). ERMI sets guiding principles for ERM functional requirements for selection, acquisition, access, administration, user support, renewal, and retention of electronic resources throughout their entire life cycle. ERMI deliverables include a road map and ERM problem definitions; workflow diagram; functional specifications; an entity relationship diagram; data elements and definitions; XML schema; and a final report. The use of standards should be maximized so that common interests of libraries and vendors can be met and development costs reduced (Jewell et al. 2004). Reactions to ERMI were very positive and it continues to shape the ERM market in significant ways.

ERMI II

Work proceeds with the DLF ERMI, Phase II. The group will review and revise the data definitions "Data Dictionary," aiming for consistency and extensibility. They will expand context and system interoperability and will incorporate licensing. This effort will explore the possibility of using the ERMI-specified data elements for license terms as a basis for a publishing industry license messaging standard in conjunction with the ONIX family of transmission standards. Also, license expression will be discussed in context with museums and archives so that cultural memory can be addressed. Usage data extraction and analysis for ARL E-metrics and Project COUNTER will be explained, as will functional requirements for incorporation of SUSHI (www.diglib.org/standards/dlf-erm05.htm) (Digital Library Federation 2005).

STATISTICS GATHERING SERVICES

New on the scene, statistics gathering services fetch COUNTER-compliant usage statistics for the library using SUSHI or parallel tools. Once the connection information, user names, passwords, time period, and types of statistics are registered, these services auto-fetch usage statistics on a regular basis. Most services then store the statistics in reportable formats; ScholarlyStats does this. Other tools (Serials Solutions 360 Counter, for example) provide a standardized container for downloaded usage statistics and accompanying cost data. Some ERMs have this functionality built in. Interoperability with ILS and other systems continues to be an issue. Even with the aid of ScholarlyStats, Washington State University had to perform a considerable amount of work in order to import usage statistics into their Innovative ERM (Chisman 2007). This is probably not uncommon. If a publisher interprets the COUNTER standard even slightly differently, perhaps by omitting a row or inserting cell contents in the header area, data automation will not work.

ARL E-METRICS

The Association of Research Libraries (ARL) has been collecting statistics about member libraries since 1961–1962 (www.arl.org/stats/annualsurveys/arlstats). Data collected describes the collections, expenditures, staffing, and service activities for ARL member libraries. Data for electronic collections began to be collected in December 2001. Questions centered on the number and value of electronic journals, resources, and e-books. ARL Statistics Series include the Academic Health Sciences Library Statistics, the Academic Law Library Statistics, the ARL Preservation Statistics, the ARL Supplementary Statistics, and the University and Library Total Expenditures. Usage statistics are also surveyed, as are the number of Web site clicks and virtual reference transactions. These efforts have helped to focus libraries' collecting and reporting activities of usage statistics, and further the momentum to find workable solutions that allow easier data collection, manipulation, and analysis (Association of Research Libraries 2008; Shim 2004). Of note, ARL statistics are based on the fiscal year and COUNTER is based on the calendar year. Collecting the data requires a great amount of work.

OPENURL

OpenURL linking was first described as reference linking by Herbert Van de Sompel and Patrick Hochstenbach at the University of Ghent, Belgium, in 1999. The first tool was SFX (for "special effects"), by ExLibris. NISO formalized OpenURL linking into a standard in 2005, Z39.88: The OpenURL Framework for Context-Sensitive Linking. OpenURL linking is a syntax that creates Web transportable packages of metadata and/or identifiers about an information object. The OpenURL consists of a base URL, that is, the URL for a specific library's link resolver.

Figure 9.1 shows the OpenURL for this citation: Herring, G. (2008). Evaluating two new methods for capturing large wetland birds. *Journal of Field Ornithology*, 79 (1), 102–10.

The base URL is http://ucelinks.cdlib.org:8888/sfx_local? The source ID is sid=CAPTURE: CAPTURE (in this case, a capture citation function, but this typically is an abstracting and indexing database or a reference citation). Figure 9.2 shows the citation information.

Libraries maintain a knowledge base of their collection holdings. When a search is executed in an OpenURL-enhanced resource, and the item is activated in the knowledge base, the OpenURL allows context-sensitive linking to library resources and services. In addition to linking to full-text or print and microform holdings, OpenURL linking can be used for interlibrary loan services, library catalogs, citation export tools, A–Z and subject lists of journals, citation linking forms, bibliographies, course tools, electronic reserves, tutorials, and other creative applications. Libraries are continually developing new uses for OpenURL linking to enhance services and access to resources (George 2006; Van de Sompel and Hochstenbach 1999a, 1999b).

Figure 9.1
OpenURL

```
http://ucelinks.cdlib.org:8888/sfx_local?sid=CAPTURE:CAPTURE&iss
n=0273%2D8570&atitle=Evaluating%20two%20new%20methods%20for%20ca
pturing%20large%20wetland%20birds&title=Journal%20of%20Field%20O
rnithology&volume=79&genre=article&date=2008&spage=102&epage=110
&aulast=Herring&auinit=G
```

Figure 9.2
Citation Information from Base URL

```
&issn=0273%2D8570&atitle=Evaluating%20two%20new%20methods%20for%
20capturing%20large%20wetland%20birds&title=Journal%20of%20Field
%20Ornithology&volume=79&genre=article&date=2008&spage=102&epage
=110&aulast=Herring&auinit=G
```

Using OpenURL linking gives an institution an additional source of usage statistics. Typical statistics collected include query numbers:

1. Number of SFX requests and clickthroughs per date.
2. Number of SFX requests and clickthroughs per source.
3. Number of SFX requests and clickthroughs per object type.
4. Number of SFX requests and clickthroughs per service type.
5. Number of SFX requests with/without full-text services.
6. Top target services shown in the SFX menu.
7. Number of clickthroughs per target.
8. Number of clickthroughs per target service.
9. Number of clickthroughs for one particular journal.
10. Most popular journals selected by target.
11. Most popular journals selected by source.
12. Journals requested but have no full text.
13. Selected document delivery targets by source.
14. Books accessed via SFX ranked by use.
15. Services preferred over full text.
16. Unused full-text journals.
17. Number of SFX requests which resulted in SFX menu screen without services.
18. Number of SFX requests and clickthroughs by IP address.
19. Most popular journals.
20. OpenURLs that resulted in no full-text services, selected by source.

These reports can do much to supplement analysis of the use of resources. Interestingly, John D. McDonald has shown that OpenURL linker statistics have a large and significant effect on publisher usage statistics (McDonald 2006).

OPENURL LINKER STATISTICS IN PRACTICE

The University of California (UC), Riverside, Libraries implemented the OpenURL linker SFX in 2004. The UC campuses are in consortium with the California Digital Library (CDL). CDL implemented a modified Model 3, a single SFX instance. Essentially, multiple UC institutions share the same instance. This means that the consortium has a common interface, but individual campuses manage local holdings. Campuses have no access to the server and read-only access to the consortial instances of licensed resources. At the time of implementation, CDL captured a few general use statistics reports including requests and clickthroughs per source (query 2) and target (query 7). The Riverside campus asked for additional statistics: journals by source (query 11), journals for which there was no full-text (query 12), books (query 14), unused full-text journals (query 16), most popular journals (query 19), and OpenURLs that resulted in no full-text services, by source (query 20). Data is entered into a Microsoft Access database, with tables for each query and year. The Electronic Resources Coordinator extracts a list of books that are not owned but sought during the research process and posts it on the intranet for collection development decisions. A similar list is generated for journals that are requested but not owned. When combined with ILL data, a threshold number of requests could be set for automatic acquisition consideration.

OpenURL linker statistics can illustrate instruction needs. In one library, for example, *Psychological Bulletin* and *Psychological Reviews* may be titles that are commonly indexed and frequently requested (via SFX requests), but not purchased (because they don't meet curricular or campus research needs). Librarians are alerted to the frequent OpenURL linker requests for these titles and the corresponding need for undergraduate instruction about why these titles do not meet assignment parameters requiring scholarly literature.

The "books requested" report shows that conference proceedings are frequently cataloged under series ISSN but indexed in databases under volume ISBN. Studying the "books requested" report led to simple workaround links in library catalog records for conference proceedings owned in print. Hopefully, future development of OpenURL linker knowledge bases will incorporate these complicated relationships among series and issues.

OpenURL linker statistics illustrate where our users are coming from at the point of research need and can direct marketing and instruction efforts. For example, of all sources, GoogleScholar ranked 19 of 163 in 2005, 7 of 175 in 2006, and 5 of 309 in 2007. This gives clear evidence that many of our users are not entering library resources through the library Web site.

For those resources that do not have publisher-provided usage statistics, the Electronic Resources Coordinator uses OpenURL Linker statistics at the target and source level to supplement data collected at publisher sites for ARL statistics, specifically target-level clickthroughs as searches and source level clickthroughs as sessions. Additionally, for resources without publisher-provided usage statistics or OpenURL linker usage statistics, the library uses clickthroughs on the library Web site links to give a picture of usage for these resources.

LOCALLY DEVELOPED SYSTEMS

Throughout the late 1990s and early 2000s, institutions invested talent, time, and energy into developing their own usage statistics management systems, in an effort to cope with the variety of data in variable formats. In the early 2000s, the University of Minnesota-Twin Cities developed a clickthrough counter for databases and article indexes based on MySQL, PHP, and EZProxy. A similar tool can also be set up through an OpenURL resolver (Stemper and Jaguszewski 2003). Abigail Bordeaux, Binghamton University, used a PHP-based counter for databases whose publishers do not provide usage reports to supplement reports from the OpenURL linker (Sullenger 2005).

Some local efforts are very focused. CLICAPS (Chemistry Library Information Control and Presentation System) was first implemented in the early 1990s by Daniel Suter, Josef Meienberger, and Martin Brändle at Swiss University (www.clicaps.ethz.ch/fmi/xsl/special_search_en.xsl). Over the years, the system has been supplemented with additional modules: OPAC functions (and links to the main OPAC), acquisitions, cataloging, serials management, a publishers' database, correspondence, a users' database (including personalized journal lists), circulation, reference linking from chemistry databases to articles and patents, balance sheets, and a visual thesaurus. MyCLICAPS is a tool for obtaining current awareness in scientific literature. The JavaScript onClick function captures link clicks (Kumar and Brändle 2007). A system like this allows focused study of resource usage.

Alfred Kraemer, at Wisconsin Libraries Medical College, developed a relational database to collect vendor price data, publisher use data, bibliographic information, Web clickthrough counts (for titles without other data available), ILL data, and print use data. The system is versatile, so he can generate new fields and tables as needed. He has written PERL scripts that pull the publication year out of print journals' use, so he can track usage by year of publication. Annual reports through a ColdFusion created Web form include complete usage reports, low use titles, high cost per use titles, high demand ILL journals, and ILL requests that can and cannot be filled. This tool is available to faculty, staff, and students (Sullenger 2005).

Beginning in 1999, Arizona State University developed an electronic use management informa-tion database that tracked vendor usage statistics by quarter and year, with customizable reports. Use ratios are generated for cost per search, per connect time, per session, per turnaway, and per full-text unit viewed or downloaded, as well as searches per session. Also reported are records viewed per search or session and full content units viewed or downloaded per session or search (Shim 2004).

ERUS (Electronic Resource Usage Statistics) began in 2003 through collaborative efforts of Caryn Anderson (Simmons College), Andrew Nagy (Villanova), Tim McGeary (Lehigh), and Lori Stethers (Trinity College). The group posted a survey to the ERIL-L (Electronic Resources in Libraries http:// listserv.binghamton.edu/archives/eril-l.html) listserv to assess current practices, challenges, and ideal conditions for collection, analysis, and utilization of e-resources usage data. The plan was to develop a relational database using the open source tools PHP, MySQL, and Apache. Plans were made for reporting both standard and custom reports; collecting and importing statistics (with the option of a paid service provided by one of the parties); profiles for vendors, resources, subjects, and institutions; and a reference area with annotated bibliography, FAQs, and links to initiatives, forums, and ERM tools. The initial focus was on indexing and abstracting databases, and to incorporate usage statistics into the larger framework of price, impact factor, and faculty interest. While perhaps naively ambi-tious, the project illustrated the many issues facing librarians trying to gather and use usage statistics (ERUS December 2004 Report; Medeiros 2005).

In 2004, Andrew Nagy at Villanova simultaneously developed LibSGR (Library Statistics Gather-ing and Reporting), which was similar to ERUS, but focused on e-journal usage. LibSGR's function-ality would be incorporated into ERUS. The system allowed users to upload .csv usage statistic files and to run reports. It also had ERMS functionality for managing a journal list, vendor list, and invoices (Riemer 2005; ERUS December 2004 Report).

MaxData, a 2005–2007 study sponsored by the U.S. Institute of Museum and Library Services, compared costs and benefits of collecting and analyzing usage data and to better understand user behavior, preferences, and use. The study compared three types of data analysis to determine what kinds of conclusions can be drawn from each type: (1) deep log analysis of e-journal usage log data collected by the OhioLink libraries; (2) analysis of usage reports from vendors, link resolvers, and proxy servers provided by the University of Tennessee; and (3) surveys of faculty and students at the University of Tennessee and Ohio Universities to probe library users' reading patterns, prefer-ences, motivations, and outcomes of readings. The surveys had demographic, general factual, and critical incident questions (Tenopir et al. 2007). MaxData may do much to focus data collection efforts; librarians are looking forward to seeing the results of this study (www.cci.utk.edu/~IMLS/ index.html).

BENEFITS OF LOCAL EFFORTS

Local efforts can be viable alternatives to vendor products. A locally developed tool can provide consistent and reliable data and allow comparison of titles across publishers. Over time, libraries have had to convince themselves that vendor data could be trusted. A 2003 study by Stemper and Jaguszew-ski comparing local and vendor counts for matching titles found a strong similarity between local and vendor data but that a critical mass of vendor data is necessary for valid comparison. It is a challenge to amass similar data for local and vendor resources. Local data may best be used to inform fund allo-cations and collection decisions, while vendor data is best used for in-depth studies. Distinct user groups may show less use in local data but higher use in vendor statistics. This may illustrate a burgeoning area of research that is reflected in small numbers but has great potential (Stemper and Jaguszewski 2003).

ISSUES WITH LOCAL EFFORTS

Is data from different sources equivalent? A study by Duy and Vaughan in 2003 found that vendor data correlated greatly with library data in showing similar use patterns, but less so with regard to specific data (vendors tended to inflate usage, libraries to undercount). Variable vendor session counting may explain this tendency (Duy and Vaughan 2003). Local efforts miss access from bookmarks and direct vendor sites, and do not reflect actual article downloads (just clicks on the links). Libraries still must depend on vendor sources for download data (Stemper and Jaguszewski 2003). For most libraries, homegrown systems are not practical due to lack of resources, support, time, and talent (Tenopir et al. 2007). Even so, some libraries may choose to depend on local systems, at least temporarily, until the market provides better solutions.

COUNTING ISSUES

Even with standards like COUNTER, there are many issues with usage statistics. Despite the COUNTER audit, definitions of elements and measures (and their interpretation) vary or may be lacking. For non-COUNTER statistics these issues become monumental. Sessions can be a problematic metric. For example, JSTOR counts any additional hits on the article home page as new sessions if they occur after 10 seconds of the initial contact. A new interface due near the time of this writing helps by changing the session length to 30 minutes, but this does not fully address the problem. An industry-wide session definition and length standard would help. Some vendors do not include titles with zero uses in the reports, while others include all journals published instead of limiting the report to subscribed titles. Some publishers provide download data but not articles, abstracts, and tables of contents viewed or other usage statistics (Moen, Oguz, and McClure 2004; Stemper and Jaguszewski 2003; Anderson 2006; Tenopir et al. 2007; Cohn, Mouw, and Stanison 2008).

Despite the COUNTER audit, format of reports may vary. Even a slight difference, e.g., a change in column heading or a missing blank row, can seriously impair automation attempts and mandate expensive and time-consuming hand manipulation. During a beta test of Library Journal Use Reports from ISI in 2007, participating campuses (including this author's) had to substitute a "standard" header on reports that would not load into the usage statistics portion of the tool. The problem headers on COUNTER Journal 1 reports had slight variations that were not machine readable by the LJUR loader. Nonstandardized data suffers even more format issues. Formatting can be presented in an inefficient structure or style that makes data manipulation very time consuming (Stemper and Jaguszewski 2003; Anderson 2006).

Delivery of data presents its own set of problems. In this author's practice (reinforced anecdotally by peers), e-mailed statistics are promptly processed, but e-mailed notifications that statistics are ready for download are not. Keeping track of where statistics are located, user names, passwords, and other data involves complicated spreadsheets or ERM systems. Varying methods of data transfer create a time-consuming, complicated, labor-intensive work environment for libraries capturing the information. Irregular deliveries further complicate the scene (Anderson 2006; Tenopir et al. 2007).

A continuously vexing problem is that data from publishers may not be equal and is difficult to compare. In their analysis of local and vendor counts for four major publishers, Stemper and Jaguszewski found that (at least in 2003) Wiley did not provide reports of titles with zero hits, and the Institute of Electrical and Electronics Engineers did not break down data by title. The American Chemical Society (ACS) combined data for a three-month period for either individual IP in the institution or for an entire regional consortium (2003). COUNTER compliance has helped to reduce this problem, but quite a bit of compliance variation continues to complicate the situation. Vendor practices of dropping leading zeros from ISSNs or reporting all titles (even nonsubscribed) require individual manipulation in order to get an accurate picture. Some publishers report ISSNs without hyphens.

For an institution without programming resources, this can be a significant hurdle to overcome. At the very least, an institution must develop customized procedures for individual reports (Moen 2002; Tenopir et al. 2007; Baker and Read 2008). Comparison of usage across years remains a challenge (Henle and Cochenour 2007). When the process of downloading and processing reports demands so much time and attention, customized procedures stretch already stressed staffing resources.

As Judy Luther said at the NFAIS (National Federation of Abstracting and Information Services) Forum on online usage statistics in 2004, "No number stands alone" (Anderson 2004, 1). Interpretation is everything. Usage must be interpreted by the number of resources available, with a perspective that includes historical context, costs, data needs, and reporting requirements. Usage data must also be linked to other usage data. It is ultimately a value judgment on what is usable data or not (Moen, Oguz, and McClure 2004). In addition to a stable, reliable storage location and accessible, reportable data, analysis is needed to notice spikes, unmet resource needs, or changes that can be used to guide collections decisions (Henle and Cochenour 2007).

With the variety and form of data streams (standards and nonstandards compliant), it is extremely difficult to get a comprehensive view of usage of an institution's entire electronic resource collection (Anderson 2006). When library staff is already stretched to the snapping point, this is even more of an issue. Libraries may need to make triage decisions about which data are vital for reporting needs or most easily captured and processed, and catch the rest later when the situation is more manageable.

Publishers and vendors face significant costs in developing the ability to collect, analyze, and host statistics. Costs can be ongoing as standards change. When value is frequently based on usage, publishers and libraries worry that data is taken out of context. Skill and insight is needed to translate data into scholarly patterns of use. Personalized services, table of content or other e-mail alerts, may retain user-specific information and raise privacy concerns (Luther 2000; Rous 2004). Libraries can address privacy issues by clearly posting notice that data is being collected and giving users the option to participate. Staff need training in policies and procedures and any data collected needs safeguarding (Anderson 2004).

WHAT USAGE STATISTICS DON'T TELL

Low usage data may not be caused by lack of use. A time frame of 12 months to 3 years is needed for users to become acquainted with a new resource (Townley and Murray 1999; Best 2007). Deficient resource marketing or promotion may also suppress usage. Interface can be a factor; if a patron must click through a "terms of use" agreement, is faced with an obtuse interface without an obvious search box, or an OpenURL linker resolves to the database level without carrying through metadata, the resource will likely be selected fewer times (Hahn and Faulkner 2002).

User preferences also factor in. For example, users prefer to browse through the HTML version of an article but download the PDF version (Blecic, Fiscella, and Wiberly 2007). A study by Tammy Siebenberg, Betty Galbraith, and Eileen Brady shows that if a journal is not available in electronic format, users will shift to another electronic journal rather than use the print format (Cooper 2007). Our patrons will make the choice with the "lowest cost in terms of time and effort with highest worth in terms of meeting the information need" (Conger 2007, 261).

As Robert Broadus observed in 1985, usage statistics measure not what should have been used but what was used. They measure the quantity but not quality of resources used (Medeiros 2005; Shim 2004). Savvier searchers will find an article more quickly, with fewer browsed articles, resulting in a lower usage count (Dubicki 2007). Jeff Shim has rightly observed that statistics cannot be taken out of context. They are not a measure of performance, but can give insight into the value of a resource. The output is not an outcome; instead, it must be interpreted within the context of a decision-making framework (Anderson 2004).

INTEROPERABILITY

Cost per use is the Holy Grail for librarians. If a journal is available from multiple platforms, some aggregated, then the actual use of the journal can be difficult to cumulate. Assigning cost and then getting cost information out of the ILS and into an analysis tool can be daunting, depending on the system used. Some tools are beginning to include the ability to calculate cost per use by combining the amount paid with COUNTER-compliant usage report data. In some cases, this is tied in with an ILS, ERM, and SUSHI; in other cases it is a separate module or tool requiring manual input of cost and/or usage statistics. This lack of interoperability between systems has far-reaching consequences for library staff in terms of time, talent, and other library resources. Libraries are buying products from an immature market in an attempt to meet pressing functional needs. One must remember that cost per use and other important information is only as good as the data is complete in these management systems. Getting the information to an acceptable level of completeness is just as important of a quest.

USAGE STATISTICS AND RESOURCE COST ANALYSIS

Cost per use is not a straightforward metric. Shim observes that a resource is a sunk cost: it is paid for up front whether it is used or not (Shim 2004). Chisman (2007) observes that cost data is inaccurate because subscriptions tend to be paid one year ahead of time. Medeiros (2007) cites Holmström's concern that cost per use is flawed because uses of journals can be from years other than the current subscription period.

Carol Tenopir and Donald W. King distinguish between purchase value of a journal and the use value of a journal for both print and electronic journals. Purchase value is the amount researchers are willing to pay to use a journal, and the use value of a journal is derived from the benefits that come from its use (Hahn and Faulkner 2002). Additionally, Medeiros notes that cost per use data ignores staff costs. Instead, Medeiros supports Holstrom's suggestion that Carol Tenopir and Donald King's algorithm from the 1990s might be more accurate. Here is an example of how it works:

- Base year: current year issues constitute 58.5 percent of all uses of X journal for the current year. The remaining 41.5% uses are from previous years.
- Base year +1: Base year issues would represent 12.3 percent of uses.
- Base year +2: Base year issues would represent 6.2 percent of all uses (Medeiros 2007).

While this use estimation method seems more realistic and accurate, it would require an information management system to track data and perform calculations.

Alfred Kraemer broke his institution's usage data into quartiles. The highest use journals make up 80 percent of the total journal use. Nearly all of the high cost journals fall into the third quartile, which accounts for only 6 percent of the total journal use (Sullenger 2005). This might be a useful method of helping to identify core journals by usage, not citations.

Print and electronic journal usage may not be equal metrics. Montgomery and King, as cited by Franklin, claim that print and electronic use are not directly comparable, mostly due to the fact that print shelving counts reflect the use of one article, while electronic journal use counts the use of each article (Franklin 2005). To compensate, the Muenster study in 2003 comparing cost efficiencies of print and electronic journals measured print usage differently by subtracting monograph copies (25 percent) from the total copy volume. The net number of journal copies was divided by 10 in an effort to estimate the number of articles copied. The Muenster study showed that users accessed electronic copies more than print and that unit cost of an online usage was significantly less than the unit cost of a print journal usage (Franklin 2005). It is best for libraries to maintain two distinct count streams.

Many institutions calculate cost per search for online databases, at times assigning cost ratios for bundled print and electronic journals. Others also capture cost per article download (Franklin 2005). There will be increasing demand for vendors to break down package costs to per-title costs, and other services that will make this process easier.

An institution must decide which methods can be accomplished and which calculations are most useful and deliverable. This is almost impossible without the use of systems that either help to gather the data in automated ways, or that tie in with existing systems (ILS, ERM, or other data repositories). Also needed are the vision and staff time and expertise to maximize the use of this data.

CITATION USE

Citation analysis, a standard methodology, is considered by some to be a valuable tool in evaluating journal quality, researcher productivity, and journal use (McDonald 2006). ISI citation data tracks citation and publishing patterns worldwide and looks at citation patterns from two perspectives. "Global citation" data, found in Journal Citation Reports, calculates the impact factor for journal X in 2000 as how often journal X is cited in 1998 and 1999 divided by the total number of articles published in those two years. "Total citations" measures citations in a journal for a year. This may be impacted by publication frequency or the number of articles per issue. However, not all journals are indexed by ISI, and also, only citations in ISI-indexed journals are counted when calculating impact factors (Duy and Vaughan 2006).

ISI citation data can be costly and thus inaccessible to some libraries. John D. McDonald observes citation analysis can be biased due to the highly individualized nature of citing material and citation culture differences between fields. Well-known authors are cited far more than others. Researchers have described issues with ISI's collection and indexing methods that factor in also (McDonald 2006). Areas with greater inaccuracy rates include papers produced by consortium, non-English journals, and journals with dual-volume numbering systems or combined volumes. News and correspondence sections may be cited but are not considered citable. Scientists also make mistakes while citing. This is complicated by naming discrepancies of authors, departments, and institutions (Adam 2002; Moen 2002). Despite these limitations, citation analysis and bibliometric information are easily gathered, obtained, manipulated, and analyzed—and will remain an aspect of the study of use of library resources (McDonald 2006).

Joanna Duy and Liwen Vaughan point out that citation data does not answer what motivates the citation. Data is not timely, nor does it reflect use by those who publish less frequently (undergraduates and staff). Impact factors are useful in that they offer a broad view of a subject for collection development, especially those titles not owned but cited. Correlation results from studies for comparing citations measures (e.g., impact factor and usage) have varied among institutions and fields. In the Duy and Vaughan study, the impact factor did not correlate with e-journal usage, but other studies have shown a correlation. More work is needed to determine the significance of field on print and electronic usage and impact factor (Duy and Vaughan 2006).

OTHER METRICS

The University of California, Riverside, Libraries participated in a beta version of LJUR from ISI in 2007, which allowed the campus to identify faculty and researchers associated with an institution, and download specific reports showing local faculty's publishing efforts indexed by ISI, the number of times cited, and usage based on COUNTER Journal 1 reports. While there were a few glitches in authority control and data loading, there is great potential for tools that combine information in this manner. After studying local data, a focused group could be identified for scholarly communication efforts on campus as well as other library initiatives. Tools like these that mine data already collected by vendors and combine it with institution-specific data have tremendous potential. We will likely see increased development of value-added products from vendors and publishers.

Researchers suggest additional metrics. Darmoni and Roussel propose the reading factor statistic, which measures the number of full-text uses of an article divided by the total number of articles in the database in which it is found. The reading factor is also combined with the impact factor (McDonald 2006). Hahn and Faulkner propose the average cost per access metric, which is the subscription price divided by the number of articles accessed. They also suggest the average cost per article, which is the subscription price divided by the number of articles online (Hahn and Faulkner 2002). Peter Shepherd (2006)would like to see the following key performance indicators added to reports: gross expenditures for staff, students, and FTE; information expenditures for staff, students, and FTE; resources per year; cost per seat hours per year; full-text downloads; downloads per FTE user; and cost per download of online journal. Additionally, he would like to see full-text requests by title; full-text requests by publisher package; full-text requests by FTE; most requested; usage of subscribed versus nonsubscribed; cost of full-text article requests; and cost per FTE. Boots et al. (2007) point out values such as cost per search and cost per article are in effect ratios that can be used to illustrate the value that our users place on electronic resources.

USAGE ANALYSIS

Usage data must be as complete as possible in order to be most informative. Vaughan points out that decisions to cancel print are often being made on anecdotal evidence and gut feelings about print use, rather than empirical data. When empirical data is difficult, labor- or time intensive to obtain, decisions will need to be based on other criteria. Transitions between formats can also make a difference. Christa Easton observes that often the electronic version will replace the print version without much publicity, so usage results may be skewed (Cooper 2007). Librarians might want to take the date of electronic availability into account when evaluating usage.

In the end, the numbers themselves provide the foundation for analysis. John D. McDonald did a significant study in 2006 analyzing usage statistics. A study of print and electronic journals' use from 1997 to 2004 tested five hypotheses:

- citations are positively correlated to print journal usage;
- citations are positively correlated to locally measured online journal usage;
- citations are positively correlated to publisher provided online journal use;
- online availability increases local journal citations; and
- tools that increase discoverability and access to online journals increase local journal citations and increase local usage.

Using Kendall's tau-b, a nonparametric correlation for non-normally distributed data, to rank correlations, and negative binomial regression for regression analysis, McDonald (2006) found that print use predicts local citations after a delay of two years. This two-year delay may be an issue for libraries that have abandoned capturing print use as online has become more prevalent and preferred.

For publisher-provided usage statistics, Kendall's tau-b correlations show high correlations between both print and electronic usage measures and citations. The study documents that online availability and tools that assist with discovery and access (including OpenURL link resolvers) substantially increase citation counts. Wilcoxon Signed-Rank test scores, used to compare a single column of numbers against a hypothetical median (GraphPad Software, Inc. 2007), were used to document the impact of the link resolver and online availability. The results of the study also show that print use declines after a journal becomes available online. Online journals are cited at a higher rate than non-online journals. Citations increase after a journal becomes available online, and print use and publisher use are highly correlated. McDonald determines that publisher use could be a valid substitute for print use. Usage is an important variable in a potential multivariable model for predicting citations. Institutional publication patterns vary over time and could affect results. This type of analysis could be built into statistical packages and collection analysis tools, helping librarians to base collection decisions on empirical data and provide the library with data for outreach programs (McDonald 2006).

In their 2003 study of the use of ACS titles, Philip M. Davis and Leah R. Solla determine that the power law, inverse square law, may be in effect when estimating the size of a user population for a title. Their data, obtained by examining the number of downloads per title, shows that each user IP can be represented by approximately 11 downloads plus or minus 3.5 downloads. There is a quadratic relationship between number of journals consulted and number of articles downloaded per user (Davis and Solla 2003). This equation may be useful to librarians when predicting user populations for other journals.

FOR THE FUTURE

Several recommendations have been made to improve current usage statistics reporting and practice. Alea Henle and Donnice Cochenour observe (2007) how informative it would be to have usage statistics sortable by subject. Joanna Duy and Liwen Vaughan (2006) would like to see citation data also grouped by subject, scope, and language. As useful as these enhancements would be, they are complicated by the fact that many publishers/vendors have proprietary subject headings. Since libraries deal with the same data, the provision of cross-mapped tables of subject headings would be most convenient.

Elise Anderson (2007) suggests a multipronged approach. Vendors should readily adopt existing standards. IP-based usage statistics may enhance identification and capture of hackers, but metasearch results must be filtered out so that only unique searches are counted. At the vendors' administrative sites, libraries should be able to select and format data to view and download, including the ability to identify time period or other elements in the report. Automatic extraction is most desirable. Data needs to be easily compatible with ILSs and ERMs so that usage, subscription, license, and financial information are available in a single interface. Data should be compatible with third party statistics reporting or modeling programs so that it is available for additional study and manipulation. Libraries should be able to easily combine data from different sources, offering opportunities for expanded analysis. There is great potential and need for outsourceable third party tools.

Peter Shepherd (2006), COUNTER expert, would like to see the journal year of publication data included in the COUNTER reports, and usage reports per article in addition to per journal. XML would make these transactions easier to record and report.

Shim (2004) encourages continued refinement and standardization of COUNTER, ARL E-Metrics, ICOLC, and ANSI measures. Additionally, these initiatives need to communicate and develop in concert with each other. Greater interoperability of vendor and library systems would help considerably. Additionally, qualitative information must be integrated with quantitative measures.

The Serials Decision Database at Washington State University (WSU) combines journal, use, and publication data from Ulrich's Serials Analysis System, ScholarlyStats, ISI's JUR, the ILS, and ERMS into one spreadsheet. The database calculates cost per use and tracks journal title, ISSN, catalog record number, fund code, cost, the number of WSU-authored articles published in a journal (from JCR), impact factor, the number of times the articles in a journal title are cited in a WSU-authored article, ILL requests by WSU faculty staff and students from a journal title, and data usage statistics for each vendor (Chisman 2007). This captures much of the data needed to make decisions, but requires staff time and expertise to load and manipulate the data (Carroll 2007).

There are opportunities for collaborative efforts, including the Usage Data Decision Framework wiki that grew out of the NISO-sponsored forum, "Understanding the Data around Us: Gathering and Analyzing Usage Data" held in late 2007 (usagedata.pbwiki.com/Usage+Data+Decision+Framework). Caryn Anderson has set up a discussion of a draft framework that proposes to

1. review organization mission outcomes and goals;
2. determine measures that indicate success in these areas;
3. consider requests for information/knowledge/action from stakeholders;
4. determine questions that need answers;
5. brainstorm measures that can answer those questions (whether feasible or not);
6. identify tools/tactics necessary for executing/collecting the measures;
7. prioritize measures based on criteria;
8. select measures and check with relevant stakeholders;
9. design full measurement plan;
10. test plan;
11. redesign plan if necessary;
12. implement (collect, analyze, present, and utilize results); and
13. evaluate if measures and process were effective.

Several months later, at Electronic Resources and Libraries 2008, following a roundtable discussion about usage statistics, a group of librarians expressed interest in developing best practices for gathering and reporting usage statistics (http://electroniclibrarian.org/forum). Virginia Kinman, Bonnie Tijerina, and the author continue this work. Efforts like these will do much to maximize knowledge, experience, energy, and efforts spent on capturing usage statistics and interpreting the data for decision-making.

CONCLUSION

Usage data will become more important as recording, reporting, and analysis of it becomes more standardized and common and opportunities for manipulation increase. Even so, libraries still struggle to capture and digest this information while expending significant amounts of staff time and energy on the process. Usage data can support empirically which collections and service directions need strengthening, and major stakeholders will benefit from continued cooperation and dialogue among publishers, vendors, libraries, and standards organizations. Continued enhancement of standards for value-added analysis, the resolution of system interoperability issues and development of best practices, and a usage data decision framework will do much to inform librarians about the use of resources. Increasingly, and with more efficiency, libraries will be able to use usage statistics, OpenURL linker and Web site usage statistics, Journal Use and Journal Citation Reports, and other tools to quantify usage, determine unmet needs, and inform strategic decisions.

REFERENCES

Adam, David. 2002. The counting house. *Nature* 415:726–29.

Anderson, Caryn L. 2004. "No number stands alone . . . " report on online usage statistics: Current trends and future directions. *NFAIS Online Newsletter* 46 (5) (September–October): 1–8.

———. 2006. Electronic resource usage statistics: Defining a complex problem. www.utip.info/erus/ ERUSlandscape.doc.

Anderson, Elise. 2007. The next steps in developing usage statistics for E-serials. In *Usage statistics of e-serials*, edited by David C. Fowler, 245–60. Binghampton: Haworth Information Press.

Association of Research Libraries. 2008. ARL statistics. www.arl.org/stats/annualsurveys/arlstats/index.shtml.

Baker, Gayle, and Eleanor J. Read. 2008. Vendor-supplied usage data for electronic resources: A survey of academic libraries. *Learned Publishing* 21 (1): 48–57.

Best, Rickey. 2007. Lies, damn lies and usage statistics: What's a librarian to do? In *Usage statistics of e-serials*, edited by David C. Fowler, 199–214. Binghampton: Haworth Information Press.

Blecic, Deborah D., Joan B. Fiscella, and Stephen E. Wiberly, Jr. 2007. Measurement of use of electronic resources: Advances in use statistics and innovations in resource functionality. *College and Research Libraries* 68 (1): 26–43.

Boots, Angela, Julia Chester, Emma Shaw, and Chris Wilson. 2007. E-journal usage statistics in action: A case study from Cancer Research UK. In *Usage statistics of e-serials*, edited by David C. Fowler, 183–98. Binghampton: Haworth Information Press.

Carroll, Diane. 2007. Tools for serials collection assessment. PowerPoint presentation presented at the Regional Medical Libraries meeting in Pullman, Washington, June 15, 2007. research.wsulibs.wsu.edu:8080/ dspace/handle/2376/1333.

Chandler, Adam, and Tim Jewell. 2006. Standards—libraries, data providers, and SUSHI: The standardized usage statistics harvesting initiative. *Against the Grain* 18 (2): 82–83.

Chisman, Janet K. 2007. Electronic resource usage data: Standards and possibilities. In *Usage statistics of e-serials*, edited by David C. Fowler, 275–85. Binghampton: Haworth Information Press.

Cohn, Kevin, James Mouw, and Christine Stanison. 2008. The usage data big picture: A look at the collection analysis tools and usage. Paper presented at Electronic Resources and Libraries, March 19–21, Atlanta, Georgia.

Conger, Joan E. 2007. Usage statistics in context: Develop effective assessment practices through collaboration. In *Usage statistics of e-serials*, edited by David C. Fowler, 261–73. Binghampton: Haworth Information Press.

Cooper, Mindy M. 2007. The importance of gathering print and electronic journal use data: Getting a clear picture. *Serials Review* 33 (3): 172–74.

Davis, Philip M., and Leah R. Solla. 2003. An IP-level analysis of usage statistics for electronic journals in chemistry: Making inferences about user behavior. *Journal of the American Society for Information Science and Technology* 54 (11): 1062–68.

Digital Library Federation. 2005. DLF Electronic Resource Management Initiation, Phase II. www.diglib.org/ standards/dlf-erm05.htm.

Dubicki, Eleonora. 2007. Statistics drive marketing efforts. In *Usage statistics of e-serials*, edited by David C. Fowler, 215–31. Binghampton: Haworth Information Press.

Duy, Joanna, and Liwen Vaughan. 2003. Usage data for electronic resources: A comparison between locally collected and vendor-provided statistics. *Journal of Academic Librarianship* 29 (1): 16–22.

———. 2006. Can electronic journal usage data replace citation data as a measure of journal use? An empirical examination. *Journal of Academic Librarianship* 32 (5): 512–17.

ERUS December 2004 Report. 2004. web.simmons.edu/~andersoc/erus/reportdec04.html.

Franklin, Brinley. 2005. Managing the electronic collection with cost per use data. *IFLA* 31 (3): 241–48.

George, Sarah E. (recorder). Morag Boyd and Sandy Roe. 2006. Beyond article linking: Using OpenURL in creative ways. *The Serials Librarian* 50 (3/4): 221–26.

GraphPad Software, Inc. 2007. Interpreting results: Wilcoxon Signed Rank Test. www.graphpad.com/help/ prism5/prism5help.html?stat_interpreting_results_wilcoxon_.htm.

Hahn, Karla L., and Lila A. Faulkner. 2002. Evaluative usage-based metrics for the selection of e-journals. *College and Research Libraries* 63 (3): 215–27.

Henle, Alea, and Donnice Cochenour. 2007. Practical considerations in the standardization and dissemination of usage statistics. In *Usage statistics of e-serials*, edited by David C. Fowler, 5–23. Binghampton: Haworth Information Press.

International Coalition of Library Consortia (ICOLC). November 1998. *Guidelines for statistical measures of usage of Web-based indexed, abstracted, and full text resources.* www.library.yale.edu/consortia/webstats.html.

Jewell, Timothy D., Ivy Anderson, Adam Chandler, Sharon E. Farb, Kimberly Parker, Angela Riggio, and Nathan D. M. Robertson. 2004. *Electronic resource management: Report of the DLF Electronic Resource Management Initiative.* Washington, DC: Digital Library Federation.

Kumar, Arun, and Martin P. Brändle. 2007. Deriving usage statistics from local library management software. In *Usage statistics of e-serials*, edited by David C. Fowler, 111–28. Binghampton: Haworth Information Press.

Luther, Judy. 2000. White paper on electronic journal usage statistics. Washington, DC: Council on Library and Information Resources. www.clir.org/pubs/reports/pub94/introduction.html.

McDonald, John D. 2006. Understanding online journal usage: A statistical analysis of citation and use. *Journal of the American Society for Information Science and Technology* 57 (13): 1-13.

Medeiros, Norm. 2005. Electronic resource usage statistics: The challenge and the promise. *OCLC Systems and Services* 21 (3): 145–47.

———. 2007. Uses of necessity or uses of convenience? What usage statistics reveal and conceal about electronic serials. In *Usage statistics of E-serials*, edited by David C. Fowler, 233–43. Binghampton: Haworth Information Press.

Moen, Henk F. 2002. The impact-factors debate: The ISI's uses and limits. *Nature* 415:731-32.

Moen, William E., Faith Oguz, and Charles R. McClure. 2004. The challenges of nonstandardized vendor usage data in a statewide metasearch environment: The Library of Texas experience. *Library Quarterly* 74 (4): 403–22.

Pesch, Oliver. 2008. Gathering the data: A look at alternatives for populating ERMs. Paper presented at Electronic Resources and Libraries, March 19–21 in Atlanta, Georgia.

Pringle, James. 2004. Secondary publishers and usage statistics. In *Online usage: A publisher's guide*, edited by Bernard Rous, 73–90. New York: Professional and Scholarly Publishing Division, Association of American Publishers.

Project COUNTER. 2008a. www.projectcounter.org/about.html.

———. 2008b. Introduction to Release 3 of the COUNTER Code of Practice for Journals and Databases. www.projectcounter.org/r3/r3_intro.pdf.

Riemer, Marilene L. 2005. Electronic resources usage analysis: A review of methods, uses, guidelines, products and reporting of statistics. http://librarytrends.net/statistics.htm.

Rous, Bernard. 2004. Introduction: Use and abuse of online statistics: Overview. In *Online usage: A publisher's guide*, edited by Bernard Rous, 1–16. New York: Professional and Scholarly Publishing Division, Association of American Publishers.

Shepherd, Peter. 2006. Using the COUNTER code of practice: A tutorial. Presentation at NISO Managing Electronic Collections, September 28, 2006.

Shim, (Jeff) Wonsik. 2004. Usage statistics for electronic services and resources: A library perspective. In *Online usage: A publisher's guide*, edited by Bernard Rous, 34–46. New York: Professional and Scholarly Publishing Division, Association of American Publishers.

Stemper, James A., and Janice M. Jaguszewski. 2003. Usage statistics for electronic journals: An analysis of local and vendor counts. *Collection Management* 28 (4): 3–22.

Sullenger, Paula (recorder), Abigail Bordeaux, and Alfred B. Kraemer. 2005. Making the most of your usage statistics. *The Serials Librarian* 48 (3/4): 295–99.

Tenopir, Carol et al. 2007. MaxData: A project to help librarians maximize e-journal usage data. In *Usage statistics of e-serials*, edited by David C. Fowler, 55–77. Binghampton: Haworth Information Press.

Townley, Charles T., and Leigh Murray. 1999. Use-based criteria for selecting and retaining electronic information: A case study. *Information Technology and Libraries* 18 (1): 32–39.

Van de Sompel, Herbert, and Patrick Hochstenbach. 1999a. Reference linking in a hybrid library environment Part 1: Frameworks for linking. *D-Lib Magazine* 5 (4) (April). www.dlib.org/dlib/april99/van_de_sompel/04van_de_sompel-pt1.html (accessed March 26, 2008).

———. 1999b. Reference linking in a hybrid library environment Part 2: SFX, a generic linking solution. *D-Lib Magazine* 5 (4) (April). www.dlib.org/dlib/april99/van_de_sompel/04van_de_sompel-pt2.html (accessed March 26, 2008).

BIBLIOGRAPHY

Abatelli, Carol. 2007. E-Resource management in Connecticut Academic Libraries: 2005 CCALD Survey Results. In *Usage statistics of e-serials*, edited by David C. Fowler, 79–109. Binghampton: Haworth Information Press.

Blecic, Deborah, Joan B. Fiscella, and Stephen E. Wiberly, Jr. 2001. The measurement of use of Web-based information resources: An early look at vendor-supplied data. *College and Research Libraries* 62 (5): 434–53.

Chemistry Library Information Control And Presentation System. 2008. www.clicaps.ethz.ch/fmi/xsl/special_search_en.xsl

Clement, Susanne K. 2007. Shared purchase-shared responsibility: A stewardship tool for consistent e-usage evaluation. In *Usage statistics of e-serials*, edited by David C. Fowler, 43–53. Binghampton: Haworth Information Press.

Gedeon, Randle. 2007. Are we really balancing the ledger with e-journals? In *Usage statistics of e-serials*, edited by David C. Fowler, 25–42. Binghampton: Haworth Information Press.

Kendall, Susan L., and Celia Bakke. 2007. Usage statistics of electronic government resources. In *Usage statistics of e-serials*, edited by David C. Fowler, 161–72. Binghampton: Haworth Information Press.

Lafferty, Cindy. 2006. Serials usage statistics in a small academic library. *The Serials Librarian* 49 (4): 45–52.

Library Technology Reports. 2002. 38 (3): 1–71.

Mercer, Linda S. 2000. Measuring the use and value of electronic journals and books. *Issues in Science and Technology Librarianship* (Winter). www.library.ucsb.edu/istl/00-winter/article1.html.

Morrison, Heather. 2007. The implications of usage statistics as an economic factor in scholarly communications. In *Usage statistics of e-serials*, edited by David C. Fowler, 173–82. Binghampton: Haworth Information Press.

Noonan, Christine F., and Melissa K. McBurney. 2007. Application of electronic serial usage statistics in a national laboratory. In *Usage statistics of e-serials*, edited by David C. Fowler, 151–60. Binghampton: Haworth Information Press.

Stengel, Mark G. 2004. Using SFX to identify unexpressed user needs. *Collection Management* 29 (2): 7–14.

PART IV

Reference and Instruction

CHAPTER 10

Moving Beyond the Hash Mark: Capturing the Whole Reference Transaction for Effective Decision-Making

DANIELLE THEISS-WHITE,
JASON COLEMAN, AND KRISTIN WHITEHAIR

INTRODUCTION

Because library systems and processes have become automated, patrons can now search more quickly and employ sophisticated search strategies (Babu and O'Brien 2000). Previously, library users were only able to search a library card catalog by an author's name, a small set of subject headings, or a title. Today's systems allow users new opportunities for finding the information they seek, through means including keyword searching, combining search results sets, setting a variety of limits, conducting faceted searches, and sorting results by relevance.

Automation need not be limited to library catalogs containing bibliographic and holdings information. Although in many libraries staff at reference desks assist patrons with the use of online catalogs and databases, information about transactions is often only recorded on paper. Frequently this information is recorded in the form of a hash mark to keep a tally of the day's reference transactions (Novotony 2002). This hash mark generally provides limited information about the date, time, and type of question asked (e.g., whether it was reference or directional). Much as automation of catalogs enabled patrons to increase the sophistication of their searches, automation of the reference transaction recording process can enhance a library's ability to make complex decisions based on easily accessible data.

The power of this data to inform decisions reaches throughout the library to include the areas of human resources, staff training, resource needs, and library instruction. Beyond the library walls, detailed reference data also provides persuasive evidence about decisions and issues impacting the entire institution or surrounding community. For example, in an academic environment, library reference transaction data can inform campus decisions regarding technology and student services, including writing and testing centers.

It has been difficult to adapt traditional methods for recording reference transactions to address the variety of recent changes to the nature of library services. A number of these changes have greatly expanded opportunities for providing reference services (one example is the increasing affordability of high bandwidth Internet connections). Systems for recording reference transactions must adapt in order to effectively capture the totality of reference services being provided by libraries.

In this chapter we will explore the value of going beyond the technology of the hash mark for recording reference transactions. We will focus particular attention on the benefits that derive from using a Web-based database to continuously record extensive data about transactions. Much of our discussion will be based on Kansas State University Libraries' experiences.

Background

In January 2007 K-State Libraries began using the open-source Web-based reference tracking system Libstats to record reference transaction data at its Hale Library Help Desk (HLHD), a general reference help desk. K-State Libraries serve a full-time equivalent enrollment of 23,332 undergraduate and graduate students in addition to faculty, staff, and community members. During 2007, the HLHD received 24,470 reference questions. Currently the HLHD is staffed by 18 employees holding MLS degrees (Master of Library Science), three employees currently pursuing MLS degrees, four other non-MLS employees, and eight undergraduate student workers. The implementation of Libstats was initially motivated by the goal of streamlining the data collection process for reference transaction data. However, the new reference transaction data recording system has profoundly impacted numerous areas of the library beyond the HLHD. As of March 31, 2008, several of K-State Libraries' other service points and branch libraries had adopted the program: Fiedler Engineering Library; the Math/Physics Library; Weigel Architecture Library; the Dow Chemical Multicultural Resource Center's Help Desk; the Government Documents, Maps, and Microforms Help Desk; Love Science Library's Help Desk; and Hale Library's Reception Desk. In addition, the remaining two branch libraries, the College of Veterinary Medicine Library and K-State University at Salina's Library, have expressed interest, but have not yet implemented Libstats.

Description of Libstats

Libstats is an open source, Web-based reference transaction database developed by the University of Wisconsin at Madison Libraries. The database makes it easy to record the communication channel through which a reference question was presented. The options employed at the HLHD are in-person, telephone, instant message, text message, and e-mail. The entry form consists of five customizable drop-down menus, a field for the initials of the staff member completing the transaction, and question and answer text boxes. Each entry also receives an automatic date and time stamp with a backdating option. Since it was designed to serve numerous users throughout the library, it allows several users to simultaneously record transactions. Recognizing the need to collect separate sets of data for each service point, Libstats allows users to create multiple "libraries" within one installation of the program. Libstats' source code is available at the Libstats Google Groups page (http://code.google.com/p/libstats). Operating the Libstats software requires a server supporting Apache, PHP, and MySQL programming languages. For authentication, users are required to enter a login and password.

For the needs of K-State Libraries, the number of selection options in each menu field was limited to five. This choice was made to help improve the consistency of data, since options not immediately visible could easily be overlooked by busy staff members. Figure 10.1 depicts the entire Libstats'

Figure 10.1
Libstats' Entry Form

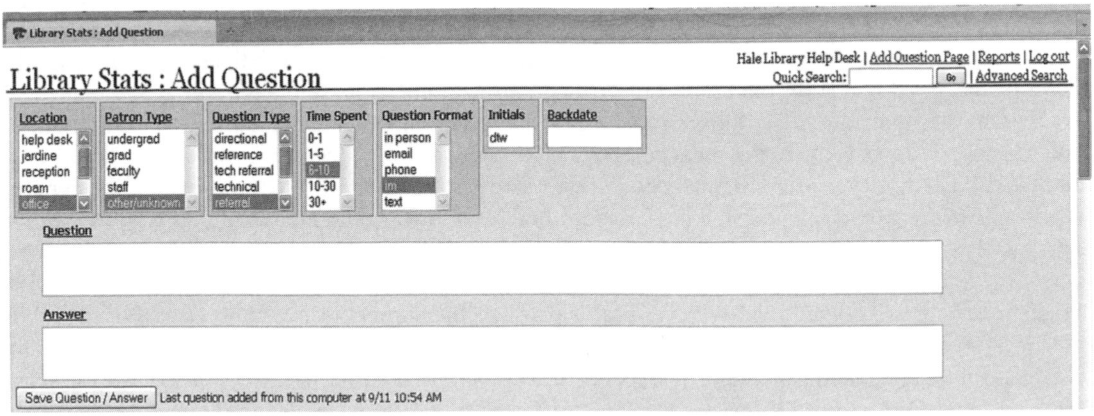

entry form and shows the options for each of the five menu fields used at the HLHD and Hale Library's Reception Desk. Staff initials are optional and the automatic time stamp can be altered if backdating is needed. The last two fields are text boxes for the reference question and answer.

Since many staff enter data into Libstats, common definitions are necessary for data to be useful. Perhaps the most problematic of the fields is patron type. For example, a nontraditional sophomore may not appear to be an undergraduate. The General Reference Unit's policy is not to ask patrons to identify themselves regarding their patron type. Nonetheless, many patrons self-identify or provide information in their questions that identify their patron type. For example, a question regarding a graduate course assignment enables staff to assume that the user is a graduate student. However, if staff are unsure, the "other/unknown" option is available. Evidence of this policy is seen in Figure 10.2, which shows that the patron type was recorded as "unknown/other" for 41.8 percent of the entered reference transactions in K-State Libraries' Libstats. Overall, general guidelines and expectations for Libstats are important to ensure data integrity. For example, at K-State Libraries guidelines have been developed for electronic reference transactions; for instant messaging (IM), text messaging, and e-mail transactions, staff are instructed to copy and paste conversation text into the question and answer text boxes. Staff are asked to remove identifying information (e.g., names and e-mail addresses) from these conversations.

Figure 10.2
Sample Libstats' Report

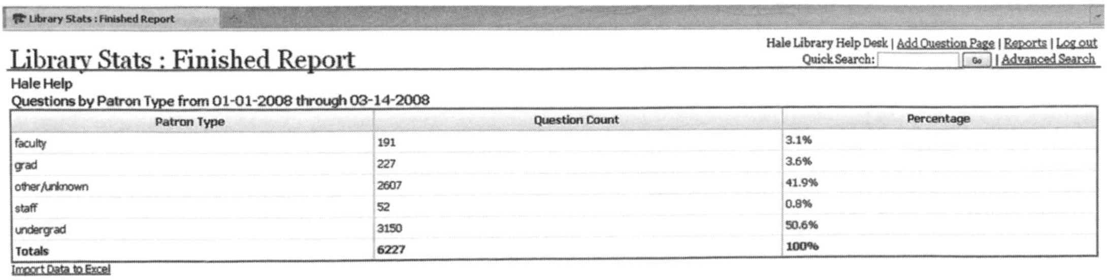

Beyond simply recording transactions, Libstats provides reports and allows users to search entries by keywords or phrases. The search feature also allows for truncation and searching by transaction dates. Libstats' initial six report types were "data dump," "questions by date," "questions by patron type," "questions by question format," "questions by time of day," and "questions by weekday." At the request of the General Reference Unit, K-State Libraries' Digital Initiatives department modified Libstats to add an additional report of "data dump with questions and answers" that includes all the data in the standard "data dump" report as well as each question and answer. The "data dump" and the added report provide the most comprehensive view of reference transaction data. Report data can be easily imported into spreadsheet software for further analysis. After selecting the type of report, users are asked to specify a date range, library, and location. Data from the narrower report options (i.e., the report options excluding the "data dump" and "data dump with questions and answers") are presented in tables that give numbers and percentages. For example, choosing the "questions by patron type" report creates a table that lists the number of questions received from each patron type during the specified time period. In another column the percentage of questions from each patron type is listed. This type of report is pictured in Figure 10.2. These reports allow for accurate and timely reporting. The reports also quickly reveal changes or trends in reference transactions.

Enhanced Data

Libstats' relatively spartan entry form records significantly more data about each transaction than traditional paper recording methods. In addition to general categories of reference questions (for example, reference or directional), Libstats captures substantially more detailed information. The richer data from each transaction can be used throughout the library in numerous ways, as this chapter explores. Libstats allows for continuous data collection and provides solid evidence documenting trends and issues. With paper reference statistics, little information about the patrons' information needs are collected; this prevents critical trends from being exposed. With Libstats, libraries no longer have to rely on anecdotal evidence, but can document and detect the trends occurring in the library during all service hours and on all days of the week. Similar questions or incidents may occur regularly, but since many different staff answer questions during various shifts, the true extent of the need may not be apparent.

LITERATURE REVIEW

Scant literature is available that explores the use of automated reference transaction software. The majority of the literature addressing reference transaction data in general has focused on analyzing and evaluating the quality of services provided (Baker and Lancaster 1991). However, there are two key works that indicate the potential and value of automated reference systems. Michael M. Smith's 2006 article in *Reference Services Review* describes the design and implementation process of an automated reference transaction recording software program at Texas A&M University Libraries. Smith describes strategies used to prevent confusion and encourage staff participation. Both of these features are critical to collecting valid and accurate data. Informing staffing decisions and identifying staff training needs are two beneficial elements of the automated system described by Smith. Notably, Smith concludes that the benefits of the new standardized system outweigh the cost of developing and implementing it.

Secondly, Lakly et al. (2008) describe the uses of a Web-based reference transaction recording system implemented at Pitts Theology Library at Emory University. Uses for the Web-based reference tracking system include recording reference transactions, communication between staff, identifying potential problems, and indicating when additional assistance is needed. The accounts that

Theiss-White reports from staff members using the Web-based system indicate its value throughout the library. These accounts from staff demonstrate that this Web-based system of recording reference transaction statistics satisfies new roles that traditional hash mark systems could not.

In response to the movement toward evidence-based decision-making, Ackerman (2007) argues that Libstats, and its commercial competitor West Campus Library RefStats, can provide valuable data that can be used for persuasive arguments for increased funding and resource allocation. This data can allow libraries to measure their services in new ways. Similarly, Lavoie, Dempsey, and Connaway (2006) outline how major competitors of libraries (such as Amazon and Google) effectively bring submerged data to the surface and employ data to enhance users' experiences. They note that libraries can easily employ similar methods, because they require fairly small investments of money and effort. An automated reference transaction recording system is one critical piece in the larger landscape that Lavoie, Dempsey, and Connaway address.

Regarding the state of reference transaction documentation, Novotony (2002) conducted a survey focusing on methods used by Association of Research Libraries (ARL) member libraries to record reference transaction data. Results from this survey indicate that 25 percent of libraries use an electronic system. At the same time, 99 percent of libraries record transactions manually (e.g., by using hash marks on paper). From these results it is apparent that some libraries are recording transaction data manually on paper and then transcribing the data into an electronic document. While this does signal a desire for complex analysis of transaction data, transcribing hash mark data into spreadsheets does not capture the additional data that can be recorded by automated systems. Notably, one survey response reported by Novotony mentioned the desire to automate the reference transaction recording process. However, on the whole, the survey reported that reference transaction data collection greatly varies in regard to frequency and method between the similar ARL member libraries.

A similar study by Phillips (2004) produced like results. Phillips conducted a survey exploring how reference transaction data is collected and used. Of the 60 public, school, special, and academic libraries that responded, Phillips notes that only a few use spreadsheets in some manner while managing reference transaction data. Automated systems capturing the same level of detail as Libstats were not identified in Phillips' study.

Some literature focusing on automated reference transaction data collection used with virtual reference software is relevant. Numerous studies using transaction logs of virtual reference systems have been conducted (Carter and Janes 2000; Arnold and Kaske 2005; Radford 2006). These studies often focus on question type, patron type, level of difficulty of question, and the type of interaction between user and library staff member. Chowdhury (2002) conducted an extensive analysis of scholarship focusing on virtual reference transaction logs. Chowdhury recognizes that the data logs contain critical information that can provide vital clues to identifying patron needs. Libstats provides similarly rich data.

Arnold and Kaske (2005) take a complementary approach by examining the quality of virtual reference transactions. They argue that virtual reference logs provide a valuable data source for determining accuracy of answers. While Arnold and Kaske only study virtual reference questions, the same opportunities afforded by virtual reference transaction data are available with the use of Libstats. While Libstats does not capture every word of all transactions like virtual reference systems do, the content and critical identifying information is recorded. Libstats does have the ability to copy electronic reference transcripts into the question and answer sections, so one could still have the entire reference transcript available. Virtual reference chat log analysis provides guidance for future scholarship regarding the use of automated reference data recording software.

Traditionally, reference transaction statistics have been reported to library organizations including the ARL and accrediting organizations. In fact, according to Novotony's survey, this is the most prevalent reason that reference transaction data is collected (2002). However, there is little confidence placed in these statistics; Smith (2006) notes that library employees generally do not believe these statistics are accurate. Compounding the data collection problem are varied policies throughout libraries for collecting data. Novotony's survey demonstrates the dissimilarities in data collection between the relatively homogenous group of ARL member libraries.

Ciucki (1977) recognizes the opportunity for standardizing reference collection practices and definitions throughout libraries and attempts to create shared definitions and practices so libraries can compare their performance with peers. Novotony (2002) notes that libraries employ varied methods to record data regarding extended reference transactions. The time limit used to differentiate short from extended reference transaction varies widely. Additionally, some libraries differentiate between simple and complex reference questions by the type of resources required by the transaction rather than the amount of time required to complete the transaction. In 1976 the American Library Association Committee on Reference Statistics surveyed current statistics collection methods to create a standardized reference transaction data collection form for all libraries. While the current status of reference data collection indicates that the 1976 initiative was unsuccessful, the opportunity still exists, and an automated system with easily accessible training and assistance resources may better reach this goal. If implemented on a broad level with shared definitions, a new level of accuracy and consistency could be brought to reported reference statistics.

2008 REFERENCE TRACKING NATIONAL SURVEY

To augment and extend the insights we have gained through our experiences, the authors developed a survey to gather information about the methods used for recording reference data at other libraries. This 10-question survey was administered from February 28, 2008, to March 13, 2008. The call for participation that went out on several major reference listservs (including LibRef-L and RUSA-L), was posted on multiple blogs and had a total of 659 respondents. The survey results show very interesting findings in reference services data collection. Seventy percent of survey participants shared that

Figure 10.3
Process of Entering Transactions in Reference Tracking System

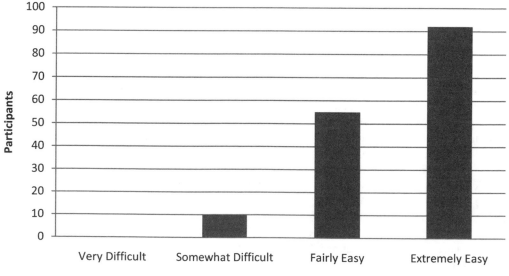

Figure 10.4
Struggle to Find Time to Enter Your Transactions?

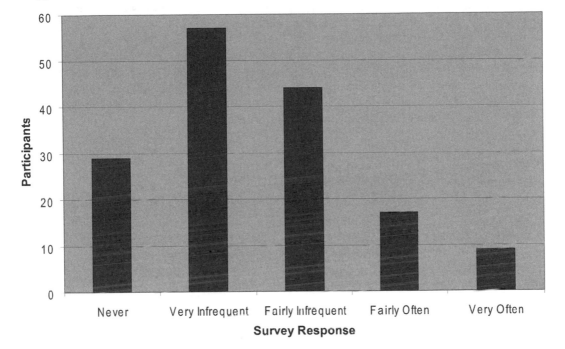

their libraries are using paper tally sheets to capture reference transactions, while the remaining claimed their libraries were using some kind of electronic method to capture reference transactions.

Of the 30 percent of survey participants who said they captured reference transactions through the use of an electronic method, 28 percent said they use a Web-based tracking system, 46 percent a desktop application, and 26 percent another type of program. Fifty-eight percent of survey participants who use an electronic or Web-based tracking system reported that entering transactions into either a Web-based tracking system, a desktop system, or another type of system is extremely easy, whereas 35 percent reported that it is fairly easy (see Figure 10.3). Do survey participants using a Web-based or electronic tracking system struggle to find time to enter transactions? Nineteen percent of survey respondents responded that they never struggle to find time to enter transactions and 64 percent that they very infrequently or fairly infrequently struggle. Only 17 percent of survey respondents noted that they struggle to enter transactions fairly often or very often (see Figure 10.4).

Of the survey participants who said they captured reference transactions through a paper tally sheet and not a Web-based or electronic tracking system, 333 responded to the follow-up question, "Is your library currently thinking of moving to a Web-based or desktop tracking system?" Seventeen percent of this group responded "yes," 4 percent "maybe," 78 percent "no," and 2 percent that they "do not know."

FINDINGS AND DECISIONS INFORMED BY A TRACKING SYSTEM

A reference desk manager can make an array of management decisions using the data found within a Web-based reference tracking software program. Through Libstats' reports a reference manager can make informed decisions based on how many questions were answered per day, per hour, or over a specific time period, and how many transactions were of a specific question type or question format.

The statistics from these reports can offer insight into when the reference desk should be staffed, how many staff should be on the desk at a particular time, and who should staff the desk. In addition, a reference desk manager can use the tracking system's searching capabilities and canned reports to gain insight into how to provide staff training and continuing education.

K-State Libraries has used the available report functions to make several evidence-based management decisions. Examples of these decisions include how and when to staff the HLHD, when to offer virtual reference services on the desk or in a library staff member's office, and when to staff the HLHD with technology adept staff members. In addition, the reports have been used to examine when an increase in IM occurred and why, and to see question patterns for faculty, graduate students, and undergraduates. K-State Libraries has also used Libstats to provide staff training and continuing education for its General Reference Unit.

Staffing the Hale Library Help Desk: Spring 2007–Fall 2007

Historically, the HLHD double-staffed its reference desk from 8 A.M. to 5 P.M. Monday through Friday. K-State Libraries began using Libstats in January 2007 and hired a new general reference coordinator later that spring. The coordinator recognized that she could use Libstats' transaction time and date stamp data to determine whether the desk should be staffed by one person rather than two for certain parts of the day. After the spring 2007 semester, she ran the "data dump" report found within the reports section of Libstats and saved the output file. She then imported the data into Microsoft Excel and sorted it according to day of the week and time of day. After sorting the transactions, she tallied the number of questions asked for each hour of the week and calculated the average number of transactions for each of those hours. She then created a chart showing these totals and averages (see Figure 10.5).

This figure reveals that only an average of one to four questions were received each hour from 8 A.M. to 10 A.M., Mondays through Fridays. It also shows that the average number of questions

Figure 10.5
Spring 2007 IM Transactions by Hour

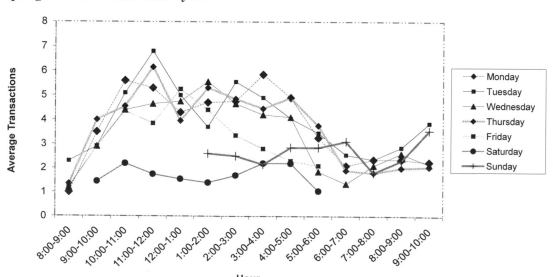

received per hour gradually decreased during the afternoon of each of these weekdays. Based on this data, the coordinator changed the fall 2007 schedule by assigning only one person to the HLHD from 8 A.M. to 10 A.M. and 5 P.M. to 6 P.M. each week day. When making these changes, the coordinator realized that they may not perfectly match the pattern of business during the fall 2007 semester; therefore she resolved to examine the data from fall 2007 and make further adjustments for the spring 2008 semester.

Staffing the Hale Library Help Desk: Spring 2008

When the general reference coordinator analyzed the fall 2007 data in order to make changes to the spring 2008 schedule, she noticed that there appeared to be additional hours throughout the week when she could safely reduce staffing on the HLHD.

The chart of average hourly transactions for fall 2007 (Figure 10.6) is markedly different than the chart for spring 2007 (Figure 10.5). The early mornings were busier during the fall 2007 semester than the spring 2007 semester. The fall 2007 chart shows that on Tuesdays, Thursdays, and Fridays, the average number of questions per hour increased rapidly over the course of the morning and then gradually decreased throughout the afternoon. For Mondays and Wednesdays, the fall 2007 chart shows the same rapid increase throughout the morning, but reveals that the average number of questions per hour remained fairly steady throughout the afternoon. Based on this data, the coordinator opted to make only one further change to the HLHD schedule: she decided to single-staff the desk from 4 P.M. to 5 P.M. each weekday.

For subsequent semesters, the coordinator will pull data from Libstats to determine appropriate staffing levels. When making these decisions, she will take into account the fact that spring semesters at K-State Libraries are usually slower than fall semesters.

Figure 10.6
Fall 2007 Average Hourly Transactions

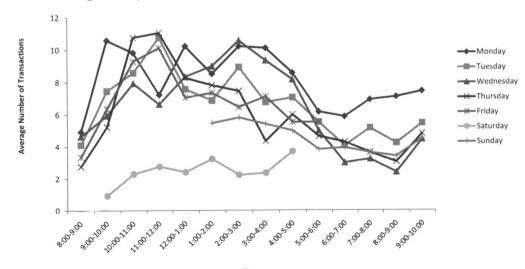

Management Decisions Based on Reference Transaction Length

K-State Libraries is currently in the process of changing its model for delivering public services. The Libraries' administration recently asked the General Reference Unit's coordinator what percentage of the HLHD transactions are actually longer than five minutes. To determine this information the coordinator conducted a "data dump," imported the resulting file into Microsoft Excel, and then sorted the data by length of transaction. Figure 10.7 shows the length of transactions at the HLHD for fall 2007.

Though data about the average number of questions asked at a reference desk during a given hour and the length of those transactions makes it much easier for a reference desk manager to make staffing decisions, this information is not sufficient to ensure that those decisions will be appropriate. This is because, by itself, length of a transaction is a poor measure of a question's difficulty. At K-State Libraries we have observed that length can vary drastically according to a staff person's level of knowledge. For example, we have observed that the average length of transactions fielded by student workers who staff the HLHD is much shorter than those fielded by staff who hold an MLS degree. An additional piece of information about the transactions that could further improve the quality of

Figure 10.7
Length of Reference Transactions, Fall 2007

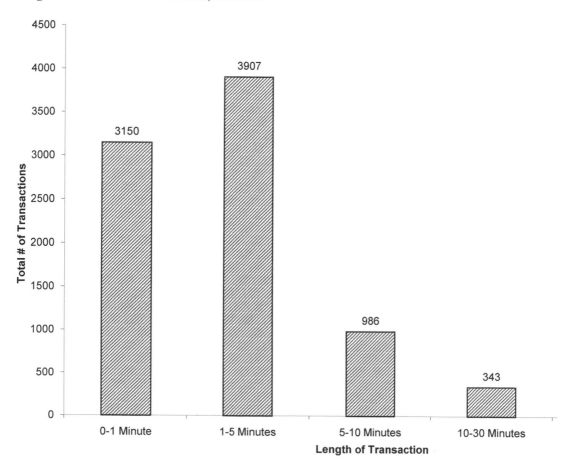

Figure 10.8
Transaction Length by Time of Day, Fall 2007

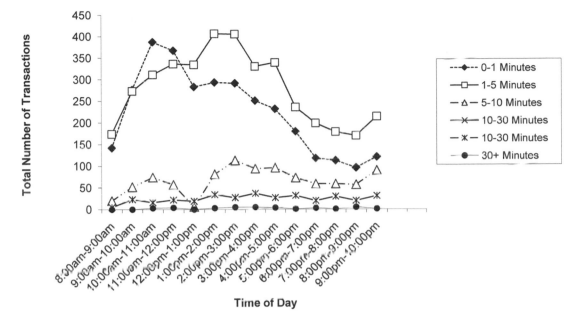

these decisions is the amount of effort it took staff to answer questions. To improve staffing decisions it is helpful to also take into account the content of questions and the effort it took staff to answer them.

To test the assumption that short reference interactions are not challenging, the general reference coordinator plans to add the READ (reference effort assessment data) scale as one of the fields offered at the top of the Libstats' transaction entry form. The READ scale was developed by Bella Karr Gerlich and G. Lynn Berard and launched at Carnegie Mellon in 2003. It measures effort used to answer a reference question. By adding this scale to Libstats, K-State Libraries would be able to see the full picture of how busy the HLHD was at a given time (see Figure 10.8) and how difficult and time consuming the questions were at that time. The scale could be added as another field in the "Add Question" section of Libstats and have a drop-down window for librarians to choose the amount of effort for that particular reference encounter.

When to Offer Virtual Reference Services at the Hale Library Help Desk

The advent of IM, text messaging, and voice-over-Internet protocol (VOIP) services has presented libraries with a number of new and exciting ways to interact with patrons. Libraries that implement these technologies will find that they are faced with several challenging management decisions. Perhaps the most difficult is deciding whether to staff virtual reference services from the main reference desk or to staff them at a location away from the public. Another important decision involves deciding when to offer virtual reference services. In particular, many libraries will need to decide whether to offer virtual reference services during the same hours that in-person reference service is offered or to extend virtual reference services to late evening hours or even to 24 hours a day through a virtual reference cooperative with other libraries.

Figure 10.9
Total IM for Fall 2007 Semester by Hour

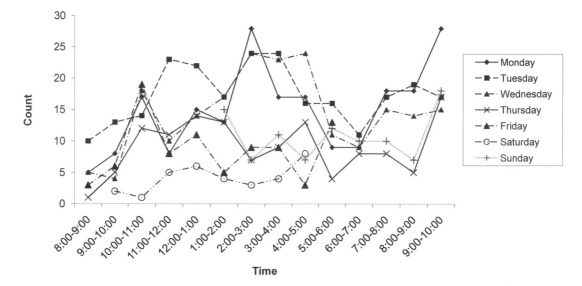

K-State Libraries' General Reference Unit implemented an IM reference service in October of 2006 and a text messaging reference service in December of 2007. These two new services have been offered during the same hours as the unit's phone, in-person, and e-mail reference services. The General Reference Unit is currently considering the possibility of extending virtual reference services for a few hours after the HLHD closes. Throughout the spring 2007 semester, the IM reference service was staffed either from the HLHD or from a computer away from the HLHD. On a typical week, the service was staffed a total of 83 hours: 43 from the HLHD, and 40 away from the HLHD.

Before creating the spring 2008 HLHD schedule, the General Reference Coordinator examined the fall 2007 IM reference transactions to see if the schedule used to staff the IM reference service was still appropriate. The goal became to staff the IM service at librarian's offices during hours when the service is very busy and to keep the IM service on the Help Desk when it is not. The coordinator performed a "data dump" report in Libstats, imported the output file into Excel, and sorted by question format and date to isolate all the IM transactions. She then calculated and graphed (see Figure 10.9) the total number of IM questions received each hour and day of the fall 2007 semester.

The resulting chart reveals that on weekdays of the fall 2007 semester the IM service remained slow until around 11 A.M. each morning, rose to a peak in the early afternoon, and then gradually became slower, until rising again later in the evening. Based on this data, the general reference coordinator decided to staff the IM service from the HLHD for an additional three hours each weekday: 9–11 A.M. and 4–5 P.M.

Increase in IM Traffic, Spring 2008

From January 17, 2007 (the start of the spring semester), to March 1, 2007, K-State Libraries' General Reference Unit received 172 IM reference questions. One year later, the unit received 439 IM reference questions during the equivalent period, an increase of 155 percent. Figure 10.10 shows the number of IM reference questions the General Reference Unit received during each of the six weeks from January 17 to March 1.

Figure 10.10
IM Transactions, January 17–March 1, by Week of the Semester, 2007 and 2008

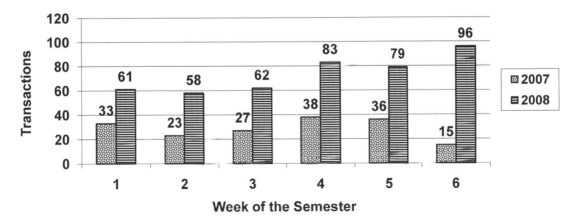

Several factors likely contributed to this 155 percent increase. In early 2008 K-State Libraries initiated an Ask a Librarian marketing campaign and added widgets to its catalog search screen and its main database page. In addition, the IM reference service has been demonstrated in several library instruction sessions conducted since the beginning of 2007.

Additional Technology Staff Members at the Hale Library Help Desk

The beginning of fall semester at Kansas State University is a busy time for new students, many of whom need to learn how to use their K-State e-mail, connect to the wireless network on campus, and use the printing system in the university's computing labs. The university's IT Help Desk, like the HLHD, is located on Hale Library's 2nd floor. Unlike the HLHD, the IT Help Desk is not visible from the public entrances to the 2nd floor. Therefore, though the IT Help Desk is the designated service point for technology questions, many students present those questions to staff at the HLHD. Staff at the HLHD answer many of those questions but refer the majority of them to the IT Help Desk.

The high number of technology questions presented at the HLHD during the first several weeks of each semester can make it difficult for the HLHD staff to provide timely, high quality service to patrons with library-related questions. Seeking a solution to this problem, the general reference coordinator asked K-State's director of information technology to schedule an IT staff member at the HLHD for the first two weeks of the semester. The director did so. The success of this request was largely due to the fact that the general reference coordinator presented the director of information technology with Libstats' data showing that the HLHD fielded a large number of technology questions during the first few weeks of the spring 2007 semester.

Figure 10.11 clearly shows that, even with the additional IT staff member for the first two weeks of the fall 2007 semester, the HLHD still fielded a large number of technology related questions (these transaction numbers do not contain questions that the IT student workers handled during this two-week period). It is interesting to note that there was a large jump (over 100) in the number of such questions from the fourth to the fifth week of the semester. This increase is likely attributable to a rise in the number of papers and presentations that were due or coming due at that time and the number of tests that were on the horizon. As a result of these demands it is likely that more students were discovering that they needed to know how to use the printing system, how to use productivity software,

Figure 10.11
Total Technology Transactions, Fall 2007

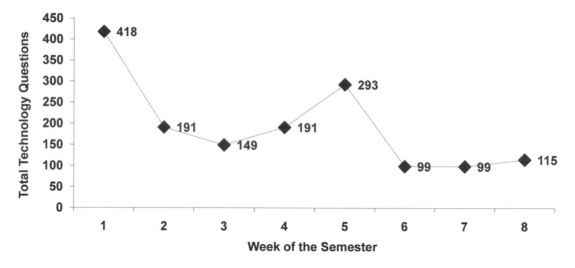

where to borrow AV equipment, and what their user name and password were to access K-State's course management system or gain remote access to K-State's electronic resources.

When Do Various Patrons Ask Questions?

Libstats' data can be used to analyze when a reference desk receives the most questions during the week from different groups (e.g., faculty members, graduate students, or undergraduates).

Figure 10.12
Fall 2007 Faculty Transactions by Day of Week

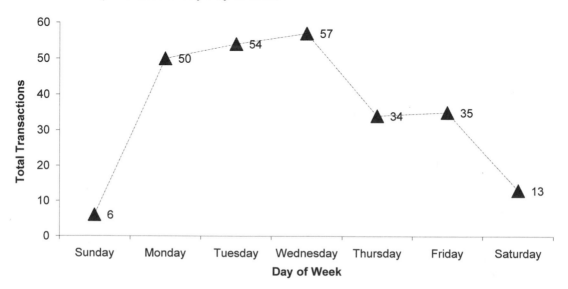

Figure 10.13
Fall 2007 Graduate Students' Transactions by Day of Week

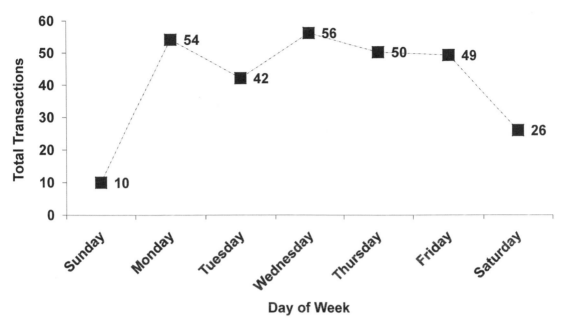

This assessment could be useful for staff scheduling purposes. To examine whether the time distribution of questions fielded by K-State Libraries' General Reference Unit differed according to the status of the questioner, the total number of questions received each day of the week can be charted by the different patron groups served.

The charts for faculty and graduate students (see Figures 10.12 and 10.13, respectively) show that throughout the fall 2007 semester each group asked the most questions on Wednesdays. K-State Libraries' reference managers could use this knowledge to strategically schedule subject librarians on Wednesdays to ensure that the most skilled librarians are available to assist the faculty members and graduate students. The reference managers could also recommend that subject librarians keep their Wednesdays open for faculty referrals and appointments. This is particularly important at K-State Libraries because the HLHD's referral policy states that all in-depth reference questions from faculty and graduate student should be immediately referred to subject specialists.

Undergraduate Students' Questions by Day of Week

Figure 10.14 shows that undergraduates' questions occurred most frequently on Mondays and decreased in frequency throughout the week. The general reference coordinator could use this data to recommend that instruction librarians work at the HLHD on Mondays, Tuesdays, or Wednesdays. This would ensure that the staff who are most adept at helping undergraduates learn to use the catalog and databases would be at the desk when their expertise is most needed.

Most Web-based tracking systems provide a way for a reference manager to export data into Microsoft Excel or an equivalent program. With Excel it is easy to manipulate the data and generate charts. This, in turn, makes it easy for a reference manager to determine staffing levels at reference desks, decide when to offer virtual reference services on or off the desk, analyze increases in particular

Figure 10.14
Fall 2007 Undergraduate Transactions by Day of Week

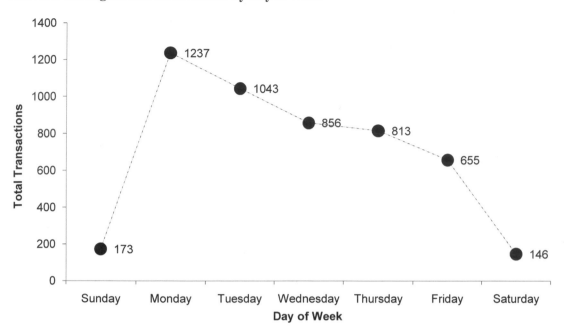

methods of contacting the reference desk, look at how to meet demands for technology expertise, or allocate staff according to question patterns from faculty, graduate students, and undergraduates. Though these are valuable applications of a Web-based tracking system, they are not the only ones. Additionally, a Web-based tracking system can also be used to make decisions about the curricula of library instruction programs and also for staff training and continuing education of library staff.

TRAINING AND CONTINUING EDUCATION

A reference manager can use a Web-based tracking system to make decisions about how to deliver training and continuing education to reference staff. The transactions log can be used to familiarize new library staff with the complexity and types of questions patrons ask. This log can also be used to inform decisions about what content to cover in continuing education sessions offered to library staff. Before providing examples of how K-State Libraries' General Reference Unit uses a Web-based tracking system for staff training and continuing education, it is helpful to discuss HLHD staff reactions to the adoption of Libstats.

K-State Libraries' Staff Perceptions of Libstats

When Libstats was first implemented, the General Reference Unit did not mandate that staff fill in the field for their initials. This was because staff were concerned that they might be penalized if they answered a question incorrectly. This worry was unwarranted, and within the first month of entering transactions into the database all library staff felt comfortable enough with the system to add their initials to each transaction. It is interesting to note that many of the reference generalists, who initially entered "RG" (for "reference generalist") into the initials field, subsequently went and identified which "RG" entries were theirs. Several have reported that they did this because they want to know the exact number of reference transactions they have handled. This number can be useful for the reference generalists to include in their yearly evaluations as a baseline for how many transactions they have fielded but should not be used for evaluation purposes by a supervisor. It also facilitates self-directed, friendly competition among them.

Training Staff to Use a Web-Based Reference Tracking Program

"It's easy to use," responded a K-State Libraries staff member who took a survey about the HLHD's use of Libstats. Thirteen HLHD staff completed the survey in July 2007. Ninety-nine percent of survey respondents reported that they found the process of entering transactions in Libstats "extremely easy" or "fairly easy." When new staff members begin to work at the HLHD, they are asked to spend several hours reading Libstats' entries to become familiar with the questions recorded in the database for the previous semester. This is a good opportunity to show the new staff member how easy the tracking system is, how to use it, and how to make corrections to a transaction entry.

Web Based Reference Tracking Systems Used for Continuing Education and Staff Training

Very few libraries are using the data from their Web-based reference tracking system for the continuing education of library staff members. Barton and Westmantel (2006) created a weblog for reference staff at Michigan State University to keep track of relevant questions so that other staff members who view the site can see what types of questions are asked and how they are answered. Barton and Westmantel (2006) note potential for this type of blog for staff training purposes but had not yet implemented a formalized program. In his article about a reference tracking system used at Texas A&M, Smith (2006) notes the potential for using a tracking system for training and continuing education purposes but has not implemented a formal continuing education and/or training program.

John Weaver, head of Public Services and reference librarian, and other library staff of Pitts Theology Library at Emory University, implemented a Web-based tracking system in 2006. This home-grown system has a free text box in which library staff can record the reference question and, if applicable, what the librarian did to answer the question. This free text box is keyword searchable and enables all public service staff to read other staff members' transactions.

Reference Batting Practice

The public service staff subsequently implemented a formalized continuing education program called "Reference Batting Practice" in 2006. Lakly et al. describe this continuing education program as "a time for us [library staff] to share both good and bad experiences—to celebrate our 'home runs' and reflect upon our 'strike outs' (the times when we felt we failed to adequately meet a patron's needs)" (2008, 168). This program worked well to introduce several new library staff members to the library's specialized reference resources. It also helped show them how to conduct an appropriate reference interview.

K-State Libraries has found many uses for Libstats' data in reference staff continuing education and training. Using Pitts Theology Library's Reference Batting Practice as a guide, the General Reference Unit implemented its own version in 2007 and added monthly subject librarian training sessions. Many of the responses to the HLHD staff survey about Libstats suggest recognition of the benefits of using Libstats' data for continuing education and staff training. Following are some suggestions:

- "I read them so I can learn how other library staff answered reference questions and to see if I could have been able to answer them the same way. I also like to learn about the technical problems the Help Desk may be having."

- "I search to find answers to frequently asked questions."

- "I like that there is a record of the actual transaction, and you can learn from what other people have done."

- "I think it's useful to know what has been going on, especially if there are ongoing or similar questions. Also, it's a learning tool because sometimes people give different answers than I would."

K-State Libraries uses Reference Batting Practice to encourage members of the General Reference team to evaluate the quality of the service they provide. Prior to a session of Reference Batting Practice, each member of the team is asked to review his or her recent transactions by searching Libstats for the initials they use when recording transactions. The member is instructed to use the criteria that were established by the entire team to identify a few exemplary transactions (grand slam, home run, double), a few moderate successes (single, walk, bunt), and a few opportunities for improvement (strike out, hitting into a double play). This introspective analysis of reference transactions helps each member of the team recognize what he or she may need to learn more about or spend more time learning how to do.

Needs and Strengths of Staff Members

A reference manager can read through the transaction entries to determine if there are individual or group training needs and identify particular strengths of a reference staff member or group of individuals. Consider, for example, a transaction in which the staff person wrote in the question field that a patron was looking for a particular American Society for Testing Materials Special Technical Publication number 1256 but notes in the answer section that he or she could not find the publication. The reference manager could see this as an opportunity to have the engineering librarian visit the General Reference Unit and explain how to handle this type of question. For another example, consider a transaction in which the staff person wrote in the question field that a patron was looking for finance journals and recorded in the answer field that he or she showed the patron how to locate the K-State Libraries homepage, how to search the catalog, the databases, and the e-journals for specific finance journals, and also gave the patron a stacks guide to help locate the journal articles the patron will need to pull from the library stacks. A reference manager could take this entry to an upcoming reference meeting and present it in as an excellent example of how to handle that type of question.

Answering Certain Types of Questions

Reference librarians in academic institutions are well aware that they may be routinely approached with questions from students who have assignments requiring them to find a particular resource in the library, use a certain database, or find documents that meet specific criteria. These assignments can be especially challenging when the faculty member has not checked to see if the library still subscribes to the particular journal listed in the assignment or to see if the library may have upgraded from providing a database on CD-Rom to providing it via the Web. An advantage to using Libstats is that staff can use a transaction's question and answer field to provide each other with useful information about these particular assignments. If the staff person used the expected keywords in the question or answer field, other staff can easily retrieve their answers by searching Libstats. An example of this practice is shown below. Here a library staff member was asked

"scavenger hunt" questions and shares how to find the answers. The staff member also notes which academic department gave the assignment.
Libstats Entry:

Question: Where can I find the volume and issue numbers for January–March 1983 issues of *Time*? Is the microfilm collection stored in alphabetical or call number order? How can I find out the major headline on the *New York Times* for December 8, 1941?
Answer: v. 121, no. 1 thru v. 121, no. 13/call number order/Microforms (3rd Floor, Hale) *Note: this is a Speech "scavenger hunt" assignment we also got thru IM last week.

If another patron came to the Help Desk after this question was recorded, and asked for help with the same assignment, the library staff member could type "scavenger hunt" into Libstats' quick search box, and very quickly benefit from the work of his or her colleague. This would save time and help the library staff member focus attention on teaching the patron how to find sources.

Use for Specific Class Assignments

A Libstats' survey respondent stated that he or she would use Libstats "in case of recurring class project questions." When questions for a class assignment are answered at the HLHD, library staff members routinely cite the department and the course number in the answer field. This allows other staff members to search for the course number and pull up all transactions that contain it. Below is an example in which the library staff member input the course number and retrieved information on how to handle the assignment.
Libstats Entry:

Question: Marketing class assignment MKTG 542—looking for industry info using list of sources from instructor
Answer: student was looking for *U.S. Market Trends and Forecasts*—it is in Stacks due to old age. We looked at the Marketing & International Business subject guide page. Used Business and Company Resource Center, Industry: Child Care—had some more recent info that looked helpful. She also used ABI/Inform for articles.

Technical Questions

The entries in Libstats often describe the current status of the public printers in Hale Library, the machines that enable patrons to add money to a Kansas State identification card, K-State's wireless network, or the scanners or copiers in Hale Library. This information is very useful to staff who work reference shifts during or shortly after the transaction occurred. When the transactions are recorded in Libstats, staff no longer need to spend a great deal of time sending out constant e-mail updates, writing notes, and repeating previous attempts to solve the malfunctions. One library staff member alluded to this in a response to the Libstats' survey when he or she wrote that one use of Libstats was to "see if there have been any computer or technical problems." This response also reveals that staff are aware that Libstats can be used as a form of staff communication. Here is an example of a Libstats' entry demonstrating use of the database for communicating about technical issues:
Libstats Entry:

Question: What does it mean when the Cash to Chip machine says "Card is Mute"?
Answer: Not sure—anyone know this? [Yes—from staff member X—it means that their chip is bad. Sometimes you can fix it by rubbing it with a piece of cloth, such as your shirt. Cotton seems to work best. But if that doesn't work, they need to go to the ID card center and get a new one].

This Libstats' entry is also an excellent example for demonstrating how the tool can be used for training and continuing education. The staff member who initially recorded the transaction did not know the printing system (Cash to Chip machine) error codes and did not know how to solve them. Another staff member read this entry and provided an excellent answer. By recording the answer in Libstats, rather than providing it only in person or by e-mail, the staff person made the knowledge available to all Libstats' users.

Monthly Subject Librarian Meetings

Since August 2007 one or two subject librarians have visited with the General Reference team once a month. Before a subject librarian visits with the General Reference team, the General Reference Unit's coordinator generates a list of Libstats' transactions related to the subject librarian's areas of responsibility by doing quick keyword searches on various topics, for example, English, modern languages, education, history, art, law, business, sociology, or music. The coordinator provides the list to the subject librarian, who evaluates the answers to see if the most appropriate resources were used to answer the questions, provides feedback about the answers, and suggests alternate resources. Since beginning these sessions in August, the General Reference team has participated in training on English, modern languages, law, history, business, economics, education, government documents and maps, art, and performing arts. Future meetings have been planned for social sciences, science, and engineering.

USES FOR INSTRUCTION

The line between reference services and library instruction is blurry; reference questions often evolve into short library instruction sessions. As an academic library, K-State Libraries focus on developing the research and information literacy skills of those it serves. Questions received by service desks indicate user instruction needs. Capitalizing on the value of the rich data held within Libstats' question and answer fields, K-State Libraries' Instruction Unit analyzed the data to inform instruction sessions.

The initial step in the instruction unit's analysis of Libstats was to export all the questions and answers using the "data dump with questions and answers" export option. All questions from the first entry on January 3, 2007, through May 3, 2007, were included in the analysis. The next step in the process was creating classification categories based on content to be applied to each question. These categories represented the information need of the user. The categories were developed by examining the first 1,000 entries in the Libstats' database. After this review the categories were examined to ensure they represented information useful for library instruction and would fully capture the information needed. The next step was time consuming and tedious but yielded valuable results: each of the 4,674 entries was analyzed and labeled with a category.

The categories for this analysis project were created with the intent of capturing the patron's initial need for instruction. For example, if a patron requested assistance locating resources on a topic, the question was classified as "Topic Research." Although the reference transaction may have also included catalog instruction and finding a call number on the shelf, the patron initially requested help with beginning topic research.

In response to common technical questions, key distinctions were made for select requests that were somewhat similar in nature. Most notably, requests for instruction regarding how to print were differentiated from reports of technical issues with printers.

The results of this analysis primarily reinforced previously assumed instruction needs. The six most common information needs expressed are, in descending order of frequency: known item request, topic research, technical assistance, assistance locating a call number, and help printing. While not unexpected, these results indicate the relative importance of instruction on these topics and support decision-making in designing library instruction curriculum.

Figure 10.15
Spring 2007 Monthly Printing Instruction Requests

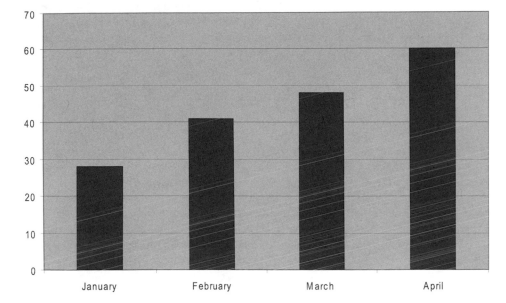

Beyond initial totals for each category, questions can also be analyzed by month, time of day, day of week, and date. This information is valuable for scheduling classes on topics including topic research or using specific databases. For example, topic research requests steadily grew in demand throughout the spring 2007 semester. The slight decline in the total number of requests for the month of March is likely attributable to spring break, as most students vacate campus for an entire week. The data for requests for the topic of how to print follow a similar pattern (see Figure 10.15). Similarly, requests for information about library service hours nearly doubled on Sundays compared to other days of the week, indicating a need for more information about library hours on Sunday.

While findings from this analysis reinforced the current direction of instruction efforts at K-State Libraries, the results also inform future choices regarding instruction services by providing precise information. Notably, analysis of reference data identified that patrons needed assistance using the printing system. Although printing had been included in introductory library tours, the data suggests that it should be addressed in detail and included in sessions beyond introductory tours.

Future analysis of Libstats' entries could identify possibly differing needs for the fall and summer semesters. Additionally, ongoing analysis could identify short-term and long-term trends in the information needs of users.

USES RELATED TO REFERENCE SERVICES

Knowledge Base

After recording transactions for several months, the database is likely to contain a wealth of useful information. The fact that staff can search the database by keyword means that they can quickly mine this information to help them assist patrons. However, it is important to realize that if the records in the database contain only the actual answers delivered by staff, then no single answer is likely to provide a comprehensive set of information about the patron's topic of inquiry. For example, no staff member is likely to answer a question about book reviews by providing a full list of all the electronic and print ources that index these, strategies for searching those sources for book reviews, and contact informa- on for other individuals in the community who are experts at finding book reviews. Indeed, the col- ctive set of recorded answers to questions about book reviews is not likely to include all this information. The same is true for nearly every other topic patrons inquire about: each answer will be customized to the unique needs of the patron and heavily influenced by the experience and prefer- ences of the staff person providing the answer. None will address all the details a staff person might need to answer other questions on the topic.

One way to solve this problem is to use an approach similar to that discussed in the next chapter of this volume: use the collection of records to identify patrons' frequently asked questions, and then create and maintain answers to these questions. In the case of the Libstats' database, these answers can be entered into the database just like any other record. Because the Libstats' database has no limit to the amount of text that can be entered in a record's answer field, the answers can provide a thorough, easy-to-read orientation to the topic in the question field. If the entries are populated with a variety of keywords and a special code that indicates the entry is artificial (e.g., "artificialentry"), then staff can quickly find up-to-date information about everything from recommended resources, to names of individuals or organizations who have expertise related to the question, to tips for searching databases, to troubleshooting instructions. For example, staff looking for information to help a patron who needs to have a test proctored could search for an artificial entry by typing "proctor artificialen- try" into the database's keyword search box. There is no limit to the number or scope of such entries.

Improved Referrals

When members of K-State Libraries' General Reference Team make a referral to another member of the staff, they often send an e-mail to give that person advanced notice. Rather than repeat the description of the question and answer they entered in Libstats, they can simply link to the record of the transaction url and provide the login and password. Since anyone with access to the database can edit a transaction, the person to whom the question was referred can add information to the record for that transaction. This practice can make the database even more useful as a knowledge base and staff training tool.

Searchable and Browsable FAQ

One way to maintain an FAQ is to create a separate installation of Libstats and provide a link to it from a Web page, along with the login and password. Although it is not easy to remove the entry fields and buttons from the interface, it is possible to make the data entry portion of the interface less con- spicuous by removing all but one element from each of the fields and renaming that element "n/a." When populating the FAQ, the actual reference transaction record could be consulted to determine which questions really are most frequently asked.

Keep Reference Desk Staff Apprised of Important Information

Some reference desks function as communication hubs, channeling and routing information among staff as well as between staff and the public. When such desks are operated by a large group of staff, it can be very difficult to make sure that all of them are kept up-to-date about time sensitive information, including the status of problems with the building or technology, messages that need to be delivered to patrons or other staff, notes about difficult questions the desk has been fielding, reminders about a change in policy or procedures, or the availability of new resources.

Libstats can be used as a platform for centralizing and archiving this communication. If all members of the staff apply the same code (e.g., "fyifyi") to information intended as internal communication, other members of the staff can retrieve the communications simply by searching Libstats for that code. Since staff can edit the message, they can append additional relevant information to the initial message, rather than create an endless string of new messages. And when the message becomes dated, the can demote it by changing the code to something else (e.g., "oldfyi"). When used in this manner, Libstats combines the best features of a wiki and a blog.

Give Insight into What Happens at the Reference Desk

If staff or members of the public ever ask what happens at the reference desk, one quick way to provide a great deal of insight is to show them the full set of reference transaction records. If staff dutifully record every transaction, it should serve as a reasonably good substitute for the experience of actually observing the desk for hours on end. If your library wishes to promote the value of reference services, the collection of records can be combed for actual transactions that clearly convey the expertise of reference staff and demonstrate the benefit the service provides to patrons. The collection of records can also be combed for examples to promote reference service to administration, friends groups, and other units within a library. And, of course, staff can facilitate this by applying a code as they record interesting transactions.

USES FOR ASSESSING SERVICE NEEDS

William A. Katz's (2002) explication of his classic categorization scheme for reference transactions reveals that the scope of questions fielded by reference services can be quite broad. More recent content analyses of reference transactions at academic libraries reveal that this diversity is found in both in-person transactions and virtual transactions (see, for instance: Fennewald 2006; Houlson, McCready, and Pfahl 2006; Mosley 2007). A portion of questions pertain to strategies, tools, and procedures for finding information resources. Others relate to the library itself, either as physical space or virtual space; these include navigational questions, questions about staff, and questions about hours and capacities of various services. Unless staff at a reference desk are intimidating, or the desk is strewn with signs advising patrons to ask only "library questions," there is also likely to be an odd mix of questions regarding needs unrelated to the library's self-described roles (Mosley 2007). At the HLHD, for example, staff field numerous questions about the location of K-State's buildings, the availability of campus services, and directions to locations in the city of Manhattan.

Managers could interpret almost every reference transaction as evidence of the need to improve some facet of some service in the library. From this perspective, the full complement of reference transactions is a lengthy testimony of shortcomings, and concomitantly a trove of data regarding opportunities to better meet patrons' needs. Below are some key categories and examples based on data from the HLHD.

Opportunities for New Services

All libraries are visited by patrons who have needs that remain completely or partially unmet. Some of these needs are revealed at reference desks. For example, any time reference staff are unable to identify a referral to a local, free service, there may be evidence of either the need for a service or a need for that service to be better promoted. At the HLHD, we are in the fortunate position of being able to give referrals to free, local services for most needs that we ourselves can not fulfill. We are not, however, always able to find such referrals for all persons who request writing assistance, test proctoring, access to textbooks, or access to test preparation materials.

Opportunities to Expand Services

Anytime reference staff provide a referral to a service that is not conveniently located or not currently available, the transaction may suggest an opportunity to establish the service closer to the library or make it available at different hours. Examples we routinely encounter at the HLHD include requests for access to a fax machine, access to a subject specialist, access to our Special Collections, and access to a place to purchase or borrow headphones.

Opportunities to Better Promote Services

It has been our experience at the HLHD that patrons are often unaware of several of the services that have been made available to them. While we enjoy informing them about our interlibrary loan services, the fact that we have scanners they can use for free, and that we can place a recall for a book that has been checked out, it is clear to us that our enjoyment is made possible only by a woeful lack of information among our current and potential patrons. Each happy revelation is evidence of an opportunity to better educate patrons through a combination of marketing and instruction.

Opportunities to Make Services Easier to Find and Use

Many of the transactions that occur at the HLHD would likely not occur if our services and systems were easier to find and more intuitive. Every request for directions to the rest room or the Reserves desk or to our collection of DVDs is a suggestion for a more intuitive spatial layout or improved access to, and promotion of, directories, maps, and signs. Each explanation of how to print, how to find articles, or what to do with a call number may be a call to make systems more intuitive or instructions more visible and easier to understand.

Opportunities to Discontinue or Reduce Services

Most of the reference transaction record speaks to the need for additions to service offerings. To a limited extent, it can also hint at the lack of need for some current offerings. These hints can take two forms: information from patrons revealing that they prefer a modern service (e.g., scanning) over an older one (e.g., photocopying), or absence of requests for a service that is mediated by reference staff (e.g., materials behind a desk with a sign directing patrons to see reference staff for access, yet the staff never has requests to access those materials, suggesting that the space may be better occupied by something else).

Opportunities to Increase Demands on Services

Absences of requests for assistance are tricky to interpret. They can arise when systems are so well promoted and so easy to use that needs are met without intervention. They can also arise when there is no demand for a service. Before concluding that the service could be discontinued it is important to consider whether or not it is a service for which a demand should exist. If it is, then the record can be taken as evidence of the need to either promote the service or change demands placed on patrons so they acquire a need for the service. At the HLHD we encounter few patrons who ask, "Can you help me find the most highly regarded works on my topic?" or "How can I be sure I have found everything about my topic?" While this absence could signify that patrons know how to do this or are contacting subject specialists directly, we suspect it indicates that not all instructors are placing high demands on the quality of evidence students present in papers. The absence could be a call to convince instructors of the value of impelling their students to learn how to find the best available evidence and how to discriminate between good evidence and that which is of questionable relevance or suspect authoritativeness.

Opportunities to Improve Collections

If reference staff record details about what patrons are trying to find and whether or not the staff are able to find enough to meet their information needs, the complete set of transaction records can become a useful aid to collection development. It can augment interlibrary loan request data by surfacing additional desired items that patrons did npt have the time or inclination to request. If course numbers are in included in records of transactions about course assignments, the approach Bennett, Berg, and Brothen describe in the next chapter can be used to improve collection support for specific courses. The complete set of transaction records can also reveal gaps in the collection's coverage of topics and information formats. For example, the records of transactions at the HLHD reveal a demand for more travel guides, audio books, online indexes to older articles, popular fiction titles, popular DVDs, and language guides in CD format.

USING LIBSTATS

K-State Libraries' General Reference Unit decided to adopt Libstats for four main reasons: (1) it is a Web-based database that supports simultaneous entries from multiple locations; (2) it is a free, open-source program that is fairly easy to install and customize; (3) its operators can easily and quickly enter transactions and edit them; (4) it has a sufficient number of fields to enable us to collect the information we want. Once we began using it, we realized that it has a number of additional properties that enable us to employ the data in creative ways, including the following:

- Its built-in export function makes it easy to export all the metadata to a program where it can be manipulated, analyzed, and combined with other data sets.
- The files it creates are small, making it easy to keep all the data in a single file.
- The fields for recording questions and answers are extremely large, making it possible to record extensive information about each transaction.
- Each record has a unique, static url.
- Operators can enter and edit transactions from any computer with Web access.
- The user interface enables keyword searching across all fields.
- The administration module makes it easy to create separate user interfaces, which can contain a unique set of elements for each field.
- Each user interface dumps data into a common database, but the search functions only search the records saved via that interface.

CAPTURING AND ANALYZING INFORMATION RELATED TO PATRONS' NEEDS

Increasing Quality and Size of Sample

To make the reference transaction records maximally useful for discerning information needs, it is essential to decrease the gap between the number of needs present among a population of patrons and the number of needs revealed in the reference transaction records. Several practices are particularly helpful. First, reference desk staff can increase the likelihood that a patron with a question will approach them by behaving in an inviting and friendly manner (Swope and Katzer 1972) by increasing service hours, by expanding access channels, and by improving desk visibility (Pierson 1985). Second, they can help patrons reveal (and sometimes discover) their information needs by conducting reference interviews that maximize use of neutral, open-ended questions (RUSA 2004; Dervin and Dewdney 1986). Third, they can ensure that expressed needs are visible in transaction records by recording the needs as fully as possible. This requires staff to refrain from the desire to record only interesting or novel information needs. It also requires them to avoid the temptation to express needs using a single term or phrase, a practice that masks the complexity of the true need. Consider, for instance, the difference in what can be learned from a record that has only the word "fax" and a record that has "Patron wanted to send a document to a person. He requested a fax machine. It turned out that a combination of scanning and e-mailing would meet his needs even better."

Facilitating Data Analysis

The data produced when staff develop their own methods for recording information needs will be rife with inconsistencies in terminology and levels of detail, rendering analysis quite difficult. One way to mitigate this problem is to develop a coding scheme for routine information needs and encourage staff to use the codes as an aid, not a substitute, for detailed description. The codes could be applied through fields or added to the text of the question or answer.

A useful approach for developing these codes is to record transactions without the codes for a period of time and then read through the collection of records and develop a list of common information needs, e.g. how to determine where to go for a call number, or how to find an article based on a

Figure 10.16
Color Printing Questions for 2007 by Hour

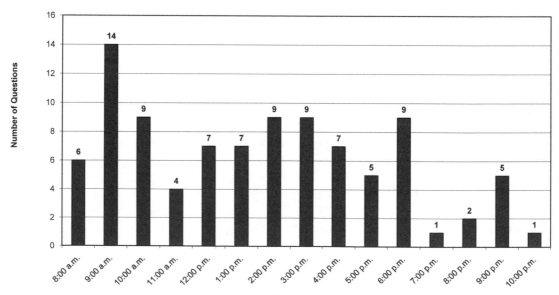

citation. Each element on the list could then be assigned an alphanumeric code, e.g. "callnum1," "direction3." Even more sophisticated schemes could be created that use faceted approaches (e.g., recording the subject of the inquiry as a word and the type of service need as a number). Regardless of what scheme is devised it is essential that the set of codes be easy to apply. Therefore, the list should be fairly short, and definitions for the codes should be easy to find.

Performing Data Analyses

Though the most compelling reason to record information needs is to see their full scope, there are also a number of questions that can be asked about the individual needs. Basic questions include how many times was the need expressed, who expressed it, and when was it expressed. More advanced questions include which needs were commonly expressed in conjunction with which others, and what external factors might influence the likelihood that a need would be expressed. Clearly, the ability to answer these questions depends on the availability of relevant data.

The exact procedure for performing the analysis will depend on the nature of the software used for recording the transactions, the procedures and policies used for expressing information needs, and the availability of software for conducting statistical analyses. If Libstats is being used to record transactions, the first steps in performing the analyses are to decide which information needs will be analyzed and to tag each manifestation of that need with a unique code. These codes can be applied at the time the transactions are recorded or at the time of analysis. Once the codes are applied (for instance,

Figure 10.17
Color Printing Questions for 2007 by Month

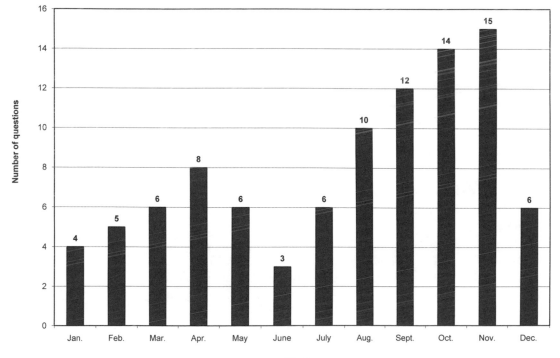

Figure 10.18
Color Printing Questions for 2007 by Patron Type

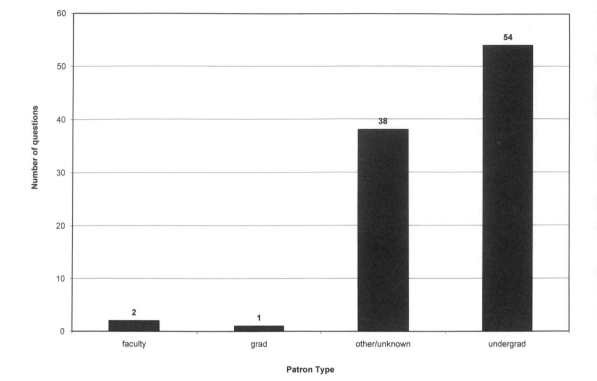

by typing them into the question field), the next step is to export the data into a program that makes it easy to manipulate and graph data, e.g., Excel, SPSS, or SAS.

Examples of graphs that can be obtained from Excel are shown in Figures 10.16 through 10.19. Figure 10.16 shows the number of times patrons asked for help sending a print job to Hale Library's color printer by hour of day. Figure 10.17 show the breakdown of these requests over the course of the 2007 calendar year. Figure 10.18 shows the breakdown of these requests by patron type. And Figure 10.19 shows the breakdown by channel through which the question was asked.

CAVEATS AND BENEFITS

Caveats

Though we are proponents of collecting and analyzing data, we must caution against implementing so many special codes and stringent rules for recording questions and answers that staff become overwhelmed and disenchanted with the tracking system. The desire to understand what is happening at the desk and why it is happening must be balanced against the much more important need to ensure that staff are able and motivated to provide high quality service. It must also be balanced against the need to ensure that a transaction will be recorded in more or less the same way, regardless of who records it. If the rules for deciding which entities to select in the metadata fields are complicated or there are numerous rules for entering the question and answer, chances are good that similar

Figure 10.19
Color Printing Questions for 2007 by Question Format

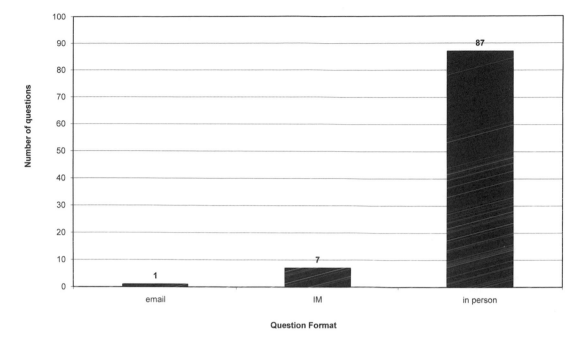

transactions are being recorded in widely disparate ways. If the variability in recording practices is especially high, it will be difficult to gain accurate insights from descriptive analyses. It will also be difficult for staff to use keyword searching to find answers to questions.

When data is used to help inform decisions, it is important to honestly appraise its reliability and validity, and adjust the influence it plays in the decision-making process accordingly. Analyses of data about patrons' needs are, in all honesty, likely to have less than complete reliability, no matter how intense the staff's training program, how thorough the policies governing recording practices, or how dedicated and vigilant the staff. There are simply too many factors at a reference desk that can prevent staff from consistently recording information needs. Validity is also likely to be lower than optimal, as expressions of needs are not always reliable indicators of actual needs. For these reasons, managers must avoid the temptation to weigh the data and the analyses based on it too heavily.

The data has one additional glaring weakness: it cannot tell a manager what decisions to make. It can suggest possible courses of action, pose questions that need to be addressed, and spark fruitful discussion. But, even under the most optimal conditions, it cannot be a substitute for wisdom, experience, and judgment.

Benefits

Based on the preceding discussion, it might seem that the entire enterprise of collecting and analyzing transaction data for evidence of service needs is a waste of time. Nothing could be further from the truth. Indeed, it is because we are so convinced of the value of collecting and considering this data that we present these caveats. We do not want uncritical use of data to cast a cloud over the entire data collection enterprise.

The value of collecting and analyzing data that contains information about patrons' information needs goes far beyond the ability of the analyses to aid decision-making. One of the greatest benefits is that it helps managers effectively present cases to administration and funding agencies. Logical arguments augmented with illustrative data are extremely compelling and speak of thoroughness and professionalism. There are several other, less obvious benefits. First, the content of the questions and answers in the database can serve as the basis for an inventory of training needs and support arguments for the need for a well-trained staff. Second, the data is likely to immediately suggest a number of low-cost, low-effort improvements to services. These improvements can bolster staff morale and promote the value of the library. Third, if the data shows that patrons have questions about services provided by individuals or organizations outside the library, managers can act on the data by establishing partnerships and information exchange procedures. Fourth, and perhaps most importantly, the practice of recording transactions and analyzing patrons' information needs helps engender a desire among staff to surface needs of patrons, rather than hide them. When managers ask reference staff to discover and record needs, they are helping the staff understand the mission of the library. They are also inspiring them to interact with patrons in a way that will clearly demonstrate that the library is dedicated to helping patrons succeed.

CONCLUSION

In this chapter we have described how both an information-rich set of records of reference transactions and the system used to create that set of records can be used to improve services, both within the library that provides the reference service and within that library's extended community. We have shown that there are numerous ways to exploit both the primary data within the set of records and the secondary data derived from analysis of that set of records. In addition, we have argued that some of the most important benefits of such a program and system extend not from its products, but from the activity itself. Hopefully, we have successfully conveyed some of the excitement for such systems that led one adoptee to call it "a godsend," another to call it "the best thing since sliced bread," and several to call it "fantastic," "excellent," or "great."

We have revealed several benefits that explain this enthusiasm. First, when transactions are recorded in a database that can be browsed and searched, reference staff can use the set of records as a knowledge base and a communication platform. This, in turn, can improve the accuracy and speed of their answers, engender a sense of community, and bolster efforts to promote the value of reference service. Second, a record with information about the nature of patrons' questions can be examined to create an inventory of patrons' information needs. This inventory can inform decisions about what content to provide in instruction sections for patrons and training sessions for staff. In addition, the ability to examine how the nature of questions varies over time makes it possible to create optimal schedules for both types of efforts. Third, the easy access to counts of questions over time and counts of question formats enables a reference desk manager to optimally staff desks and services. Intelligent decisions about which staff to place at which points at which times are more possible when information about the nature of questions over time and across formats is added to the mix. Fourth, details about the needs that led patrons to seek assistance can be used to develop new services, modify existing services, and in some cases, eliminate services.

It is important to realize that we have only touched on a small portion of the possible ways reference transaction records can be used. Collectively, the full set of records provides a rich source of information about patrons' needs, attitudes, and understandings of library systems. A library that is committed to doing all it can to reach out to patrons will mirror Google and Amazon in investing significant resources in merging this data with other information about patrons' needs and leveraging the data to increase the relevance of its services. Such a library could also strive to improve the accuracy and reliability of its reference transaction records through means such as training to standardize the way transactions are recorded and validation studies to provide feedback about the accuracy of the records.

Even as we have laid out arguments for implementing and creatively using reference transaction recording systems, we have also cautioned against misuse of these systems and misapplication of the information contained in the records. It is vital that the system not be applied in a way that burdens staff, engenders fear, or impedes performance. Attempts to exert too much control and to record too much data will likely stifle creativity, prevent buy-in, and compromise both reliability and validity. It is equally important to recognize the limitations of statistics extrapolated from a set of records that is not completely reliable or accurate. Statistical data should contribute to wisdom, not trump it.

Though we are data enthusiasts, we acknowledge that our arguments for following our lead rest almost entirely on the testimony of reference staff and appeals to logic. In the future we would like to put this hypothesis to the test by evaluating the impact of reference services before and after reference units implement a program of recording and mining reference transaction data. If the before and after comparisons were to show no significant improvements in subjective or objective outcome measures, we would be among the first to cease our data mining programs and look for more fruitful means of making our services more valuable to patrons.

We believe that the results of such a test would show that libraries and their communities have much to gain by investing time and effort in recording the content of reference transactions. Though we know that some libraries will await such evidence, we encourage them to take a bold leap. The risks are minimal, but the potential gains are enormous. And interestingly, the likelihood that gains would accrue increases as more libraries take this leap and share ideas about best practices for recording and analyzing data from reference transactions.

REFERENCES

Ackerman, Erick. 2007. Program assessment in academic libraries: An introduction for assessment practitioners. *Research & Practice in Assessment* 1 (2): 1–9.

Arnold, Julie, and Neal Kaske. 2005. Evaluating the quality of chat service. *Portal: Libraries and the Academy* 5 (2): 177–93.

Babu, B. R., and Ann O'Brien. 2000. Web OPAC interfaces: An overview. *The Electronic Library* 18 (5): 316–30.

Baker, Sharon L., and F. Wilfrid Lancaster. 1991. *Measurement and evaluation of library services*. Arlington, VA: Information Resources Press.

Barton, Emily, and Arlene Westmantel. 2006. Ref logs now. *Library Journal (1976)* 131 (16): 28–30.

Carter, David S., and J. Janes. 2000. Unobtrusive data analysis of digital reference questions and service at the Internet Public Library: An exploratory study. *Library Trends* 49 (2): 251–65.

Chowdhury, Gobinda. 2002. Digital libraries and reference services: Present and future. *Journal of Documentation* 58 (3): 258–83.

Ciucki, Marcella. 1977. Recording reference/information service activities: A study of forms currently used. *Reference Quarterly* 16 (4): 273–83.

Dervin, B., and P. Dewdney. 1986. Neutral questioning: A new approach to the reference interview. *Reference Quarterly* 25 (4): 506–13.

Fennewald, J. 2006. Same questions, different venue: An analysis of in-person and online questions. In *Assessing reference and user services in a digital age*, edited by Eric Novotny. Binghamton, NY: Haworth Information Press.

Gerlich, Bella Karr, and G. Lynn Berard. 2007. *The READ (reference effort assessment data) scale study, 2007*. http://bkarrgerlich.googlepages.com/ (accessed March 16, 2008).

Houlson, V., K. McCready, and C. S. Pfahl. 2006. A window into our patron's needs: Analyzing data from chat transcripts. *Internet Reference Services Quarterly* 11 (4): 19–39.

Katz, William A. 2002. *Basic information services*. Vol. 1 of *Introduction to reference work*. 8th ed. Boston, MA: McGraw-Hill.

Lakly, David, Aimee Morgan, Danielle Theiss-White, and John Weaver. 2008. Refereed reference: Measuring and enhancing library services through a Web-based tracking system. In *Summary of proceedings, 61st annual conference of the American Theological Library Association*, 163–72. Chicago: American Theological Library Association.

Lavoie, Brian, Lorcan Dempsey, and Lynne Sillipigni Connaway. 2006. Making data work harder. *Library Journal* 131 (1): 40–42.

Mosley, P. A. 2007. Assessing user interactions at the desk nearest the front door. *Reference & User Services Quarterly* 47 (2): 159–67.

Novotony, Eric. 2002. *Reference service statistics & assessment: Executive summary, SPEC Kit 268*. Washington, DC: ARL.

Phillips, Sarah M. 2004. The search for accuracy in reference desk statistics. *Community & Junior College Libraries* 12 (3): 49–60.

Pierson, R. 1985. Appropriate settings for reference service. *Reference services review* 13 (3): 13–29.

Radford, Marie. 2006. Encountering virtual users: A qualitative investigation of interpersonal communication in chat reference. *Journal of the American Society for Information Science and Technology* 57 (8): 1046–59.

Reference and User Services Association (RUSA) of the American Library Association. 2004. *Guidelines for the behavioral performance of reference and information service providers*. www.ala.org/ala/mgrps/divs/rusa/resources/guidelines/guidelinesbehavioral.cfm.

Smith, Michael M. 2006. A tool for all places: A Web-based reference statistics system. *Reference Services Review* 34 (2): 298–315.

Swope, M. J., and J. Katzer. 1972. Why don't they ask questions? The silent majority. *RQ* 12 (2): 161–66.

CHAPTER 11

Maximizing the Value of Reference Data: A Case Study

ERIKA BENNETT, SOMMER BERG, AND ERIN BROTHEN

ABSTRACT

Reference interactions typically produce vast quantities of data, and reference activity levels are frequently cited when reporting on library usage. This is only half the picture that reference data can provide. Reference interactions offer a unique opportunity for librarians to learn what gaps exist from users' perspectives. Strategic collection of detailed reference interaction data is central to practical decision-making about library services. By analyzing reference data the librarians at Capella University's online library have been able to strategically schedule reference hours, save reference transaction time through a knowledge base, produce relevant guides and tutorials, provide concrete evidence for course development participation, modify research assignments, improve collection development, and better market the current collections. This chapter will explain what reference data is collected, how it is analyzed, and the specific activities that have been implemented based on that data.

INTRODUCTION

A greater call for accountability, affecting educational and government institutions, has forged the ideal of a library "culture of assessment." In this climate discussions about libraries resonate of Darwinism; contributors to the 2005 Library Assessment Conference in Thessaloniki, Greece, characterized the increasingly competitive struggle for diminishing resources in libraries across the world as a battle for survival (Kyrillidou 2005).

Nurturing a "culture of assessment" has been presented as a solution for libraries struggling to prove their worth (Jourbert and Lee 2007; Lakos 1999; Lakos and Phipps 2004). In practice, however, this state of perpetual evaluation may feel like pointless busywork if it does not yield pragmatic results. Electronic resources and measuring equipment allow us to collect more information than ever about the habits of our users, but there is no accepted standard for determining which of these data sets convincingly demonstrate the value of library services to our stakeholders. Different institutions maintain different institutional goals. Additionally, the sheer variety of library interactions can lead to confusion, since not every library query contributes to a measurable learning outcome. Some simply lead to the bathroom; others unlock the capacity for lifelong learning. As Schrader asks when reviewing Canada's library data, "What do these numbers really tell us?" (Schrader 2006).

In this frenzy of counting and tallying, the human element of library services can be lost. Assessment that is geared toward an internal or administrative audience risks losing its relevance for inspiring responsive user services. In contrast, Capella University librarians use reference statistics to energize their activities in myriad ways. Instead of the traditional assessment route (deciding what value we want to get from a data assessment, then mounting a major data collection effort, and finally analyzing the results through one specific lens), we err on the side of overcollection. Data that can be gathered easily are saved, so that there is an existing pool of information that can be queried when necessary. We maximize the value of reference information by applying it to questions we have in all areas of library services, including liaison flexibility, library knowledge management, instruction efforts, reference scheduling, and even course development.

CAPELLA UNIVERSITY LIBRARY

Capella University is an online institution with primarily masters and doctoral students; as of December 2007, 87 percent of Capella students were enrolled in a graduate level degree program (Capella Education Company 2008). Accredited by The Higher Learning Commission, Capella is a member of the North Central Association of Colleges and Schools. The university is divided into five schools: Undergraduate Studies, Business and Technology, Education, Human Services, and Psychology. The approximately 20,000 students are scattered throughout the United States with a small percentage of students abroad. The Capella University Library exists entirely online, and includes nearly 30 research databases, with interlibrary loan service available for items outside of our digital collections.

For most of the Capella Library's history, library services were supported by off-site, contract reference staff. These services were provided by the University of Alabama until 2002 and then by Johns Hopkins University from 2002 to 2007. In January 2007 the Capella Library services were brought inhouse to the Minneapolis, Minnesota, headquarters. Since the very first week of the transition, Capella's new librarians have answered the dozens of reference questions that arrive each day.

The reference tallies kept rising from the moment the new library opened. The total number of reference questions in the fall academic quarter of 2007 (Quarter 4) was 74 percent higher than the first quarter of the same year. Though our staff ultimately reached 11 librarians, the increasing number of reference calls meant we needed truly pragmatic assessment measures. With the number of reference questions rising each quarter, our data had to immediately inform our service decisions. In the long term, these same assessment measures are allowing us to expand services in a manner that maximizes the value of the library when there are few increases in available resources.

LITERATURE

In many libraries, two obvious reference assessment tracks prevail: reference desk tally sheets that record the total number of questions, and satisfaction surveys. Both assessment methods are reported to library administrators as a way to justify library services, but they have serious drawbacks. Monitoring total reference queries may be the easiest library assessment strategy. However, assessment that stops with total reference queries at best paints an incomplete portrait of learning outcomes, since users may be utilizing library reference in many ways.

The second conventional path of library reference assessment attempts to capture reference quality through satisfaction surveys. However, survey design and distribution practices are often tightly regulated inside academic institutions, hindering assessment speed. The service package LibQUAL+ is increasingly being adopted by university libraries (Cook 2001; Cook and Heath 2001). While thorough, LibQUAL+ and similar organizational assessment tools take years to cycle, administer, and interpret. As a new library program, Capella needs a more swiftly strategic assessment tool, and one that is easy to modify and provides constant feedback. Though we are looking into satisfaction surveys in the long term, this approach does not provide the quick assessments needed in these first few years. The Capella Library's reference assessment measures help inform multiple levels: both long-term administration decisions and practitioner-level daily service considerations. The reference assessment outcomes guide both reference and nonreference services, as well.

Very few articles in the library science literature focus on reference data as a direct launching point for multilevel service considerations. Some look at the practice of data collection and the many ways it can align services to user needs (Cheng, Bischof, and Nathanson 2002). Others look at very narrow activities such as "mining syllabi for library service opportunities" (Williams, Cody, and Parnell 2004). Capella Library treats data collection and analysis more broadly, by collecting data on all reference interactions and gleaning from them useful information about user preferences, information literacy needs, and course-related issues.

REFERENCE SERVICES AND DATA COLLECTION

Because all Capella courses are online, librarians work with students almost exclusively at a distance.[1] Capella University Library currently provides e-mail and phone reference 50 hours each week. Reference services are offered to students, faculty, and staff. "Ask a Librarian" reference contact information is posted throughout the library Web site, inside Capella's online courserooms in Blackboard, and is linked within several of the library databases.

As soon as the Capella Library came inhouse, the librarians began to collect information about every reference transaction, manually entering information for each transaction into a database created using Microsoft Access software. Our database was inspired by the Libstats open source software used at the University of Wisconsin-Madison. The statistics database has prepopulated fields and is easily updated to include new data or remove unnecessary information. While the specific pieces of data that we collect have changed slightly since we began, the basic type and amount of information collected remains very similar. The data we currently collect includes time received, time answered, the time it takes to answer the question, the course number, question type, patron type, school, and question format (see Figure 11.1 for entry options).

Librarians can enter their transaction data into the Access database at any point during or after a reference transaction. The database automatically populates the current date and time when opened, so some librarians open the program before each reference call, and then use the open fields to take notes. E-mail transaction times have to be entered manually, so many librarians enter an entire day's transactions when convenient. An estimate of the time it takes a librarian to enter the data is included as a part of the recorded amount of time spent answering the question, so the data reflects the total time spent on reference activities.

While we do not include personally identifying data in our Access database (e.g., names, phone numbers, or e-mail addresses), we do collect information of a somewhat personal nature (e.g., school, degree program, and course number). We have found that knowing this type of specific information not only increases the usefulness of data, but also the quality of the answers we provide as well. For this reason, we attempt to collect this information for every reference transaction. The "Ask a Librarian" link takes students to a form that has required fields for school, degree program, and course number. For phone questions, the caller ID function of our customer management software frequently recognizes a student's phone number and triggers the student's information record to appear. Since the information we store cannot identify an individual student, our data collection meets both Capella University's privacy policy (2008) and Reference and User Services Association's Guidelines for Implementing and Maintaining Virtual Reference Services (2004).

Since the inception of reference data collection, librarians have recognized new information needs and changed the reference data categories accordingly. Students do not always phrase questions clearly, and e-mail renders the reference interview moot. Many e-mails arrive outside of library reference hours, and our practice of answering e-mail reference in the order that it arrives means that e-mails are typically answered eight hours after receipt. To improve the relevance of our responses, course numbers are now required, and students can also include the class week from the syllabus if they have an assignment-specific question (courses contain standard content across all course sections at Capella, so a course's week number is much more important than section number for locating assignment directions). Although students may override the required fields by entering any keystroke combination, many do include course information. Librarians at Capella have access to all course content through moderator log-ins to the course software. We can look at the exact assignment in question before creating a reference response. This makes course numbers particularly useful.

Figure 11.1
Reference Transaction Data Recorded

Free Text Entries	Restricted Text Entries				
Date/Time Answered	Question Type (may pick two)	Format	Location	Patron Type	Time Spent
Date/Time Received	APA	E-mail	Business & Technology	BS	00–05 minutes
Librarian Initials	Course Readings	Phone	Education	MS/MBA	05–10 minutes
Course Number	Full Text	Fax	Human Services	PhD/PsyD	10–20 minutes
Question	ILL	Colloquia	Psychology	Faculty	20–30 minutes
Answer	Liaison	Embedded	Undergraduate Studies	Alumni	30–45 minutes
	Other	Liaison	Other	Staff	45–60 minutes
	References		Unknown	Unknown	60+ minutes
	Reference – Instruction				
	Technical – Databases				
	Technical – Other				
	Writing Center				

At first, librarians only collected data on questions that came in through the "Ask a Librarian" Web form and phone services. Due to increasing volumes of reference questions from other sources, librarians now also collect data on questions from embedded librarian discussion boards in courses, individual reference appointments at colloquia, and questions from faculty and staff that come to liaison librarians directly. By recording these nontraditional reference questions, we hope to develop a better understanding of future instruction needs, collection and service development opportunities, and the demands placed on our current staff.

DATA ANALYSIS

Data from our Access database is pulled on the tenth of each month for the previous month and saved in Excel worksheets. We analyze our reference data on different levels, depending on the audience for the conclusions. First, the data is used to create a monthly report that is shared with the entire library. The report highlights the total number of reference transactions via phone, e-mail Web form, or other format. It also lists the number of questions from each school or degree program, and the turnaround time for a student to get a response to a reference question. Enrollment data from the university is added to the report to measure our service demand against enrollment increases. This monthly, aggregate data allows the librarians to quickly see what is happening in reference, and is also used when reporting to university administration.

The liaison librarians are also able to look at the raw data of reference transactions placed by members of their respective schools. This data can be sorted by course number or question type to provide information specific to the liaison librarian's interests. This school-specific data is used by the liaison librarian to create quarterly reports that identify trends within the school. The librarian can quickly identify popular question types, specific courses that prompt frequent questions, or areas potentially in need of expanded instruction materials. These reports can be used in interactions with faculty or school administrators to drive collaboration efforts and information sharing. The number of times a question is asked can be a powerful illustration that an assignment could benefit from more extensive instructions or links to library guides. Finally, data can be pulled from the database to answer specific questions that arise about reference activities. Our current reports do not include the average time spent on reference questions, the number of questions answered by individual librarians, or the hourly reference load. This type of detailed information has been compiled and analyzed as needed when special projects demand it. By analyzing reference data the librarians at Capella University's online library have been able to strategically schedule our reference hours, streamline reference services, produce instructional material tailored to student needs, and improve the content and usage of the library's collection.

STRATEGIC SCHEDULING

The first major use of the reference data was to help inform library hours. Cheng, Bischof and Nathanson (2002) have looked at automatically captured reference statistics as a basis for cutting back or expanding services. In spring 2007 the library decided to expand reference services to include evening and weekend hours. Instead of simply picking new hours based on intuition, we chose to let our reference data inform the decision. With several months worth of data it was possible to analyze non-business-hours "Ask A Librarian" requests over the course of a quarter. The analysis pointed to providing longer hours on Mondays and expanding services to include a midday Saturday shift. Not only were a greater number of e-mails arriving during these hours (or in the wee hours of the morning prior to the Saturday shift), but these new hours also allowed students to receive reference help in advance of the common assignment due dates of Wednesday and Sunday.

Reference librarians typically have multiple job duties, many of which directly compete with reference services. Our reference librarians are involved in the course development process, participate in doctoral colloquia, engage in collection development activities, and create a variety of instructional materials for faculty and course developers. Each of these activities has its own schedule, and requires varying levels of librarian time. Knowing the ebb and flow of reference demand can help boost reference services while reducing librarian stress and distraction. This involves more than simply counting up reference transactions; the nature of the transaction and the time spent answering the query are significant as well. Because questions via phone are answered immediately and can be lengthy, better management of scheduling can relieve some of the pressure and time management issues that on-call status creates. In our data there are clear patterns of reference usage over the course of the day, week, and quarter. For example, phone reference requests rise over the lunch hour, when many working students have time to devote to homework.

While it is impossible to know with certainty what reference demand will be like on any given day, there are some general trends that can influence planning for other library activities. Meetings can be organized at times that are typically slow for phone reference, and deadlines for large projects can be shifted to avoid the busiest parts of the quarter. Since our reference data includes both the time of receipt and the time of response, we can calculate how long students have to wait for a response from a librarian, both in total hours and in business hours. Increases in reference volume and changes in services show up in these turnaround times.

Strategic scheduling has been implemented to decrease the number of calls abandoned or sent to voicemail, and to reduce e-mail turnaround times to about two business hours. We hypothesize that this drop in response time has actually encouraged our students to use e-mail reference more. E-mail reference is easier for the reference librarians to manage while working on other projects, and the reference data shows that student preference has switched from phone calls to e-mails over the course of the year.

REFERENCE KNOWLEDGE BASE

As a new library, with increasing demand and a static staffing level, our first order of business was to boost operational efficiency. With 10 librarians answering reference questions, not every librarian experiences a particular recurring question. Nor is it guaranteed that a liaison librarian will ever encounter a repeated reference question related to her school or subject specialty. By reviewing all of the questions together and sending them to the individual liaison librarians through monthly reports, it is easier to identify and address recurring questions. The question of how to maintain flexible, point-of-need, responsive service is not singular to our profession. Librarians have started to look to corporate models to help enhance the management of internal knowledge. Knowledge innovation culture provides precedents for collecting tacit and piecemeal staff knowledge and organizing it into a usable format (Sheng and Sun 2007; Wen 2005).

At the inception of the Capella Library, several librarians created individual shortcuts for dealing with recurring questions. These included personal "cheat sheets" that gave basic outlines of the responses to frequently asked questions. Other librarians routinely searched e-mail sent files for previous reference answers. These methods produced a significant amount of duplication, as each librarian recreated similar answers and lacked the more in-depth knowledge a liaison librarian might have about a particular assignment, database, or subject area. In the same way that the library has a systematic method for collecting reference data, the librarians also developed a process for streamlining answers to frequent questions.

Some questions recur, but not frequently enough to warrant a specific guide. To prevent the librarians from continually reinventing the wheel on each reference shift, the Reference Knowledge Base was created. This is a document containing a list of standardized responses to frequent reference questions, located in a network shared folder. Links to buried department pages of the university and Snag-it images of sample searches in databases are particularly time consuming to create for individual reference questions, but the Knowledge Base allows us to house extensive contextual and assignment-specific advice for a variety of common questions. The answers in the Knowledge Base can be cut and pasted directly into an e-mail, modified to fit the particular needs of the student, and sent. This way our most frequent and difficult questions often receive the quickest and most thorough answers.

When a question recurs frequently, the basic topic of the question is added to the Reference Knowledge Base word processing document. The appropriate liaison librarian is assigned to the topic, explores the assignment thoroughly, and then produces a generic response to the question, including images and links. Once added to the Reference Knowledge Base, which is located in a shared network folder, any reference librarian can grab the response, modify it to meet the present circumstances, and quickly send it out. The Knowledge Base's answers can quickly be modified to meet other needs. Several have been repurposed as customized assignment guides and included with the assignment directions in the Blackboard courseroom. The simplicity of the Knowledge Base format and the informality of creating entries make it fast and easy for the librarians to adapt to increasing demands for reference services.

While designed to speed e-mail reference, the Reference Knowledge Base is also used by librarians answering phone reference questions. Since the amount of time spent answering a question is recorded in the database, and the resulting Excel worksheet is searchable, it is easy to approximate how much time is saved by adding a particular Knowledge Base entry. One popular library research assignment from a first course in the psychology program first appeared in the fall quarter 2007. The first librarian to answer the question took 20–30 minutes to craft a response. In the winter quarter 2008, the question appears 45 times in the reference data, with a median answer time of less than 10 minutes. The Knowledge Base maintains the quality of reference answers, while simultaneously improving response turnaround time.

GUIDES AND TUTORIALS

Since library guides and tutorials are available at any hour, and Capella students are working on course work at all hours, the guides and tutorials page provides help when librarians are not available. Additionally, when a single assignment prompts several similar reference questions, but the school wants to keep the original assignment requirements, the liaison librarian can create a special research guide that is inserted as a PDF into the course. This happens most frequently in the mandatory first courses when students are asked to perform their initial library research. Some repeated reference questions reflect the more advanced library research tasks required of graduate students. Masters and doctoral students in all schools must identify seminal research, scan bibliographies to find related articles, and limit their research to peer-reviewed journals.

By knowing which courses are appearing most often in reference questions, librarians can look at the reference questions in light of what the courses actually require, and then try to provide library instructional aids in anticipation of student needs. Liaison librarians create guides or tutorials that are placed on the library Web site and inserted in specific courses as appropriate. These guides can be specific to a topic, or provide more general instructional assistance. A guide or tutorial that is more general may prove to be useful in multiple courses (e.g., guides to searching for articles utilizing a specific research methodology or to organizing citations).

COURSE AND ASSIGNMENT DEVELOPMENT

Contextual information enhances library interactions between librarians and users. Knowing course numbers and degree programs not only increases the usefulness of our reference data, but it also improves the immediate reference transaction. Poorly worded reference questions become understandable when the librarian can see the directions and requirements for a course assignment, and librarians can tailor their responses to the resources best suited to the level of the student.

In turn, point-of-need library instruction has become a burning theme in distance librarianship (Drumm and Havens 2005; Kelly and Gronemyer 2006; Kinnie 2006). As Steven Bell (2007) writes in response to a recent research survey, "Perhaps it's time you considered strategies for connecting with students in their courses. That's what students really want . . . course specific resources." Of course, in an online university, invisibility in the online Blackboard courseroom means invisibility in the curriculum.

In their seminal article on the importance of establishing a library presence in the courseroom, Shank and Dewald (2003) make a widely cited distinction between microlevel courseroom involvement (i.e., librarians collaborating with individual instructors), and macrolevel courseroom involvement (i.e., impacting the structure of the courseroom systematically). As mentioned previously, Capella courses are different than traditional university courses in that they contain standard content across all course sections. Courses are developed through a tightly structured process (detailed below). In effect, the standardized nature of the Blackboard courseroom environment means that any improvements we make to individual courses are electronically preserved for future sections without having to continually convince or remind faculty to include these library elements quarter after quarter. Course assignments remain static until a scheduled course revision, so any changes the library implements become permanent features of the course.

At Capella, the course development process involves a subject matter expert (SME), a course developer, instructional design staff, and other key players, collaboratively creating course outcomes and media content. The library's reference data for specific courses helped us make the first inroads into the formal course development process, by offering the evidence that a high volume of questions were stemming from a few courses. One library liaison sent a summary of the high volume of reference calls that had resulted from a course's difficult assignments to the appropriate course developer and SME prior to a scheduled revision of the course. The SME and course developer were alarmed at the number of distressed calls related to the current assignments and decided more library research instruction would be helpful in the new version of the course. As a result, we were sporadically invited as consultants for individual course development meetings. Armed with the success of this initial collaboration, we met with course development administration to discuss a wider pilot effort. As of October 2007, we became more systematically involved in course development. Librarians are now invited to nearly every initial development meeting for new courses and course revisions.

Currently, librarians are involved in drafting and testing research assignments and have the opportunity to recommend or create general guides and tutorials for specific assignments. As appropriate, the liaison librarian can also create an assignment-specific guide for inclusion in any given course. For course revisions especially, our ability to review reference statistics ahead of time, searching for how many and what type of calls the specific course has generated in the past, makes our advice to the development team more customized. In these cases, we not only offer our expert opinion, but we also support our diagnosis with evidence.

While proactive library involvement in courses is preferable, librarians can also be reactive when necessary. When questions about a particular course consistently appear in the reference data, we look at the assignment to determine how the assignment may be confusing students. As noted before, because all courses are online, their contents (including assignment instructions) are available to librarians. Instructors typically do not give extra guidance about research unless they are asked questions by the students; therefore, librarians are often the first to find out that students are confused by an assignment or do not know how to conduct research in an online library.

An online library can cause confusion on two levels: some students have never conducted scholarly research before, while others have never translated those skills to an online environment. In introductory courses, the liaison librarian may offer suggestions for rewording assignments to include database hints or potential research topics. As mentioned above, targeted library guides and tutorials can also be added; for example, including a guide to finding peer-reviewed articles in the first assignment that requires this skill can help ease a student's transition into higher level course work.

Once a research assignment is identified as generating confusion or questions, the liaison librarian has several options according to the degree of revision needed. Misinformation that is tangential to learning outcomes, including broken links to library articles, can be corrected quickly with an online form submission to IT. More extensive revisions are reviewed quarterly by the individual schools, but librarians can submit a request form with our revision recommendations at any time. Our recommendations are typically implemented quickly, and without further changes. Finally, we can always contact faculty members with suggestions, citing the calls and e-mails we have received.

Capella librarians with experience at traditional universities have noticed little difference between the courseroom issues encountered in our online courses and those at other institutions. Learners experience trouble selecting appropriate topics, navigating controlled vocabulary, widening or narrowing their search results efficiently, or using advanced search techniques. Our reference data efforts simply allow us to be more responsive in targeting and fixing issues by spotlighting reference themes and problem courses quickly. Our activities fit well with the data-driven culture of the university and help us prioritize our efforts.

As with any academic institution, faculty and course developers do not know the library's collections as well as the librarians and may not be aware of changes to the library that affect student ability to succeed with an assignment. Most faculty are also experienced researchers, so they may not immediately recognize which research tasks are difficult for a novice researcher to perform (Manuel, Molloy, and Beck 2003). Reference data can illuminate situations where there is a mismatch between the library collection and either the assignment requirements or student skills. Since so many Capella courses are designed to appeal to working professionals, they often emphasize emerging trends and current industry interests. Thus, some research assignments clash with the long delays common in academic publishing or with electronic database embargoes. Librarians can recognize, and work to mitigate, resulting research frustrations.

Our exclusively online courses and standardized course development process may be unique to Capella, but other academic libraries can easily copy aspects of our involvement in courses. We are using data to identify where library involvement is most needed, and then citing that data to communicate those needs to faculty. Librarians at any university can approach faculty with data that show students' information literacy gaps and then offer suggestions for library content in the course. Those types of liaison activities may even be easier in a traditional university, where faculty have offices near the library and more casual conversations are possible. Many universities also have online courses that remain relatively unchanged from quarter to quarter. Librarians adding content to those online courses can achieve the same level of consistency we have in Capella's Blackboard courserooms.

COLLECTION DEVELOPMENT AND MARKETING

While the liaison librarians do receive collection development suggestions from faculty, reference transactions are one way to learn about areas that are popular research topics for learners, especially doctoral students. Academic libraries have looked at dissertation bibliographies for collection development analysis (Haycock 2004; Gooden 2001). Because all material in the Capella library is held within databases, we have limited ability to identify which items are used frequently. While we are able to track the number of times a specific database is accessed, there is often no way for us to know how often individual journal titles or e-books are accessed or downloaded. By looking at common topics that appear in the reference questions we receive, we have been able to not only find areas that need greater collection support, but also work on highlighting and promoting the high-interest items we already have.

Many graduate students do not realize that we have e-books that explain research methodology and technique. Analysis of reference questions highlighted the need for these types of materials, so librarians began advertising current holdings through guides and library blog posts, as well as adding more titles to the existing collection.[2] Students also frequently request background information for their research. This need for scholarly encyclopedias and other reference sources has also been answered by this two-pronged approach of marketing and collection development.

The library's data also showed less library usage by undergraduates relative to their registration numbers. This prompted the librarians to reach out to undergraduates by embedding a librarian in several first courses and adding library guides and tutorials to course assignments. By measuring undergraduate question rates against total undergraduate enrollment, we are able to see that our outreach methods are having a significant impact. Undergraduates are contacting the librarians for help at almost twice the rate of a year ago.

FUTURE POSSIBILITIES

Due to our extensive collection of reference data, the librarians now know much more about our students and their habits. Human Services and Psychology graduate students generally contact us very early in their degree programs, while Business students wait until their methodology courses or when they begin dissertation research. Technology undergraduate and graduate students almost never contact librarians directly. Undergraduates choose to e-mail their reference requests more often than any other group. This information can help us determine which courses may need more library involvement, focus future outreach projects, and anticipate the likely consequences of service changes on specific groups of students.

Librarians are increasingly asked to defend their services in a data-driven environment. Return on investment, usage increases, and other numerical objectives are central to promoting and sustaining library services. Many academic libraries need to produce evidence for requests for more funds. The Capella Library is no exception; by harvesting usage data early in the library's history we hope to have a significant amount of comparison data to back up future budgetary requests (including for additional staff, new technologies to improve service, and collection development).

CONCLUSION

While very few librarians share our experience of starting a library from scratch, our experience can offer lessons for libraries dealing with enormous change. We successfully used data to learn about our situation and then adapted quickly to the new environment. By keeping track of our reference activities, we will be able to better manage future changes to the library, including major reductions or additions to budgets, staff changes, and new technology. We can strategically choose what services need to be removed or expanded and will be able to see the consequences of any changes quickly. This will help us quantify successes and failures in the course of any major library change.

Monitoring reference data not only allows us to more effectively address the needs of learners and faculty, but also ultimately saves time. Collecting and analyzing detailed reference transaction data has given Capella librarians the information needed to maximize time-saving measures, including strategic scheduling and a Reference Knowledge Base. These activities both improve response turnaround time and help manage librarian workload. Our data provides impetus to address troublesome course assignments and has become part of the course development process. It also helps us quickly gain an understanding of the skills needed by our student population, thus directing the focus of the information literacy and instruction materials we create. Similarly, liaison librarians are able to identify gaps in our library collection relative to student interests and inform students of useful materials we already have. The data collected in the first year of the inhouse Capella Library created a strong basis for our initial activities and has created a foundation for future assessment and service changes.

ENDNOTES

1. Capella PhD students also participate in three in-person colloquia during their course work, where they may choose to attend a library instruction session or schedule a one-on-one reference appointment with a librarian. Otherwise, all communication between students and librarians occurs remotely.

2. Off the Shelf: The Capella Library Blog is available at www.capella-id.com/library.

REFERENCES

Bell, Steven. December 10, 2007. Pay some attention to the research. http://acrlog.org/2007/12/10/pay-some-attention-to-the-research/.

Capella Education Company. 2008a. Capella University media fact sheet. February 14. www.capellaeducation.com/news/assets/Media_Fact_Sheet_Q401.pdf.

———. 2008b. Privacy policy. www.capellaeducation.com/footer/privacy.aspx.

Cheng, Rachel, Steve Bischof, and Alan J. Nathanson. 2002. Data collection for user-oriented library services: Wesleyan University Library's experience. *OCLC Systems & Services* 18 (4): 195–204.

Cook, Colleen, ed. 2001. The maturation of assessment in academic libraries: The role of LibQUAL+TM. *Performance Measurement and Metrics* 3 (2): 34–112.

Cook, Colleen, and Fred Heath. 2001. Users' perceptions of library service quality: A "LibQUAL+™" qualitative study. *Library Trends* 49 (4): 548–84.

Drumm, Michelle, and Barret C. Havens. 2005. A foot in the door: Experiments with integrating library services into the online classroom. *Journal of Library & Information Services in Distance Learning* 2 (3): 25–32.

Gooden, Angela M. 2001. Citation analysis of chemistry doctoral dissertations: An Ohio State University case study. *Issues in Science & Technology Librarianship* 32. www.istl.org/01-fall/refereed.html.

Guidelines for implementing and maintaining virtual reference services. 2004. *Reference & User Services Quarterly* 44 (1): 9–13. http://ezproxy.library.capella.edu/login?url=http://search.ebscohost.com/login.aspx?direct=true&db=aph&AN=15078345&site=ehost-live.

Haycock, Laurel A. 2004. Citation analysis of education dissertations for collection development. *LRTS: Library Resources Technical Services* 48 (2): 102–6.

Joubert, Douglas J., and Tamera P. Lee. 2007. Empowering your institution through assessment. *Journal of the Medical Library Association* 95 (1): 46–53.

Kelly, Maureen, and Kate Gronemyer. 2006. Courseware connections: Reaching and teaching students through blackboard. Paper presented at the Online Northwest 2006 conference. http://hdl.handle.net/1957/1798.

Kinnie, Jim. 2006. The embedded librarian: Bringing library services to distance learners. Paper presented at the 22nd Annual Conference on Teaching and Learning, Madison, Wis. http://ir.library.oregonstate.edu/dspace/handle/1957/1798.

Kyrillidou, Martha. 2005. Library assessment: Why today and not tomorrow? Paper presented at the Library Assessment Conference held at Thessaloniki, Greece, June 13–15, 2005. http://www.libqual.org/documents/admin/KyrillidouGreecePapers.doc.

Lakos, Amos. 1999. The missing ingredient: Culture of assessment in libraries, performance measurement and metrics. *International Journal for Library and Information Services* 1 (1): 3–7.

Lakos, Amos, and Shelley Phipps. 2004. Creating a culture of assessment: A catalyst for organizational change. *Portal: Libraries and the Academy* 4 (3): 345–61.

Manuel, Kate, Molly Molloy, and Susan Beck. 2003. What faculty want: A study of attitudes influencing faculty collaboration. In *11th ACRL National Conference Proceedings*, edited by H. Thompson, 292–306. Chicago: American Library Association.

Reference and User Services Association. 2004. Guidelines for implementing and maintaining virtual reference services. American Library Association. www.ala.org/ala/mgrps/divs/rusa/resources/guidelines/virtrefguidelines.cfm.

Schrader, Alvin M. 2006. 400 million circs, 40 million reference questions. *ARGUS* 35 (1): 15–22.

Shank, John D., and Nancy H. Dewald. 2003. Establishing our presence in courseware: Adding library services to the virtual classroom. *Information Technology and Libraries* 22, no. 1 (March 1): 38–43. www.proquest.com.library.capella.edu/.

Sheng, Xiaoping, and Lin Sun. 2007. Developing knowledge innovation culture of libraries. *Library Management* 28 (1/2): 36–52.

Wen, Shixing. 2005. Implementing knowledge management in academic libraries: A pragmatic approach. *Chinese Librarianship: An International Electronic Journal* 19. www.white-clouds.com/iclc/cliej/cl19wen.htm.

Williams, Lisa M., Sue Ann Cody, and Jerry Parnell. 2004. Prospecting for new collaborations: Mining syllabi for library service opportunities. *Journal of Academic Librarianship* 30 (4): 270–75.

BIBLIOGRAPHY

Aranda, Daniel A. 2003. Service operations strategy, flexibility and performance in engineering consulting firms. *International Journal of Operations & Production Management* 23 (11): 1401–21.

Barsky, Jonathan D., and Richard Labagh. 1992. A strategy for customer satisfaction. *Cornell Hotel and Restaurant Administration Quarterly* 33 (5): 32–39.

Barth, Jennifer, and Kate Bejune. 2003. The virtual reference librarian's handbook. *D-Lib Magazine* 9 (2). www.dlib.org/dlib/february03/02bookreview.html.

Campbell, John P., Peter B. DeBlois, and Diana G. Oblinger. 2007. Academic analytics: A new tool for a new era. *EDUCAUSE Review* 42 (4): 41–57. http://connect.educause.edu/Library/EDUCAUSE+Review/AcademicAnalyticsANewTool/44594?time=1207597026.

Carter, David S., and Joseph Janes. 2000. Unobtrusive data analysis of digital reference questions and service at the internet public library: An exploratory study. *Library Trends* 49 (2): 251–65. http://ezproxy.library.capella.edu/login?url=http://search.ebscohost.com/login.aspx?direct=true\&\#38;db=lxh\&\#38;AN=4110986\&\#38;site=ehost-live.

Donham, Jean, and Corey Williams Green. 2004. Developing a culture of collaboration: Librarian as consultant. *Journal of Academic Librarianship* 30 (4): 314–21.

Gilbert, L. M. 2006. Assessing digital reference and online instructional services in an integrated public/university library. *Reference Librarian* 46 (95/96): 149–72.

Gray, Sharon A., Stewart Brower, Heather Munger, Amanda Start, and Pamela White. 2001. Redefining reference in an academic health sciences library: Planning for change. *Medical Reference Services Quarterly* 20 (3): 1–11.

Jantz, Ron. 2001. Knowledge management in academic libraries: Special tools and processes to support information professionals. *Reference Services Review* 29 (1): 33–39.

King, Helen. 2000. The academic library in the 21st century: What need for a physical place? In Virtual libraries: Virtual communities. Abstracts, fulltext documents and PowerPoint presentations of papers and demos given at the International Association of Technological University Libraries (IATUL) Conference (Brisbane, Queeensland, Australia, July 3–7), ED447820. www.eric.ed.gov/ERICWebPortal/custom/portlets/recordDetails/detailmini.jsp?_nfpb=true&_&ERICExtSearch_SearchValue_0=ED447820&ERICExtSearch_SearchType_0=no&accno=ED447820.

Massey-Burzio, Virginia. 1998. From the other side of the reference desk: A focus group study. *Journal of Academic Librarianship* 24 (3): 208–16.

Nicholson, Scott. 2006. The basis for bibliomining: Frameworks for bringing together usage-based data mining and bibliometrics through data warehousing in digital library services. *Information Processing and Management* 42 (3): 785–804.

Pomerantz, Jeffrey. 2005. A linguistic analysis of question taxonomies. *Journal of the American Society for Information Science and Technology* 56 (7): 715–28.

Sampson, Scott E. 1996. Ramifications of monitoring service quality through passively solicited customer feedback. *Decision Sciences* 27 (4): 601–23.

Scherrer, Carol S. and Susan Jacobson. 2002. New measures for new roles: Defining and measuring the current practices of health sciences librarians. *Journal of the Medical Library Association* 90 (2): 164–72.

Shankar, Venkatesh, Amy K. Smith, and Arvind Rangaswamy. 2003. Customer satisfaction and loyalty in online and offline environments. *International Journal of Research in Marketing* 20 (2): 153–75.

Stover, Mark. 2004. Making tacit knowledge explicit: The ready reference database as codified knowledge. *Reference Services Review* 32 (2): 164–73.

Tax, Stephen S., Stephen W. Brown, and Murali Chandrashekaran. 1998. Customer evaluations of service complaint experiences: Implications for relationship marketing. *Journal of Marketing* 62 (2): 60–76.

Tennant, Michele R., Tara Tobin Cataldo, Pamela Sherwill-Navarro, and Rae Jesano. 2006. Evaluation of a liaison librarian program: Client and liaison perspectives. *Journal of the Medical Library Association* 94 (4): e201–4.

Yi, Kwan, Jamshid Beheshti, Charges Cole, John E. Leide, and Andrew Large. 2006. User search behavior of domain-specific information retrieval systems: An analysis of the query logs from PsycINFO and ABC-CLIO's Historical Abstracts/America: History and Life. *Journal of the American Society for Information Science and Technology* 57 (9): 1208–20.

CHAPTER 12

Instruction by the Numbers: Using Data to Improve Teaching and Learning

WENDY HOLLIDAY, ERIN DAVIS, AND PAMELA MARTIN

Outcomes assessment has been a mandate across higher education for at least a decade, and instruction librarians are no strangers to the call to show what their students have actually learned. Most libraries keep general statistics on instruction, including the number of class sessions librarians teach and the number of students in attendance. These numbers, however, reflect only "outputs" of an instruction program. Administrators call upon librarians (and other faculty) to measure student learning and the impact of specific programs on student retention. Educational theory and practice provide models for assessment, yet librarians face significant challenges in this environment. Librarians often teach only single sessions of courses conceived, created, and controlled by traditional teaching faculty members, with little control over course pedagogy or learning outcomes, and limited opportunities to assess students.

The Library Instruction Program at Utah State University (USU) uses a wide-ranging approach to assess student learning and measure programmatic effectiveness. We gather multiple data sources to inform our efforts to improve classroom teaching and persuade administrators and faculty to integrate information literacy (IL) instruction into the larger university curriculum. Some of these data sources are more traditional, including citation analysis of student papers and LibQUAL+[1] survey results. Other sources are more creative, including analysis of syllabi to assess the degree to which faculty incorporate IL into general education classes. Librarians weave this data together with anecdotal and other qualitative evidence from the classroom. Librarians then use the data to change individual teaching practice, develop new IL curricula in collaboration with faculty, and make recommendations for change to campus-wide programs.

CITATION ANALYSIS

Citation analysis is a common means of assessing IL. Most of these analyses look at what kinds of sources students cite, including books, articles, or Web sites, and other markers of quality, including the currency or scholarly nature of the cited sources. Several recent studies show that students do seem to increasingly rely on the World Wide Web rather than books or scholarly articles (Davis 2003; Ursin, Blakesley-Lindsay, and Johnson 2004). Some studies show that strict guidelines on sources from instructors and library instruction can increase students' use of library information sources (Davis 2003; Hovde 2000; Hurst and Leonard 2007; Robinson and Schlegl 2004). Librarians use the results of such studies to change, or advocate for change, in IL instruction (Mohler 2005).

At USU we use citation analysis in a similar fashion. Using various samples of student work from the past three years, we have been able to tease out interesting, and sometimes quite subtle, aspects of students' information behavior. Rather than relying on black and white numbers to denote "good" or "bad" outcomes, we use citation analysis, in combination with other quantitative and qualitative evidence, to help us tell stories. We then communicate these stories to other librarians, faculty, and the students themselves to improve instructional practice and promote greater student learning.

Librarians at USU embarked on our first citation analysis as part of a wider assessment project in 2004. We partnered with the English Department to conduct a value-added assessment of Introduction to Writing (English 1010) and Intermediate Writing (English 2010). In fall 2004, all Introduction to Writing students wrote a prompted essay before receiving any substantive instruction. At the end of that semester, all Intermediate Writing students wrote an essay in response to an article by Derek Bok about free speech on college campuses. The premise of the value-added approach is that any improvement in the quality of papers between an entering and exiting cohort (students completing Intermediate Writing) reflects that learning has taken place. The English Department scored a random sample of 400 essays (200 from Introduction to Writing and 200 from Intermediate Writing) according to a standard rubric that addressed elements of style, organization, and use of evidence. Librarians saw this sample as an opportunity to conduct a citation analysis to determine if there were differences in the number and types of sources cited by Introduction to Writing and Intermediate Writing students. We compiled an Excel spreadsheet, recording each of the 242 citations from the sample of 400 essays. We also recorded standard citation information (author, title, and date) for each source. We then classified these sources by type (for example, Web site, book, or scholarly article). For the Web sites, we also classified subtypes, including news sources, primary sources, and reference sources.

The results show that Intermediate Writing students were more likely to cite sources than Introduction to Writing students. Very few Introduction to Writing students cited any sources (only 16 percent), while Intermediate Writing students were more likely to cite at least one source (45 percent). Even so, the vast majority of students (70 percent) failed to cite any outside sources of information. This might reflect the fact that the essay instructions did not explicitly require research. Of the students who did cite sources in their essays, there was little difference between the introductory and intermediate students in the number of sources cited (see Figure 12.1).

Web sites were, by far, the most common type, comprising 54.5 percent of the total citations (see Figure 12.1). The next most common type was the essay referred to in the essay prompt (10.3 percent

Figure 12.1
Percentage of Students Citing Sources in Writing Classes

	All	**Introduction to Writing**	**Intermediate Writing**
Did not cite sources	70%	84%	55%
Cited one source	10%	7%	13%
Cited two sources	11%	3%	19%
Cited three or more sources	10%	6%	13%

of all citations), which we placed in its own category because it was commonly cited. Students cited books or book chapters 9.9 percent of the time. Assuming that most students found books, articles, and print reference sources in the library, we classified 31.4 percent of the total 242 sources as coming from the library. Web sites were a slightly larger percentage of the Introduction to Writing citations (62.1 percemt versus 51.7 percent for Intermediate Writing), but the remaining categories were cited at similar frequency in the Introduction to Writing and Intermediate Writing samples (see Figure 12.2).

One of the most interesting findings was the fact that several students cited the same sources repeatedly. All of these repeated citations, with the exception of the prompt essay, were Web sites. Nearly half of the Web citations (49 percent) came from only 16 different Web sites. In fact, 25 percent of all sources cited came from these 16 Web sites. The fact that so many of these sites appeared again and again suggests that many students were only using the most convenient sources.

In order to investigate this hypothesis further, we used Google to recreate some of the most likely searches that might yield results on the essay topic: free expression on campus. We did several searches and looked to see if some of the repeated Web sites were on the first page of results. Indeed, 9 of the 16 repeated sites were in the top 10 Google results. The most popular Web site (cited 10 times) was the Legal Information Institute, a digital library of legal materials from Cornell University Law School. It was the first result for a search on "first amendment." The second most popular source was www.firstamendmentcenter.org (nine citations). It was either the second or third result in Google searches for "speech codes," "hate speech campus," "freedom speech," and "first amendment."

The citation analysis confirms the trend, noted anecdotally by both librarians and writing instructors, that students tend to skim the surface of Google. Librarians at USU were able to leverage the citation analysis into actual curricular change. Partly as a result of the value-added assessment, librarians and writing instructors designed a much more intensive research component for Introduction to Writing. This included a problem-based group research project, where students spent two to four class sessions in the library conducting research with the help of a librarian. For Intermediate Writing,

Figure 12.2
Types of Sources Cited

Types	All	Introduction to Writing	Intermediate Writing
Web sites	54.5%	62.1%	51.7%
Bok essay	10.3%	9.1%	10.8%
Books	9.9%	6.1%	11.4%
Newspapers	6.6%	4.5%	7.4%
Popular magazines	4.5%	0.0%	6.3%
Primary sources	4.1%	6.1%	3.4%
Reference books	3.3%	6.1%	2.3%
Scholarly articles	2.9%	1.5%	3.4%
Film or song	1.7%	0.0%	2.3%
Unknown	1.7%	4.5%	0.6%
Personal interview	0.4%	0.0%	0.6%

we developed a range of lesson plans designed to introduce students to the wide range of resources available in the library. In both composition classes, focus shifted from one-shot demonstrations to several integrated sessions throughout a research assignment.

Our next citation analysis project focused on actual assignments from Introduction to Writing and Intermediate Writing from the 2005 to 2006 academic year. This sample was not random, but rather a convenience sample of papers from instructors who were willing to supply us copies of student work. We analyzed 39 bibliographies (with a total of 358 sources cited) from two different Intermediate Writing sections. We only classified the citations by type, including books, articles, and Web sites. We did not classify the sample by mode of access (library versus the World Wide Web). Students participated in two library instruction sessions, one on concept mapping and one on searching the catalog and library databases. Most students cited articles (42.2 percent of all citations). Web sites followed closely behind (35.2 percent of all citations). Books were a distant third (12 percent of all citations). Of the articles cited, slightly more were scholarly (51.2 percent) than popular (48.8 percent). The fact that many students cited scholarly articles suggests that students learned the difference between scholarly and popular publications, and that they used library databases to conduct their research (see Figure 12.3).

Both the value-added assessment and the smaller sample of actual papers were suggestive of trends in student citation patterns. The smaller sample of actual papers from 2005 to 2006 was tantalizing but did not provide any clues about instruction across the wide range of nearly 100 Intermediate Writing sections that we teach each year. We also wanted to assess the impact of changes to the Introduction to Writing curriculum, by analyzing citation patterns from the problem-based group research projects.

In 2006–2007 librarians collected final papers and annotated bibliographies from a much larger sample of 14 sections of Introduction to Writing and 18 sections of Intermediate Writing. This sample included bibliographies and papers from 112 Introduction to Writing students and 249 Intermediate Writing students. Citations from the bibliographies were entered into a Microsoft Excel spreadsheet for a total of 574 citations for Introduction to Writing and 1,949 citations for Intermediate Writing. Librarians then classified each citation with regard to the following parameters:

Figure 12.3
Intermediate Writing Bibliographies, 2005–2006

Type	Percentage
Article	42.2%
Web site	35.2%
Book	12%
Interview	6.7%
Unknown	2.5%
Government document	0.8%
Presentation	0.3%
Dissertation	0.3%
n = 358	

- *Type*: These included books, scholarly journals, magazines, newspapers, reference works, and Web sites. Web sites were defined as general sites freely available via the World Wide Web. Each source was classified by its primary type (e.g., newspaper article) rather than the mode of access (e.g., the Web or a library database).

- *Print or Electronic Format*: In many cases, we could determine that students accessed sources electronically because of a URL provided as part of the citation. In other cases, we assumed that if a title was available electronically and in print, students accessed the electronic copy (for example, it is unlikely that students used microfilm to retrieve articles from the older newspapers and magazines when an electronic option was available). This likely skewed the final analysis toward electronic sources, but format was unclear in only about 10 percent of the citations.

- *Library-Provided*: For all electronic journals, magazines, newspapers, and reference works, we determined whether the source was freely available on the Web or provided through a library subscription database. URLs often provided clues to how students accessed electronic articles. We could determine, for example, whether a student accessed a *New York Times* article from the *New York Times* Web site or from our library subscription by looking at the URL in a citation.

Web sites were the most popular type of source in both composition classes, comprising around 40 percent of the total citations. Of these Web sites, most were authored by private organizations or individuals, rather than government or educational organizations. We did not analyze the credibility of each Web site. Many did seem to include reliable and high-quality information. Students might be missing more subtle forms of bias and perspective, however, on sites authored by organizations and private individuals with an advocacy agenda. Students might find a study on the Cato Institute or Brookings Institute Web site, for example, and not understand that these studies are guided by the underlying philosophy of each organization.

Figure 12.4
Introduction to Writing and Intermediate Writing Bibliographies, 2006–2007

Type	Introduction to Writing	Intermediate Writing
Web sites	40.94%	38.58%
Journals	21.6%	15.34%
Magazines	17.07%	15.24%
Books	7.49%	11.08%
Newspapers	6.45%	6.46%
Personal Interview	0.35%	3.75%
Wikipedia	0.35%	2.72%
Reference Sources	2.09%	2.21%
Movie, music, or television	0.35%	1.69%
Government or ERIC document	3.31%	0.77%
Other	0.00%	2.16%
n for Introduction to Writing = 574		
n for Intermediate Writing = 1,949		

For both courses, the rate of citing Web sites was lower than the rate in the value-added assessment. For Intermediate Writing the rate of citing Web sites dropped from 51.7 percent to 38.6 percent; for Introduction to Writing the rate dropped from 61 percent to 41 percent. This suggests that our new curriculum and teaching approach succeeded in steering students away from free Web resources.

Journals were the second most popular type of information source. More Introduction to Writing students (22 percent) used scholarly journals than Intermediate Writing students (15 percent). Intermediate Writing students cited a slightly higher percentage of books than Introduction to Writing Students.[2] See Figure 12.4 for a complete summary of the different types of sources.

Students overwhelmingly favored electronic sources. For both writing classes, more than 90 percent of the citations to periodicals and reference works were electronic (90 percent in Introduction to Writing and 94 percent in Intermediate Writing). Introduction to Writing students were more likely to use the library to find electronic periodicals. Seventy-nine percent of the citations to periodicals came from a library subscription resource. For Intermediate Writing, library resources comprised 69 percent of the electronic citations. Introduction to Writing students generally received more intensive and consistent instruction, including up to three library research days when they worked closely with librarians. This might explain their greater use of library resources.

For the Intermediate Writing citations, we also analyzed the variety of sources used by each individual student. We categorized the range in variety of each student's sources as "all library"; "mainly library" (more than 67 percent of sources were library sources); "mixed" (between 33 percent and 67 percent from the library); "mainly Web" (more than 67 percent from the Web); and "all sources from the Web." Thirty-three percent of students used all library sources and 18 percent used mainly library sources. The heavy use of library sources suggests that library instruction introduced or reinforced the need to look beyond Google for academic research. Books and scholarly journals also seemed to serve as a "gateway" to using a wider range of resources. Of the 89 Intermediate Writing students who cited a book, 58 percent used mainly library (or non-Web site) information sources. Only 7 percent of these students used Web sites as their primary sources of information. The picture was similar for the students who cited a journal, with 56 percent using library sources more frequently than Web sites. Eighteen percent of the students used primarily Web sources, however, suggesting that some students might need further instruction and encouragement to use library sources (see Figure 12.5). We found similar results for Introduction to Writing, although the group projects made it harder to identify trends for individual students.[3]

All of these citation analysis projects combine to provide a complex picture of student behavior at USU. They generally confirm national trends, including students' strong preferences for electronic sources, especially freely available Web sites. But rather than simply bemoaning students' reliance on simple Web searching, librarians use our citation analysis data to tell stories to various

Figure 12.5
Variety of Sources Used in Intermediate Writing, 2006–2007

All Library	33%
Mainly Library	18%
Mixed	28%
Mainly Web	3%
All Web	18%
n = 249 students	

constituencies and make an argument for radical change in the way we approach library instruction. The first value-added assessment shows us that entering USU freshmen are not likely to use outside sources of information unless explicitly required to do so. In an assessment using the same value-added methodology during the following year, the exact same percentage of entering Introduction to Writing students (84 percent) failed to cite an outside source. This result provides librarians with a baseline figure to argue that entering freshmen require IL instruction because they are not in the habit of using research in their writing.

The heavy reliance on Web sites among both Introduction to Writing and Intermediate Writing students in the value-added citation analysis also highlights the impression that students do not use scholarly and comprehensive library resources when not required by the assignment. We reported these results to the English Department at a time when instructors were debating when and how to introduce research into the composition course sequence. Some instructors argued that library research skills should only be taught in Intermediate Writing, when students learn formal persuasive writing. Research suggests the importance of transforming college student study habits early (Kuh 2005; Tinto 1993). Librarians cited this broader research in combination with the citation analysis to make a much more powerful case for introducing research early, in Introduction to Writing. If students have no exposure to library resources before they reach Intermediate Writing, it is harder to persuade them of the value of searching more deeply than the World Wide Web. Librarians and writing instructors then developed the problem-based learning activity for Introduction to Writing that includes multiple library visits and team teaching with librarians.

Subsequent citation analysis of actual student work helped us assess our new approach to Introduction to Writing. The results showed that Introduction to Writing students relied heavily upon library information sources for their problem-based group projects in 2006–2007. Indeed, they cited a higher percentage of library sources than several Intermediate Writing classes. Instead of analyzing only the types of sources cited, we traced sources back to their origin (freely available on the Web versus in a library subscription database). Students in Introduction to Writing, who generally spent more one-on-one time with a librarian, used the library as their avenue to information rather than the World Wide Web and search engines like Google. In the past, many writing instructors at USU required that students use certain types and numbers of sources for their papers. Students often saw this as arbitrary and selected sources only on the basis of whether they met the required criteria. With more intensive coaching by librarians, students could see the value of high-quality reference sources, books, and scholarly articles in the context of their actual use for an assignment. Librarians are now able to show that intensive, personalized librarian coaching serves as an important means of teaching the value of using library resources.

In Intermediate Writing, the 2006 citation analysis suggests that our instructional approach is yielding mixed results. Some students heavily relied on the World Wide Web alone, while others used the library as a gateway to information. In order to understand this better, librarians used a standard rubric to score Intermediate Writing bibliographies for the quality and variety of sources used. We found that Intermediate Writing students scored better in the "use of a wide range of sources" measure when they participated in a greater number of library sessions.

Librarians at USU used the stories emerging from citation analysis to persuade English instructors to include more library instruction sessions in Intermediate Writing, and to include opportunities for one-on-one coaching. The citation analyses also changed actual classroom practice. At USU we had been conducting fewer one-shot demonstration sessions over the past several years, but many librarians still felt the need to do some type of search demonstration. Librarians saw, both anecdotally in their classes and through the citation analysis results, that a coaching model was more effective in getting students to actually use the library. Librarians now make passive database demonstrations a much smaller part of their instructional approach in all classes, focusing instead on more critical issues of discussing information needs and relevancy and providing point-of-need assistance for more mechanical information search skills.

Citation analysis was even used by some librarians to provide feedback to students, an important and often overlooked aspect of the assessment process. Several librarians shared with students the results of the first citation analysis for the value-added assessment using the prompted essay. Librarians described how many students cited the same Web site and that this Web site appeared as the first result for a Google search using keywords from the prompt. While many students understood that only looking at the first page of Google results translated into shallow research, they did not think about how the originality of their thinking and writing might be affected by citing the easiest to find sources. In a reflective essay at the end of the semester, one Intermediate Writing student wrote that the story of the value-added assessment opened his eyes to the need to dig deeper in his research so that he could develop more original insights in his writing.

At a time when many library instruction programs are moving towards online tutorials for delivery to general education classes like these, librarians at USU are moving in the opposite direction, arguing for a "high touch" approach to instruction for lower-level undergraduate students. When librarians, library and university administrators, and faculty members suggest that librarians should move toward online delivery of instruction, we can counter with a complex and rich story of the value of intensive, personalized one-on-one instruction with librarians, building upon the data of thousands of citations from student papers.

GENERAL EDUCATION SYLLABI AUDIT

In 2006 the Library Instruction Program completed an audit of syllabi for approved University Studies (general education) courses. Our goal was to see where information literacy (IL) was being taught throughout the general education curriculum. The development of IL skills, defined as "an understanding of the nature, organization, and methods of access and evaluation of both electronic and traditional resources in the subject area," is a university requirement for integrated breadth

Figure 12.6
Syllabi Analyzed by Curricular Area

Areas	Number of Syllabi	Percentage of Courses Offered in Each Area
BAI: Breadth American Institutions	8	86%
BHU: Breadth Humanities	19	67%
BLS: Breadth Life Science	15	73%
BPS: Breadth Physical Science	16	88%
BSS: Breadth Social Science	20	62%
DHA: Depth Humanities and Arts	35	63%
DSC: Depth Science	21	66%
DSS: Depth Social Science	58	77%
Total	192	

courses (Utah State University General Education Subcommittee). At USU general education includes both breadth courses and depth courses, the latter building upon the knowledge and skills introduced at the breadth level. We examined syllabi from both breadth and depth courses. While syllabi are only one view into the curriculum, they are a relatively accessible and concrete source of information. The audit provided a broad picture of IL opportunities, both taken and missed, at USU.

We collected syllabi for the general education courses approved as of 2004. We analyzed a total of 192 syllabi, representing 68 percent of the 238 courses approved for general education. The syllabi represented all of the general education areas, with the exception of Breadth Creative Arts (BCA). We had received only two syllabi for BCA and decided not to include them because the small sample might not represent course offerings in that area. The total number of syllabi covered between 62 percent and 88 percent of the courses offered in each of the remaining areas. See Figure 12.6 for a complete breakdown of the coverage of syllabi in each area.

For each syllabus, we recorded the following information:

- Does the syllabus include a clear statement of learning goals? If so, is information literacy an explicit part of those goals?
- Are information literacy assignments included? IL assignments are defined as anything that requires students to find, evaluate, or use information sources in some final product (e.g., a paper or presentation).
- How many information literacy assignments are required?
- Do the assignments have clear grading criteria, and are information literacy skills measured by those criteria?
- Do information literacy assignments require that students find outside sources of information (rather than evaluating and synthesizing information provided by the instructor)?
- Do instructors require certain types or numbers of sources?
- Are information literacy assignments broken up into stages (for example, is an annotated bibliography required before a final paper is due)?
- Which Association of College and Research Libraries Information Literacy Standards for Higher Education (ACRL Standards) are covered in the assignments?
- Does the syllabus explicitly mention the library as a useful resource for students to complete their assignments?

We also wanted to measure the rate of participation in library instruction for all general education courses, regardless of whether a syllabus was available. If a syllabus was not available, we still wanted to know if a class included IL through a formal library instruction session. So, we compiled a list of all approved general education courses that included a library instruction session between 2003 and 2005. This provided an additional measure of the degree to which IL was integrated into the general education curriculum at USU during these years.

Most of the syllabi included clear learning outcomes or objectives for the course (69 percent). Of the syllabi with learning goals, 39 percent included IL goals as part of their larger course objectives. Fewer than half of the total 192 syllabi, however, had any IL assignments (46 percent). IL assignments were included in some syllabi from each of the subject areas. The sciences had the smallest percentage: 3.4 percent of the Breadth Life Science and 2.2 percent of the Breadth Physical Science syllabi included IL assignments.[4] The Depth Social Science classes included the largest percentage of IL assignments (42.7 percent) (see Figure 12.7). Large class sizes, especially in the breadth areas, likely account for the lack of IL assignments in some cases. Some breadth classes enroll 500 students, making it difficult for instructors to grade even short written assignments (many of these large classes have no teaching assistants to help with grading).

The most common assignments (47) were research papers, which required students to research a topic related to the class. Papers responding to or summarizing weekly readings were also popular

Figure 12.7
Syllabi with Information Literacy Assignments

Area	Number	Percentage in curricular area
BAI: Breadth American Institutions	3	3.4%
BHU: Breadth Humanities	6	6.7%
BLS: Breadth Life Science	3	3.4%
BPS: Breadth Physical Science	2	2.2%
BSS: Breadth Social Science	9	10.1%
DHA: Depth Humanities and Arts	20	22.5%
DSC: Depth Science	8	9.0%
DSS: Depth Social Science	38	42.7%
Total	89	

(24). Six classes required an annotated bibliography, and six classes included a presentation assignment. Other assignments were book reviews, literature reviews, posters, editorials, memos, and company or product research.

Slightly more than half of all the IL assignments (55 percent) required some type of outside sources, meaning that the instructor required students to seek information beyond class texts or reserve readings. In other cases, instructors recommended that research using outside sources might help, but it was not a requirement. Most of the assignments that did not use outside sources were critical readings of instructor-provided texts. We classified these as IL assignments because they required critical reading and synthesis of information. All Breadth and Depth science courses, if they had IL assignments,

Figure 12.8
Assignments Requiring Outside Sources

Areas	Number of assignments	Percentage in curricular area
BAI: Breadth American Institutions	0	0%
BHU: Breadth Humanities	4	66.7%
BLS: Breadth Life Science	3	100.0%
BPS: Breadth Physical Science	2	100.0%
BSS: Breadth Social Science	6	66.7%
DHA: Depth Humanities and Arts	6	30.0%
DSC: Depth Science	6	75.0%
DSS: Depth Social Science	22	57.9%
Totals	49	

required outside sources 75–100 percent of the time. Depth humanities courses with IL assignments, however, were less likely to require outside sources (only 30 percent of the time; see Figure 12.8); these courses tended to assign critical readings of required texts.

Only 22 percent of syllabi with IL assignments mentioned the library in any capacity. Other syllabi mentioned the library as the source of course reserve readings but did not have any IL assignments. Of the 49 assignments that required outside research of some type, only 29 percent mentioned the library. Most often, the library was noted as the best place to find the kinds of scholarly sources required for the assignment. Five syllabi included library skills as a specific competency to be achieved by the end of the course. One suggested that the subject librarian was a useful resource for completing the research assignment.

Few of the IL assignments (20 percent) were assigned in stages. Usually, this meant preparing a topic proposal, outline, or annotated bibliography before the final paper was due. Assigning a paper in stages forces students to reflect on their sources and do their research in advance of writing the final draft. Annotated bibliographies also deter plagiarism, as they require that students reflect on and summarize the sources they find. Twenty IL assignments required a certain number of outside sources; the average number was 4.5. Nearly the same number of assignments (22) either required certain types of sources, especially scholarly articles, or forbade or limited the use of Web resources. Thirteen assignments required a certain number and made specifications as to the types of sources students could use.

Thirty-five percent of the 89 IL assignments stated clear criteria for grading, and IL requirements were included in 19 of these. These criteria often addressed the use of credible sources and proper citation mechanics. Most of the courses with IL grading criteria (16) were either Depth Social Science or Depth Humanities courses.

The 89 IL assignments addressed, as a whole, the entire range of the ACRL Standards. Standard Three (i.e., the evaluation of information for credibility and usefulness) was the most commonly addressed standard (75 percent). Sixty-three percent covered Standard Two (i.e., selecting search tools and searching effectively).

Very few general education courses included a formal library instruction component. Only 8.4 percent of the approved general education courses brought classes to the library for instruction between 2003 and 2005. Most of these classes were in the Depth Humanities and Depth Social Science areas (60 percent).

The results of the general education syllabi audit suggest that little formal IL instruction was taking place across the general education curriculum between 2003 and 2005. While a syllabus does not reflect the full range of instruction that occurs in a class, its descriptions of assignments, learning goals, and content coverage provide one view of the way that IL may be integrated into a course. Furthermore, librarians are not the only ones who teach IL skills, and looking at syllabi may fail to completely capture whether instructors are teaching students about the nature of information and knowledge in a discipline, how to use search tools and evaluate information, or how to document sources.

Nevertheless, the audit suggests that many general education courses were not fulfilling the mandate to teach IL skills. The audit confirms that most students receive formal, integrated IL instruction only in the two required composition courses: Introduction to Writing and Intermediate Writing. Approximately half of students test out of Introduction to Writing, so a large number of students receive IL instruction only in Intermediate Writing. Depending on their major, some USU students receive additional library instruction in introductory upper division and disciplinary classes. Yet, students can graduate from USU with virtually no formal IL instruction, depending on their major and their instructor's approach to Intermediate Writing. The sciences were especially underrepresented in both the number of IL assignments and in offering formal library instruction (science classes represented only 9 of 188 subject-specific library sessions taught in 2004–2005, for example).

We presented the result of the syllabi audit to the General Education Subcommittee at one of their regular meetings. The results were surprisingly well received, despite the potentially critical tone of the audit. Committee members were surprised to hear about the peripheral nature of IL in so many of the general education courses. Librarians suggested that one of the reasons that faculty members might not include IL components into their courses was that the original requirements, written 10 years before, were overly broad and hard to interpret. The committee then charged a smaller, informal task force to investigate how to clarify those broad requirements. The task force first sent an e-mail to several general education instructors, asking for the following information:

In your own words, briefly describe what students should know or be able to do in terms of information literacy by the end of an integrated breadth course. Please feel free to focus on your particular disciplinary area of science, social science, or the humanities. Please provide some concrete or specific examples, if possible.

We then met with these instructors and clarified some of their IL learning goals. Using the information from these discussions, we wrote the following preliminary learning goals for breadth courses:

- Students need to know that there are a variety of information sources, many available only through the library.
- Students need to understand something about the context of how information gets produced, so that they can differentiate between opinion, informed opinion, research-based findings, and so on.
- Students need to learn that librarians who specialize in different subjects are available for help.

We also identified barriers to integrating IL into general education courses. The most common barrier was large class size. Some general education classes enroll 100–500 students, and faculty members cannot easily grade written assignments or conduct in-class discussions. Several instructors felt time pressure, particularly in breadth classes, to cover a large amount of material. Librarians also identified the problem of repetition. Some students receive the same kind of instruction about using library resources in Introduction to Writing, Intermediate Writing, and then some general education and other discipline-specific courses. Any solution to integrating IL in the breadth courses had to develop a more sequenced approach, introducing basic ideas in general education courses and building on these with greater sophistication in the major. Librarians and faculty members were in strong agreement that IL, in some form, is vital in the breadth courses. The task force felt that if students are not at least introduced to library resources early in their careers, it is harder to move them beyond general Web resources and Google. Finally, the task force brainstormed some general ideas about practical activities and assignments that might serve as a model for general education courses. In the humanities, for example, we proposed that students read one classic work (or primary source) and then read one scholarly article about that source, in order to see how humanities scholars "work."

The task force presented a summary of their discussions and ideas to the General Education Subcommittee. The summary was also distributed to all instructors of general education courses. In response, one general education instructor took up our proposed humanities assignment. We also saw an increase in requests for library instruction from general education classes in 2007–2008.

Building on this momentum, librarians decided to tackle the general education classes as part of an annual instructional design program. Each year librarians determine an area for developing or improving IL instruction. We select, through an application process, three to five IL Fellows (generally faculty members in the "target" area) to work with librarians to design instruction. We provide them with a small stipend ($500). General education was the focus of our efforts for the 2007–2008 academic year. We hired three general education instructors to develop concrete models (including lesson plans and classroom activities) for integrating IL into breadth general education courses. The Fellows worked closely with librarians in the sciences, social sciences, and humanities to develop model instruction. In Fall 2008, these ideas were posted to the Library and General Education Web sites, and we offered outreach and training opportunities to help instructors adapt various instructional models and ideas into their courses.

The general education syllabi audit resulted in concrete change at USU. Although some instructors might have read the results as critical of their practice, many were instead motivated to change their approach to IL. The audit led to productive conversations between librarians and faculty members about what it means to be information literate in a discipline. The results provided impetus for sustained and creative collaboration between librarians and instructors through the IL Fellows program. The results continue to provide concrete data for outreach to faculty. In 2009, the General Education Subcommittee will consider changing the language of the IL requirement to better match what librarians and faculty members identified as their common learning goals.

LIBQUAL+

In Spring 2007 the USU Library conducted a LibQUAL+ survey to assess library services to the university community. Almost 20 percent of USU's population responded to the survey. There were no questions in the LibQUAL+ survey that asked directly about library instruction. However, there were five "Information Literacy Outcomes Questions"; respondents were asked to rate their satisfaction levels from one to nine, one representing the least satisfaction and nine representing the most.

Figure 12.9 shows the USU ratings by population (undergraduates, graduates, faculty), and the overall average for each question. Compared to American Research Libraries averages, USU scored slightly lower on all of the outcomes statements but one: "The library helps me distinguish between trustworthy information and untrustworthy information." The undergraduates scored higher than graduate students and faculty for these statements, generally, suggesting that undergraduates saw the library as playing a role in their development of information literacy skills, and that the library was doing a slightly better job at meeting these needs for this population. It also suggests that the library needs to better focus on IL outcomes, especially for graduate students and faculty.

Of 2,537 responses, 1,192 include comments. Of these comments, 26 dealt directly with library instruction. Twenty of these were by undergraduates, four by faculty, and two by graduate students. Instruction comments fit into one of three categories: positive, negative, and "want more instruction." Positive comments generally retold helpful experiences of working with librarians in the classroom and made up the majority of instruction comments. Negative comments portrayed disappointing experiences with library instruction; only two comments fit into this category. Nine respondents said they wanted more library instruction opportunities in their classes.

Seventy-five percent of instruction comments left by faculty were positive. These comments commended the instruction librarians for their efforts, e.g., "Your greatest resource is the teaching librarians. They are so helpful, thoughtful, and knowledgeable. My students love our library visits, and so do I" (Faculty, Humanities, Arts, & Social Sciences, age 31–45, female). One faculty comment was "want more instruction," indicating the faculty member's need for personal library instruction: "I haven't had time to learn how to access it [the library]. I am constantly overwhelmed by work pressures and even though the library is a great resource, I can't stop long enough to get oriented" (Faculty, Education and Human Services, age 46–65, male). While this faculty member seemed to think this problem was theirs and not the library's, the library instruction program can do a better job to alleviate faculty confusion. There were no negative instruction comments left by faculty.

Graduate students left the fewest instruction comments. The two comments received were split: one respondent praised library instruction ("I also appreciate the classes offered on specific topics" [Graduate, Science, age 23–30, male]) and the other requested more instruction opportunities

Figure 12.9
USU LibQUAL+ Survey Ratings by Population

Statement	Undergraduate mean	Graduate mean	Faculty mean	Overall USU mean	Overall ARL mean
The library helps me stay abreast of developments in my field(s) of interest.	6.23	6.36	6.07	6.24	6.85
The library aids my advancement in my academic discipline.	6.89	6.87	6.40	6.85	7.34
The library enables me to be more effective in my academic pursuits.	7.18	6.95	6.58	7.11	7.47
The library helps me distinguish between trustworthy information and untrustworthy information.	6.24	5.91	5.64	6.16	6.10
The library provides me with the information skills I need in my work or study.	6.65	6.41	5.92	6.57	6.82

("Provide at least one formal library orientation session to new students for them to easily get acclimatized to the library" [Graduate, Engineering, age 31–45, male]).

Undergraduates wrote the majority of comments, and they mentioned library instruction 20 times in the LibQUAL+ survey. Fifty-five percent of undergraduate comments were positive, 35 percent stated "want more instruction," and 10 percent were negative. Positive comments often referred to librarians by name and sometimes mentioned takeaway messages from library instruction sessions. For example, two students referred back to the Information Literacy Outcome question about source accuracy. One wrote, "I was never aware that some sources, even though they are published, can be totally inaccurate. A librarian showed me this when I came with a class one time" (Undergraduate, Natural Resources, age 23–30, male).

The very personal nature of several comments suggests that our high-touch approach to Introduction to Writing and Intermediate Writing is helping us meet one of our primary goals for these classes: to portray the library as a welcoming and user-friendly environment. One way to do this is by assigning librarians to the writing classes. Comments show that students responded favorably to one-on-one interaction with librarians and many students felt "ownership" of librarians, especially after multiple class visits. Many of the LibQUAL+ comments included positive comments about specific librarians: "Jane[5] was very helpful when I was researching for one of my papers. She knew exactly where to look and how to go about it" (Undergraduate, Undecided, age 18–22, male). Our citation analysis suggests that more time spent with a librarian might lead to greater use of library resources. The LibQUAL+ comments help explain how the personalized, high-touch approach contributes to greater library use.

Many undergraduate students noted the benefits of "point-of-need" instruction: "It's often too much information having someone verbally teach you all the library can do. It's easier to go in, learn how to get the one type of resource you're there for, get it, and go" (Undergraduate, Education and Human Services, age 23–30, male). To address this, the library recently started holding evening point-of-need instruction sessions twice a week, called "Find It Fast." In these sessions, library peer mentors (student employees trained to provide reference and instruction assistance) demonstrate how to find books and articles quickly and then help students with individual research needs. Some instructors offer extra credit if students attend these sessions, while other students attend if they have a paper due and need general help accessing articles or other resources. The "Find It Fast" sessions were implemented after receiving the LibQUAL+ comments, but attendance has been light. These sessions need to be better marketed in order to reach students in need.

While some undergraduates clearly benefited from making a personal connection to a librarian, others felt lost. Several undergraduates identified the need for general orientation sessions, in addition to the point-of-need sessions and the integrated Introduction to Writing and Intermediate Writing curriculum. The seven "want more instruction" comments left by undergraduates confirm the library can be perceived as a very intimidating and overwhelming place for many students, particularly incoming freshmen. The "want more instruction" comments often conveyed feelings of confusion and apprehension concerning library resources: "I would guess that the most common concern for people using the library is the sense of intimidation they feel in not knowing how to properly use the library's resources" (Undergraduate, Education and Human Services, age 23–30, male). These undergraduates suggested that general workshops could be offered each semester to alleviate this stress. In Fall 2009, the library instruction program will expand the marketing for "Find it Fast" to address the needs of undergraduates, and institute a series of workshops for graduate students and faculty.

LibQUAL+ comments from undergraduates also suggest a need to cleverly market library services as "user friendly" to all of our students, especially nontraditional (distance education and returning) students. Students want to feel comfortable navigating the library and we want them to keep coming back. As one nontraditional student commented, "I might use the library more often if I felt more comfortable looking up information." Technology, combined with the general size of the collection, tends to block access for some students who opt for Google's instant gratification over scholarly, reliable sources available from library databases. LibQUAL+ comments indicate student frustration with technology issues, including difficulty using Article Linker (our open URL resolver), navigating the library Web site, and finding books using the Library of Congress system. According to one student, "While I need the library to have the tools I need for my education, the library feels too big to be able to find anything in there for anyone who has not been initiated to the university library circle" (Undergraduate, Humanities, Arts, & Social Sciences, age 18–22, female).

There were also two negative comments from undergraduates. Some students who visited the library for both Introduction to Writing and Intermediate Writing felt that attending one "library day session" was sufficient for their research needs: "I wish teachers wouldn't make students sit through the library tours after they have been to some. I have had to go to more than a couple" (Undergraduate, Education & Human Services, age 18–22, female). Another undergraduate lamented that the library instructor treated her like "an elementary school child." These comments were similar to those we receive on teaching evaluations and one-minute surveys that ask students to reflect on their learning at the end of an instruction session. Two types of students emerge from all of this data: a group that desires more "basic" instruction, including library tours and help with locating material in the print and electronic collections, and a group that finds library instruction too repetitive and elementary.

Although the LibQUAL+ comments that focus on library instruction were few, they provide clues on how to best serve our different populations of students. The comments directly addressing instruction generally validate our high-touch approach to library instruction. The majority of instruction sessions we teach at the Merrill-Cazier Library are coordinated with specific classes and instructors.

These sessions seem to have a lasting impact. In their comments, faculty members appreciated collaboration with the librarians, and students recalled not only librarians' names, but also the lessons that those librarians taught.

The comments also highlight the need for better "orientation" sessions and suggest that nontraditional, distance, and graduate students might be particularly underserved by the library instruction program. The value of even a few negative instruction-related comments is significant. They give voice to students whom we might not be reaching effectively, especially nontraditional students. They also highlight barriers that we might not identify through methods like citation analysis. We often assume that students do not use the library because of the convenience of Google, but the LibQUAL + comments suggest that perceived barriers, including a large building and overly complex search interfaces, might contribute to this as well. The LibQUAL+ results point to some concrete areas where we can change our practice in instruction, but they also highlight systemic issues that go beyond instruction.

CONCLUSIONS

Most teachers have a good sense of when instruction is or is not working simply by spending time with students in the classroom, but in our contemporary educational context, numbers are often what count most. Our assessment approach at USU tries to build upon the insights and instincts of librarians in the classroom and at the reference desk and the power of data to report our successes and persuade librarians, faculty, and administrators when change is needed. We focus on the entire picture before us, using qualitative sources to help us better read our data and inform and enliven our practice. With citation analysis, we get a large-scale look at the search behavior of our students and their preference for electronic sources and Google. Our LibQUAL+ survey results suggest ways in which that preference might be due to barriers to using the library, some related to the instruction program's failure to reach certain populations of students, and some related to confusing library interfaces. Faculty members often bemoan their students' inability to use scholarly resources, but our syllabi audit suggests that this might be because students are not provided with meaningful activities and assignments that encourage the use of scholarly resources. Likewise, in designing curricula to promote IL in general education courses, our LibQUAL+ survey data, teaching evaluations, and classroom anecdotes all tell us that we need to avoid repetition. We need to have clear learning goals for each class and design activities that account for different levels of skill and experience among our students. Some students will require very basic introductory instruction, while others will need meaningful opportunities to practice and apply what they learned in previous library sessions.

All of these cases suggest the ways in which we learn from multiple sources and readings of data. Assessment is never a finished product at USU. We continually expand and circle back on our understanding of our students, our faculty, and our own teaching practice. We use this understanding to communicate to our entire community of librarians, faculty, students, and administrators rich and complicated stories with concrete numbers and nuanced qualitative readings of our data. We use the data to try to tease out the "why" as well as the "what happened" so that we can effectively improve our practice and identify potential partners, allies, and opportunities for change.

ENDNOTES

1. LibQUAL+ is a registered trademark by the Association of Research Libraries.

2. We categorized Wikipedia as a separate type of source, just to see how many students cited it. None of the Introduction to Writing students cited it, and it represented only 3 percent of the total Intermediate Writing citations.

3. In Introduction to Writing it was more difficult to determine the variety of sources used by individual students because the bibliographies were submitted as part of a group project. Some students submitted bibliographies as a group, so we could only assess the variety of sources used by the entire group. Other students submitted a bibliography for their individual contribution to the larger group project. These bibliographies usually included only two citations. Percentages of the types of sources cited in a two-item bibliography were always 50 percent (two different types of sources) or 100 percent (both sources are of the same type). These percentages are misleading, so they are not reported here.

4. This percentage only reflects the inclusion of information literacy assignments in the syllabi from our sample, which is a convenience sample of all the syllabi we could locate. We analyzed syllabi from 73 percent of the Breadth Life Science and 88 percent of the Breadth Physical Science courses approved for general education. The percentage of courses represented by syllabi in the two breadth science areas is higher than the average of 73 percent across all subject areas (see Figure 12.6).

5. Names have been changed for privacy.

REFERENCES

Davis, Philip M. 2003. Effect of the Web on undergraduate citation behavior: Guiding student scholarship in a networked age. *Portal: Libraries and the Academy* 3:41–51.

Hovde, Karen. 2000. Check the citation: Library instruction and student paper bibliographies. *Research Strategies* 17:3–9.

Hurst, Susan, and Joseph Leonard. 2007. Garbage in, garbage out: The effect of library instruction on the quality of students' term papers. *E-JASL: Electronic Journal of Academic and Special Librarianship* 8 (1). http://southernlibrarianship.icaap.org/content/v08n01/hurst_s01.htm.

Kuh, George D. 2005. *Student success in college: Creating conditions that matter.* San Francisco: Jossey-Bass.

Mohler, Beth A. 2005. Citation analysis as an assessment tool. *Science & Technology Libraries* 25 (4): 57–64.

Robinson, Andrew M., and Karen Schlegl. 2004. Student bibliographies improve when professors provide enforceable guidelines for citations. *Portal: Libraries and the Academy* 4:275–90.

Tinto, Vincent. 1993. *Leaving college: Rethinking the causes and cures of student attrition.* Chicago: University of Chicago Press.

Ursin, Lara, Elizabeth Blakesley-Lindsay, and Corey M. Johnson. 2004. Assessing library instruction in the freshman seminar: A citation analysis study. *Reference Services Review* 32:284–92.

Utah State University General Education Subcommittee. "Criteria for Integrated Breadth Course." Utah State University. www.usu.edu/provost/academic_programs/geduc_univstud/designation_criteria.cfm .

PART V

Specific Methods and Issues

CHAPTER 13

If the Library Were a Business, Would It Be Profitable?: How Businesses Go Beyond Numbers

MICHAEL A. CRUMPTON

The comparison of library operations to businesses, in particular retail businesses has been a subject of debate over the past several years. Especially with the development of the bookstore superstore and the perceived competition for "users," some libraries have looked at such models in order to adapt useful elements to help "patrons" identify with user services and available materials that fit current needs and lifestyles. Like businesses that are driven by a need to be profitable, libraries also have to look for the means by which to gather useful data and persuade funding authorities to spend money or invest in the organization. Can you compare business incentives for capital expenditures with justification of expenses that a library needs by creating data-driven arguments? The answer is yes; similarities do exist between libraries and businesses for the use of data that can influence decisions regarding sustainability and growth. Businesses, however, have learned to look beyond quantitative numbers in order to provide qualitative data that can add detail and depth to justifications and proposals.

Librarians debate the use of the term "customer" in referring to library users because the commercial aspect of a business (sales), or services for profit, differs from a library's function as a nonprofit organization that in most cases is providing materials and services for free. Opinions in the field vary, with those that disagree focusing on the preservation and cultural aspect of libraries and on the flexibility that comes with not having to answer to shareholders or other established business standards. As a thriving organization, however, the library must generate customer- or user-driven data that can become the means by which measurable standards are created and maintained, justifying the use of funds, resources, and time. What happens when those resources are threatened or compromised? Has the organization experienced growth or change which needs to be funded? Can typical library statistics provide a persuasive argument for obtaining needed resources or funding?

Libraries control a large amount of money that is used within the scope of operations for buying collections, paying staff, marketing, equipment, maintaining facilities, and other businesslike activities. What kinds of data are needed to support these spending decisions in libraries, and how does the effective management of finances compare to data-driven decisions in business? Businesses are expected to earn profits, while libraries are expected to serve their designated clientele. Businesses must develop a degree of efficiency in order to be profitable; libraries must also be efficient in order to make the best use of existing resources as well as explore patrons' requests for the newest and latest information resources and accompanying technology. This chapter will look at techniques used in business environments that provide information beyond statistics, which is used for acquiring and evaluating data to make profitable decisions. This type of decision-making is also useful in a library environment to marshal resources and justify expenditures needed to support services and the information needs of patrons.

ECONOMIC UTILITY

Most business models start with determining how products and services will ultimately affect customer satisfaction. A basic economic utility model for the marketing of retail businesses determines if goods or services can satisfy one or more needs or wants of a consumer. Major elements including time, place, form, and possession are the broad categories that need to be addressed in order to obtain and sustain a profitable operation. Keeping in mind that library users are also retail customers, a comparison of these broad categories used in business can also be used by library organizations seeking to satisfy patron needs. Figure 13.1 shows the economic utility element and its business definition, as well as how it could be defined and used by libraries.

To be considered successful, businesses strive to make sales and conduct business efficiently, and libraries seek to satisfy patrons, determine information needs, and serve a variety of interests. A business must make a financial investment in each of the elements that support all of the economic utilities: having merchandise on time, a nice place or Web site to attract shoppers, enough of an assortment for customers to generate interest, and of course the overhead needed (including personnel, equipment, and fixtures) to interact with the customer and make the sale. Business activities will generate some data and statistics related to the process of doing business and that provides the basis for determining ongoing operational decisions. Beyond the basic operations, further financial decisions require additional data regarding activities such as consumer behavior, shopping patterns, and customer predictability, which justify additional investment into the business. This additional data is needed to persuade investors that the business is making sound decisions and that objectives are being met successfully, as indicated by the possession utility.

The economic utility of a library revolves around the same four elements identified by businesses: time, place, form, and possession. These elements are what customers or users relate to and expect. Therefore, if users do not get resources when needed, cannot obtain access or visit during library

Figure 13.1
Economic Utility Element

Utility	Business Definition	Library Interpretation
Time	Having merchandise when customers want it	Providing resources when requested
Place	Store locations, Web sites, easy accessibility	Hours and access efficient for patron use
Form	Merchandise mix or service assortment that complements and supports total experience	Array of information resources available to support mission of library and expectations of clientele
Possession	Sales and other business objectives are met successfully	Patron's information need was met or satisfied

hours, cannot find the type of information desired, or simply do not get their information need satisfied, they will not return or encourage others to use the library. Do typical usage statistics generated by library operations provide enough data for future decision-making in terms of having met patrons' information needs? Not completely. Knowing about user behaviors and information need patterns could provide strong arguments for requesting funds and resources for a library.

Businesses and libraries depend upon statistics generated by the activities of their organization to make daily decisions on operational issues. In a global, competitive society which is constantly changing, trends, fads, and personal habits are critical for analyzing the customer or end user to satisfy the economic utility. While usage statistics might support a particular course of action, generating additional data related to anthropological measurements will ensure those actions are relevant, efficient, and cost effective.

An example for libraries might be identifying the economic utility for satisfying user needs by making a decision to convert resources from print to electronic resources. Timing relates to understanding a patron's need for resources quickly, place relates to ensuring accessibility when needed, form relates to the general selection of resources available, and possession relates to the user's ability to be satisfied with the resources offered. Looking beyond usage data can help focus trends and user habits into data that supports more efficient decisions.

WHAT YOUR STATISTICS DON'T TELL YOU

Businesses generate many figures related to their operation. The basic ones are merchandise purchases and the resulting gross margin, costs, and expenses associated with doing business, and the all-important sales figures, which indicate money or cash flow coming into the business (hopefully more than is going out). To ensure that the figures generated are in keeping with the need for profitability, statistics are created with various sets of data to project trends and provide the basis for analyzing numbers and decision-making. These statistics can come in the form of cost ratios, sales trends by merchandise type, percent of shoppers using cash versus credit cards, or even number of people who enter a store in a day. But these are just a few of the data types needed for making decisions; businesses also look for other ways to analyze customer behavior and buying patterns.

Similar statistics generated by libraries might include the number of hits on a database, circulation data, number of reference questions, and gate counts. But can statistics alone tell a business that it will continue to be profitable, predict merchandise trends, or identify problems within the business that are festering? Can statistics alone tell library administration that users are satisfied with their services? In this new information age, libraries are competing not only with bookstore superstores, but also with the Internet and the tools and portals that support access to information from a multitude of locations. What else would a business need to know in order to maximize operational efficiency and ensure success through profitable activities?

Many elements can affect a customer's buying decision. Activities including analyzing the customer's experiences or perceptions, determining why they are purchasing, and uncovering environmental or comfort factors that can affect customers can all give new meaning or depth to statistics. Businesses look beyond operational activity generated or quantitative data to determine consumer buying behaviors and predict product and usage trends in order to maximize the organizational effort put forth through marketing, facility standards, employee training, display standards, and merchandise assortment. Libraries can also look beyond statistics and operational numbers to learn what customers/patrons need and desire.

Statistics alone do not tell the entire story of consumer or library user activity. Statistics do not tell about the human behavior side of activities associated with doing business or providing library services. Statistics is about reporting the results of actions taken in a specific period of time, in specific environmental conditions, and under certain circumstances. Many people use these types of statistics to predict future actions or needs. While that is not wrong, it can be incomplete in providing comprehensive support for major decisions. Qualitative research helps not only support and justify decisions made based on quantitative statistics, but also helps one truly understand if actions taken or activities produced have the desired result: profit for a business or satisfying an information need for a library.

THINKING LIKE THE USER

Librarians traditionally go to library school to learn the how, what, when, and where of information resources. The "who" is the end user, whose information needs the librarian is learning how to satisfy. Typical interactions with library users focus on the librarian teaching, training, and showing users how to access information resources, locate materials, conduct electronic searches, and evaluate results. These typical interactions can illustrate that the user is expected to learn how to think like the librarian. The librarian is sharing his or her knowledge through personal instruction, presuming that users will emulate those skills in future situations as information needs occur.

Businesses are now learning that to achieve their goals of profitability and efficiency, they must learn to think like their customers. This knowledge goes beyond gathering and analyzing numbers on activities; for example, how much of a certain brand of toothpaste is sold, or at what discount you can sell the most pairs of shoes and still make a profit. It is about understanding the customer and what makes the customer choose that brand of toothpaste, or what factors influence a shoe buying decision. This focus also seeks to discover what a customer is thinking in terms of product need, shopping environment, convenience, staff interaction, marketing effort, and online support, as well as to recognize when customers begin to change their habits, needs, and desires so as to predict future buying habits and thus adapt operations and decision-making early for greater efficiency.

The field of librarianship has also begun looking at tools that focus on the attributes that users value. One of the most popular is LibQUAL+, an academic library tool for determining user perceptions about materials and resources, staff assistance, and facilities. LibQUAL+ is a suite of services that libraries can use to solicit feedback, track and gather response information, understand and interpret results, and act upon users' opinions of service quality. It is a Web-based survey tool that asks about patron expectations and their perceptions of the institution's success at meeting each expectation. Many institutional participants in the LibQUAL+ survey will follow up the survey results with focus group and interview activities to gain further insight into the data generated by the survey.

ANTHROPOLOGY OF SHOPPING

The "anthropology of shopping" is the study of humans while in an environment perceived to be retail in nature, or which provides the opportunity to buy goods and services. This type of study goes beyond using statistics for decision-making in order to incorporate observing what humans do and how they go about doing it, so as to predict and influence future decision-making. This has been made famous by Paco Underhill's book *Why We Buy: The Science of Shopping* (1999) in which he identifies close to 900 aspects of shopping, including atmospherics and environment, shoppers' perceptions, service implications, and product attributes. These concepts also have applications to other service-based organizations concerned about assessment of activities beyond numbers.

Studying and observing retail shopping in depth helps distinguish what works from what does not work in the execution of a business plan. The focus of conducting qualitative research is obtaining evidence gathered by observation and utilizing a variety of senses (smells, temperature, and visually pleasing displays) in order to capture the attention of patrons and better understand their actions and intentions. This type of approach also draws conclusions that directly affect business decisions. For example, in Underhill's book, he concludes that merchandise placed in narrow spaces, which can cause customers to be "butt brushed," will not meet its full potential of sales because of customers' discomfort with being touched. This type of conclusion is based on statistics gathered from observing individual actions, e.g., shoppers trying to read labels in narrow aisles. Another example found that men are shopping for underwear themselves now, identifying a change from the past norm by which women were the primary purchaser of men's underwear. This conclusion affected how underwear manufacturers marketed men's underwear: to men (using sports figures), instead of to women (with healthy looking models).

Pursuing Underhill's lead of observing customer shopping habits, Herb Sorensen (2003) makes some additional conclusions that could be helpful in a library environment. Sorensen looks more globally, at the entire store, as opposed to specific product categories. He investigated the idea that with traditional marketing you either brought merchandise to the customer or you brought the customer to the merchandise. Based upon observing customer behaviors, Sorensen advocates maximizing exposure to specific products by their placement in the building with relation to natural traffic patterns within. This means that you can gather data that supports where services or materials should be located internally.

Sorensen's focus is inside of the facility (wall-to-wall and entrance-to-exit), which takes the focus off of where the building is located and places it on where items are located within the building. Libraries are usually not able to make general location decisions due to established institutional and community situations. He used an electronic tracking system to monitor shopper behavior, providing a large amount of data to establish traffic patterns and how they impact business decisions. He concludes that he needed to see where the customer went in the store so that appropriate merchandise is placed where customers are expected to travel internally.

Could this same philosophy apply in a library environment? Are we placing materials and services within the building in locations where users are walking, or are we simply modernizing traditional spaces in their traditional locations without thought to traffic patterns? Libraries are typically "destination locations," which means the user is coming to the library for a specific purpose, even if that purpose is leisure. Once users are in the library, opportunities exist to maximize their experience and strengthen their net gain from each particular visit by addressing the placement of services and materials based on observed needs.

Francine Fialkoff (2008), editor for *Library Journal*, writes that we must overcome our fear that our values as publicly supported agencies will be compromised by using the methods of experts like Underhill to promote library service. With that in mind, let's look at the anthropology of library use.

STUDYING LIBRARY USER BEHAVIORS

Businesses focus on the needs, desires, and behaviors of their customers in order to make decisions for profitability. Libraries have an opportunity as well to focus on users and understand the details of information and resource use from a user perspective. Business news is full of examples of what can happen when the focus is taken off the customer. A recent example is Ford Motor Company, which had continued to do business the same way it had for years. When business and profits dropped, the company set forth to analyze the problem. They determined that Ford was doing business with an "if we build it they will buy" mentality. They had not studied the thoughts and desires of customers to predict behaviors, buying patterns, or automobile needs and desires. Libraries also have a tendency to believe that just because they are there, users will come and be happy with what they find.

Studying library users' behaviors can provide some valuable data to help with decision-making in a variety of areas. Anthropological research can be conducted on humans from the point of view of culture, which in this case could be to study the research and information habits of library users. That is what Underhill and others have done with shopping, and they've used their findings to influence decisions regarding goods and services based on anthropological research. Components of anthropological research that could apply to library environments are sampling, interviewing, and participant observation.

Sampling can be important for a couple of reasons. First, you can use sampling to give your statistical data and measurements enhanced meaning by identifying how the data represents the context in which it was collected. You can take generalized information and create persuasive arguments targeted to specific needs or audiences. Sampling also can help identify the attributes of individuals or materials involved so as to create a relationship between the numbers and what the numbers mean. This is called probability sampling and according to sampling theory can be an accurate assessment of your data in relation to the sample size. Sampling theory is about interpreting distributions to extract the needed relationships between sets of data. If you are interested, for example, in learning if users will use a new database and want to sample a group of trial users, the larger the sample group of users, the more accurate their feedback will be in response to your questions regarding the database.

You can also sample with nonprobability expectations in a library environment by creating a focus group of experts in a particular area to establish culture data. Culture data takes into account the subject expert's topic expertise and can be helpful in making observations about particular resources, formats, space considerations, or technical areas in which special knowledge or skills are needed. This also allows you to address subcategories of the population (children, for example), to provide the expert knowledge or experience regarding the data in which you are interested. Much information exists regarding sampling, how to design and conduct sampling, and how to evaluate results. The intention here is to introduce it as a tool, once again used commonly in business, but also useful for strengthening other types of data and supporting arguments.

A simple example of using sampling to support and give depth to quantitative data regards gate counts. If you know your gate counts are X by hour or day (however you document), you could sample the users counted and create categories by demographics. If you sampled for number of patrons coming through the gates over age 50, this adds to your data.

For another example, a gate count on Monday of 100 people tells you that 100 people came in and out of your library. But by sampling 20 of those people and creating a distribution of who they are, you could instead say that on Monday we have a high probability (standard deviation) that 75 students and 15 faculty and 10 staff members come in and out of the library. Time of day, age, destination, and purpose are all possible elements that could be included. This is how businesses create demographic profiles for product development and marketing activities. In this example, by determining through sampling that 15 percent of Monday's traffic is faculty, decisions could be effected related to staffing (who to schedule), instructional classes, material displays, meetings to be scheduled, or other activities.

Interviewing is another type of anthropological research that is very useful in developing persuasive data. Paco Underhill's company Envirosell places a big emphasis on interviewing with formal methodologies, documentation, and trained staff that provide structure and credibility to the process, as listed on their Web site, www.envirosell.com. Examples of Envirosell's interview methods include "Shop-Along" interviews, accompanying shoppers through the store; location interviews, targeting of particular locations within the store; and sales associate interviews (talking to employees who interact with customers and know the kinds of questions that customers are asking).

Like sampling, interviewing can range from simple to complex, and a great deal of literature exists on managing the interview process. The purpose of interviewing is to extract useful information from conversation between two or more people. The amount of control desired for the interview could dictate the interview method used and the process in which it is executed. The amount of control and structure might also focus results into seeking more specific or targeted responses based on the information need.

Many libraries are already familiar with the use of focus groups for interviewing, which can be more efficient and timely by interviewing multiple people at once, but other types of interviewing are important as well. Underhill and his company focus on individual interviews that are structured to occur quickly and efficiently. Just like sampling, the more interviews conducted the more credible and authoritative the results will be.

Also important in both individual and focus group activities is "probing" for additional information. The art of probing involves learning how to stimulate responses in order to produce more information or details from the answers to each question. It is also important that questioners not allow too much of themselves to bleed into conversations and influence probed responses. But probing is an effective way to gain additional or detailed information from customers or library users.

Participant observation is considered to be at the core of conducting cultural anthropology studies. Participant observation is defined by Bernard (2006) as a set of research strategies which aim to gain a close and intimate familiarity with a given group of individuals. Examples are religiously, occupationally, or culturally different groups, or particular communities of common interest. Observation of their practices through an intensive involvement with people in their natural environment over an extended period of time allows the observer to be treated as a participant within the group. This is an important part of Envirosell's strategy in commercial research, and they have developed proprietary tools and guidelines for collecting data in this manner.

Envirosell calls this "tracking" and has trained professional teams making up the The Envirosell Tracker Pool that specialize in the detailed observation of customers interacting with both macro- and micro-elements within store environments. Envirosell clients credit many changes to their strategic planning process or changes in direction to the results delivered by Envirosell.

This type of data collecting is considered fieldwork, and much of the information gathered will be qualitative in nature, thus adding "personality" to the numbers generated from operational activities. This fieldwork can be important in making better persuasive arguments by providing detail and substance to quantitative data.

SOME OTHER TECHNIQUES TO CONSIDER

Mystery shopping is a popular assessment technique, used by businesses to evaluate services from a customer's perspective. Criteria are defined, format and process selected, and then trained employees posing as customers "shop" a store or business to observe and record their findings. Kate Tesdell (2000) describes how the Willard Library's reference service was "shopped." The shoppers were looking for accuracy of information, degree of helpfulness, and added distinction provided in routine transactions. This data, along with observational data during the "shops," was used to address building improvements and create strategic planning opportunities.

Another technique used in business for decision-making is learning to recognize changes, or more specifically, paying attention to trends. Dr. Dale Achabal, Associate Dean of the Retail Management Institute, discusses the trend of multichannel models, stating, "I can't think of a significant retailer today that is not operating under a multi-channel model because the data shows that customers are shopping in multiple channels" (Chandler 2005, 12). This should certainly apply to libraries, whose users are utilizing multiple resources and formats to get the information they need. Recognizing those trends in use can help a library make decisions related to the investment of equipment, space, and resources.

One of the largest operating expense items in a retail store is payroll. Depending on the type of retail, payroll expenses can be 50–75 percent of a store's controllable costs and thus have a direct impact on profit. Likewise, in a library model, control of payroll is important for efficiency; payroll dollars must be stretched to fulfill the labor need related to the work needing to be done. Retail businesses use a combination of analyzing traffic patterns, peaks, and valleys during any given time frame and calculating an average hourly rate of pay to project needs and move staff accordingly. It is also understood at the time of hiring that staff work within a range of time, instead of set shifts, so as to remain flexible for future adjustments to peaks and valleys of customer traffic or operational activity.

SOME DIFFERENCES TO BE AWARE OF

A big difference in businesses studying their customers and libraries studying their patrons is uniqueness. Many businesses, especially retail, are chain driven or utilize the same operational model in multiple locations. This means that information learned within a given set of circumstances can be duplicated across a wide number of locations. Libraries, even larger systems, tend to focus on the unique aspects of their local community, school, or patron base and thus must have the ability to customize data gathering to reflect local attributes and situations. Whereas businesses hold industry-wide meetings to implement and execute research methods or activities, librarians hold workshops and conferences to "share" what they've done individually or locally, with the intended result of participants taking the ideas and techniques back home and adapting them to their institutions' own individual needs and goals.

Vendor relationships can be different as well. Library vendors are not only developing product for end users but also for the librarians themselves. Some vendors might have a tendency to offer products based on their perception of the purchaser (librarian), not the end user. This can result in products that do not fulfill the need appropriately for the user and is a good reason to provide the vendor with qualitative data to better support the need.

CONCLUSIONS

In this brief comparison of retail businesses and library operations, the objective has been to encourage anthropologically driven measurements of performance that will provide statistical data to enhance the value or substance of numerical data when used in making persuasive arguments or proposals for increased financial investment. Businesses, in particular retail related businesses that have direct contact with customers, have developed strategies and methods that provide the means to learn more from their customers, in order to justify investment in their businesses. The basic economic utility model discussed above can be applied to libraries seeking to compete for users just as retailers must compete for customers. The use of anthropological type data can give credence to persuasive arguments for decision-making within the organization.

The science of thinking like a library user takes analyzing quality data beyond the techniques used in LibQUAL+. But the information gained from a LibQUAL+ survey can be used to create a program of anthropological data collection (e.g., sampling, interviewing, and observation) that will give more depth and detail to survey data and the interpretation of the results. Library users are becoming more sophisticated in their information needs, and information resources are becoming more accessible and openly available. In order for libraries to compete in attracting and retaining users who seek library services, it will become increasingly crucial to know how users think, what motivations and factors affect users' decision-making, and how users view the role that the library should perform within their lives. Anthropological methods of gathering data to learn more about users and their needs can make a tremendous difference in an organization's ability to compete for users and resources in order to sustain and grow.

REFERENCES

Bernard, H. R. 2006. *Research methods in anthropology: Qualitative and quantitative approaches*. Lanham, MD: Alta Mira Press.

Chandler, Michele. 2005. Multi-channel merchandising essential. *Mercury News*, December 11. As cited in *The 2006 retail business market research handbook*. Loganville, GA: Roger K. Miller & Associates.

Fialkoff, Francine. 2008. Giving good library. *Library Journal* 129 (12): 8.

Sorensen, H. 2003. The science of shopping—location is important, but it's not everything. *Marketing Research* 15 (3): 30. www.retailwire.com/Downloads/ScienceOfShopping.pdf.

Tesdell, K. 2000. Evaluating public library service—the mystery shopper approach. *Public Libraries*, 39 (3): 145.

Underhill, P. 1999. *Why we buy: The science of shopping*. New York, NY: Simon & Schuster.

CHAPTER 14

The Use of Grounded Theory in Interlibrary Loan Research: Compliance Always Occurs

DAVID E. WOOLWINE AND JOSEPH A. WILLIAMS

INTRODUCTION

Library science employs a variety of methodologies when conducting research (Woolwine 2007). Prior studies on doctoral theses in library and information science indicates that surveys as well as historical and bibliographic methods were used from 1977 to 1994, with the survey method being dominant (Blake 1994, 2003). Other research indicates that various qualitative methodologies were common in the 1980s, including symbolic interactionism, ethnomethodology, phenomenology, discourse analysis, and sociolinguistic analysis (Fidel 1993; Kim 1996; Powell 1999). Hjørland (1998; 2000) and Benoît (2002) describe the philosophical and theoretical underpinnings of various methodologies which Benoît broadly categorizes as positivist versus hermeneutical. There is clearly a division between quantitative and qualitative methods as indicated by Trosow (2001) and Mansourian (2006) but interestingly, outside of Mansourian's work, there is little documentation on the use of grounded theory in library science.

Grounded theory (which will be discussed in more detail later in this chapter) is a sociological methodology that is "grounded" in data which has been obtained by sociological research. This type of methodology contrasts with "formal abstract theory obtained by logico-deductive methods." It was an important development in sociological research in the 1970s that sought to unite "uninformed empirical research and empirically uninformed theory by grounding theory in data" (Abercrombie 2006, 174). Grounded theory by its nature is more pragmatic than other sociological methodologies. What this chapter will do is present an analysis of data on interlibrary loan departments as a model of how grounded theory may be used in library science research.

PROBLEM BACKGROUND

As the full-text availability of scholarly journals has increased due to the presence of licensed databases in academic libraries, two questions have emerged in interlibrary loan research. The first concerns whether the presence of such databases, which also contain indexed and abstracted articles, has caused an increase or decrease in the number of interlibrary loan transactions in aggregate. Wiley and Chrzastowksi (2005) find a 20–26 percent decline occurring in requests between the years 1995 and 2003 in a sample of Illinois libraries. Egan (2005), in a study of requests made by faculty and graduate students at John Jay College/City University of New York for the years 1994–2004, finds that faculty requests initially increased or stayed consistent from 1994 to 1998, then increased greatly until 2000, followed by a substantial decline by 2002 (which may be due partly to the fact that in 2000 JSTOR was added to the library resources at John Jay). Changes in graduate student requests at John Jay were not as dramatic but also showed substantial reductions from 2001 onward.

The second major issue concerning interlibrary loan practices in an increasingly electronic environment is whether the presence of licensing agreements and restrictions led to changes in practices within these departments. Wiley's (2004) study, based on a survey of 13 major research libraries in the Midwest, finds various steps taken to deal with restrictions in the licenses. These include checking an internal list on paper or in a database, using a specialized software package, and keeping notes in the local holdings field of OCLC. Her major point is that licensing agreements constitute a problem for interlibrary loan departments. Croft (2005) argues that interlibrary loan departments use three possible responses to licensing restrictions: avoidance, reaction, or proactive behavior. She defines avoidance as not lending anything from electronic resources. Reactive steps are those detailed by Wiley above. Proactive behavior means negotiating terms with vendors to reduce restrictions.

RESEARCH BACKGROUND

As part of a study of academic libraries to determine whether the presence of electronic databases has decreased or increased interlibrary loan usage, we initially developed an open-ended questionnaire addressing the issue of licensing agreements and how they might impact departmental practices. It addressed governance of interlibrary loan departments (e.g., headed by a full-time MLS-holding librarian or not, duties of paraprofessionals), where licenses were physically held, and actions taken in regard to them when filling requests (e.g., checked every time a request came in, not checked, or final verification of compliance with licensing restrictions by library administrators). The questionnaire was posted on ILL-L, the major listserv for interlibrary loan librarians in the United States. The survey yielded 21 usable responses.

The initial intention, as laid out by Woolwine (2007), was to produce an ethnomethodological account of how social rules are constructed and followed in interlibrary loan departments. Developed by Harold Garfinkel (1984, 2002), ethnomethodology is premised on the assumption that social order arises out of the methods of regulating action used in everyday life. Such rules are not to be understood as residing somehow in the mind. They are embedded in, arising out of, and are understood only within social life (Frohmann 1990). Staged events, close observation of established situations or contexts, and discourse analysis are the usual means to uncover or elicit the types of methods (or rules) used to bring about the ordering of behavior and the continuation of shared action. In a famous study by Garfinkel (1984), regularly occurring "errors" or "omissions" in clinical medical records can be understood not as mistakes in a sort of actuarial record, but rather a record may be seen as a type of a contract produced, and then read, by competent clinic members, who follow implicit rules. As Garfinkel explains, "Folder contents are assembled against the contingent need, by some clinic members, to construct a potential or past course of transactions between the clinic and the patient as a 'case,' and thereby as an instance of a therapeutic contract . . . the clinic member 'makes a case' from the fragmented remains in the course of having to read into documents their relevance for each other as an account of legitimate clinic activity" (1984, 203). In order to read the record the clinic member must have a specific purpose in mind but also have an overriding interest in proving that implicit or explicit contractual agreements were kept with the patient. Furthermore, the "reader" of the clinic record must have background knowledge of the patient, of those who have recorded the information, the actual operating procedures of the clinic, and of standard procedures used in the clinic in order to "read" records (1984, 206).

So that we might reach a number of librarians, and thus have cases for comparison, we used a survey in the present study. We thought that, because of the survey format, a full ethnomethodological study of interlibrary loan practices might not be possible, primarily because close observations of an interlibrary loan department over a period of time were not done, and also because the type of narrative usually used in discourse analysis would not be forthcoming. However, a survey did not rule out interpreting the results in some ethnomethodological manner, or in a manner influenced by ethnomethodological concerns. But, given the type of data collected, a method other than a standard ethnomethodological one was needed to analyze the data.

The question became: What to do with the data? Finding an approach, or set of theories, useful for analysis became the task at hand. Grounded theory appeared to offer at least some assistance. The goal here would be to produce an initial interpretation, refine the analysis of interlibrary loan practices, and perhaps produce something that might aid in constructing a better quantitative questionnaire for the larger project. If the interpretation fit an ethnomethodological account, then fine, but if not, then we would go where the data led us. Admittedly this is a mixture of approaches, goals, and methods. It is carried out in the spirit of Liebscher (1998), who argues for a "between methods," approach or combination of methods in library science. Our overall approach, therefore, laid aside issues of ontology or schools of thought and became pragmatic through the use of grounded theory. We decided to use NVivo, a software program by QSR International that is often used by sociologists for analyzing qualitative data. The use of the software forced us to think seriously about our final codes. NVivo also allows, among other things, for matrix analysis of researcher-defined variables or attributes. Although such matrices can be constructed manually, using a program like NVivo produces "cleaner" and quicker results.

GROUNDED THEORY

Grounded theory originated in the work of Barney G. Glaser and Anselm L. Strauss (1967) and was later restated by Strauss (1987), Strauss and Corbin (1990, 1997) and Glaser (1992). Grounded theory consists of guidelines for collecting and analyzing qualitative data. Its goal is to develop middle-range theories that "fit" the data at hand. Charmaz, a major interpreter of grounded theory, argues that it can be used with both quantitative and qualitative data. In her summary of its steps she writes, "The strategies of grounded theory include (a) simultaneous collection and analysis of data, (b) a two-step data collection process, (c) comparative methods, (d) memo writing aimed at the construction of conceptual analysis, (e) sampling to refine the researcher's emerging theoretical ideas, and (f) integration of the theoretical framework" (2003, 251).

Glaser, Strauss, and Charmaz recommend the coding of data, sometimes line by line, as it is collected. One may go back and re-code if clear categories develop. Memo-writing is the recording of observations, initial interpretations, analysis, questions, conditions, and circumstances. It should be kept separate from the coding to not influence it too greatly. At later stages re-sampling or re-observation, guided in part by the interpretative categories that have emerged, can take place. Later samples or observations might alter the overall interpretation. The final stage would usually be the production of a more integrated theoretical framework.

Not all of these steps are taken here. For instance, we did not re-sample our respondents. We believe that these further steps may be satisfied by incorporating some of the interpretive insights, refined categories, and questions to be incorporated in a larger, quantitative survey of interlibrary loan departments which will be conducted in the near future.

STEP ONE: CODING AND NVIVO

Initial coding was developed on the basis of the questions themselves. In the act of framing a question, investigators usually have some idea of the types of answers that are to be expected, even if the questions, as in this case, are open-ended ones. Questions about interlibrary loan departments included "[I]s it headed by a full-time professional librarian (holding the MLS) for whom this is his/her primary responsibility?" and "What are the daily duties of the professional librarians working in interlibrary loans?" Examples of questions related to practices included "Does a member of the staff (including the librarian) check licensing agreements every time your department receives a request for a loan from an outside contact . . . ?" and "If not every time then when are such agreements consulted?" The responses given led to coding differently than what was expected. For instance, the simple distinction "MLS headed" and "non-MLS headed department" was almost immediately changed into "Heavily-involved MLS headed," "Detached MLS headed," and "non-MLS headed" departments. Likewise, licenses themselves were almost never consulted, but respondents often noted that they either employed a local printed list or an electronic solution (e.g., information in OCLC records or SFX) which summarized license restrictions and was either always or sometimes consulted. Questions about the skill levels of paraprofessionals, if answered at all, were usually brief and devoid of information. Questions about training and information given to paraprofessionals about licensing restrictions were indirectly useful, in that responses often revealed other practices in the department, e.g., the use of technological solutions instead of training.

Another question concerned whether licensing agreements were physically kept in the interlibrary loan department or elsewhere. Most were kept elsewhere, making direct consultation of the license on a regular basis almost impossible. Finally, respondents were asked if library administrators verified that licensing agreements were being followed. Since 18 of the 19 institutions answering this question indicated that there was no verification, our initial thought was that this "variable" was unimportant. However, it later emerged that this was a significant factor in our interpretation of the data.

STEP TWO: MEMO WRITING

Grounded theory's suggestion that memos be made simultaneously with coding but kept separate turned out to be beneficial. For example, in memos one can enter observations that the current codes do not fit or that categories are not easily definable. More general speculation and interpretation can be a part of memo-writing. As noted, we initially rejected the simple distinction between MLS headed and non-MLS headed departments and broke that category into three types: those headed by heavily involved librarians, those whose librarian was detached (performing multiple roles in the institution and leaving day-to-day ILL operations to the staff), and those where a non-MLS director ran the department (reporting, most often, to a high-level administrator at the institution). However, memo-writing soon showed us that some difficulty occurred in trying to place every department into even these three categories. The realities of daily life have a way of not lending themselves to categorization. So we decided to code both ways, using both a simple MLS/non-MLS code, as well as one that divided MLS headed departments into detached and involved librarians. In the end the detached/involved distinction proved to be the more useful one and we ultimately felt that the criteria were both clear enough and applied consistently enough to warrant keeping the distinction.

Another characteristic which emerged in the responses was the claim that the department was moving toward a technical solution or had requested one (from another department or from library administrators) but had been rebuffed. While there were not enough responses indicating this to re-code the data, it was filed away as a possible contribution to some theory or interpretation which might emerge.

A similar pattern was the occasional use of the phrase, "We check when questions arise." It did not occur frequently enough to be coded but arose often enough to be noted.

It was in memo-writing that a question arose which was to have major significance in the primary interpretation: should we take an "objectivist" or a "constructionist" position with regard to respondents' reported understanding of licenses? Could we take at face value one respondent's assertion that vendors X and Y never allow interlibrary loan requests to be filled from their databases, as well as the assertion of another that all vendors, including presumably X and Y, allow some filling from their databases? Was it the case that respondents did not know what was in the licenses, or that we did not know how much variation existed among licensing agreements? We decided that since we did not have access to the licenses and, therefore, could not determine what was "objectively true" about them, that we must suspend any doubts about the accuracy of various assertions. This led to a more "constructionist" way of thinking. To follow a "constructionist" position we would necessarily interpret the answers through the social framework by which those answers were given. We want to emphasize that the issue was revealed not through coding but rather through memo-writing. Our decision influenced the ultimate interpretation of the data; once we had accepted a general constructionist notion of interlibrary loan departmental practices, it became easier to define "compliance" in the manner that we ultimately did.

Even more importantly, the interplay of coding and memo-writing forced us to grapple with an issue that appeared at first to be an intractable problem, but later became useful in constructing the core interpretative category. The issue arose at the point in the survey where respondents were asked to "Describe any 'shortcuts,' 'rules of thumb,' or 'unofficial procedures' used in attempting to comply with licensing restrictions." Most respondents listed nothing or said they did not follow rules of thumb. Some of the same respondents indicated elsewhere in the survey that they did not seek to know what licensing restrictions existed and yet nonetheless filled requests from electronic databases. Others said they never followed "rules of thumb," but elsewhere gave statements that could be considered "rules of thumb." Finally, a small number explicitly said they followed "rules of thumb" and listed them. This indicated that not all the respondents agreed upon what constitutes a "rule of thumb." We began to think about how this interacted with the notion of "compliance" and how it was achieved in the social framework of these departments.

STEP THREE: PRIMARY INTERPRETATION

The practices Wiley (2004) notes (namely, keeping a local hardcopy list or using a technological solution) were employed by some of our respondents. One of the additional practices that Croft (2005) lists (refusal to loan any article from electronic databases) was also reported. Both Wiley and Croft argue that licensing restrictions on the loaning of articles from electronic databases pose problems for interlibrary loan departments. However, only four institutions reported never filling requests from electronic database holdings. If nonfilling is taken as the major problem produced by licensing restrictions we did not find strong evidence of it. Furthermore, even "time spent dealing with licenses" may not be a major problem. All the practices reported appear to allow loans to be filled with relative ease and in compliance with licensing restrictions in the vast majority of departments. Licenses themselves are almost never consulted, consulting lists or using technical solutions is not particularly time consuming, and all other practices reported appear to have been developed to allow quick decisions and actions to take place.

This leads to our major interpretive insight: compliance is a broad and subjective category and is always a matter of interpretation. The use of "rules of thumb, shortcuts, and hearsay" can be reinterpreted by interlibrary loan departments as types of compliance. As an initial interpretation we would argue, therefore, that in the area of filling requests from electronic databases the primary goal of the interlibrary loan department is to never see itself, or to be seen by others, as noncompliant (or at least not egregiously noncompliant). We argue that compliance is always achieved and that its achievement has emerged as one of the more important goals in an interlibrary loan department. Compliance can be interpreted as simply "not breaking the law" (achieved with most certainty by never filling from electronic databases), as using "good faith" shortcuts (through lists or technical solutions, either of which may or may not be completely accurate), by using memory (which may or may not be accurate), or as believing what one's administrator, or another librarian, says about the licenses (which may or may not be accurate). The important point is that these practices are almost never defined as "shortcuts," "rules of thumb," or "hearsay." When a respondent did indicate that their compliances practices followed a "rule of thumb," it was presented as being reasonable and at the worst case, a form of "harmless deviance" and "essentially compliant." Here, respondents stated, "I assume that online is like print . . . don't send if not allowed, but expect to be allowed to send," "Only fill requests that I know are 'free for all' or in our print collection," "Use electronic if we have print. Justification—we have the print and are using the electronic as a timesaver," and "If an issue [is] in the bindery we will use the electronic form . . . to fill a request. We feel this is justified since the print version is temporarily unavailable."

A department may also present itself as in compliance by stating that it is "moving in the direction of a technological solution" or has asked a librarian outside the department or an administrator to help them to do so. This response indicates that to the department they are "essentially compliant," even though the librarian and staff in the department may not be sure what the licensing restrictions are in any given instance.

Another way to establish compliance is to follow the rule "Consult when a question arises." This is a useful rule, since the conditions for following it cannot be established. In order to establish those conditions (which are rules themselves) one would have to list in advance all possible cases of "questions which arise" and determine in advance when particular cases, or types of cases, are sufficiently important to invoke the rule. Such conditions cannot be fully specified in advance because of their multiplicity. Finally, the fact that 18 of the 19 departments responding reported that no higher administrator verified that the department complied with licensing restrictions turns out to be further support for the notion that compliance always occurs. Nonverification is an active practice in itself and is necessary if compliance is always to be achieved. It is not a mistake on the part of library administrators, nor is it something that should be corrected. It is a means by which library administration guarantees that compliance always takes place.

The primary interpretation which has emerged, at this stage, therefore, is in line with other ethnomethodological accounts. Namely, when presented with a disruptive situation (new technology in the form of electronic databases, and new legal restraints in the form of licensing agreements), communities of practice (interlibrary loan departments) develop new practices to allow action to go forward. Furthermore, a new goal for ILL departments was made paramount, i.e. compliance with licensing restrictions. That goal is so important that it is always achieved even when licenses are not consulted, not consulted regularly, not available, or never looked at. Finally, library administrators ensure that compliance is always achieved by active nonverification.

STEP FOUR: SECONDARY HYPOTHESES

Another set of interpretations has emerged which take the form of hypotheses for future research. As Figure 14.1 indicates, the presence of a heavily involved librarian meant that the department was unlikely to be a "never-filler." On the other hand, only four of the six departments where the librarian played a more detached role reported filling from electronic databases, and only three out of five non-MLS headed departments reported filling from electronic databases. The numbers in every category are too small for serious comparison but the 100 percent willingness to fill from electronic databases for departments headed by heavily involved librarians leaps out as a possible place for future research. If filling all requests where one holds the item and compliance with licensing restrictions are both goals for interlibrary loan departments (and sometimes competing goals), then departments headed by heavily involved librarians appear to be those most likely to find some way to achieve both goals. Either such departments manage to get licenses which allow filling more often than do other departments (they are proactive in Croft's sense), or heavily involved librarians are better at performing interpretative acts which ensure both compliance and filling. The question naturally arises whether they are most willing to sacrifice legal compliance for accessibility but this is moot here, because this research examines the questions from a constructionist view. If a goal of interlibrary loan librarians, as a collective group, is to keep the national system of interlibrary loans running, to have as many loans requests filled as possible, and to stay out of trouble with vendors, then this model of administration may be best. This hypothesis may be worthy of future research.

However, departments headed by heavily involved librarians appear as likely to fill under some ideal version of best practices as by "rules of thumb." These "best practices" are understood as taking steps in accord with the belief that it is better to fill a request after making an effort to consult the license directly or a list, paper or electronic, of restrictions. Departments headed by detached librarians appear less likely to invoke rules of thumb. Such departments preferred to either not fill at all from electronic databases or fill using lists or technical solutions. Interestingly, none in this category consulted licenses directly before filling. Non-MLS headed departments invoked rules of thumb two out of five times. Again the numbers are small in each category, so strict numerical comparisons are unwarranted. Since heavily involved librarians are willing to invoke rules of thumb and consult licensing sources equally, this leads one to speculate about the nature of the professional expertise of these librarians.

Therefore, as another area of future investigation, one might look at how professional expertise is understood or exhibited by librarians. One could hypothesize that, among librarians who are heavily involved in their subarea of expertise, there are two ways of exhibiting professional knowledge. One involves attempts at control. This would include establishing regular, transparent, and clearly defined procedures which they or their staff must follow in a consistent manner. The second way of exhibiting professional knowledge is to use something which we will call at this point in the analysis "trained judgment." "Trained judgment," we hypothesize, is that which allows for the creating of rules of thumb which are not seen as rules of thumb, stating what is "justified" beyond the strict statements in contracts or other documents and of knowing "when the question arises." These are merely ideas to pursue in further research and of course these are also ideal types of professionals, but it would be interesting to see whether some librarians exhibit one type of professionalism rather than the other, and under what conditions one type is more likely to emerge.

Figure 14.1
Professional Librarian Involvement and Interlibrary Loan Fills

	Heavily involved MLS	Detached MLS	No MLS
Never fills from electronic databases	0	2	2
Fills after consulting licenses or lists, or use of technological solution	5	3	1
Fills by rules of thumb or hearsay	5	1	2

STEP FIVE: MORE RESEARCH

At its heart, grounded theory seeks to build from the initial data and experiences of the investigators' research to produce more refined research projects. The founders of this theory suggest that re-sampling is necessary once an interpretive framework, categories, and suggested hypotheses emerge. Using this theory and the current research, it is possible to consider different areas of study that might be carried into a larger survey.

First, as noted, the difference between heavily involved versus detached librarians is an interesting distinction that needs to be further examined. Internal definitions of duties and of rule-following within a department might have different meanings according to the level of responsibility of library professionals. This calls for more in-depth research.

Second, the primary interpretation of the data (namely, that compliance always occurs with regard to licenses) strongly suggests further avenues of research. Is such compliance isolated to interlibrary loan departments, or does it extend to other parts of the institution as well? While extending this hypothesis to other areas may be a broad assumption, it is a worthy area of study so long as the researchers stay attuned to evidence that contradicts it or sets points or conditions under which compliance issues might not occur. An integrated middle-range theory that consists of smaller working hypotheses integrated with abstract conceptual schemes might include this as a central component.

Grounded theory also suggests that at some point theoretical integration should occur and that middle-range theories be developed. Beyond the speculation above, it is impossible to determine at this point what such a theory might look like. This is not a weakness of grounded theory. One of its strengths is that it asks the researcher to resist the erection of premature frameworks or hypotheses. Insights and, ultimately, theory are allowed to emerge from the process. By using pragmatic approaches like grounded theory, it is hoped that research in library science would be carried out in ways which reduce the intrusion of too hastily adopted models and allow instead for the emergence of more accurate explanations. This particular study is one example of how such a pragmatic model might work.

REFERENCES

Abercrombie, Nicholas, Stephen Hill, and Bryan S. Turner. 2006. *The Penguin dictionary of sociology.* New York: Penguin (Non-Classics).

Benoît, Gerald. 2002. Toward a critical theoretic perspective in information systems. *Library Quarterly.* 72: 441–47.

Blake, Virgil L. 1994. Since Shaughnessy: Research methods in library and information science dissertations, 1975–1989. *Collection Management.* 19:1–41.

Blake, Virgil L. 2003. Dissertations in library/information science: 1975–1994. In *Encyclopedia of library and information science*, 2513–23. New York: Marcel Dekker.

Charmaz, Kathy. 2003. Grounded theory: Objectivist and constructivist methods. In *Strategies of quantitative inquiry*, ed. Norman Denzin and Yvonna S. Lincoln, 249–91. Thousand Oaks, CA: Sage Publications.

Croft, Janet Brennan. 2005. Interlibrary loan and licensing: Tools for proactive management. *Journal of Library Administration* 42:3–4, 41–54.

Egan, Nancy. 2005. The impact of electronic full-text resources on interlibrary loan; A ten-year study at John Jay College of Criminal Justice. *Journal of Interlibrary Loan, Document Delivery & Information Supply* 15:23–41.

Fidel, Raya. 1993. Qualitative methods in information retrieval research. *Library and Information Science Research* 15:219–47.

Frohmann, Bernd. 1990. Rules of indexing: A critique of mentalism in information retrieval theory. *Journal of Documentation* 46:81–101.

Garfinkel, Harold. 1984. *Studies in ethnomethodology.* 4th ed. Oxford: Polity Press.

Garfinkel, Harold. 2002. *Ethnomethodology's program: Working out Durkheim's aphorism*, edited by Anne Warfield Rawls. Lanham, MD: Rowman & Littlefield.

Glaser, Barney G. 1992. *Emergence vs. forcing: Basics of grounded theory analysis*. Mill Valley, CA: Sociology Press.

Glaser, Barney G., and Anselm L. Strauss. 1967. *The discovery of grounded theory: Strategies for qualitative research*. Chicago, IL: Aldine Publishing Company.

Hjørland, Birger. 1998. Theory and metatheory in information science: A new interpretation. *Journal of Documentation* 54:605–21.

Hjørland, Birger. 2000. Library and information science: Practice, theory, and philosophical basis. *Information Processing and Management* 36:501–31.

Kim, Mary T. 1996. Research record. *Journal of Education for Library & Information Science* 37:376–86.

Liebscher, Peter. 1998. Quantity with quality? Teaching quantitative and qualitative methods in an LIS masters program. *Library Trends* 46:668–80.

Mansourian, Yazdan. 2006. Adoption of grounded theory in LIS research. *New Library World* 107:386–402.

Powell, Ronald R. 1999. Recent trends in research: A methodological essay. *Library & Information Science Research* 21:91–119.

Strauss, Anselm L. 1987. *Qualitative analysis for social scientists*. Cambridge: Cambridge University Press.

Strauss, Anselm L., and Juliet Corbin. 1990. *Basics of qualitative research: Grounded theory procedures and techniques*. Newbury Park, CA: Sage Publications.

Strauss, Anselm L., and Juliet Corbin, eds. 1997. *Grounded theory in practice*. Thousand Oaks, CA: Sage Publications.

Trosow, Samuel E. 2001. Standpoint epistemology as an alternative methodology for library and information science. *Library Quarterly* 71:360–82.

Wiley, Lynn N. 2004. License to deny? Publisher restrictions on document delivery from e-licensed journals. *Interlending and Document Supply* 32:94–102.

Wiley, Lynn N., and Tina Chrzastowski. 2005. The impact of electronic journals on interlibrary lending: A longitudinal study of statewide interlibrary loan article sharing in Illinois. *Library Collections, Acquisitions, and Technical Services* 29:364–81.

Woolwine, David. 2007. Sociological approaches to library science: Researching interlibrary loan practices in an electronic environment. *International Journal of Technology, Knowledge & Society* 3:51–58.

CHAPTER 15

Investing in Electronic Resources Using Capital Budgeting

TIMOTHY M. MCGEARY

INTRODUCTION

The struggle to financially manage subscriptions to electronic resources (Leonard 1994; Prabha and Ogden 1994) has created a long period of "professional anxiety" within libraries (Meyer 1997). Despite steadily, sometimes aggressively, increasing journal costs compared to remarkably small increases in collection budgets, libraries are tasked with managing the dual supply and demand environment of academic research publications and collections (Henderson 1999). Libraries, as suppliers of journals and databases for researchers, are unable to meet the demand from researchers. Conversely, the supply of research is greater than the demand of libraries based on their relatively shrinking budgets (McGeary and Hartman 2006). While Tenopir and King (1998), based on decades of lessons learned from print journals, describe in excellent detail the costs of electronic journals, the problem is larger than just cost alone. Researchers in universities are producing 70 percent of articles and citations in U.S. natural science and engineering journals; from 1976 through 1990, research doubled, while library spending only rose 50 percent.

It is time to change the modus operandi of collection management, specifically collection management of electronic resources, from mere year-to-year survival, which requires annual cuts of subscriptions, restrictive bundling of journals, and wishful longing for less-than-expected price increases, to proactive evaluation of electronic resources as a large capital investment portfolio that gains returns on investment. It is crucial that libraries discover and use available objective information to show the value of electronic resources when seeking funding for collections. What is even more important is how that information can be modeled and analyzed to not only show the worth of specific electronic resources, but also indicate the worth of more funding to the library and research communities overall. We can no longer focus simply on tying library budget requests to journal price increases. As Landesman (2004) eloquently states:

This focus also feeds the perception that the library is a "black hole." Campus administrators despair of effecting long-term improvements in their libraries because, no matter how often the money is found, the library needs more the next year. There has to be a return to our institutions beyond simply stopping cancellations. We need to look for ways to show that the investment of new funding brings new titles and/or a new level of service. (3)

Electronic resources are investments, very large investments totaling millions of dollars a year in many cases. It is therefore appropriate that we begin to use capital budgeting models to manage and analyze these investments and, hopefully, persuade administrators to increase funding based on these models.

WHAT IS CAPITAL BUDGETING AND WHY USE IT IN LIBRARIES?

Capital budgeting, by definition, is the investment of available capital in projects whose benefits will be realized in the future (Park and Sharpe-Bette 1990; for detailed examples and descriptions, see also Unger 1974; Hayes 1984). The vast majority of capital budgeting models are used in for-profit financial and engineering firms that have capital to invest and want a future return on that investment. Capital budgeting decisions often affect multiple entities (for instance, departments or divisions) (Baldenius, Dutta, and Reichelstein 2007). In the case of libraries, the multiple entities are academic departments and research disciplines. Due to limited investment budgets, factors external to capital budgeting decisions can present themselves because investment opportunities are mutually exclusive. But it is also possible that firms may be able to acquire assets applicable to multiple entities (Baldenius, Dutta, and Reichelstein 2007). Each of these cases can be easily translated to libraries investing in electronic resources, from mutually exclusive, competing journals from multiple disciplines, to aggregate databases that include more than one subject area and field of study.

There are several reasons for the importance of capital budgeting decisions to the success of a firm or organization. The first is that investments often require a large amount of capital, and it is important to base such large investment decisions on as much objective information as possible, information which capital budgeting models provide. Second, firms need to find the best way to acquire the money for these investments and determine how to repay it. Capital budgeting models will show you the projects that will have the best return on investment (ROI), and therefore best fulfill the repayment requirement. The need to repay investments in a for-profit business is assumed based on its overarching goal of making a profit, which would exceed simply repaying the investment. But as libraries are specifically spenders of budgets without a financial return, it is crucial that collection managers have objective information proving how investments of budgetary allocations are being returned through usage and research. Third, capital budgeting decisions typically require a long-term commitment, and this is true in electronic resource management (ERM) at least in that it requires investment over multiple time periods (e.g., budgetary cycles or fiscal years). Finally, the timing of capital budgeting decisions is important, as firms need to base decisions on the current interest rate in the financial markets (Cooper et al. 2002). The last reason is how using capital budgeting models in for-profit firms differs from applying them to libraries. Where investment and engineering firms have financial returns and gains on investments, libraries have nonfinancial returns in usage that often cannot even be measured in financial units. However, as Cooper et al. state, "The need for relevant information and analysis of capital budgeting alternatives has inspired the evolution of a series of models to assist firms in making the 'best' allocation of resources." The venture of applying capital budgeting modeling to libraries is just that type of alternative use and has been previously introduced using the classical capital budgeting or knapsack model (McGeary and Hartman 2006). The goal of this chapter is to reinforce that initial offering with a revised data sample and analysis of the optimized results to develop the proof-of-concept as a persuasive argument that collection management decisions for electronic resources ought to include capital budgeting modeling and analysis. Furthermore, with two more years of data available from the previous study, the results of the models can now be analyzed for trends, or at least the foundations of possible trends. Examining the worth of a journal over time by its selected ranking compared to the rest of the collection can provide excellent foresight for collection management decisions in the near future.

CLASSICAL CAPITAL BUDGETING: THE KNAPSACK MODEL

Simply stated, the knapsack model has N number of resources available but is only able to fit a limited number (X) of them, constrained by the size of the knapsack. This is a clear summary of the annual collection management decision process. In the classical form of capital budgeting, the objective is to maximize the returns of the X number of N resources that can fit in the knapsack. This can be accomplished by a number of measures. Taylor (1998) provides short, simple descriptions of various capital budgeting models, but I will be discussing the net present value (NPV) model. While using the NPV model, a firm will discount income from the project by a minimum acceptable rate of return. This is typically done by using an interest rate based on the current market. The NPV of a project is calculated as the difference between the present value of the income and the cost of the project. The project is accepted if the difference is positive (a profit) and rejected if negative (a loss). In capital budgeting, the terms "accepted" or "selected" are used synonymously when discussing projects that meet the objective (i.e., would result in a profit) (Cooper et al. 2002). Using a discount factor within the ERM capital budgeting model will not only work, but also is vital to evaluating the relative worth of a journal or resource. Adding the discount factor will not only show if a journal is accepted into the knapsack, but also in what order it is selected based on a journal's worth relative to the budget and to other journals. Each library may determine a different rate for its discount factor. In the models I present here, the first determines the discount factor as the mean price increase of journals per year, while the other model uses a predefined constant in the data file. In the latter example, the discount factor could be set to the rate of increase in the collection budget. By definition, this rate should be the minimum acceptable rate of return in growth of usage expected by the library for its electronic collection.

Cooper et al. also describe using capital budgeting models while deciding about a comparable new project not available or accepted in a previous time period. An example of this would be selecting a journal not previously available in electronic format, or a database competing with one currently in a library's collection. Despite its perception, a new project is not as discrete or independent from the list of the current projects as decision makers sometimes assume. Therefore, it is important to give careful consideration to what conditions will exist with or without the new, or replacing, project so that appropriate benchmarks of value can be applied. Such appropriate benchmarks will be discussed later in this chapter. Understanding these benchmarks of value are crucial to applying this model to libraries where, again, returns are nonfinancial. As Hartman and I stated in our initial publication of this model, the objective of modeling ERM through capital budgeting is to maximize usage, a measure of value of journal subscriptions.

Libraries are constantly in a position that requires justification of the levels of funding allocated to them and how those funds are used. As the shift of funding continues toward electronic collections, external administrators expect to receive evidence proving the wisdom of this shift towards electronic resources (Breeding 2002). Breeding states that electronic resources take the form of renewable subscriptions or investments, not one-time-only purchases. Decisions regarding continuing these investments from year to year can be made by measured usage, which is the ROI available to libraries. This is exactly why capital budgeting should be used in evaluating electronic resources. Because library decision makers are a main consumer of statistics, and because the objective of this model is to maximize usage, it is important to evaluate the statistics to determine the best measure of value. Breeding comments that "Library directors, unit managers, and others in positions with the authority to allocate resources rely on data regarding the relative importance of competing interests. A detailed understanding of the levels of use of electronic resources is vital to ensure the appropriate levels of funding are provided in the budget process" (2002, 9). Cost per use is one possible measure, and can at least be helpful in this process. When faced with a budget crunch, it is tempting to immediately look at highest priced resources to cut first, but expensive resources could also have a high volume of use, and thus a low cost per use. Cost per use seems rather straightforward but is an indication of a specific period of that investment, and we know that electronic resources are multiple-year invest-ments, therefore, more detailed and objective information is warranted in analyzing the worth of these investments.

Capital budgeting allows us to have a deeper look at the relative value of each investment using a discount rate, and through the outputted results of dual variables we can see another angle on just how valuable (or costly) is a subscription. The discount rate, also known as an interest rate, is simply the cost of money for a specific period of time. A perfect example of how to apply a discount rate to a capital budgeting model is the chief financial officer of a firm who knows that if he invests all of his firm's available capital in a guaranteed interest-bearing account, he would receive a Y% return; there-fore, he requires that a discount rate be applied to proposed projects to ensure that these investments will yield a greater return than the interest rate investment. This is a very important element and distinction of capital budgeting versus just using a yearly cost per use analysis.

Likewise, dual variables offer similar elements. In every capital budgeting model that is solved through linear algebra, there are two sets of results: the primal and the dual results. The primal results include the main objective, which in our case is the maximum usage obtained by investing in the X number of resources that fit in our budget. The dual results indicate the cost of each resource, so that the minimum total possible is paid for the investment in these resources (Park and Sharpe-Bette 1990). What the dual variable result indicates is the upper-bound (UB) constraints of each project, or the highest value a project will have to the overall objective. The dual results will be impacted by the discount rate applied to the investments, and together these will provide excellent data to objectively analyze the value of electronic resource investments.

DEFINING THE VALUE OF AN ELECTRONIC RESOURCE

Capital budgeting models objectively indicate the value of financial investments, and it is clear now more than ever that libraries must prove how well they are using financial resources. Duy and Vaughan (2006) discuss how librarians and information scientists struggle in determining the worth or value of a journal. Previously, methods of measuring this were print reshelving or circulation data (where seri-als are allowed to circulate). E-journals present the same problem of valuation and comparison as print journals: what a publisher charges does not indicate the journal's relative value (Hahn and Faulkner 2002). The important question to answer is what an e-journal's value is relative to, which is why col-lection management of electronic resources is a perfect capital budgeting problem. Although the capital budgeting model cannot describe the value of the content, it can indicate the value within the budget from the point of view of usage within the time period analyzed.

Hahn and Faulkner also focus on new benchmarks and metrics to compare existing resources to potential new and replacement resources. They describe three foundations for determining the value of print journals, one of which is comprised of two metrics by Tenopir and King (1998) that reflect the *purchase value* of a journal, which is based on the amount that patrons are willing to pay for use of the journal, and *use value*, which is based on the benefits that come from using the journal. When the purchase value is greater than the use value, use of that journal will decrease, and researchers will find alternative sources. Tenopir and King suggest that this foundation is appropriate for evaluating e-journals, and I would argue that using a capital budgeting model is a natural extension of this foun-dation. This will be evident in the results of my capital budgeting model, specifically in the order in which journals are accepted based on their relative value as shown by the duality results, a key element to capital budgeting (as described above).

The need for a method to employ usage statistics is also well documented. Noonan and McBurney (2007) discuss the necessity of usage statistics within collection management to indicate trends in research, assist in collection decisions, and to highlight necessary changes in Web site usability and the promotion of resources. Hahn and Faulkner point out that there have been few applications of the lessons of assessment of print journals to e-journals, but rather a focus on standardization of the usage statistics. At this point in time with COUNTER statistics widely available, this discussion of standardization should go to the background. It is time to apply evaluation applications to the usage statistics that we do have at our disposal. As cited by Hahn and Faulkner, Blecic, Fiscella, and Wiberley (2001), note that if a library is unable to reinvest in all of the titles in its collection, it must decide what is the goal of usage and what resources it can afford to retain to meet that goal. But this does not describe the whole scenario that the library faces because a high-priced journal could be more valuable than a host of cheaper journals whose sum cost is equal to or greater than the high-priced journal. Hahn and Faulkner follow up with an excellent discussion of new metrics that should be investigated and could possibly be included or used as a complementary element of this capital budgeting model.

Finally, Medeiros (2007) discusses the flaws of simple cost per use interpretation. He correctly points out that usage reported by vendors does not indicate the volume and issue level of electronic journals, yet it is commonplace to measure that against the cost of maintaining a current subscription. In his article, he details a variation of the simple cost per use metric to more precisely reflect usage of specific volumes of an electronic resource. While it may be important to understand the value of specific volumes and issues within a resource, that measure does not allow opportunity for investigating the relative value of that resource, as a whole, within the confines of a collection budget. Defining the relative value of maintaining current subscriptions is the objective of using a capital budgeting model. What capital budgeting can address is whether maintaining the active subscription is worthwhile or if canceling a title and depending on interlibrary loan would be more cost efficient. Such analysis might also indirectly assist the library in defining the value of maintaining access to back files.

USAGE STATISTICS AS RETURN ON INVESTMENT

The sum of HTML and PDF (full-text) downloads is the most commonly discussed usage data, specifically in the discussion of cost per use. Duy and Vaughan (2006) state, "Also according to Shim et al. these numbers 'provide a circulation count for electronic contents in a way analogous to the tradition of circulation of books,' with the difference that these counts are obtained at an article level rather than a whole journal level." Duy and Vaughan (2006) continue by showing how electronic usage is highly correlated with print reshelving data, thus allowing for full-text (FT)/download usage to replace an expensive reshelving statistics collection, despite no indications of a relationship between journal impact factor and electronic usage data. They also report that popular titles in print continue to be popular in electronic format. Their article offers a discussion of impact factors and their worth as a ROI of journal subscriptions, and they also indicate that more research is needed to see if the model of "content adjusted usage" by Hahn and Faulkner (2002) has any correlation to impact factors.

Duy's 2004 article shows that vendor-provided statistics can give libraries accurate indications of the usage of their virtual collections which will justify the increasing dollars spent on electronic resources. Duy also shows how libraries can gain understanding of patron use of electronic resources, specifically what is used most often, and therefore libraries can redesign or restructure their own Web interfaces to promote access to lesser used, yet important resources. Duy also details the unfortunately nonstandardized nature of the usage data, including log-ins, sessions, and number of searches. While COUNTER has standardized the formatting of usage reports, aside from FT/download statistics, what the other data represent may vary from vendor to vendor. Number of searches is particularly troubling depending on how the searches are handled on the vendor's Web site. Are searches for the whole product or an individual title? Do searches of the whole product count as one total search, or one search per each title within the product? Vendors can define usage in various ways, which can make search statistics nearly unusable for capital budgeting.

Many authors detail the growth of standardization of these statistics through efforts like the JSTOR Web Statistics Task Force, International Coalition of Library Consortia efforts, ARL E-Metrics (Measures for Electronic Resources), and Project COUNTER. Henle and Cochenour (2007) describe the importance of standardization of usage data at a local level that fits the needs of an individual library and encourages a "keep it simple" approach to processing and disseminating usage data related to collections. The most useful measurement of electronic journal usage is the "number of full content units examined, downloaded, or otherwise provided to the user" (ICOLC) or "items request in electronic databases" (E-Metrics), which are often reported as FT articles viewed (Duy 2004). It is a goal of this model to eventually include other factors, as Medeiros (2007) alludes to in describing my participation in 2004 and 2005 with Caryn Anderson (Simmons College) and Andrew Nagy (Villanova University). The efforts of the Anderson/Nagy/McGeary model stalled mostly due to the variations of access protocols vendors were opening to libraries, making a consistent approach to download statistics nearly impossible. While COUNTER Level 1 compliance was steadily increasing, an idea that later became the SUSHI protocol was merely a hope of Anderson, Nagy, and me, as well as the Digital Library Federation. It is becoming clear that FT downloads, above all other available measures, offer the best indication of the use of an electronic resource.

Hahn and Faulkner (2002) stress the importance of collection and assessment of usage data, but also the importance of weighing the data against quality and price measurements. But until vendors start to provide standardized information about their content (e.g., the number of articles, pages, or words within a particular journal) these measurements will be difficult to balance. Duy suggests two key questions in the face of usage assessment presented by Hahn and Faulkner: What kinds of use are valued, and what type of use is the library able to support? We know that a journal was useful if cited in research, but a citation could be considered as an "end point" in terms of usage, an end point which may not be reached even if the journal was useful. Libraries should work to meet the information needs of students and faculty who are not actively researching and publishing, yet are using journals for continuing education, course work, or keeping up with the current research in their disciplines. If a journal in this category were not available in print or electronically, would the user bother to request it through interlibrary loan? Would research and/or knowledge of their field of study suffer as a result?

Duy emphasizes that these are questions that we must address within collection management. Hahn and Faulkner (2002) indicate that while there are difficulties standardizing the metrics of the variety of usage statistics, these usage statistics do offer new opportunities in the collection management work of assessing relative value. The advantage of the capital budgeting model using a discount factor is that usage can been measured by its relative worth within the constraining budget and its growth or decline over multiple periods. As I will show in the results below, this model can even out the worth of a journal based on its usage despite variances in price from one journal to another, thus allowing trend analysis (which was not done when this model was presented previously, as only two years of data was available at that time).

To summarize the above, an important caveat of usage data is that it is quantitative not qualitative; and it does not describe how a resource was used. There is no indication that usage was satisfactory, nor does low usage definitively show an electronic resource is not useful. The latter could be a result of the resource not being visible or marketed properly on the library Web site. Duy cites Bernard Rous's cautions that heavy usage could be a measure of the size of the research community within a discipline or of the ease with which its research results translate to publication, and also that high usage, measured against price, could drive out less-used titles that are crucial to specialized or newly defined research fields. The balance that subject librarians bring to the collection management process is the expertise and knowledge of the quality of resources, which cannot be measured by usage statistics alone. Duy includes a study that shows that other factors influence use of electronic resources, including the length of time that an electronic resource has been available to users; it is suggested that a minimum of 12–18 months is necessary before indicative usage will be observed. Breeding (2002) warns not to take too simplistic a view of the usage statistics but to investigate the more complex relationships of the use. This is indeed the goal of using a capital budgeting model to evaluate electronic resources. Despite these caveats some believe FT usage to be the best indicator of quality and utility. Hahn and Faulkner claim that, since libraries are subscribing rather than owning this material, it makes little sense to continue to invest in access to resources not used. Therefore, to examine the impact capital budgeting can have on collection management of electronic resources, we will use FT usage as our ROI.

THE MULTIPERIOD CAPITAL BUDGETING MODEL

McGeary and Hartman (2006) provide an in-depth mathematical discussion of the multiperiod capital budgeting models. Figure 15.1 shows the classical knapsack, quasi-NPV model with no discount factor. This model produces a solution of year-to-year selections of materials. Therefore, there is no connection between the periods of usage statistics u_{jn}. Figures 15.2 and 15.3 show a different objective statement than Figure 15.1, introducing a discount factor z_n that forces continuity into the model, rewarding growth in usage and penalizing a decrease in usage. Hartman and I also introduce this discount factor to emulate the impact of financial gains and losses compounded over multiple periods. Because we are going to invest Z% more per year into the budget to accommodate price increases, the discount factor indicates a demand for usage to maintain a level worthy of investment. Therefore, the discount factor promotes journals that have growth in usage in each period and demotes journals with decreases in usage, thus highlighting the ROI per journal per period.

The discount factor of z_n in Figure 15.2 is calculated by the percentage of annual average journal price increase from one year to the next, and in Figure 15.3 z_n is a fixed parameter that can be changed in a data file to test various discount rates. As mentioned above, the discount rate should represent the minimum acceptable rate of return of usage for the library, which could equal the mean price increase of the electronic resource collection, the budget increase from one period to the next, or a goal rate decided upon by the collection managers. The results of the model represented in Figure 15.1 will produce results close to a cost per use model, but for each year separately. The results for the models in Figures 15.2 and 15.3 are affected directly by growth and decline in both usage and journal pricing.

Figure 15.1
Capital budgeting model 1: Maximizing present usage

$$\max \sum_{n \in N} \sum_{j \in J} u_{jn} x_{jn}$$

$$s.t.$$

$$\sum_{j \in J} a_{jn} x_{jn} \leq b_n \qquad \forall n \in N$$

$$x_{jn} \in (0,1) \qquad \forall j \in J, \forall n \in N$$

where:

u_{jn} = present usage value of journal j at time n
x_{jn} = journal selection variable of journal j at time n
a_{jn} = annual cost of journal j at time n

b_n = budget limit on supplied funds at time n
z_n = constant discount rate
J = set of journals
N = set of time periods

Figure 15.2
Capital budgeting model 2: Maximizing present usage with annual discount rate of usage growth over time

$$\max \sum_{n \in N} \sum_{j \in J} z_n \left(u_{jn} - u_{jn-1} \right) x_{jn} + u_{jn-1} x_{jn-1} + u_{jn} x_{jn}$$

$s.t.$

$$\sum_{j \in J} a_{jn} x_{jn} \leq b_n \qquad\qquad \forall n \in N$$

$$\left(\sum_{j \in J} a_{jn} - \sum_{j \in J} a_{jn-1} \right) / \sum_{j \in J} a_{jn} = z_n \qquad \forall n \in N$$

$$x_{jn} \geq 0 \qquad\qquad \forall j \in J, \forall n \in N$$

$$x_{jn} \leq 1 \qquad\qquad \forall j \in J, \forall n \in N$$

where:

u_{jn} = present usage value of journal j at time n
x_{jn} = journal selection variable of journal j at time n
a_{jn} = annual cost of journal j at time n
b_n = budget limit on supplied funds at time n
z_n = the discount rate as the average cost increase from time $n-1$ to time n
J = set of journals
N = set of time periods

Figure 15.3
Capital budgeting model 3: Maximizing present usage with a fixed discount rate of usage growth over time

$$\max \sum_{n \in N} \sum_{j \in J} z_n \left(u_{jn} - u_{jn-1} \right) x_{jn} + u_{jn-1} x_{jn-1} + u_{jn} x_{jn}$$

$s.t.$

$$\sum_{j \in J} a_{jn} x_{jn} \leq b_n \qquad\qquad \forall n \in N$$

$$x_{jn} \geq 0 \qquad\qquad \forall j \in J, \forall n \in N$$

$$x_{jn} \leq 1 \qquad\qquad \forall j \in J, \forall n \in N$$

where:

u_{jn} = present usage value of journal j at time n
x_{jn} = journal selection variable of journal j at time n

a_{jn} = annual cost of journal j at time n
b_n = budget limit on supplied funds at time n
z_n = constant discount rate
J = set of journals
N = set of time periods

It is very important to note that this model is intended to work for individual journals despite the fact that they may be part of bundles or packages. It is important to know the value of each title in order to examine whether the bundle or package has been a wise investment strategy. Because historical and retail prices are available for individual titles, and it has already been shown that usage statistics are widely available for individual titles, even within packages, it is prudent to examine the collection in this way. Noonan and McBurney (2007) suggest that low usage by titles in bundles/packages can add negotiation power. And knowing the relative value of the titles as they stand alone can add even more knowledge for negotiations, especially if only a small number of the titles within a package are of worth, and they could be subscribed to separately at a lower cost.

DATA SAMPLE

The sample, as shown in Figure 15.13 (Appendix 1), differs slightly from that of McGeary and Hartman (2006). Two of the 52 journals in the first publication were cancelled, as McGeary and Hartman indicated they were slated to be by the Lehigh University collection management team; these were not replaced. Two other titles were replaced based on usage data for certain publishers not being available because of interface changes and system faults. This unfortunate situation highlights the crucial need for a systematic solution for logistical management of electronic resources, and at the time of this writing, there is not yet one in place. It is also important to note that prices listed may vary from what other libraries pay. Some of the prices listed come from EBSCO's historical price listing, some are actually invoice-line prices, and some are retail prices. In all cases, the variance of the sample price to the actual price Lehigh University is paying is small and does not have a significant impact on the optimal solution of the model.

RESULTS AND TRENDS

The results of the second and third model with the discount factor z_n, listed fully in Appendix 1, show just how much impact the discount factor z_n has on rewarding usage growth and penalizing declines in usage. Figure 15.14 (Appendix 2) shows the journals accepted in period 2007 as ordered by cost per use, which is equivalent of the discount factor $z_n = 0$. Figures 15.15 through 15.18 (Appendices 3 through 6) display the results of various discount factors ordered by the upper-bound dual result to full-text ratio. The UB dual result represents the amount of usage calculated in the objective based on the impact of the discount rate to a specific journal's usage between periods. To find the relative impact of that journal to the budget, we take the ratio of the UB dual results to the reported FT usage. This ratio levels the sample of journals outside of price because the ratio shows whether the UB value met the expectation of the reported FT usage. This ratio is impacted by the discount factor z_n and constrained by the budget. Sorting the list of journals in descending upper-bound dual value to full-text (UB/FT) ratio order indicates the order in which the journals are accepted into the collection. For Figures 15.15 through 15.18 (Appendices 3 through 6), the cost per use figure is also shown. It is evident that the capital budgeting model does not follow cost per use, because of the applied discount factor.

Having two more years of data than when the model was run by McGeary and Hartman provides opportunity to evaluate some trends (or at least the beginnings of trends, as four years of data may not be sufficient to identify real trends). The most significant trend to analyze would be what position a resource was accepted for each period and for each value of z_n. In McGeary and Hartman (2006), we showed how the journal *Statistical Science* was affected by the different discount rates (see Figure 15.4). To reevaluate *Statistical Science* with more data, we can see that it has climbed in relative importance but still is adversely affected as z_n increases (see Figure 15.5). It is very important to note that *Statistical Science* is a very inexpensive journal, priced from $110 in 2004 to $164 in 2008. But despite its economic value, the worth of *Statistical Science* to the collection relative to the budget and discount factor is not very strong.

In contrast, the *Journal of Crystal Growth* is the most expensive journal of the sample, with a price of $12,176 in 2004 to $14,373 in 2008. Figure 15.6 shows its value based on z_n.

The journal's UB/FT ratio does not change much, mainly because of the high cost of the journal. It is important to remember that the UB dual value represents the modeled value of the journal based on the discount factor z_n, and the ratio represented the relative value of that journal within

Figure 15.4
Upper-Bound Dual Variable/Full-Text Ratio Value of *Statistical Science* Per Discount Rate z Weight in 2005

z	UB dual/FT	Rank
0%	82.23	27/39
6%	44.35	35/38
8%	31.87	35/38
10%	19.28	37/37
50%	0	not selected

Figure 15.5
Upper-Bound Dual Variable/Full-Text Ratio Value of *Statistical Science* Per Discount Rate z Weight for 2007

z	UB dual/FT	Rank
0%	76.30	17/39
6%	64.38	28/39
8%	60.40	28/38
10%	56.43	31/38
50%	0	not selected

Figure 15.6
Upper-Bound Dual Variable/Full-Text Ratio Value of *Journal of Crystal Growth* **Per Discount Rate z Weight for 2007**

z	UB dual/FT	Rank
0%	68.25	25/39
6%	67.74	24/39
8%	67.57	25/38
10%	67.40	25/38
50%	69.46	17/35

the constrained budget. With budgets of $70,500 in 2004 to $80,100 in 2008, the *Journal of Crystal Growth* takes over 17 percent of the sample budget. The steadiness of its relative worth shows that this journal is valuable to the collection because it is not adversely affected or significantly promoted by the discount rate. The key to analyzing the optimized solution is to see what the duality results indicate for each resource, as this goes beyond straight cost per use. This shows a perspective of the journal's growth or decline in usage compared to the other journals while being constrained by the annual budget.

Expanding this analysis to the full sample, Figure 15.7 displays the accepted order of each journal through each period in the model based on the ratio of the UB dual value to the FT usage reported value when the discount rate $z_n = 6\%$. The simplified view of this data shows the relative worth of each journal for each period constrained by the available budget for each period. Dashes in a column indicate that a journal was not accepted in that period. It is possible to discover trends over multiple periods of this model, and more importantly, lay the foundation of analysis to continue over a substantial number of years. Within this table, the consistency of *Journal of the American Chemical Society*, *Applied Optics*, *Foreign Policy*, and *Journal of School Psychology* (the last two after 2004) are clear. The lack of relative worth of *Annals of Physics*, *Journal of Approximation Theory*, *Information Sciences*, *Applied Economics*, and *Journal of Scientific Computing* is just as evident, as none of them were accepted for any period within this sample constrained by this budget.

Looking at the journals accepted in the model graphically can help you visualize possible trends. Figure 15.8 displays the top 10 journals accepted in 2007 based on the UB/FT ratio when $z_n = 6\%$. You can see some volatility in this third of the journals accepted in 2007, with the exception of the top three resources, which are consistently at the top.

Figure 15.9 graphs the UB/FT ratio for the journals ranked 11–20 as accepted in 2007. Overall there is more consistency in the year-to-year rankings of these journals, showing steady performance of this tier of journals from the sample.

Figure 15.10 graphs the UB/FT ratio for the journals ranked 21–30 as accepted in 2007. It may be expected that the lowest tier of journals accepted would show the most volatility in value, and this graph indeed indicates that. These journals are trending toward decline in usage, and while their relative value to the collection was enough to be accepted in 2007, a continuing decline in usage will likely find these journals outside of the accepted resources in future periods.

Figure 15.7
Select Order Based on Dual Upper Bound/Full-Text Ratio

Journal	2004	2005	2006	2007
Journal of the American Chemical Society	1	4	4	1
Foreign Policy	—	1	2	2
Journal of School Psychology	30	3	3	3
Journal of Politics	—	24	20	4
Industrial Marketing Management	14	19	35	5
Journal of Memory and Language	9	6	19	6
Journal of Fluid Mechanics	32	35	11	7
Applied Optics	3	5	5	8
Journal of Accounting Research	23	23	—	9
Optical and Quantum Electronics	—	—	32	10
Chemical Engineering Science	8	10	16	11
Water Research	10	13	8	12
ABA Journal	—	30	9	13
Journal of the American Ceramic Society	—	7	1	14
Journal of Financial Economics	12	26	22	15
Annals of Statistics	4	11	14	16
European Journal of Political Research	31	—	27	17
Computers and Education	13	22	13	18
Cognitive Psychology	11	12	23	19
American Journal of Political Science	19	18	17	20
Journal of Microscopy	6	15	21	21
Journal of Small Business Management	28	34	15	22
Modern Asian Studies	24	25	25	23
Journal of Crystal Growth	16	16	34	24
Computers and Operations Research	21	17	18	25
Composite Structures	22	21	28	26
Computer Communications	—	—	38	27
Statistical Science	2	29	7	28
Engineering Fracture Mechanics	15	20	33	29
BioEssays	—	—	29	30
British journal of special education	18	—	24	31
Physics Reports	27	32	31	32
Journal of Manufacturing Systems	—	36	—	33
Politics and Society	—	—	39	34
Adolescence	—	2	6	35
Mechanical Engineering	—	9	10	36
Journal of Advertising	—	8	12	37
Computers and Industrial Engineering	17	14	30	38
Materials Letters	7	33	37	39
Journal of Communication	5	28	36	—
International Economic Review	20	27	—	—
Journal of Theoretical Biology	25	—	—	—
Journal of Economic Theory	26	31	—	—
Psychophysiology	29	—	26	—
Annals of Physics	—	—	—	—
Journal of Approximation Theory	—	—	—	—
Information Sciences	—	—	—	—
Applied Economics	—	—	—	—
Journal of Scientific Computing	—	—	—	—
Information Systems	—	—	—	—

Figure 15.8
Trend Graph of Top 10 Journals Selected in 2007, for z = 6%

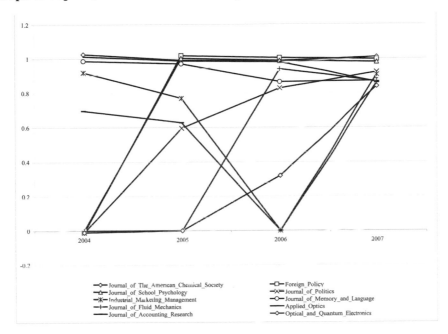

Figure 15.9
Trend Graph of Top 11–20 Journals Selected in 2007, for z = 6%

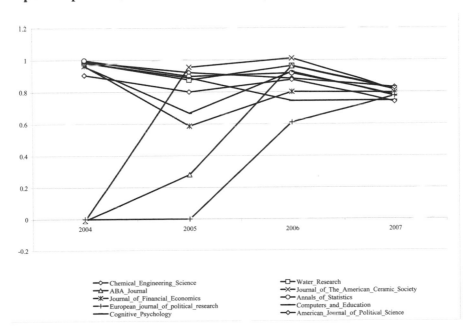

Figure 15.10
Trend Graph of Journals 21–30 Selected in 2007, for z = 6%

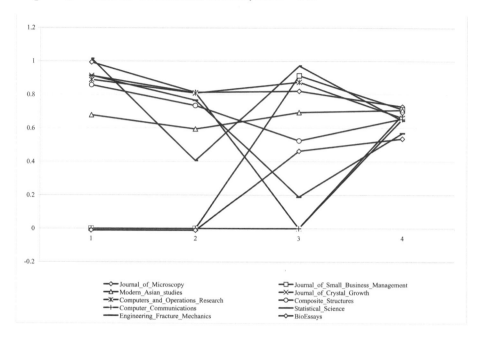

Having this information available for the entire collection will be extremely valuable to subject librarians and collection managers. I stress, again, the importance of modeling library collections individually in spite of the bundles and packages that make up parts of the electronic collection, as full-text usage data is largely reported for individual titles with the COUNTER Journal Report 1. But that said, with a little effort it is feasible to expect this model to work just as effectively with each bundle included as a single investment. Just as important as the upper bound duality results of the journals accepted are the duality results of the budget constraint. The dual value of the budget constraint is the value of the capital in the budget and represents the value of gained resources if more capital is contributed to the budget. This is a key element, as it is objective evidence that collection managers can use to petition for more funding. Looking at the data results, Figure 15.11 shows us the dual variables for the budget for all solutions.

Figure 15.11
Budget Dual Variables for all Solutions

	2004	2005	2006	2007
z = 6%	0.008258	0.024968	0.021719	0.016548
z = 8%	0.008339	0.025045	0.021605	0.016797
z = 10%	0.008419	0.025122	0.021491	0.017046
z = 50%	0.010022	0.026668	0.017423	0.019319

Figure 15.12
Expected Increase in Usage for Every $1,000 Added to the Budget

	2004	2005	2006	2007
z = 6%	8.25835	24.9678	21.7193	16.5478
z = 8%	8.33853	25.0451	21.6052	16.7967
z = 10%	8.41871	25.1224	21.4911	17.0457
z = 50%	10.0223	26.6684	17.4233	19.3185

When the variables are multiplied by $1,000, Figure 15.12 shows how much more usage can be expected for every $1,000 more put into the budget.

This information can be very powerful in negotiating or requesting an increase in collection funds. Within this sample, this information is not as helpful because it is showing that the budget is fairly saturated and that increases in this budget would allow for an acceptance of a journal that costs $40–$65 per use. But expanded to a full collection, it is expected that this result will show a much more favorable and persuasive value.

CONCLUSION

These results are just the tip of the iceberg as to the uses of capital budgeting for evaluating electronic resource collections. In general, unlike discussions of the types and standards of usage statistics, studies of applying usage data of electronic resources are uncommon in literature (Duy 2004). As time progresses and usage data is collected and stored for better accessibility, I believe there will be a stronger motivation to continue this type of capital budgeting research across the library industry.

I have examined the current and past efforts of determining the value of electronic resources for collection management. There have been no small inquiries and examinations of this issue, but what has been missing is the strategic method of analyzing these collections as financial investments. Basing collection decisions on objective data obtained through capital budgeting can change the landscape of budgeting and subscription negotiations throughout the library industry. Using FT usage data as the ROI, this technique can give a clear hope that libraries can go from merely surviving year to year to making proactive and confident renewal and acquisition decisions.

While this capital budgeting model is still in a proof-of-concept phase, with only four years of data available within a small sample, I believe that it lays a strong foundation for a new standard of collection management of electronic resources. Requirements to expand this model are a viable systematic solution for collecting both cost and price information on an entire collection, as well as testing the scalability of this model over thousands, or tens of thousands, of electronic resources and over long periods of time. But just as usage statistics will become even more readily available, and hopefully continue to increase in accessibility, the ability to analyze collections through capital budgeting will also increase. The time has come to change the nature of analyzing electronic collections, to value these collections as significant financial investments with expected returns, and to make forward-thinking decisions based on as much objective information as possible.

APPENDICES

Appendix 1

Figure 15.13
Data Sample with Annual Prices

Journal	2004	2005	2006	2007
ABA Journal	$120	$120	$120	$120
Adolescence	$143	$143	$153	$164
American Journal of Political Science	$242	$275	$308	$335
Annals of Physics	$4,490	$4,827	$4,726	$5,010
Annals of Statistics	$220	$240	$250	$270
Applied Economics	$3,228	$4,741	$4,741	$5,301
Applied Optics	$2,680	$2,894	$3,108	$3,338
BioEssays	$895	$999	$1,149	$1,250
British journal of special education	$362	$407	$435	$465
Chemical Engineering Science	$5,189	$5,578	$5,461	$5,788
Cognitive Psychology	$653	$702	$687	$728
Composite Structures	$4,442	$4,775	$4,675	$4,535
Computer Communications	$1,618	$1,740	$1,703	$1,805
Computers and Education	$1,478	$1,589	$1,556	$1,648
Computers and Industrial Engineering	$2,711	$2,914	$2,853	$3,025
Computers and Operations Research	$2,944	$3,164	$3,099	$3,006
Engineering Fracture Mechanics	$4,311	$4,634	$4,537	$4,809
European Journal of Political Research	$636	$694	$757	$818
Foreign Policy	$25	$25	$25	$25
Industrial Marketing Management	$859	$923	$904	$958
Information Sciences	$4,091	$4,398	$4,306	$4,177
Information Systems	$1,636	$1,759	$1,722	$1,825
International Economic Review	$324	$352	$383	$408
Journal of Accounting Research	$404	$438	$565	$599
Journal of Advertising	$90	$135	$149	$199
Journal of Approximation Theory	$2,241	$2,498	$2,446	$2,592
Journal of Communication	$219	$227	$808	$759
Journal of Crystal Growth	$12,176	$12,815	$13,200	$13,585
Journal of Economic Theory	$2,498	$2,685	$2,629	$2,786
Journal of Financial Economics	$1,909	$2,128	$2,084	$2,045
Journal of Fluid Mechanics	$1,805	$1,920	$2,264	$2,700
Journal of Manufacturing Systems	$721	$759	$799	$827
Journal of Memory and Language	$793	$883	$865	$917
Journal of Microscopy	$1,301	$1,463	$1,566	$1,667
Journal of Politics	$145	$139	$175	$191
Journal of School Psychology	$380	$425	$416	$440
Journal of Scientific Computing	$915	$1,198	$1,249	$1,348
Journal of Small Business Management	$158	$171	$205	$223
Journal of the American Ceramic Society	$1,131	$1,131	$1,246	$1,378
Journal of the American Chemical Society	$2,939	$3,165	$3,387	$3,624
Journal of Theoretical Biology	$3,687	$3,881	$4,075	$4,279
Materials Letters	$2,450	$2,730	$2,673	$2,624
Mechanical Engineering	$125	$125	$127	$129

Modern Asian Studies	$256	$272	$319	$367
Optical and Quantum Electronics	$1,721	$1,895	$1,999	$2,188
Physics Reports	$5,683	$6,335	$6,202	$6,574
Politics and Society	$569	$569	$604	$653
Psychophysiology	$317	$344	$368	$401
Statistical Science	$110	$130	$140	$150
Water Research	$4,605	$5,133	$5,026	$5,327

Appendix 2

Figure 15.14
Journals Selected in 2007, Ordered by Cost Per Use

Journal	Cost/Use	x
Foreign Policy	$0.57	1
Journal of the American Chemical Society	$0.73	1
Journal of School Psychology	$0.91	1
Mechanical Engineering	$1.26	1
Adolescence	$1.29	1
Journal of the American Ceramic Society	$4.15	1
Applied Optics	$4.64	1
Materials Letters	$6.53	1
Journal of Politics	$7.07	1
Industrial Marketing Management	$7.26	1
Journal of Fluid Mechanics	$8.04	1
Journal of Memory and Language	$8.26	1
Water Research	$8.51	1
ABA Journal	$9.23	1
Chemical Engineering Science	$10.26	1
Journal of Advertising	$11.06	1
Annals of Statistics	$11.74	1
Journal of Accounting Research	$11.75	1
Computers and Education	$12.30	1
Optical and Quantum Electronics	$12.72	1
Journal of Financial Economics	$13.37	1
Statistical Science	$15.00	1
American Journal of Political Science	$15.23	1
European Journal of Political Research	$15.73	1
Journal of Small Business Management	$15.93	1
Cognitive Psychology	$16.18	1
Journal of Microscopy	$16.67	1
Computers and Operations Research	$18.56	1
Modern Asian Studies	$19.32	1
Journal of Crystal Growth	$20.10	1
Composite Structures	$22.45	1
Computer Communications	$23.75	1
Computers and Industrial Engineering	$27.75	1
Engineering Fracture Mechanics	$28.29	1
BioEssays	$29.76	1
British Journal of Special Education	$51.67	1

Physics Reports	$55.71	1
Journal of Manufacturing Systems	$59.07	1
Politics and Society	$59.36	1
Information Sciences	$63.29	0.14508
Journal of Theoretical Biology	$66.86	0
International Economic Review	$81.60	0
Journal of Scientific Computing	$122.55	0
Journal of Communication	$151.80	0
Journal of Economic Theory	$154.78	0
Annals of Physics	$238.57	0
Information Systems	$260.71	0
Journal of Approximation Theory	$518.40	0
Applied Economics	$1,767.00	0
Psychophysiology	—	0

Appendix 3

Figure 15.15
Ratio of Dual Variable (UB) to Usage with z = 6%, for Period 2007

Journal	Full Text					z = 6%	
	2004	2005	2006	2007	Cost/Use	UB	UB/FT
Journal of the American Chemical Society	3,124	3,370	3,242	4945	$0.73	4,987.21	100.85%
Foreign Policy	0	25	40	44	$0.57	43.8263	99.61%
Journal of School Psychology	362	582	526	482	$0.91	472.079	97.94%
Journal of Politics	0	4	10	27	$7.07	24.8594	92.07%
Industrial Marketing Management	32	48	75	132	$7.26	119.567	90.58%
Journal of Memory and Language	75	222	97	111	$8.26	96.6657	87.09%
Journal of Fluid Mechanics	309	197	336	336	$8.04	291.321	86.70%
Applied Optics	630	1,288	1,440	720	$4.64	621.564	86.33%
Journal of Accounting Research	5	14	5	51	$11.75	43.8479	85.98%
Optical and Quantum Electronics	0	10	31	172	$12.72	144.253	83.87%
Chemical Engineering Science	521	788	569	564	$10.26	467.922	82.96%
Water Research	415	496	1,044	626	$8.51	512.77	81.91%
ABA Journal	0	2	20	13	$9.23	10.5943	81.49%
Journal of the American Ceramic Society	0	189	990	332	$4.15	269.717	81.24%
Journal of Financial Economics	118	68	108	153	$13.37	121.86	79.65%
Annals of Statistics	28	29	32	23	$11.74	17.9921	78.23%
European Journal of Political Research	5	5	20	52	$15.73	40.3839	77.66%
Computers and Education	87	62	180	134	$12.30	103.969	77.59%
Cognitive Psychology	57	74	34	45	$16.18	33.6132	74.70%
American Journal of Political Science	8	16	25	22	$15.23	16.2765	73.98%
Journal of Microscopy	144	104	96	100	$16.67	72.6549	72.65%

Journal of Small Business Management	3	4	20	14	$15.93	9.94985	71.07%
Modern Asian Studies	3	8	11	19	$19.32	13.407	70.56%
Journal of Crystal Growth	425	784	564	676	$20.10	457.919	67.74%
Computers and Operations Research	86	190	252	162	$18.56	106.857	65.96%
Composite Structures	106	212	113	202	$22.45	132.296	65.49%
Computer Communications	5	4	19	76	$23.75	49.5513	65.20%
Statistical Science	29	4	28	10	$15.00	6.43784	64.38%
Engineering Fracture Mechanics	152	236	67	170	$28.29	96.6018	56.82%
BioEssays	0	0	22	42	$29.76	22.5153	53.61%
British Journal of Special Education	12	1	16	9	$51.67	0.885291	9.84%
Physics Reports	38	84	100	118	$55.71	10.295	8.72%
Journal of Manufacturing Systems	0	15	0	14	$59.07	1.155	8.25%
Politics and Society	0	4	10	11	$59.36	0.254312	2.31%
Adolescence	0	103	84	127	$1.29	0	0.00%
Computers and Industrial Engineering	91	196	64	109	$27.75	0	0.00%
Journal of Advertising	0	20	22	18	$11.06	0	0.00%
Materials Letters	251	182	255	402	$6.53	0	0.00%
Mechanical Engineering	0	17	24	102	$1.26	0	0.00%
Information Sciences	12	12	14	66	$63.29	0	0.00%
Annals of Physics	18	24	20	21	$238.57	0	0.00%
Applied Economics	2	10	12	3	$1,767.00	0	0.00%
Information Systems	2	3	0	7	$260.71	0	0.00%
International Economic Review	10	8	4	5	$81.60	0	0.00%
Journal of Approximation Theory	2	4	2	5	$518.40	0	0.00%
Journal of Communication	26	6	16	5	$151.80	0	0.00%
Journal of Economic Theory	21	44	29	18	$154.78	0	0.00%
Journal of Scientific Computing	0	0	2	11	$122.55	0	0.00%
Journal of Theoretical Biology	33	48	38	64	$66.86	0	0.00%
Psychophysiology	8	2	10	0	—	0	—

Appendix 4

Figure 15.16
Ratio of Dual Variable (UB) to Usage with z = 8%, for Period 2007

Journal	Full Text					z = 8%	
	2004	2005	2006	2007	Cost/Use	UB	UB/FT
Mechanical Engineering	0	17	24	102	$1.26	106.073	103.99%
Journal of the American Chemical Society	3,124	3,370	3,242	4,945	$0.73	5,020.37	101.52%
Adolescence	0	103	84	127	$1.29	127.685	100.54%
Foreign Policy	0	25	40	44	$0.57	43.9001	99.77%
Journal of School Psychology	362	582	526	482	$0.91	471.089	97.74%
Journal of Politics	0	4	10	27	$7.07	25.1518	93.15%
Materials Letters	251	182	255	402	$6.53	369.685	91.96%

Journal							
Industrial Marketing Management	32	48	75	132	$7.26	120.469	91.26%
Journal of Accounting Research	5	14	5	51	$11.75	44.6188	87.49%
Journal of Memory and Language	75	222	97	111	$8.26	96.7174	87.13%
Optical and Quantum Electronics	0	10	31	172	$12.72	146.529	85.19%
Applied Optics	630	1,288	1440	720	$4.64	606.332	84.21%
Water Research	415	496	1,044	626	$8.51	503.084	80.36%
ABA Journal	0	2	20	13	$9.23	10.4244	80.19%
Journal of Financial Economics	118	68	108	153	$13.37	122.251	79.90%
Journal of Advertising	0	20	22	18	$11.06	14.3374	79.65%
European Journal of Political Research	5	5	20	52	$15.73	40.8203	78.50%
Journal of the American Ceramic Society	0	189	990	332	$4.15	256.214	77.17%
Computers and Education	87	62	180	134	$12.30	102.639	76.60%
Cognitive Psychology	57	74	34	45	$16.18	33.652	74.78%
Journal of Microscopy	144	104	96	100	$16.67	72.3198	72.32%
Modern Asian Studies	3	8	11	19	$19.32	13.4756	70.92%
Journal of Crystal Growth	425	784	564	676	$20.10	456.776	67.57%
Computer Communications	5	4	19	76	$23.75	50.2419	66.11%
Composite Structures	106	212	113	202	$22.45	132.947	65.82%
Computers and Operations Research	86	190	252	162	$18.56	104.309	64.39%
Statistical Science	29	4	28	10	$15.00	6.04049	60.40%
Engineering Fracture Mechanics	152	236	67	170	$28.29	97.4645	57.33%
BioEssays	0	0	22	42	$29.76	22.6041	53.82%
Journal of Manufacturing Systems	0	15	0	14	$59.07	1.22909	8.78%
Physics Reports	38	84	100	118	$55.71	9.0182	7.64%
British Journal of Special Education	12	1	16	9	$51.67	0.629514	6.99%
American Journal of Political Science	8	16	25	22	$15.23	0	0.00%
Annals of Statistics	28	29	32	23	$11.74	0	0.00%
Chemical Engineering Science	521	788	569	564	$10.26	0	0.00%
Computers and Industrial Engineering	91	196	64	109	$27.75	0	0.00%
Journal of Fluid Mechanics	309	197	336	336	$8.04	0	0.00%
Journal of Small Business Management	3	4	20	14	$15.93	0	0.00%
Politics and Society	0	4	10	11	$59.36	0	0.00%
Information Sciences	12	12	14	66	$63.29	0	0.00%
Annals of Physics	18	24	20	21	$238.57	0	0.00%
Applied Economics	2	10	12	3	$1,767.00	0	0.00%
Information Systems	2	3	0	7	$260.71	0	0.00%
International Economic Review	10	8	4	5	$81.60	0	0.00%
Journal of Approximation Theory	2	4	2	5	$518.40	0	0.00%
Journal of Communication	26	6	16	5	$151.80	0	0.00%
Journal of Economic Theory	21	44	29	18	$154.78	0	0.00%
Journal of Scientific Computing	0	0	2	11	$122.55	0	0.00%
Journal of Theoretical Biology	33	48	38	64	$66.86	0	0.00%
Psychophysiology	8	2	10	0	—	0	—

Appendix 5

Figure 15.17
Ratio of Dual Variable (UB) to Usage with z = 10%, for Period 2007

Journal	2004	2005	Full Text 2006	2007	Cost/Use	z = 10% UB	UB/FT
Journal of the American Chemical Society	3,124	3,370	3,242	4,945	$0.73	5,053.53	102.19%
Adolescence	0	103	84	127	$1.29	128.505	101.19%
Foreign Policy	0	25	40	44	$0.57	43.9739	99.94%
Journal of School Psychology	362	582	526	482	$0.91	470.1	97.53%
Journal of Politics	0	4	10	27	$7.07	25.4443	94.24%
Materials Letters	251	182	255	402	$6.53	371.972	92.53%
Industrial Marketing Management	32	48	75	132	$7.26	121.37	91.95%
Journal of Accounting Research	5	14	5	51	$11.75	45.3896	89.00%
Journal of Memory and Language	75	222	97	111	$8.26	96.7691	87.18%
Optical and Quantum Electronics	0	10	31	172	$12.72	148.804	86.51%
Journal of Fluid Mechanics	309	197	336	336	$8.04	289.977	86.30%
Chemical Engineering Science	521	788	569	564	$10.26	464.839	82.42%
Applied Optics	630	1,288	1,440	720	$4.64	591.101	82.10%
Journal of Financial Economics	118	68	108	153	$13.37	122.641	80.16%
European Journal of Political Research	5	5	20	52	$15.73	41.2566	79.34%
Journal of Advertising	0	20	22	18	$11.06	14.2079	78.93%
ABA Journal	0	2	20	13	$9.23	10.2545	78.88%
Water Research	415	496	1,044	626	$8.51	493.397	78.82%
Computers and Education	87	62	180	134	$12.30	101.309	75.60%
Cognitive Psychology	57	74	34	45	$16.18	33.6907	74.87%
Journal of the American Ceramic Society	0	189	990	332	$4.15	242.711	73.11%
American Journal of Political Science	8	16	25	22	$15.23	15.9897	72.68%
Modern Asian Studies	3	8	11	19	$19.32	13.5442	71.29%
Journal of Small Business Management	3	4	20	14	$15.93	9.5988	68.56%
Journal of Crystal Growth	425	784	564	676	$20.10	455.634	67.40%
Computer Communications	5	4	19	76	$23.75	50.9325	67.02%
Composite Structures	106	212	113	202	$22.45	133.598	66.14%
Computers and Operations Research	86	190	252	162	$18.56	101.761	62.82%
Engineering Fracture Mechanics	152	236	67 -	170	$28.29	98.3271	57.84%
Computers and Industrial Engineering	91	196	64	109	$27.75	61.9367	56.82%
Statistical Science	29	4	28	10	$15.00	5.64314	56.43%
BioEssays	0	0	22	42	$29.76	22.6928	54.03%

Journal of Manufacturing Systems	0	15	0	14	$59.07	1.30318	9.31%
Physics Reports	38	84	100	118	$55.71	7.74139	6.56%
British Journal of Special Education	12	1	16	9	$51.67	0.373737	4.15%
Annals of Statistics	28	29	32	23	$11.74	0	0.00%
Journal of Microscopy	144	104	96	100	$16.67	0	0.00%
Mechanical Engineering	0	17	24	102	$1.26	0	0.00%
Information Sciences	12	12	14	66	$63.29	0	0.00%
Annals of Physics	18	24	20	21	$238.57	0	0.00%
Applied Economics	2	10	12	3	$1,767.00	0	0.00%
Information Systems	2	3	0	7	$260.71	0	0.00%
International Economic Review	10	8	4	5	$81.60	0	0.00%
Journal of Approximation Theory	2	4	2	5	$518.40	0	0.00%
Journal of Communication	26	6	16	5	$151.80	0	0.00%
Journal of Economic Theory	21	44	29	18	$154.78	0	0.00%
Journal of Scientific Computing	0	0	2	11	$122.55	0	0.00%
Journal of Theoretical Biology	33	48	38	64	$66.86	0	0.00%
Politics and Society	0	4	10	11	$59.36	0	0.00%
Psychophysiology	8	2	10	0	—	0	—

Appendix 6

Figure 15.18
Ratio of Dual Variable (UB) to Usage with z = 4.74% (Average Price Increase 2006 to 2007), for Period 2007

Journal	2004	Full Text 2005	2006	2007	Cost/Use	z = 4.74% UB	UB/FT
Journal of the American Chemical Society	3,124	3,370	3,242	4,945	$0.73	4966.3	100.43%
Foreign Policy	0	25	40	44	$0.57	43.7798	99.50%
Adolescence	0	103	84	127	$1.29	126.35	99.49%
Journal of School Psychology	362	582	526	482	$0.91	472.703	98.07%
Journal of Politics	0	4	10	27	$7.07	24.675	91.39%
Materials Letters	251	182	255	402	$6.53	365.957	91.03%
Applied Optics	630	1,288	1,440	720	$4.64	631.168	87.66%
Journal of Fluid Mechanics	309	197	336	336	$8.04	291.745	86.83%
Chemical Engineering Science	521	788	569	564	$10.26	468.893	83.14%
Optical and Quantum Electronics	0	10	31	172	$12.72	142.819	83.03%
Water Research	415	496	1,044	626	$8.51	518.878	82.89%
ABA Journal	0	2	20	13	$9.23	10.7014	82.32%
Journal of Advertising	0	20	22	18	$11.06	14.5487	80.83%
Journal of Financial Economics	118	68	108	153	$13.37	121.613	79.49%
Annals of Statistics	28	29	32	23	$11.74	18.148	78.90%
Computers and Education	87	62	180	134	$12.30	104.808	78.21%
European journal of Political Research	5	5	20	52	$15.73	40.1088	77.13%
Cognitive Psychology	57	74	34	45	$16.18	33.5888	74.64%

American Journal of Political Science	8	16	25	22	$15.23	16.3669	74.40%
Journal of Microscopy	144	104	96	100	$16.67	72.8662	72.87%
Journal of Small Business Management	3	4	20	14	$15.93	10.0605	71.86%
Modern Asian Studies	3	8	11	19	$19.32	13.3637	70.34%
Computers and Operations Research	86	190	252	162	$18.56	108.464	66.95%
Statistical Science	29	4	28	10	$15.00	6.68839	66.88%
Composite Structures	106	212	113	202	$22.45	131.885	65.29%
Computer Communications	5	4	19	76	$23.75	49.1158	64.63%
Engineering Fracture Mechanics	152	236	67	170	$28.29	96.0579	56.50%
Computers and Industrial Engineering	91	196	64	109	$27.75	61.5504	56.47%
BioEssays	0	0	22	42	$29.76	22.4593	53.47%
Physics Reports	38	84	100	118	$55.71	11.1001	9.41%
Journal of Manufacturing Systems	0	15	0	14	$59.07	1.10828	7.92%
Politics and Society	0	4	10	11	$59.36	0.34422	3.13%
British Journal of Special Education	12	1	16	9	$51.67	0	0.00%
Industrial Marketing Management	32	48	75	132	$7.26	0	0.00%
Journal of Accounting Research	5	14	5	51	$11.75	0	0.00%
Journal of Crystal Growth	425	784	564	676	$20.10	0	0.00%
Journal of Memory and Language	75	222	97	111	$8.26	0	0.00%
Journal of the American Ceramic Society	0	189	990	332	$4.15	0	0.00%
Mechanical Engineering	0	17	24	102	$1.26	0	0.00%
Information Sciences	12	12	14	66	$63.29	0	0.00%
Annals of Physics	18	24	20	21	$238.57	0	0.00%
Applied Economics	2	10	12	3	$1,767.00	0	0.00%
Information Systems	2	3	0	7	$260.71	0	0.00%
International Economic Review	10	8	4	5	$81.60	0	0.00%
Journal of Approximation Theory	2	4	2	5	$518.40	0	0.00%
Journal of Communication	26	6	16	5	$151.80	0	0.00%
Journal of Economic Theory	21	44	29	18	$154.78	0	0.00%
Journal of Scientific Computing	0	0	2	11	$122.55	0	0.00%
Journal of Theoretical Biology	33	48	38	64	$66.86	0	0.00%
Psychophysiology	8	2	10	0	—	0	—

REFERENCES

Project COUNTER. www.projectcounter.org.

Baldenius, Tim, Sunil Dutta, and Stefan Reichelstein. 2007. Cost allocations for capital budgeting decisions. *Accounting Review* 82 (4): 837–67.

Blecic, Deborah D., Joan B. Fiscella, and Stephen E. Wiberley. 2001. The measurement of use of Web-based information resource: An early look at vendor-supplied data using ICOLC guidelines. *College & Research Libraries* 62 (5): 434–53.

Breeding, Marshall. 2002. Strategies for measuring and implementing e-use. *Library Technology Reports* 38 (3): 1–70.

Cooper, William D., Robert G. Morgan, Alonzo Redman, and Margart Smith. 2002. Capital budgeting models: Theory vs. practice. *Business Forum* 26 (1–2): 15–20.

Duy, Joanna. 2004. Usage data: Issues and challenges for electronic resource collection management. In *E-serials collections management: Transitions, trends, and technicalities*, edited by David C. Fowler, 111–38. New York, NY: The Haworth Information Press.

Duy, Joanna, and Liwen Vaughan. 2006. Can electronic journal usage data replace citation data as a measure of journal use? An empirical examination. *Journal of Academic Librarianship* 32 (5): 512–17.

Hahn, Karla L., and Lila A. Faulkner. 2002. Evaluative usage-based metrics for the selection of E-journals. *College and Research Libraries* 63 (3): 215–27.

Hayes, James W. 1984. Discount rate in linear programming formulations of the capital budgeting problem. *Engineering Economist* 29 (2): 113–26.

Henderson, Albert. 1999. Information science and information policy: The use of constant dollars and other indicators to manage research investments. *Journal of the American Society for Information Science* 50 (4): 366–79.

Henle, Alea, and Donnice Cochenour. 2007. Practical considerations in the standardization and dissemination of usage statistics. In *Usage statistics of e-serials*, edited by David C. Fowler, 5–23. New York: Haworth Information Press.

Landesman, Margaret M. 2004. Libraries investing in the future first—some practical suggestions. *ARL Bimonthly Report* 234 (June): 1–7.

Leonard, Barbara G. 1994. The metamorphosis of the information resources budget. *Library Trends* 42 (3): 490–98.

McGeary, Timothy M., and Joseph C. Hartman. 2006. Electronic resource management: A multi-period capital budgeting approach. *Engineering Economist* 51 (4): 325–46.

Medeiros, Norm. 2007. Uses of necessity or users of convenience? What usage statistics reveal and conceal about electronic serials. In *Usage statistics of e-serials*, edited by David C. Fowler, 233. New York: Haworth Information Press.

Meyer, Richard W. 1997. Monopoly power. *Library Quarterly* 67 (4): 325–49.

Noonan, Christine F., and Melissa K. McBurney. 2007. Practical considerations in the standardization and dissemination of usage statistics. In *Usage statistics of e-serials*, edited by David C. Fowler, 151–60. New York: Haworth Information Press.

Park, Chan S., and Gunter P. Sharpe-Bette. 1990. *Advanced engineering economics*. New York: Wiley.

Prabha, Chandra, and John E. Ogden. 1994. Recent trends in academic library materials expenditures. *Library Trends* 42 (3): 499–512.

Taylor III, Lloyd, J. 1998. A comparison of capital budgeting models: Local versus global viewpoints. *Business Process Management Journal* 4 (4): 306–14.

Tenopir, Carol, and Donald W. King. 1998. Designing electronic journals with 30 years of lessons from print. *Journal of Electronic Publishing* 4 (2).

Unger, V. E. 1974. Duality results for discrete capital budgeting models. *Engineering Economist* 19 (4): 237–51.

BIBLIOGRAPHY

Conyers, Angela. 2006. Usage statistics and online behaviour. In *The e-resources management handbook*. Newbury (UK): UK Serials Group.

Ladwig, J. Parker, and Andrew J. Sommese. 2005. Using cited half-life to adjust download statistics. *College & Research Libraries* 66 (5): 527–42.

Wood, Elizabeth J., Rush Miller, and Amy Knapp. 2007. *Beyond survival. managing academic libraries in transition*. Westport, CT: Libraries Unlimited.

PART VI

Emerging Contexts

CHAPTER 16

Data for Repositories: Making the Case and Integrating into Practice

HILARY DAVIS

It is unlikely that any serious research-based institution will not have its own digital repository by the end of this decade.

—Swan and Carr 2008, 31

INTRODUCTION

Given the continuing trend of academic institutions to deploy institutional repositories, it is critical to consider the role of data in making the case for repositories and building success stories. This chapter reviews the role that data can play in institutional repositories, from planning to implementation, and in assessment for sustainability. While there are many other valuable sources on how to create repositories (e.g., Ferreira et al. 2008; Stanger and McGregor 2006; Barton and Waters 2004–2005; Crow 2002a), this chapter sets out to show how to use data analysis, evaluation, and assessment to make the case for institutional repositories and to demonstrate tried and true methods for integrating data analysis into the day-to-day practice of running repositories. Many of the practices described within this chapter are covered in far more depth in the literature; the aim here is to review the tools used and how their use can impact repository development and guide the reader to expert resources to learn more.

SPARC (Scholarly Publishing & Academic Resources Coalition) defines institutional repositories as "digital collections capturing and preserving the intellectual output of a single or multi-university community" (Crow 2002b, 4). An institutional repository may also be conceived as a set of services and content inherently unique in their collocation. While some of the content may have been previously published in peer-reviewed journals or performed as a presentation at a conference, the collocation of the content that represents the intellectual output of an institution (e.g., published research, data, and images) is the unique advantage of an institutional repository. A repository can include a variety of intellectual output from class lectures, data sets, course Web sites, peer-reviewed and non-peer-reviewed journal articles, book chapters, and technical reports, as well as theses, dissertations, capstone papers, and conference presentations. The content can be made fully, openly accessible to anyone, accessible to only certain IP (Internet protocol) ranges, to a discrete group of users with unique authentication profiles or secured in a dark archive. The services that support a repository can take a wide array of forms, including full library-mediated support for copyright management; a suite of resources for authors that includes the ability to make customizable profiles to promote their research and teaching activities; statistical evidence showing the number of downloads of content in a repository; assistance in adhering to the National Institutes of Health mandated deposit requirements; or even a self-service model where the authors are responsible for contributing the content to the repository and maintaining their own copyright issues.

Institutional repositories have traditionally been developed to meet several specific goals, including support open access to government-funded research, promote the intellectual output of a college or university, assess return on investment of research funding to outputs (e.g., peer-reviewed publications) and subsequent uptake by consumers, and preserve and archive the intellectual property of a research institution. Funding bodies and institutional administrators in the United Kingdom have taken a more aggressive and more deliberate approach toward research assessment and serve as especially interesting models for making compelling use cases for institutional repositories. Edinburgh University Library has been partnering with universities in the United Kingdom to provide data management of research outputs by capitalizing on their existing repository services. The resulting comprehensive collection of intellectual output helps to determine the level of grant funding provided to researchers and their institutions (Higher Education Funding Council for England et al. 2008).

DATA FOR FEASIBILITY TESTING AND PLANNING

Many repositories are developed using a "build it and they will come" strategy and thus lack a ready set of content. Many of these repositories have received little buy-in or appreciable press due to their evident lack of content and activity. Swan and Carr posit that institutions that launch repositories in the absence of an inaugural corpus of content and without a well-conceived content recruitment strategy are "actively projecting a very poor image of their institutions to the world" (2008, 32). More successful methods of developing repositories have focused on collecting and analyzing data about the potential content and use of the repository.

When assessing the readiness of an institutional community for committing to a repository, an environmental scan can help to envision the "who" (content providers, audience, other stakeholders), "what" (the type of content the institution will promote), "when" (reasonable timelines for implementation, launch, and outreach), and "where" (the unit on campus that is going to maintain the technical and administrative aspects) of a repository initiative at your institution.

Some questions to help identify opportunities for data analysis include, "Who is the intended audience?" "What content is anticipated?" and, "Will that kind of content attract use?" Having clear answers to these kinds of questions will make it much easier to identify key stakeholders and attract potential initial users while concomitantly formulating policies on matters including content, participants, and terms of use.

Data to Identify Early Adopters

Early adopters are often major proponents for a budding repository and can help drive buy-in from departments across campus. A thorough search for researchers, faculty, and students who are already engaged in self-archiving practices—posting full-text copies of their intellectual output on publicly available Web sites (e.g., personal Web sites or disciplinary repositories)—can lead to a solid set of contacts as well as potential sources for repository content. It is imperative to work with early adopters to build a strong set of content for the repository prior to launch. This critical mass of content aids in testing submission workflows; troubleshooting display and access issues; and in thinking through

Figure 16.1
Suggested metrics to track for a repository outreach project

Author metrics	Content metrics
Number of authors targeted for outreach	Issues regarding full-text inclusion into repository
Number of authors successfully contacted	Number of citations and full-text content in repository before outreach
Number of positive responses/Number of negative or null responses	Number of citations and full-text content in repository after outreach
Number of authors not contacted (and why)	Frequency of Web visits to repository pre- and post-outreach

intellectual property and copyright questions. Initial outreach efforts can also help identify early successes (see Figure 16.1).

Data to Aid in Identifying Content

Doing the legwork up front to identify potential key content for a repository will not only help show stakeholders that there is valuable content that would be well served by repository services, but also help identify a ready set of content to target for inclusion prior to public launch of the repository. Locally developed technical reports series, research reports series, cooperative extension reports, and capstone papers are often easily discovered by searching your institution's Web site and library catalog. The copyright for these types of series is typically owned by the university, thereby making the content well suited for inclusion in the repository. These collections can often yield thousands of full-text documents, a portion of which may need to be digitized, but a large portion of which may already be in digital format. Theses and dissertations also offer opportunities to grow a repository. A quick estimate of the number of graduating masters and doctoral students each year can help predict the number of possible items that could represent core repository content. Jones, Andrew, and Mac-Coll (2006) describe the method used at the University of Edinburgh to encourage commitment to developing an institutional repository. They estimate cost of resources and staff over a five-year period, showing that it would cost between 1.43 percent and 1.64 percent of the materials budget from year one to year five of implementation. By multiplying the number of active researchers on campus by the average number of publications each year per researcher, they postulate a potential number of full-text objects that could be deposited over a five-year period. Complementing this estimate with the projection of anticipated theses and dissertations helped them to justify that a repository could achieve a core set of content upon which to build value-added services and future content.

Building a repository on top of a collection of citations is another approach to identifying content. The North Carolina State University (NCSU) Libraries' Scholarly Publications Repository is based on a collection of citations of faculty publications at NCSU since 1997. Citations are added to the repository by harvesting citations from common indexes, including the Web of Science, Agricola, Medline, World Textiles, Zoological Record, and ERIC. Outreach and promotion efforts have sought permission from NCSU authors to integrate full-text objects with existing citations.

Taking a broad and deep sample of publishing activity of researchers on campus can also help identify a large set of potential content. Searching indexes (e.g., Web of Science) for publications associated with the institution's address can capture most of the published works associated with an

Figure 16.2
Publishers' Copyright Policies for a Sample of Publications Authored by NCSU Researchers from 2000 through 2004 (Number of Journals in Sample: 1568; Number of Publishers in Sample: 349)

# Journals	Self-Archiving Rights	# Articles
200	Allow use of publisher's version	727
38	Allow use of publisher's version after embargo	303
645	Allow use of postrefereed version	2,451
194	Allow use of postrefereed version after embargo	614
272	No use allowed without fee or letter of permission	1,126
219	Unknown	1,385

institution. In preparation for the NCSU Libraries' repository of scholarly publications, an initial data set included articles published across five years, from 2000 through 2004. Because publishers' copyright policies are clearly defined at the journal level, it is a relatively straightforward task to identify those journals that allow the posting of content in a repository by matching an institution's body of research output to journal copyright policies available from sources including the publishers and SHERPA/RoMEO (a database of copyright policies, available at www.sherpa.ac.uk/romeo.php). The sample collected for the NCSU Libraries' repository yielded over 1,500 different journals in which NCSU authors published.

Open access publishers' versions of articles are advantageous, as they do not require authors to locate a preprint or precopyedited version of a paper. Figure 16.2 summarizes copyright policies for a sample of publications authored by NCSU researchers. This small sample shows that there are over 6,600 publications authored by NCSU researchers from this five-year window, 1,030 of which (15 percent) are publisher's versions and therefore immediate potential content for the repository.

DATA FOR THE IMPLEMENTATION STAGES

> A great deal of research and imagination are needed to attempt to counter the initial reluctance of researchers to begin depositing their research materials in the institutional repository. Simply breaking the barrier of inertia is probably the most difficult challenge of all
> —Ferreira et al. 2008, "Conclusion"

Davis and Connolly (2007) assessed possible reasons for the underused and underpopulated repository at Cornell University. Understanding publishing patterns for specific disciplines, offering support for understanding copyright restrictions, and demonstrating that contributing works to a repository is worth the time and effort are all important factors to consider when positioning a repository for success.

Repository administrators and proponents at the University of Minho in Portugal reported that, as the number of full-text items in their repository (RepositoriUM) increased, the number of uses (measured by downloads) also increased (Ferreira et al. 2008). Comparing citation rates across a sample of articles made openly available through a service like an institutional repository versus articles accessible only through traditional means (publisher subscription), Antelman (2004) suggests that openly available articles have greater research impact as measured by citation rates. This research may serve as further justification for encouraging authors to deposit their works as a means to increase the consumption of their research, while contributing to continued growth and sustainability of the repository.

A clever way to integrate popular content into a repository is to target highly cited publications. Using Web of Science, for example, search for the top 100 or 1,000 most cited articles affiliated with your campus and determine which can be posted as publishers' versions. Including highly cited content in a repository may not only help promote and market the institution but also the value of the repository, since these articles in particular are likely to be highly sought after.

DATA FOR ASSESSING SUCCESS

Many repositories include a portfolio of value-added services that demonstrate use of the service and make this information publicly available. Evidence of use across different levels of granularity (e.g., visits to an author's list of works or downloads of a specific full-text article from the repository) can make a very compelling case for continued and increasing support for a repository. The California Institute of Technology's portfolio of value-added services is an excellent example of some of the more common site traffic statistics that can be used to demonstrate overall use, specific searches, and information about users' technical specifications (CalTech University Libraries 2008). Web site traffic statistics may include temporal activity, locations of visitors, specific files accessed, referring Web sites, and helpful troubleshooting data. Figure 16.3 shows statistics that are available from most Web site analyzing applications.

Specific statistics that report on the usage of individual content within repositories, or for a collection of content, are often made available as part of many repository software programs. For example, ePrints, an open source repository software solution, includes a service layer that tracks usage of individual full-text objects in the form of downloads from all sources, as well as downloads from distinct countries. These kinds of statistics can demonstrate not only trends in consumption of intellectual outputs over time (as measured by page loads or downloads), but also the level of accessibility of content

Figure 16.3
Common Web Site Traffic Statistics to Consider for Repositories

Temporal Data	Number of unique visitors over year, month, day, hour
	Number of returning visitors over year, month, day, hour
	Duration of visits
Content Data	File types accessed
	Entry pages and exit pages used by visitors
Visitor Data	Top 10 countries of visitors
	Identification of robots and spiders visiting web site
	Browsers, operating systems, screen resolution used by visitors
	Referring search engines and Web sites
	Keywords and phrases searched that led to the visit
Troubleshooting Data	HTTP error messages encountered by users accessing the Web site
	Identifies pages not found by visitors

Figure 16.4
Repository Statistics Available in Repository Software Portfolios

Metrics	DSpace	ePrints	Digital Commons
Number of cumulative downloads	✓	✓	✓
Number of downloads registered over years or months	✓	✓	✓
Views of document abstracts	✓	✓	✓
Number of distinct countries from which a document is accessed/downloaded	✓	✓	
Most viewed documents	✓	✓	✓
Most viewed authors	·	✓	
Most popular searches	✓		

via the repository service. A measure of "most viewed" or "most accessed" documents can be a very compelling invitation for authors to self-archive their works in a repository and for users to explore content in a repository. The University of Tasmania, UTas ePrints, and the University of Southern Queensland repository, USQ ePrints, are good examples of institutional repositories capitalizing on these "vanity" measures as a way to demonstrate and drive usage (University of Tasmania 2008; University of Southern Queensland 2008). The University of Southampton developed an open source tool known as IRStats (Interoperable Repository Statistics), available at http://trac.eprints.org/projects/irstats, that analyzes and reports on use of documents in repositories (University of Southampton 2008). Targeted for administrators and users of repositories, IRStats works across both DSpace and ePrints platforms and provides high impact graphs and tables of usage activity for individual documents or collections of documents. Figure 16.4 illustrates the availability of repository statistics in common software portfolios.

Other value-added metrics discussed as integral to repository environments are commonly found in bibliometric databases, including Web of Knowledge and Scopus. Citation counts for each full-text object might very well complement download, page view, and other data but may be costly to obtain, as it may be difficult to negotiate reuse of this data from proprietary sources. Leveraging citation data from Google Scholar may be a more practical option. Problems noted with this approach are that Google Scholar does not reveal how citations are collected, and searching for citations from the perspective of a particular institution or author can yield misleading or duplicative results. The School of Electronic and Computer Science repository at the University of Southampton currently embeds a link to Google Scholar from each repository record to show citation metrics via Google Scholar (http://eprints.ecs.soton.ac.uk). Another approach is to use as a baseline the citation rate via a bibliometric database and/or the number of downloads (where available from publishers' servers) and compare those metrics to the number of downloads after submission to a repository.

CONSIDERATIONS FOR SMALLER SCHOOLS

The Repositories Support Project, a Joint Information Systems Committee-funded project based in the United Kingdom that is aimed at enabling the implementation and sustainability of institutional repositories, provides a collection of case studies, first developed to foster discussion for the Open

Repositories 2008 conference and now available as a resource for those seeking ideas, advice, and best practices guidelines (Repositories Support Project 2008). Across the board, case studies demonstrate strongly the benefit of using data to help promote and drive the use of repositories. In one of the case studies, the University of Strathclyde reported that leveraging the data included in the ePrints statistical service layer was key to providing evidence to their faculty and researchers that the works for which full-text access was made available were those that also showed the greatest increase in use as measured by downloads (Dawson 2008).

FINAL THOUGHTS

Institutions and managers of digital repositories have an obligation to recognize and seize opportunities to enhance the value of an institution's intellectual output and help researchers and other information seekers tap into, evaluate, and fully exploit the value to knowledge and learning that can come from openly accessible research. A repository offers an opportunity and a venue for showcasing the collective contributions of an entire community or the individual scholarship of a single researcher. Campus administrators, researchers, faculty, IT staff, librarians, students, and users all have a stake in the success of repositories—from the content selected to highlight the research outputs of a campus community, to how the outputs are presented, to how they are contextualized to show impact, and finally, to how information is shared and preserved.

REFERENCES

Antelman, Kristin. 2004. Do open access articles have a greater research impact? *College & Research Libraries* 65 (5): 372–82, www.lib.ncsu.edu/resolver/1840.2/85 (accessed July 6, 2008).

Barton, Mary R., and Margaret M. Waters. 2004–2005. Creating an institutional repository. LEADIRS workbook. MIT Libraries, http://hdl.handle.net/1721.1/26698 (accessed July 6, 2008).

CalTech University Libraries. 2008. Statistics for CalTech Authors. http://gwaihir.library.caltech.edu/statistics/authors/current/awstats.authors.html (accessed July 6, 2008).

Crow, Raym. 2002a. *SPARC institutional repository checklist & resource guide*. Scholarly Publishing & Academic Resources Coalition. www.arl.org/sparc/bm~doc/IR_Guide_&_Checklist_v1.pdf (accessed July 6, 2008).

———. 2002b. The case for institutional repositories: A SPARC position paper. *ARL Bimonthly Report* 223. http://works.bepress.com/ir_research/7 (accessed July 5, 2008).

Davis, Philip M., and Matthew J. L. Connolly. 2007. Institutional repositories: Evaluating the reasons for non-use of Cornell University's installation of DSpace. *D-Lib Magazine* 13 (3/4). www.dlib.org/dlib/march07/davis/03davis.html (accessed July 6, 2008).

Dawson, Alan. 2008. Repository case history: University of Strathclyde Strathprints. Repositories Support Project, www.rsp.ac.uk/repos/casestudies/strathclyde.php (accessed July 6, 2008).

Ferreira, Miguel, Ana Alice Baptista, Eloy Rodrigues, and Ricardo Saraiva. 2008. Carrots and sticks: Some ideas on how to create a successful institutional repository. *D-Lib Magazine* 14 (1/2). www.dlib.org/dlib/january08/ferreira/01ferreira.html (accessed July 6, 2008).

Higher Education Funding Council for England (HEFCE), the Scottish Funding Council (SFC), the Higher Education Funding Council for Wales (HEFCW) and the Department for Employment and Learning, Northern Ireland (DEL). 2008. RAE2008. Research assessment exercise. www.rae.ac.uk (accessed July 5, 2008).

Jones, Richard, Theo Andrew, and Jon MacColl. 2006. *The institutional repository*, 41–46. England: Chandos Publishing.

Repositories Support Project. 2008. Case studies. www.rsp.ac.uk/repos/cases (accessed July 6, 2008).

Stanger, Nigel, and Graham McGregor. 2006. Hitting the ground running: Building New Zealand's first publicly available institutional repository. *Information Science Discussion Paper Series* 2006/2007. http://eprints.otago.ac.nz/274/1/dp2006-07.pdf (accessed July 5, 2008).

Swan, Alma, and Leslie Carr. 2008. Institutions, their repositories and the Web. *Serials Review* 34 (1): 31–35.

University of Southampton. 2008. Interoperable Repository Statistics (IRStats). http://trac.eprints.org/projects/irstats (accessed July 6, 2008).

University of Southern Queensland ePrints. 2008. Usage statistics for USQ ePrints repository. http://eprints.usq.edu.au/authstats1.php (accessed July 6, 2008).

University of Tasmania ePrints. 2008. Usage statistics for UTas ePrints repository. http://eprints.utas.edu.au/es/index.php?action=show_detail_date (accessed July 6, 2008).

CHAPTER 17

How Library Homepage Vocabulary Influences Database Usage: Use of Vendor-Provided Usage Data for Homepage Design

MELISSA JOHNSON

BACKGROUND

Research surrounding vendor-provided usage data has primarily focused on its strengths and weaknesses and how it can be used to influence financial decisions in the selection of electronic resources. Other research has focused on how to set up a local usage data system instead of using data provided by vendors in order to obtain more reliable data. While both of these practices have had significant impact on financial and other decisions, there is room for more research in analyzing the data vendors provide and how it can be used in creative and innovative ways. The same can be said for library Web site data. Assessment of Web site data has primarily focused on usability to determine what pages are being used and how to better serve the needs of the users. Academic libraries have conducted many usability studies focusing on user behavior to help determine the best possible design and content for a Web site. Vocabulary used on library home pages has been determined to be a significant factor in library Web site usability (Spivey 2000). Integrating vendor-provided usage data with Web site data can help provide insight into database usage.

A survey of the Abilene Christian University (ACU) Brown Library homepage found that the language used on the site was unfamiliar to many users and the categories used were difficult to interpret (Brown Library 2007). In one section of the library homepage, 11 natural language subject links were provided to databases instead of their names. Vendor-provided usage data from August to December 2006 (before the redesign) was compared to data from August to December 2007 (after the redesign). This data, along with counts of page views of the library homepage, was analyzed to determine the impact the redesign had on usage. Vendor-provided usage data from institutions of comparable size were also measured as standards to the study. A "Top Databases" section, which included many highly used resources not included in the natural language subject links section, was also added to the homepage after the redesign. Vendor-provided usage data for these links will also be analyzed. Conclusions suggest that language and page layout used on the library homepage impact effective use of databases. Final thoughts describe innovative ways libraries can integrate vendor-provided usage data into the design and content of library Web pages.

LITERATURE REVIEW

Libraries collected data and analyzed usage of library resources before vendor-provided electronic usage data was available. Libraries have developed methods of extracting data to determine what content should be available to their users in the most efficient way in order to "save the time of the user" and make decisions about which "books are for use," as first suggested by Ranganathan (Steckel 2002). Vendor-provided usage data has been criticized for its lack of standardization and "limited statistical data," leading libraries to create their own locally based usage data programs (White and Kamal 2006). However, vendor-provided usage data is readily available from most vendors and is fairly simple to use. While collecting locally produced usage data may be the most comprehensive method of evaluation, some libraries do not have the staff or funding to create or use their own. Finding creative and innovative ways to use vendor-provided data may prove to be the most economical and efficient method for most libraries.

Subscription databases are expensive, so libraries try to promote use of them in many different ways. One way is to provide links on library Web pages. Library terminology or jargon is not easily interpreted by many users, and some do not even know what a database is (Cobus, Dent, and Ondrusek 2005). Library terminology or jargon on Web pages is one of the most significant problems users encounter and one of the easiest to fix (Kim 2006b). Library homepages can vary in the information they provide, from a short menu with few categories to a more robust menu with drop-downs to deliver more choices. Trying to find the right balance of menus, categories, and labels used on a homepage can be difficult (McGillis and Toms 2001). Usability studies have become a standard practice among information professionals. Whether using surveys, focus groups, usage data, or a combination, these studies provide valuable data for Web designers in determining layout and content. However, how do you know if your redesign has had the intended impact without conducting another usability study? Using vendor-provided data can provide a starting point to help determine the success of a usability study or Web site redesign.

METHODOLOGY

The 11 natural language links placed on the Brown Library homepage were an effort to market expensive databases while eliminating library jargon that may be confusing to users, especially students. Also, when talking with students at the research desk it was clear that database names often did not have significance to them. When most students are familiar with searching for information on Google, the library homepage can seem daunting and confusing (Augustine and Greene 2002). By changing the links to natural language, an increase in usage (searches run, sessions, and articles requested) was expected. Five of the 11 links to databases were not linked to the homepage before the redesign: BasicBiosis (FirstSearch), American Chemical Society, Health Source: Nursing/Academic Edition (EBSCO), Information Science & Technology Abstracts (EBSCO), and Science & Technology Collection (EBSCO). Six of the links, American Theological Library Association Serials Religion Database (ATLAS from EBSCO), Business Source Complete (EBSCO), Communication & Mass Media Complete (EBSCO), ERIC (EBSCO), Literature Resource Center (Gale), and PsycINFO (EBSCO) had previously been listed by name on the homepage. Of the 11 natural language links, only two (ATLAS and ERIC) showed decreased usage in searches run and sessions. ERIC and ATLAS also showed a decrease in articles requested. As Figure 17.1 shows, nine of the databases had an increase in searches run (BasicBiosis, Business Source Complete, American Chemical Society, Communication & Mass Media Complete, Information Science & Technology Abstracts, Literature Resource Center, Health Source: Academic/Nursing Edition, and PsycINFO), five of which had an increase in searches run of more than 50 percent. Eight of the databases had an increase in sessions (BasicBiosis, Business Source Complete, Communication & Mass Media Complete, Information Science & Technology

Figure 17.1
Searches Run, 2006 Versus 2007

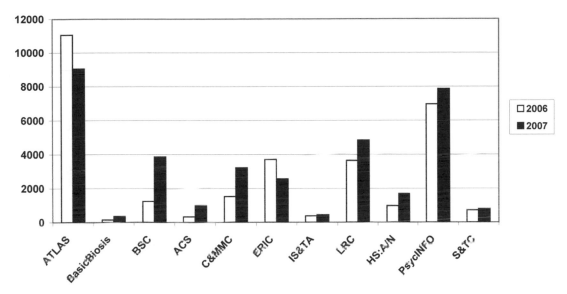

Abstracts, Literature Resource Center, Health Source: Academic/Nursing Edition, PyscINFO, and Science & Technology Collection), two of which had an increase in sessions of more than 50 percent, as shown in Figure 17.2. Six of the databases had an increase in articles requested (Business Source Complete, American Chemical Society, Communication & Mass Media Complete, Literature

Figure 17.2
Sessions, 2006 Versus 2007

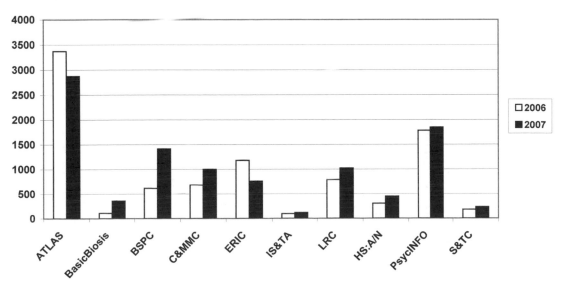

Resource Center, Health Source: Academic/Nursing Edition, and Science & Technology Collection), all of which had an increase in articles requested of more than 50 percent, as shown in Figure 17.3. The homepage views also increased by 414 percent from August–December 2006 to August–December 2007. Before the redesign, page views on the ACU Brown Library homepage had averaged an increase of 41 percent per year.

Vendor-provided usage data and Web sites from universities of comparable size were examined as benchmarks. The universities provided usage data for a one-year period for each database used in the study, although some universities did not have subscriptions to all of the same databases as the ACU Brown Library. Figure 17.4 shows the ACU Brown Library is noticeably lower than most of the other universities in searches run for ATLAS, Business Source Premier/Complete, Communication & Mass Media Complete, ERIC, Health Source: Nursing/Academic Edition, and PsycINFO. Some universities used a fiscal year and one used the calendar year. ACU used the calendar year for the purpose of comparison to the other universities. The usage data for the Business Source Premier/Complete database is where the most dramatic gap is found. ACU also is noticeably lower than the other universities in searches run by an average of 422 percent and in sessions by an average of 600 percent. The homepages of all but one of these universities did not include links to databases, yet their usage was considerably higher than ACU's usage. This may suggest that the ACU Library needs to promote database use more extensively and effectively among students and faculty.

Another method of examining data provided by vendors is to compare titles used from each database. Even if searches run, articles requested, and sessions may not have increased, if more titles have been accessed, then more of the subscribed titles have been used. Most vendors provide data on title usage including abstracts, articles requested, and table of contents. By comparing the percentage of titles used, a more complete picture of usage may be determined. Out of the 11 natural language links, two databases did not report data on title usage. As Figure 17.5 shows, for the remaining nine links, three databases decreased in percentage of titles used, five increased, and one remained the same. In the "Top Databases" section, only one database (eLibrary) reported title usage, and its title usage

Figure 17.3
Articles Requested, 2006 Versus 2007

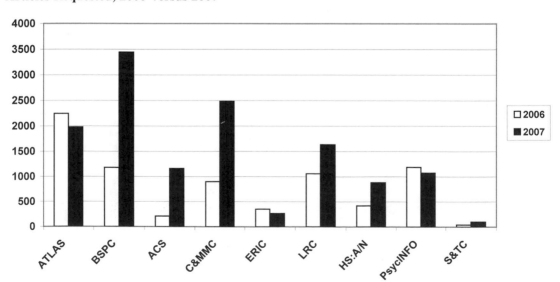

Figure 17.4
Data of Other Universities Versus ACU

	Creighton University	Harding University	Drake University	Stetson University	Saint Joseph's	ACU
	Jan07–Dec07	Jun06–May07	Jul06 Jun07	06–07	FY07	Jan07–Dec07
American Chemical Society						
Searches Run	1,528	1,479	1,590		603	1,436
Articles Requested	2,635	789	2,193		775	1,518
ATLAS or ATLA						
Searches Run	5,976	23,995		40,707	9,988	20,738
Articles Requested	90	377		236	145	4,847
Sessions		5,971		10,987	2,066	6,545
Business Source Premier/ Complete						
Searches Run	13,482		37,663	39,786	35,943	6,077
Articles Requested	13,555			8,822	35,343	5,751
Sessions			24,724	11,259	14,736	2,415
Communication & Mass Media						
Searches Run	7,883		9,297	40,201	962	4,862
Articles Requested	3,075			3,000	262	3,750
Sessions			7,054	11,303	925	1,693
ERIC						
Searches Run	16,818	13,894	29,559	7,866	22,001	5,746
Articles Requested	54	424		187	689	674
Sessions		3,238		2,101	5,360	1,727
Health Source: Academic/ Nursing						
Searches Run		3,275	18,527		8,206	2,635

Articles Requested		2,045			5,793	1,331
Sessions		1,147			2,288	775
Literature Resource Center						
Searches Run				6,653	20,432	16,350
Articles Requested				1,887		5,040
Sessions				1,027	3,035	4,036
PsycINFO						
Searches Run	35,401	11,681	39,683	44,319	33,934	15,840
Articles Requested	1,480	1,125		1,126	2,445	3,391
Sessions		2885	13,803	12,056	7,896	3,928
Science & Technology Collection						
Searches Run		1,075				1,731
Articles Requested		27				258
Sessions		307				525

increased from 3 percent to 21 percent. Increases in title usage in addition to increases in articles requested, as revealed in four of the five databases, may indicate a considerable impact on student and faculty use that was anticipated from the homepage redesign.

Another benchmark for this study is the use of the "Top Databases" section on the ACU Brown Library homepage. This section lists nine of the top databases (according to vendor-provided usage data and faculty requests) and also includes a link to the ACU Brown Library's own "Trial Databases" page. Of the nine databases listed, three did not have any usage data provided by the vendor, and one link to FirstSearch did not directly connect to a single database but to a list. Searches run for two of the six remaining databases increased (eLibrary and Marcive), while four decreased (Lexis-Nexis, New Testament Abstracts, Old Testament Abstracts, and Thesaurus Linguae Graecae), as shown in Figure 17.6. Searches run for eLibrary increased by 792 percent and Marcive increased by 56 percent. Figure 17.7 shows that only four database vendors reported usage for sessions and out of the four, two increased (eLibrary and Marcive) and two decreased (New Testament Abstracts and Old Testament Abstracts). Only one database (Lexis-Nexis) reported articles requested and that increased by 17 percent.

Figure 17.5
Percentage of Titles Used, 2006 Versus 2007

Database	2006	2007
ATLAS	51%	40%
BasicBiosis	N/A	N/A
Business Source Complete	11%	16%
American Chemical Society	86%	92%
Communication & Mass Media Complete	25%	35%
ERIC	26%	5%
Information Science & Technology	2%	6%
Literature Resource Center	N/A	N/A
Health Source: Academic/Nursing Edition	6%	29%
PsycINFO	41%	37%
Science & Technology Collection	4%	4%

Figure 17.6
Top Databases, Searches Run, 2006 Versus 2007

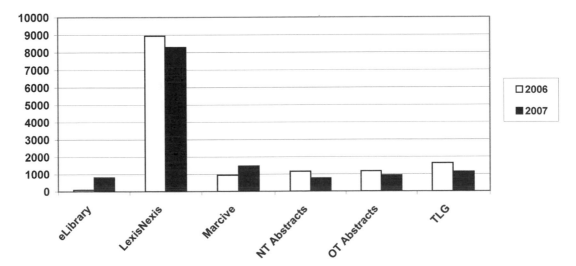

Figure 17.7
Top Databases, Sessions, 2006 Versus 2007

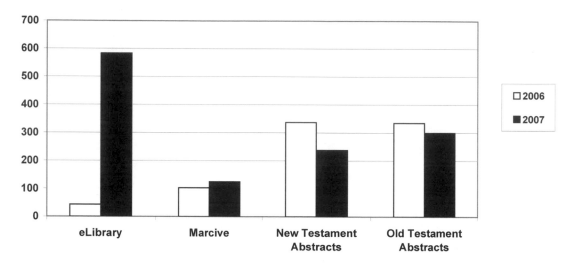

DISCUSSION

From August–December 2006 to August–December 2007 homepage views dramatically increased. This may be due in part to the ACU Brown Library homepage automatically displaying when students log into computers in the library, a practice that started in September 2007. It is also possible that Web "bots" and "spiders" could be responsible for inflation in page views (White and Kamal 2006). A combination of both of these possibilities might provide insight as to why a 414 percent increase in page views from 2006 to 2007 did not make our usage data more comparable to the other universities. With such a significant increase in page views of the homepage, an increase in database use would be expected. ACU and Creighton University are the only universities that had a link to Business Source Premier/Complete and PsycINFO on their homepages, and yet data from each institution showed that neither university had the most searches run or articles requested. The decrease in searches run, articles requested, and sessions for ERIC might be explained by the familiarity of the name ERIC to faculty and students in the Education Department. Library instruction has been greatly emphasized in this department in the past, so the name ERIC may be a highly recognizable name at ACU. However, research has shown that the name of the ERIC database is generally not well known by students (Cobus, Dent, and Ondrusek 2005). ATLAS also may be a highly recognizable database name at ACU. Library instruction for undergraduate and graduate theology classes is conducted on a regular basis. The theological librarian teaches an introduction to graduate studies course and uses the name "ATLAS" as the preferred database for religious studies. As reported by the EBSCO support site, some full-text links found in the ATLAS database reside on a non-EBSCO server (full-text residing on an ATLAS-owned server), so this usage is not reported in the EBSCO-provided data (EBSCO 2008). Though not specifically found on the EBSCO support site, similar nonreported usage for full-text from the ERIC database also may exist. The use of a database by librarians may determine how heavily it is used, which could explain the 792 percent increase in eLibrary and 56 percent increase in Marcive. Marcive is used by Government Documents library staff and has consistently been in the ACU Brown Library "Top 15 Databases by Number of Searches" (a yearly listing of highly used databases) for the last five years. eLibrary has been used frequently by librarians at the research desk to help undergraduates find information and has been requested by one librarian as a link on the homepage in the "Top Databases" section.

CONCLUSIONS

Vendor-provided usage data can be limiting in its scope and purpose, but when this data is easily accessible and available, knowing how to use it can be advantageous in making Web site design decisions. Not all vendors provide the same information, but most report searches run. The International Standards Organization, which publishes standard practices for "information and documentation—international library statistics," suggests in document 2789 (2003) that core data sets include sessions and documents downloaded (White and Kamal 2006). Some of the vendors in this study did not provide this data, which hindered the ability to compare and analyze usage of the databases. The data that was obtained from the vendors provided a basis on which to make Web site design decisions. As is clear from this study and others, having links on the homepage, whether they are natural language or not, should increase use (Kim 2006a). All four of the databases that were not on the homepage before the redesign showed an increase in usage for searches run, articles requested, and number of sessions (where applicable). When having a link on the homepage did not increase database use, this may be due to several factors: poor marketing to students and faculty, lack of knowledge of the database or databases in general, the hindrance of library terminology, or hesitation in navigating the homepage. The massive differences in the data from the other universities proves to the ACU Brown Library that more marketing of databases is needed. Comparing marketing strategies with the other universities may provide successful methods of encouraging database use. If students are more familiar with Google's simple search interface they may hesitate to use the library homepage when numerous links (including database names) are present. The best method for evaluating a homepage redesign is to gather data from vendors, server logs, surveys, focus groups, and assessments (White and Kamal 2006). While searches run, articles requested, or sessions alone should not be used to determine a database's value, these do provide insight into what students are using. While increase in database use does not guarantee whether searches were successful, it does provide hope that students and faculty are using the resources to which we subscribe. The ACU Brown Library homepage, along with other access points on its Web site, will continue to market its databases and strive to increase usage of these invaluable resources. Studying past vendor-provided data can also help librarians discover the behavior of users. When integrated with Web site data including page views and surveys, vendor-provided usage data (including searches run, articles requested, sessions, and percentage of titles accessed) can be used for future home page design. When links to databases are not included on a homepage, vendor-provided usage data may help determine best practices in Web site evaluation and redesign. More research integrating vendor-provided usage data with library instruction, assignments, faculty use, and more will most likely be needed as these were not thoroughly measured in this study.

REFERENCES

Augustine, Susan, and Courtney Greene. 2002. Discovering how students search a library Web site: A usability case study. *College & Research Libraries* 63:354–65.

Brown Library. 2007. New home page online survey. Abilene Christian University. www.acu.edu/academics/library/homepagesurvey/index.html (accessed April 25, 2008).

Cobus, Laura, Valeda Frances Dent, and Anita Ondrusek. 2005. How twenty-eight users helped redesign an academic library Web site: A usability study. *Reference and User Services Quarterly* 44:232–46.

EBSCO. 2008. *Is it possible to obtain statistics for ATLAS?* http://support.epnet.com/knowledge_base/detail.php?id=2764 (accessed August 14, 2008).

Kim, Jong-Ae. 2006a. Capturing metrics for undergraduate usage of subscription databases. *Online* 30:32–39.
———. 2006b. Toward an understanding of Web-based subscription database acceptance. *Journal of the American Society for Information Science and Technology* 57:1715–28.
McGillis, Louise, and Elaine G. Toms. 2001. Usability of the academic library Web site: Implications for design. *College & Research Libraries* 62:355–67.
Spivey, Mark A. 2000. The vocabulary of library home pages: An influence on diverse and remote end-users. *Information Technology and Libraries* 19:151–56.
Steckel, Mike. 2002. *Ranganathan for IAs*. October 7. www.boxesandarrows.com/view/ranganathan_for_ias (accessed April 25, 2008).
White, Andrew, and Eric Djiva Kamal. 2006. *E-metrics for library and information professionals: How to use data for managing and evaluating electronic resource collections.* New York: Neal-Schuman.

BIBLIOGRAPHY

Blecic, Deborah D., Joan B. Fiscella, and Stephen E. Wiberley, Jr. 2001. The measurement of use of Web-based information resources: An early look at vendor-supplied data. *College & Research Libraries* 62: 434–53.
Coombs, Karen A. 2005. Lessons learned from analyzing library database usage data. *Library Hi Tech* 23, no. 4, ACU Brown Library.
Ghaphery, Jimmy. 2005. Too quick? Log analysis of quick links from an academic library website. *OCLC Systems & Services* 21, no. 3, ACU Brown Library. http://firstsearch.oclc.org/;FSIP.
Tenopir, Carol, and Eleanor Read. 2000. Patterns of use in academic libraries. *College & Research Libraries* 61:234–46.
Townley, Charles T., and Leigh Murray. 1999. Use-based criteria for selecting and retaining electronic information: A case study. *Information Technology and Libraries* 18:32–39.

CHAPTER 18

NUC Accreditation Data and Evidence-Based Library Management in Nigerian University Libraries

SAMUEL C. UTULU

INTRODUCTION

The heterogeneous nature of university library users requires that librarians use good and accurate evidences. This is necessitated by the need to ascertain what users want, how they want it, and when they want it. Information and communication technologies (ICTs) and the Internet have also increased the possibility of distant learning and distributed campus systems which makes it easily possible for a deluge of people to be enrolled in universities. Consequently, university library users' characteristics have become synonymous with those of public library users. Teenagers, adults, and the elderly have various programs-certificates, diplomas, predegrees, degrees (undergraduate, masters, PhD), part time and full time, and specialized executive programs. As a result, university libraries are now faced with the challenge of understanding students', lecturers', and researchers' diverse characteristics in order to be able to meaningfully provide them with the information they require to learn, teach, and do research.

Thus, Fabunmi (2004) points out that Nigerian university libraries are challenged by the need to assist universities to perform the following statutory functions, as presented by Ifidon and Okoli (2002):

1. teaching, research, and public service,
2. pursuit, promotion, and dissemination of knowledge,
3. manpower development,
4. promotion of social and economic modernization, and
5. promotion of intra- and inter-continental and international understanding.

They do this by taking up and performing the following responsibilities:

1. provision of materials for undergraduate instruction as well as supplementary reading,
2. provision of materials in support of faculty, external and collaborated research,

3. provision of materials in support of postgraduate research,

4. provision of materials for personal and self-development,

5. provision of specialized information, and

6. cooperating and developing networks with other libraries for resources and knowledge sharing.

The roles above correspond with those outlined by Altbach (2007) as roles contemporary university libraries play in making a university a high-class university. The trends in globalization, ICTs, and competition among universities all over the world have also placed a strong challenge on how Nigerian university libraries must respond to the issue of providing information to support students, faculty, administrators, and proprietors. Uvah (2007) submits that in the bid to make Nigerian universities globally competitive the Nigerian National Universities Commission (NUC) initiated the following "quadrangle" concepts: Nigerian Universities Computer Literacy Project (NUCompulit), Nigerian Universities Network (NUNet), Nigerian Universities Management Information System (NUMIS), and Nigerian Virtual Library (NaViLib). These programs are aimed at promoting functional computer and information technology literacy, taking full advantage of ICTs to enhance university education performances in Nigeria, inculcating the culture of ICT in the Nigerian university system and enhancing the development of a knowledge-based society. The quadrangle concepts are very good examples of recent development in the nation that university libraries are expected to support with appropriate information management strategies.

Consequently, the NUC has designed accreditation guidelines and programs that will spur Nigerian universities into greatness through appropriateness of physical infrastructure, information provision, and alignment of objectives with set national and international university education goals. NUC's accreditation lays strong emphasis on library staff quality, standard collections, and development of innovative information management policy. It positions Nigerian university libraries to understand that a "self directed and lifelong learning system is the preferred learning system in the present age. Library resources should foster independent, self-paced and more distributed learning . . . in [a] network environment and [should] be accessed remotely" (Adeogun 2006, 49). This had compelled Nigerian university libraries to consider the human capital, social capital, technological capital, and economic capital required to run an ICT-driven library system.

This chapter, therefore, provides an overview of evidence-based library management practice in Nigerian university libraries. It identifies two basic types of evidence-based library management prevalent among Nigerian university libraries: evidence drawn from empirical research carried out by practicing academic librarians and faculties in Nigerian Library Schools, and evidence derived from data collected in the course of providing library services to users, otherwise known as innovative and core evidence-based library management. The chapter presents how NUC accreditation data requirements influence and give direction to evidence-based management practices in Redeemer's University, Mowe, Nigeria. It also develops a theoretical framework based on literature review and observation of evidence collection instruments adopted in the case study library.

THOUGHTS ON EVIDENCE-BASED MANAGEMENT

Evidence-based library management occurs when librarians develop alternatives in the course of making decisions by relying on facts systematically generated as evidence(s) to support their information delivery objectives. It simply describes a deliberate effort made to gather facts and data on any particular aspect of library operations or administration in which the generated facts and data are used as the basis of making decisions. Lucas defines operations as the "task of keeping existing applications running" (1989, 115). Library operations in Nigerian university libraries are carried out in the technical services and readers/public services units. They collate data regarding selection; cataloging and classification; and charging and discharging books. These library operations are defined and could be statistically estimated and therefore present an easy-to-know framework for making decisions required to carry them out. Generally, decision-making involves definition of problems, statement of hypothesis, data collection to test hypothesis, and drawing conclusion on issues relating to operations and management. This makes the act of decision-making scientific in nature (Adebayo, Ojo, and Obamiro 2006).

University libraries in Nigeria have been facing the challenge and the consequent result of budget cuts. Irrespective of this, the demand for high performance placed on Nigerian university libraries by users and parent institutions requires that accurate and informed decisions are taken on resource allocation and operations management. This is why evidence-based management has become *sine qua non* and a very good management alternative available to these libraries. It enables library management to allocate resources more accurately and assess the effect of the resources allocated on library service output. Haglund and Olsson write that "to be able to further develop the functions of the university libraries, it is necessary to be attentive to the changing needs and methods of work of . . . researchers; otherwise university libraries cannot contribute to the competitiveness of its [sic] university's research" (2008, 52).

Nigerian university libraries over the years have been engaged in activities that will enable them do exactly what Haglund and Olsson proposed. This quest, together with NUC's accreditation demands has influenced their adoption of evidence extraction culture and strategy. This is because it enables them to collect and use data for definition of decision problems, stating alternative causes of action, analysis of feasible alternatives, selection of best optimal actions, implementation, and evaluation of results. Common library operations that involve gathering data used as evidences are as follows:

- acquisition,
- exhibition and displays,
- use of reserve materials,
- catalog data,
- reference resources use,
- electronic database use,
- reprography/reproduction of library materials,
- circulation/collection management, etc. (Blake and Schleper 2004).

However classified, all forms of data drawn from library operations fit into five types:

- circulation data,
- electronic resources use data,
- subject and subject analysis data,
- library collection data, and
- patron opinion data and overall library service evaluation data.

In Nigeria, relying on data collected from library operations, in combination with positions expressed in library science studies published in formal outlets (including journals and newsletters) has become a culture. The evidences have been used to elicit users' opinions, understand usage patterns, and to evaluate library management trends. They have been used to identify users' needs and their patterns and to know how these factors mirror current operations effectiveness and users' satisfaction. However, evidence-based library management in Nigerian university libraries is mostly geared towards answering questions relating to negative challenges and on few occasions, successes and what formed part of the operational line and decisions that led to the result in question. The consequence of this is that areas prone to problems are evaluated for problem solving, but successful areas become very difficult to sustain.

Nevertheless, Koufogiannakis (2007) proposes a model for evidence-based collection management that encompasses core information needs and innovative information needs (see Figure 18.1). Koufogiannakis acknowledges two types of decision information needs: core decision information needs and innovative decision information needs. Although he emphasizes collection management, his model is also applicable to other aspects of evidence-based library management. Core decision information needs relate primarily to operations decisions which are taken on a daily basis. Hence, data collection relating to the practice of evidence-based management in core areas is carried out by documenting day-to-day library operations like circulation, reprography, and library use analysis records. Koufogiannakis specifically states that

Core information needs are those that are central to everyday practice and decision making. These types of information needs are embedded within the day-to-day operations of collection works. Core questions are likely to be directly relevant to subject librarians and collection managers' daily work (2007, 4).

On the other hand, innovative decision information needs are occasional. They are addressed at the managerial and strategic level and deal with medium- and long-term decisions which may affect the library. As the name implies, they also deal with new innovations that are to be introduced into the body of services the university library offers to its users. In most cases, innovative decision

Figure 18.1
Koufogiannakis's Evidence-Based Collection Management Model

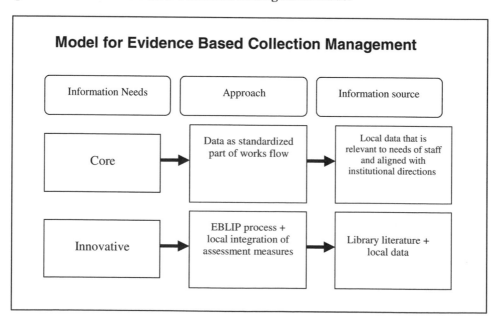

information needs also look at assessing already deployed library services through more established processes of establishing needs, evaluating the needs, applying appropriate evidence-based data collection method or research strategies, and assessing outcomes. In Nigerian university libraries, innovative evidence-based library management has become profound. This culture is supported by the fact that librarians are required to publish. As academics, librarians' major research activities are geared towards improving their profession and services to users.

In a study, Mabawonku (2005) lists 16 library and information science journal titles published in Nigeria and observes that only 5 are being published by academic institutions and private organizations, while the remaining 11 are published by library and information science associations (Nigerian Library Association state chapters). She notes that the articles are based on case studies on local issues in libraries within the locality of their publication, and not on theoretical bases or large-scale empirical studies. The implication of this is that evidence-based library management practice in Nigerian university libraries adopts more of the innovative model. Librarians study scenarios peculiar to their local library setups and report them in journals, which are in turn used for understanding management challenges and decision-making. The use of literature has been helpful irrespective of objections made by Tranfield, Denyer, and Smart (2003) on the use of literature review as evidence. Tranfield et al. consider facts presented in the literature to be often contradictory evidence.

Blake and Schleper (2004) note that librarians sometimes wander through the collections on shelves to evaluate by examining volumes that are worn out or dusty from disuse. Consequently, evidence-based decisions are sometimes carried out by simply observing scenarios, even though the scenarios may have been aroused by studies reported in librarianship journals. Situations like this are very prevalent in Nigerian university libraries. The need to use evidence has often resulted in situations in which basic strategies rooted in simple observations, like the one expressed by Blake and Schleper, are used.

METHODS AND TOOLS FOR COLLECTING EVIDENCE DATA

There are various methods and tools available for generating data used in Nigerian university libraries for evidence-based management. These, however, depend largely on the administrative structure and the peculiarity of the library in question. Aina (2004) suggests that there are three kinds of administrative structures and approaches prevalent in African university libraries: functional approach, subject approach, and hybrid approach. Functional approach occurs when a university library's administrative structure is developed around basic functions like acquisition; circulation; serials management; readers' services; and cataloging and classification. Subject approach occurs when a university library is managed based on broad subject areas offered in the university and are often spelled out by faculties or colleges. Hybrid approach takes place in university libraries that have structural balance between the functional approach and subject approach. In university libraries that have adopted hybrid approach, elements evident in the functional approach and subject approach are combined together to determine the administrative and management structure. The functional approach is adopted by older university libraries in Nigeria. The evolving private university libraries are the ones adopting the hybrid approach skewed towards subject approach, but with a bit of functional approach.

Administrative approach notwithstanding, the kinds of data collection methods and tools required are dependent on the evidence model (core or innovative) in use in a university library at a particular time. For instance, data collection is expected to take longer when it is for innovative evidence. Also, a collection of data gathered at various times for various reasons may be put together to produce the evidence required for a long-term decision. As well, a collection of core evidence may be gathered over a period of time. Therefore, method relies more on proper and formal documentation, which could be in the form of questionnaires or interviews of users or staff over a period of time. Haglund and Olsson (2008) argue that questionnaires, interviews, and focus groups are among the most widely used methods of collecting evidences in contemporary university libraries around the world.

Nevertheless, the relationship that exists between departments in a university library may determine the method of data collection used. In a university library where subject approach has been adopted, with the cycle of library functions carried out in each subject library, evidence-based library management approaches would be carried out along subject areas. Under this condition, information needs and information behavior may be influenced by the peculiarity of the subject area in question. Also, subjects influence the use of certain kinds of information resources. For example, in Nigerian university libraries transparencies are much more useful in science subjects, which deal more often with diagrams and figures, than humanities subjects, which deal more often with texts. Hence, collecting data on transparency use may require methods appropriate to science scholars and their information use behavior.

MANAGEMENT STRUCTURES AND FUNCTIONS

Management has been classified into three levels: operational, tactical/managerial, and strategic. Curtis (1995) claims that senior management (in this case, the university librarians and deputy librarians) deal with broad issues affecting an organization in the long term. Decisions, therefore, revolve around introducing new library and information services, resources allocation, administrative and managerial structural changes and their financial implications, and choice of particular investment projects. On the other hand, the tactical level involves breaking down long-term decisions to medium-term decisions at the departmental level. Tactical level decisions involve the allotment of budgets at the departmental level, scheduling, and forecasting, planning, and implementing cash flows. These functions are performed mostly by principal librarians, senior librarians, and sometimes deputy librarians who monitor library services outcomes at the large departmental level.

OPERATIONAL LEVEL

Operations in acquisition departments involve collating selection data, preparing order, monitoring the order, receiving the order, checking supplied order against order list, and so on. In circulation departments, operations primarily involve charging and discharging information resources, and thus the collection and collation of evidences on library resources usage. Regardless of the department in question, the operational level deals with short-term decisions and operations geared towards achieving operations and service efficiency and effectiveness. A deluge of data is generated and little analysis is carried out on the data. Curtis (1995) notes that data generated are exclusively within the organization and therefore very detailed, and of immediate relevance. For instance, the number of library users in a particular week can be compared with previous weeks and used to understand a fall or rise in the number of those who read in the library, who borrowed books, or the subject(s) that were mostly borrowed.

Keyes (2006) uses levels of management to define the kind of decisions employees make: operational, tactical, and strategic. She notes that operational level tasks are usually carried out in a routine fashion and are therefore not subject to complex decision-making, while middle level managers deal with analyzing and turning data carefully into finished, accurate, and usable formats for senior managers who make decisions on service delivery and projection, cost-benefit balancing, and key competitive issues. It is rational, therefore, to have operational, tactical, and strategic evidences.

As a result of the use of computers in contemporary university libraries five tools have been identified to be usable across all the three levels of management to collect library management evidences. At the operational level, transaction processing systems (TPS) are used to build up data for the upper levels. Office information systems are used to facilitate organizational communication and data transfer, while knowledge management systems help tap, accumulate, and manage a library's knowledge base. At the strategic level are management reporting systems that provide summarized reports of data from TPS into forms convenient for executive uses. Decision support systems (DSS) deal with data-driven and model-driven systems that can simulate and provide intelligent decisions. All these systems provide different methods and tools for capturing, managing, and disseminating evidences used for decision-making at all levels of Nigerian university library management.

Ifidon (2007) presents sample statistics of the number of librarians that is required at each level of management in a Nigerian university library, based on NUC requirements for a user body that is made up of more than 18,000 users:

1. University Librarian and Deputy Librarian (6)—strategic level

2. Principal/Senior librarians (12)—tactical

3. Librarian I, Librarian II, and Assistant Librarian (15)—operational

It is important to note that the categories enumerated above function as heads and supervisors at different levels and are responsible for managing and deploying the tools enumerated above. For instance, librarians in the Librarian II and Librarian I cadres may be asked to supervise circulation operations or cataloging data entry operations and make periodic reports to a staff coordinator, who may be a principal librarian. The practical situation in level of management analysis is that there appears to be a thin line separating some cadres and levels of staff. Senior supervisors at a level may be performing supplementary functions at the base of a higher level, thereby becoming a link between levels of management.

It will be appropriate to conclude this segment with Winkworth's (1999) proposition on the use and management of evidences in modern organizations. The possibility of producing performance statistics of impressive arithmetical precision should not delude anyone into thinking that performance measurement is an exact science. It is not. Performance measurement is about logic and judgment. Thinking through the logic of using particular performance indicators is far more important than precise calculation or acres of computer-produced data.

Regardless of methods and tools adopted for capturing evidence data in university libraries, the ability to accurately interpret these data and apply them is much more important in the practice of evidence-based library management. Consequently, most university libraries in Nigeria have used and continue to use nonconventional and manual methods of capturing evidences. Once the methods and tools provide evidences mirroring the questions they intend to answer, logical conclusions on the effects are then used to make decisions.

STATISTICAL MODELS ADOPTED BY NIGERIAN UNIVERSITY LIBRARIES

Evidence-based management is primarily about collecting evidences and quantifying or putting them into descriptive and measurable forms. It is therefore based on using appropriate statistical models to measure elements that have been collected as evidences. According to McClare and Sincich (2000), statistics are used to describe (descriptive statistics) and/or to make inferences (inferential statistics). Descriptive statistics uses numerical and graphical methods to trace and understand patterns in data sets. This involves summarizing the data and presenting it in forms that are convenient and easy to understand. Inferential statistics deal with generalization, estimation, decisions, and predictions. It is more quantitative in nature than descriptive statistics. LIS (library and information science)

Figure 18.2
Simple Percentage Score Formula

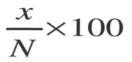

$$\frac{x}{N} \times 100$$

research adopts mainly descriptive approaches, thereby laying very little emphasis on quantification and generalization (Olorunsola, Ibegbulam, and Akinboro 2005).

Qualitative data could be generated as nominal data or ordinal data. Nominal measurements treat data by identifying or classifying the category of each unit in the sample, whereas ordinal data measures data by ordering or ranking units. Nigerian university libraries often ask users to rank the usefulness of a new or existing library service or an information resource by scaling, that is, 1 as the least value to 5 as the highest value. They also collect ordinal data that are primarily based on ranking or ordering, and therefore allow little room for arithmetic calculations. When such ranking or ordering is made they are then measured in simple percentage scores. For example, 50 users of *Chemical Abstracts* were asked their opinion of its relevance to their information needs. Thirty of them ranked its relevance as 5 (highest value), 15 ranked it as 3 (mid value), and 5 ranked it as 1 (low value). These are calculated using the formula in Figure 18.2.

In the formula above x = number of users who ranked *Chemical Abstracts* as 5 and N = total number of library users that were observed. It therefore means that 60 percent of those observed found *Chemical Abstracts* very relevant, 30 percent found it relevant, while only 10 percent did not find it relevant.

It is common to see examples such as this being used by librarians to elicit evidences. Statistics help the library to ascertain "origin," or the beginning point on a scale, an order that allows for positioning on the scale and distance of variables from one another. The example above, where 60 percent approve of the high value of *Chemical Abstracts*, shows the distance of the approval from the point of disapproval in terms of number of users who find it very valuable. Some occasions also warrant the use of the measurement of relationship, that is, the evaluation of factors that affect dependent variables (Asika 1991).

In research leading to evidence evaluation, especially in LIS which is social science based, relationships are also sought. Asika (1991) defines dependent and independent variables as constructs or concepts that have numerical value. Examples are age, number of books, or number of staff. He further states that a variable becomes dependent when its value depends on other factors or independent when its value is not affected by other factors. For instance, previous computer/CD-ROM database use can influence a library user's ability to use Internet-based databases. In Nigeria, university libraries have raised concerns about users' nonuse of electronic information sources due to their computer use ability and past experience of electronic resources. Apart from usage ability and past experience, other factors also affect library use variables. Ogunbameru (2004) recognizes six types of relations:

- reversible and irreversible relations, that is, if x then y and if y then x.
- deterministic or stochastic relation, that is, if x then always y.
- sequential or coexistence relation, that is, if x then later y or if x then also y.
- sufficient or contingent relation, that is, if x then y, regardless of anything else.
- necessary or substitutable relation, that is, only if x then y.
- interdependent relation, that is, if x changes from x1 to x2 then y changes from y1 to y2.

Those attempting to use evidence in Nigerian university libraries frequently encounter a need to analyze and consider relationships like the above. For instance, it is common among Nigerian university libraries to test the relationship between users' browsing speed and frequency of use of Internet-based databases. Over time, Nigerian university libraries, through evidence collection, have established that the reliability of Internet access actually determines its use (Ojokoh and Asaolu 2005). Other areas of relationship that are commonly evaluated using evidences by Nigerian university libraries are accessibility and availability effects on library use (Tamuno 1992).

UNIVERSITY LIBRARIANSHIP RESEARCH IN NIGERIA

The year 1998 marked the fiftieth year of university librarianship and libraries in Nigeria. Agboola observes that "Nigerian university libraries have over the last fifty years been a major component of the university scene . . . [and] been the most vibrant sector of the library and information profession in the country" (2000, 280). In terms of funding, professionalism, staffing, coordination, stock, and services, Nigerian university libraries have been in the forefront. For example, the University of Ibadan Library was the first in the country to begin an automated serials catalog in 1975. Libraries in universities have also pioneered the evolution of electronic information services in Nigeria by establishing and coordinating initiatives that have aided technology transfer and the acquisition ICTs for library management and operations (Ikem and Ajala 2000). Research on university libraries in Nigeria has therefore covered major aspects relating to staffing, technology, and information resources and services. Examples include Olorunsola and Ibegbulam's (2003) study of flexible working hours for academic librarians and Olorunsola's (2000b) evaluation of job rotation in Nigerian university libraries. The two studies sought to seek librarians' opinions on flexible working hours and job rotation in order to see how these factors might help ensure high productivity among librarians.

Other areas where research has been carried out are on use of computers in libraries, databases, and ICTs in Nigerian university libraries, for example, a study of librarians' attitudes to the use of computer-based information systems in the University of Ibadan (Adedeji, Longe, and Fabunmi 2005). Anasi (2005) evaluates how ICT application has aided the contribution and relevance of university library services to university education in Nigeria. Her research revealed that Nigerian university libraries have developed a strong ICT usage despite the fact that ICT use is still adopted at a low level compared to university libraries in Europe, the Americas, and Asia. Nwezah (2005) assesses how decisions to adopt ICTs are taken and the role local conditions and needs assessment play in the final decision reached in Nigerian university libraries. Iweha's (2005) research addresses the impact of electronic information systems (EIS) on the research output, job performance, and skills acquisition among librarians in Obafemi Awolowo University, Ile-ife, Nigeria. His evaluation also touches on the problems associated with the use of EIS among librarians. Utulu (2006) evaluates the existence and use of ICT policies in academic and research libraries and finds that only 60 percent of the libraries studied have functional and documented ICT policies, while the other 40 percent have adopted informal and undocumented policies.

From the perspective of university library users, Ojo-Ade and Jagboro (2000) examine the extent to which the subject catalog in Obafemi Awolowo University, Ile-ife, Nigeria, is used, the extent to which the catalog meets users' needs, and the effectiveness of subject classification in the library. Obajemu, Ogunyade, and Nwoye (2004) appraise the acceptance and use of CD-ROMs in 15 selected academic and research libraries in Nigeria. Their objective was to investigate the factors relative to availability and appropriateness of facilities, resources, and other necessary ingredients required for the optimum utilization of CD-ROMs. Similarly, Igbeka and Okpala (2004) analyze patterns of CD-ROM database usage among University of Ibadan, Nigeria, library users. The study was a result of the need to ascertain users' satisfaction and knowledge of CD-ROM technology and literature search. Their study also looked at the influence of database abstracts citation on the collection development activities of the case study library. Olorunsola (2000a) studies magazine users in University of Ilorin, Nigeria, in order to know the categories of library users who use magazines and what they use them for. Although the review of studies above is not exhaustive, a look at them confirms the fact that in Nigeria, a lot of evidence exists in the literature. This is why many university libraries adopt as primary evidence research published in journals, although locally generated evidences are also taken seriously.

NATIONAL UNIVERSITIES COMMISSION ACCREDITATION

The Nigerian university environment is epitomized by academic and political drama which the country was thrown into in the first 20 years of her independence. The establishment of the National Universities Commission (NUC) in 1974, the eventual takeover of regional and state government owned universities by the federal government, and the ban on private university establishment with Decree No. 19 of 1984 meant that the federal government had to impose tighter supervision on universities, using the NUC as an instrument to achieve global standards. Hence, Ifidon describes NUC as a "buffer body between the government and the universities" (1996, 5). Political as this may sound, the NUC accreditation has been designed in recent years to meet global accreditation standards and has helped the Nigerian university education sector retain its competitiveness among other African nations and the world.

Commenting on the important role NUC plays through accreditation, Ifidon (1996) points to the rush with which 26 private universities sprang up six months after the Nigerian Supreme Court ruled in favor of private university establishment without formal and regulated accreditation during the late 1970s. Basic requirements like legal basis, university governance, quality and nature of academic programs, quality and nature of staff, infrastructure (including laboratories and libraries), and funding available to sustain projects were not properly addressed. It thus became important to have an established and ongoing academic standards policy to guide Nigerian universities and also serve as a foundation for accreditation. Common areas covered in NUC's accreditation guidelines for Nigerian universities are academics, administration, staffing, infrastructure, library and information provision, and funding and fund administration. Following is a comprehensive breakdown of accreditation requirements for Nigerian university libraries:

1. staff/students ratio
2. information resources (books and electronic)
3. information services and their relevance to current trends and available programs
4. infrastructure (building, reading capacity, etc.)
5. university policy on library, especially funding and budgeting
6. students and academic programs
7.
    a. ratio of students and information resources available in the library
    b. ratio of information resources and each program in the university
8. academic staff research trend and available information resources and services

Nichols (1989) submits that accreditation sought to focus on and assess accomplishment of an institution's statement of purpose or mission. Because of NUC accreditation requirements, Agboola (2000) argues that the governance of Nigerian university libraries can be considered from three angles: external governance, internal governance, and departmental administration. The NUC oversees the external governance by proposing and supervising standards that specifically spell out funding, infrastructure (physical, ICTs, and information resources), and policies. A very good example of this is the NUC's proposal that 10 percent of Nigerian universities' recurring budgets must be set aside for their libraries. In recent times, the rigorous course accreditation requirements involve visits to university libraries to examine the quality and quantity of their books, journals, and electronic resources collections (Ifidon 1996 and NUC 1991 cited by Agboola 2000). University library management and the university library committee, comprising academic staff representatives from all faculties, are in charge of the internal governance of Nigerian university libraries. The university library committee is chaired by the deputy vice-chancellor, academics. However, in smaller universities, professors with adequate administrative experience are asked to chair the University Library Committee. Departmental governance involves day-to-day internal activities involving various departments or subject libraries that make up the university library.

Ifidon and Ifidon (2007) highlight NUC requirements (which they vehemently criticize) for university libraries with regard to their building and staffing:

1. the ultimate student enrollment figure for the new university will be 10,000;
2. 10 percent of the ultimate undergraduate enrollment represents the enrollment figure for postgraduate and certificate courses;
3. staff to student ratio will be 1:10;
4. the main library would be capable of ultimately housing 500,000 volumes;
5. seating provision should be made for 1,500 readers or 15 percent of the student population;
6. the main library should be centrally air-conditioned with the provision of a standby power generator;
7. an additional provision of 186 m^2 should be made for a student common room in each hall to include a television, lounge, and a library;
8. the total usable area would be derived from the application of the formula 1.25 m^2 per full time equivalent student;
9. where a separate audiovisual center exists, it should consist of a bindery and small printing and publishing facility (the formula of 0.06 m^2 per student [full time equivalent] should be used);
10. addition of 35 percent% of the net floor area should be allowed; and
11. cost should be calculated on the basis of ₦ 535:00 (US$5.00) per m^2, which includes variation cost.

They further present NUC's submission on staffing thus:

1. one librarian to 400 users, up to a maximum of 20 ibrarians for 8,000 users;
2. one librarian to 800 users after the first 8,000 users, up to a maximum of 30 librarians for 16,000 users;
3. one librarian for every additional 1,000 users after the first 16,000 users;
4. one paraprofessional staff to four librarians;
5. one senior administrative staff to 10 librarians;
6. one secretary to each university librarian, deputy university librarian, and dead of division or department of a deputy university librarian status; and
7. five junior staff (including janitorial staff) to one librarian.

Therefore, a university with a user population of 18,600 will be required to have

1. 33 librarians,
2. 8 paraprofessional staff,

3. 3 senior administrative staff,

4. at least 6 secretaries, and

5. 161 junior staff.

These requirements are still the standard adopted by NUC as basis for accreditation. They predetermine and shape evidence needs and methods used to elicit them in Nigerian university libraries in relationship with infrastructure, staff, and acquisition of library information resources. A good example is the position of Ikem and Ajala (2000) on University of Ibadan Library staff strengths and student population:

The library system serves a student population established at 22,782 (full-time and part-time) and a virile academic community (teaching and non-teaching) of over 2,000 staff . . . contains approximately 542,888 volumes, and receives about 600 titles of journal and stocks about 4,000 audio visuals . . . staff strength is about 160 with 26 professionals while others are para-professional, secretarial, technical, and junior staff (18).

This brings us to the conclusion that NUC accreditation data requirements are used by Nigerian universities to set out policies and long-term plans. NUC accreditation guidelines are used to form the basis of long-term, innovative, and policy-based evidence. Its requirements help libraries to evaluate how adequate their stocks are, as well as the appropriateness of their staffing and space available for office use and readers' services. It has also gone a long way to influence benchmark setting for empirical studies on major aspects of university library management in Nigeria.

In conclusion, NUC accreditation data has a very profound effect on trends in Nigerian university libraries. From infrastructure-building and ICTs, through staff requirements, to number of books to be acquired, NUC accreditation data have been used to determine and shape major policy statements. Regardless of the fact that the autonomy to decide what works for a particular university library is assured, strategic immediate management decisions are particularly shaped towards meeting up with NUC standards.

CASE STUDY: RUN LIBRARY, REDEEMER'S UNIVERSITY, NIGERIA

The Redeemer's University (RUN) came into existence in January 2005 after received a license from the Federal Government of Nigeria (through the NUC) to run as one of the private universities in Nigeria. The university was established by the Redeemed Christian Church of God, Nigeria, as its contribution to university education in Nigeria and Africa. The university library (RUN Library) opened officially on September 1, 2005, with the primary aim of providing information resources for learning, teaching, and research. At its inception, Mrs. F. Tamuno, a retired University Librarian from the University of Ibadan, and two librarians from the University of Ibadan were engaged to set up the RUN Library. They were supported by the first set of library staff, comprised of two academic librarians, one graduate assistant, one higher library officer, and five support staff. Currently, RUN Library staff comprises one university librarian, one deputy librarian, one principal librarian, one senior librarian, two librarians I, three librarians II, one assistant librarian, two library officers, 12 library attendants, one secretary, one office assistant (for administration), and three porters. In all, there are 28 members of the staff.

As a typical Nigerian university library, the development of the RUN library has been under NUC's strict supervision. NUC has strictly supervised RUN Library in the following areas:

A.) Library Building
   1. Space
      a. space for shelving books

    b. space for reading

    c. administrative work and offices

  2. Seating Capacity

    a. ultimate capacity

    b. present number of seats

  3. Population Served

    a. academic staff

    b. nonacademic staff

    c. students

    d. others

B.) Stocks/Accessions: Books and Journals: The Collection

  1. Book (volume and number of titles)

  2. Available Journals (paper based)

    a. local

    b. foreign

  3. Current Subscription

    a. local

    b. foreign

  4. Electronic Journals

    a. full text

    b. others (abstracts)

C.) Nonbook and Special Resources (CD-ROM, Video, Transparencies, Slides, etc.)

  1. birtual library workstation and accommodation

    a. available technology

    b. number of workstations

  2. Use Statistics

    a. loans

    b. reserved resources

    c. consulted resources

    d. examination period

    e. normal academic period

    f. vacation

D.) Interlibrary Cooperation Services

E.) Staff

  1. librarians

  2. paraprofessionals

  3. administrative

  4. others (RUN Library Annual NUC Report)

These areas have influenced RUN Library's practice of evidence-based library management, which takes two dimensions: core and innovative evidence management. In its endeavor to practice core evidence-based library management, both automated and manual systems of data collection methods are used. The College Portal, a university-wide integrated information system, is used as the automated evidence collection tool. Simply known as the RUN Library Portal, it functions as TPS, MIS, and IRS. All transactions including selection, acquisition, circulation, and administration are carried out using the RUN Library Portal.

Consequently, all data required on these transactions can as well be retrieved and used as evidences. Selection transaction data that could be processed using the RUN Library Portal are subjects, book vendor/suppler, college, and generating a general list of selected library resources. For instance, before an order is placed, a count of books to be ordered is carried out based on subject. This makes it possible for the acquisition librarian to have equal representation in terms of budget expenditure by subject (i.e., by colleges and departments). Evidences on cost differences, quality of library resources supplied by vendor/book supplier, and cost of doing business with vendors can also be retrieved and used to categorize vendors and the kind of library resources a vendor can be approached to supply.

On the other hand, manual systems are also used to collect evidences which complement those collected using the RUN Library Portal. An area where this is carried out is mostly on use of special resources and the Internet. Special resources include slides, transparencies, and video discs. Data is also collected on the use of the Virtual Library. Data sets that are collected manually include name of users, college, reason for use, search engine used, number of minutes spent, topic browsed, workstation used, and date. These sets of data provide firsthand information on RUN Library usage patterns and trends. All of these manual transaction data fall under core evidence-based data.

However, like other university libraries in Nigeria, innovative evidence data are elicited by putting together all the core data collected over a period of time; also, formal research carried out by academic librarians (either on library operations on a wide scale or research involving other university libraries) is used as a platform to collect innovative evidence data. Collaborative research among academic librarians and academics in other disciplines is encouraged. Library seminars, university seminars, conference paper submissions, independent research reported in journals, and e-print deposits are among the ways innovative evidence information are disseminated. Hence, there is also the possibility of using related research reported in journals and other outlets as sources of innovative evidence. The research that has been carried out in the last two years at RUN Library includes the following:

1. The Use of Faculty Opinion for Collection Evaluation at RUN Library
2. Cataloguing and Classification Online: The Experience of Redeemer's University Library
3. Library Collection and Personnel Characteristic in Nigerian Private Universities
4. Internet Technology and Nigerian Universities' Web Characteristics
5. Attitude of Librarians in Selected Nigerian Universities Towards the Use of Information and Communication Technology
6. Access to Information for Research in University Libraries

As shown by the titles above, some aspects of RUN Library management have been covered by empirical studies. New areas are still being looked at for possible research. They form an ample part of the library's evidence development initiative. Both core and innovative evidences are concatenated to provide evidences required for decision-making in the short term, medium term, and long term. It is good to conclude that the use of ICTs for evidence tracking and management is still at the base when compared with what is observable in the literature of developed countries. RUN Library, like other Nigerian university libraries, is at the verge of adopting advanced computerized systems like expert systems and decision support systems that have been adjudged as very reliable for analyzing data for evidence-based management.

CONCLUSION

In the present age, where information is considered the most important resource available to organizations, Nigerian university libraries have tried to inculcate the use of information as a management resource. By tagging this form of information as management evidence, university libraries in Nigeria try as much as possible to proffer methodology solutions to the gathering and management of evidences used for decision-making. The NUC accreditation data requirements have influenced to a large extent the pattern and shape of evidence data in Nigerian university libraries. Major management challenges are therefore set on meeting NUC's requirements for comprehensive collection development, qualitative staffing, appropriate infrastructure and environment conducive for reading, adoption of ICTs, and local and international information management collaboration. Within the limits of their abilities, Nigerian university libraries have been able to address the challenge of setting up libraries that meet considerable regional standards, especially in the areas of meeting the needs of their users for teaching, learning, and research. The struggle is still on to improve performances to international standards.

REFERENCES

Adebayo, O., O. Ojo, J. Obamiro. 2006. *Operations research in decision analysis and production management.* Lagos: Pumark Nigerian Limited.

Adedeji, B., B. Longe, and B. Fabunmi. 2005. Attitude of librarians to the use of computerized information systems in Kenneth Dike Library, University of Ibadan, Ibadan, Nigeria. *Information Technologist* 2 (2): 29–44.

Adeogun, M. 2006. The challenges of a modern tertiary education system: Paradigm shifts for educators and information professionals in sub-Saharan Africa. *African Journal of Library, Archival and Information Science* 16 (1): 45–52.

Agboola, A. T. 2000. Fifty decades of Nigerian university libraries: A review. *Libri* 50:280–89.

Aina, L. O. 2004. *Library and information science text for Africa.* Ibadan: The Third World Information Services Limited

Altbach, P. 2007. *The costs and benefits of world class universities.* www.aaup.org/AAUP/pubsres/academe/2004/ JF/Feat/altb.htm (accessed February 28, 2008).

Anasi, S. 2005. The potentials of ICT application to increased relevance and sustainability of University Library Services in Nigeria. *Information Technologist* 2 (2): 50–70.

Asika, N. 1991. *Research methods in the behavioral sciences.* Ikeja: Longman Nigeria Plc.

Blake, J., and S. Schleper. 2004. From data to decisions: Using surveys and statistics to make collection management decisions. *Library Collections, Acquisitions, & Technical Services* 28:460–64.

Curtis, G. 1995. *Business information systems: analysis, design and practice.* 2nd ed. Reading, MA: Addison-Wesley.

Fabunmi, B. 2004. Planning university libraries for effective customer services in Nigeria. In *Technology for information management and service: Modern libraries and information centers in developing countries,* edited by E. C. Madu, 147–58. Ibadan: Evi-Coleman Publications.

Haglund, L., and P. Olsson. 2008. The impact on university libraries of changes in information behavior among academic researchers: A multiple case study. *Journal of Academic Librarianship* 34 (1): 52–59.

Ifidon, B. 1996. The effects of accreditation on university library book stock: The Nigerian experience. *International Information and Library Review* 28:1–21.

Ifidon, S. and E. Ifidon. 2007. *New directions in African library management.* Ibadan: Spectrum Books Ltd.

Ifidon, S., and G. Okoli. 2002. 40 years of academic and research library service to Nigeria: Past, present and future. Paper presented at the 40th national conference and annual general meeting of the Nigerian Library Association, Topo, Badagry, 22–33.

Igbeka, J., and A. Okpala. 2004. Analyses and patterns of CD-ROM database use in Kenneth Dike Library, University of Ibadan, Nigeria. *Information Technologist* 1 (1 & 2): 39–50.

Ikem, J., and E. Ajala. 2000. Some developments in information technology at the Kenneth Dike Library, University of Ibadan. In *Information technology in library and information science education in Nigeria*; papers presented at the 10th biennial conference of the National Association of Library and Information Science Educators (NALISE), 21–31.

Iwcha, C. 2005. Utilization of electronic information sources (EIS) by the academic staff of Hezekiah Oluwasanmi Library, Obafemi Awolowo University, Ile-Ife, Nigeria. *University of Dares Salaam Library Journal* 7 (1): 47–56.

Keyes, J. 2006. *Knowledge management, business intelligence and content management: The IT practitioner's guide.* New York: Auerbach Publications.

Koufogiannakis, D. 2007. Establishing a model for evidence based collection management. In Proceedings 4th international evidence based library and information practice conference, Durham, North Carolina.

E-prints in Library and Information Science: http://eprints.rclis.org/archive/00010935/ (accessed on February 19, 2008).

Lucas, H. 1989. *Managing information services*. New York: Macmillan.

McClare, J., and T. Sincich. 2000. *A first course in statistics*. 7th ed. New Jersey: Prentice Hall.

Nichols, J. 1989. *Institutional effectiveness and outcomes assessment implementation on campus: A practitioner's handbook*, 194. New York: Agathon Press.

Nwezah, C. 2005. Nigerian university libraries and information and communication technology (ICT). *University of Dares Salaam Library Journal* 7 (1): 32–46.

Obajemu, A., T. Ogunyade, and E. Nwoye. 2004. Assessment of CD-ROM usage in academic and research libraries in Nigeria: A case study. *Information Technologist* 1 (1 & 2): 17–24.

Ogunbameru, O. 2004. *Research methods in social sciences*. 2nd ed. Hommersaak: D-Net Communications.

Ojo-Ade, C., and K. Jagboro. 2000. Subject catalogue in the Hezekiah Oluwasunkanmi Library, Obafemi Awolowo University, Ile-Ife, Nigeria. *African Journal of Library, Archival and Information Studies* 10 (2): 177–86.

Ojokoh, E., and M. Asaolu. 2005. Studies on Internet access and usage by students of the Federal University of Technology, Akure, Nigeria. *African Journal of Library, Archival and Information Science* 15 (2): 149–53.

Olorunsola, R. 2000a. A survey of news magazine users at the University of Ilorin library. *Serials Review* 26 (2): 15–20.

———. 2000b. Job rotation in academic libraries: The situation in a Nigerian university library. *Library Management* 21 (2): 94–98.

Olorunsola, R., and I. Ibegbulam. 2003. Flexible working hours for academic librarians in Nigeria. *Library Review* 52 (2): 70–75.

Olorunsola, R., I. Ibegbulam, and E. Akinboro. 2005. Qualitative and quantitative methods in library and information science. *Library Progress (International)* 25 (2): 141–49.

Mabawonku, I. 2005. Quality assurance of library and information science journals. In *Improving the quality of library and information science journals in West Africa: Proceedings of stakeholders conference, 7–8 December*, 19–34.

Tamuno, O. G. 1992. Availability and accessibility of biomedical information for teaching, research and service in Nigeria. *Workshop on Access to Science and Technology Information, Bauchi*, February 9–13.

Tranfield, D., D. Denyer, and P. Smart. 2003. Towards a methodology for the developing evidence-informed knowledge management by means of systematic review. *British Journal of Management* 14:207–22.

Utulu, S. 2006. Information and communication technology policy in academic and research libraries in Oyo and Ogun States, Nigeria. http://eprints.rclis.org/archive/00006894/01/nla.pdf (accessed March 26, 2008).

Uvah, I. 2007. The role of academic planning in university development. Paper presented at the annual conference of the Committee of Directors of Academic Planning of Nigerian Universities held at Bells University of Technology, Ota, Nigeria.

Winkworth, I. 1999. Performance measurement and performance indicators. In *Collection management in academic libraries*, 2nd ed., edited by Clarke Jenkins and Mary Morley, 71–105. Hampshire: Gower Publishing Limited.

BIBLIOGRAPHY

Adeleke, A. 2001. *Management concepts and applications*. Lagos: Concept Publications.

Hoadley, I. 1999. Reflections: Management morphology—how we got to be who we are. *Journal of Academic Librarianship* 25 (4): 267–73.

Lawal, A. 1993. *Management in focus*. Lagos: Abdul Industrial Enterprise.

Oyelude, A. 2004. Academic libraries: The state of the art. In *Technology for information management and service: Modern libraries and information centers in developing countries*, edited by E. C. Madu, 121–45. Ibadan: Evi-Coleman Publications.

Saints, W., T. Hartnett, and E. Strassner. 2003. Higher education in Nigeria: A status approach. *Higher Education Policy* 16:259–81.

Index

About the Contributors

TRACIE J. BALLOCK is Head, Collection Management Department, Duquesne University.

ERIKA BENNETT is Reference and Instruction Librarian—Liaison to the Schools of Psychology and Human Services, Capella University.

SOMMER BERG is Reference and Instruction Librarian—Liaison to the School of Undergraduate Studies, Capella University.

JAMENE BROOKS-KIEFFER is Resource Linking Librarian, Kansas State University Libraries.

ERIN BROTHEN is Reference and Instruction Librarian—Liaison to the School of Business & Technology, Capella University.

MONICA CLAASSEN-WILSON is Collection Development Information Specialist, University of Kansas Libraries.

SUSANNE K. CLEMENT is Director, Quinney Natural Resources Research Library, Utah State University. She was Head of Collection Development at the University of Kansas at the time of writing.

JASON COLEMAN is Service Coordinator, Kansas State University Libraries.

MICHAEL A. CRUMPTON is Assistant Dean for Administrative Services, University Libraries, The University of North Carolina—Greensboro.

ERIN DAVIS is a Reference Librarian at Utah State University.

HILARY DAVIS is Assistant Head for Engineering & E-Science, Collection Management Department, North Carolina State University Libraries.

ANNE C. ELGUINDI is Acting Director of Information Delivery Services, American University Library.

ERIN L. ELLIS is Coordinator of Instructional Services, University of Kansas Libraries.

NIKHAT J. GHOUSE is Social Sciences Librarian, University of Kansas Libraries.

MARGARET HOGARTH is Electronic Resources Coordinator, Science Library, University of California, Riverside.

WENDY HOLLIDAY is Coordinator of Library Instruction, Utah State University.

MELISSA JOHNSON is Electronic Services & Serials Librarian, Abilene Christian University.

LUCY ELEONORE LYONS is Coordinator for Collection Analysis, University Library, Northwestern University.

PAMELA MARTIN is a Reference Librarian at Utah State University.

BILL MAYER is University Librarian, American University Library.

TIMOTHY M. MCGEARY is Team Leader of Library Technology, Lehigh University Libraries.

DAVID A. NOLFI is Health Sciences Librarian, Duquesne University.

ANDRÉE J. RATHEMACHER is Head of the Serials Unit and Electronic Resources Librarian, Department of Technical Services, University Libraries, University of Rhode Island.

JOHN M. STRATTON is Social Sciences Librarian, University of Kansas Libraries.

DANIELLE THEISS-WHITE is General Reference Coordinator, Kansas State University Libraries.

SAMUEL C. UTULU is Acquisition Librarian in the RUN Library, Redeemer's University (RUN), Redemption Camp, Ogun State, Nigeria.

MICHAEL C. VOCINO is Collection Management Officer in the Department of Technical Services, University Libraries, University of Rhode Island.

KRISTIN WHITEHAIR is Biomedical Librarian and School of Nursing Liaison at the University of Kansas Medical Center Dykes Library.

JOSEPH A. WILLIAMS is Collection Development and Acquisition Librarian at SUNY Maritime College, Stephen B. Luce Library, Throggs Neck, New York.

DAVID E. WOOLWINE is Assistant Professor of Library Services and Reference Librarian, Axinn Library, Hofstra University, Hempstead, New York.

CARMEL YUROCHKO is Serial/Electronic Resources Librarian, Duquesne University.

KATE ZOELLNER is Education & Psychology Librarian/Assessment Coordinator, Maureen and Mike Mansfield Library, The University of Montana.

About the Editor

DARBY ORCUTT is Senior Collection Manager for the Humanities & Social Sciences, North Carolina State University (NCSU) Libraries, where he previously held the positions of Collection Manager for Data Analysis and NCSU Libraries Fellow. He has written on a variety of topics in the library literature and beyond, is a frequent reviewer for *CHOICE*, *Library Journal*, and other publications, and teaches in the NCSU Department of Philosophy & Religious Studies, the NCSU University Honors Program, and the School of Information & Library Science at The University of North Carolina at Chapel Hill (UNC-CH). He holds the Master of Science in Library Science and the Master of Arts in Communication Studies from UNC-CH. His experience prior to his professional library career includes work as a vendor to libraries and as a rare book scout.